D0722434

FRENCH ANTI-SLAVERY

Some works have examined the first and temporary abolition of French Colonial slavery during the French Revolutionary era, but relatively little is known about the second French abolitionist movement that culminated in the freeing of a quarter of a million slaves in 1848. This book fills the huge gap in existing historiography by providing the first detailed study of French anti-slavery forces during this period of the first half of the nineteenth century, explaining why France abolished colonial slavery fifteen years later than Britain but fifteen years before emancipation in the United States. It traces the largely political struggle of a cautious, elitist group of humanitarians against a well-organized colonial lobby and a largely indifferent July Monarchy government. The few radical, determined abolitionists, like the black Cyrille Bissette, were too marginal to move French public opinion and bring about abolition until the Revolution of 1848 brought the Second Republic to power.

Lawrence C. Jennings is Professor of History at the University of Ottawa in Canada. A frequent traveler and researcher in France over the past forty years, he has published on various aspects of nineteenth-century French and French colonial history. He is the author of *France and Europe in 1848* (1973) and *French Reaction to British Slave Emancipation* (1988). His numerous articles have appeared in *French Historical Studies*, *American Historical Review*, *French History*, *Journal of Modern History*, *Slavery and Abolition*, *Journal of African History*, *Canadian Journal of History*, and several French language journals.

FRENCH ANTI-SLAVERY

THE MOVEMENT FOR THE ABOLITION OF SLAVERY IN FRANCE, 1802–1848

LAWRENCE C. JENNINGS

University of Ottawa, Canada

CAMBRIDGE
UNIVERSITY PRESS

PUBLISHED BY THE PRESS SYNDICATE OF THE UNIVERSITY OF CAMBRIDGE
The Pitt Building, Trumpington Street, Cambridge, United Kingdom

CAMBRIDGE UNIVERSITY PRESS
The Edinburgh Building, Cambridge CB2 2RU, UK
http://www.cup.cam.ac.uk
40 West 20th Street, New York, NY 10011-4211, USA
http://www.cup.org
10 Stamford Road, Oakleigh, Melbourne 3166, Australia
Ruiz de Alarcón 13, 28014 Madrid, Spain

First published 2000

Printed in the United States of America

Typeface Sabon 10.25/13.5 pt.   *System* QuarkXPress [TW]

A catalog record for this book is available from the British Library.

Library of Congress Cataloging in Publication Data
Jennings, Lawrence C.
French anti-slavery : the movement for the abolition of slavery in France, 1802–1848/
Lawrence C. Jennings
p. cm
Includes bibliographical references.
ISBN 0-521-77249-4 (hardback)
1. Slaves – Emancipation – France – History – 19th century – Sources. 2.
Slavery – France – History – 19th century – Sources. I. Title.

HT1178.J46 2000
326´.8´094409034 21–dc21   99-045555

ISBN 0 521 77249 4 hardback

CONTENTS

Preface   *page* vii

1   Napoleonic and Restoration Anti-Slavery   1

2   The Revolution of 1830 and the Colonies   24

3   Formation of the French Abolition Society   48

4   Procrastinations, Consultations, and Interpellations   76

5   Abolitionist Proposals and Parliamentary Commissions   103

6   Stalemate and Regression   142

7   Crisis and Further Setbacks   165

8   Redefining Abolitionism   193

9   Toward Immediatism   229

Conclusion   285

Bibliography   291

Index   309

Figure section begins on page 135.

PREFACE

Enlightenment thought and the growth of evangelicalism sparked anti-slavery and anti-slave trade activity in the eighteenth century. The formation of a British abolitionist organization in the late 1780s was imitated in France, where the process accelerated because of the Revolution of 1789 and especially the slave revolt in Saint-Domingue. Faced with a fait accompli in Saint-Domingue, France in 1794 became the first great power to abolish colonial slavery. However, this achievement was undone by Napoleon. He reestablished both colonial slavery and the slave trade in 1802, before proceeding to repress the remnants of the first French abolitionist groupings. It was not until the latter part of the Restoration monarchy of Louis XVIII and Charles X, and especially after the advent of the July Monarchy of King Louis Philippe in 1830, that French anti-slavery was reborn. This book examines this second French abolitionist movement from its inception until the final abolition of colonial slavery by France in 1848.

Such a study is sorely lacking in the current state of historiography. Indeed, no aspect of the vast history of abolitionism has been so neglected by scholars treating either the anti-slave trade or anti-slavery movements of the eighteenth and nineteenth centuries. A large number of monographs published over the past decades have helped us to understand the American and British efforts to abolish both the slave trade and slavery. The first French abolitionist movement in the eighteenth century has also been covered by numerous articles and a handful of books. The question of French slave trade abolitionism in the nineteenth century, which culminated in the 1820s and 1830s, has found its historians in a series of French scholars. Those seeking a detailed overall view of the process that led to the definitive eradication of French colonial slavery in 1848, however, have had to resort until now to scattered chapters or limited studies on the subject.

The ground-breaking historian André Jean Tudesq, in a section of his richly documented magnum opus, *Les grands notables en France*, offered a brief and largely accurate analysis of French abolitionism under the July Monarchy as dominated by conservative *notables* unwilling to operate outside legislative channels and incapable of effecting slave liberation. Similarly, Seymour Drescher, in his study on Tocqueville, provides a chapter outlining the general development of anti-slavery prior to 1848.[1] Still, these studies offer mere glimpses of the second French abolitionist movement and whet the reader's appetite for a more complete discussion and profound analysis. The appearance of a group of publications, coinciding with the sesquicentennial of French emancipation, has not filled this lacuna. Anxious to provide rapid, all-encompassing overviews of a question on which relatively little groundwork has been done, publishers have often turned to anthropologists or political scientists rather than historians for explanations. The most noticeable results have been the studies by David Rigoulet-Roze and Fabienne Federini, which put forth the politically correct hypothesis that blacks were agents of their own liberation in 1848 as in 1794 by sparking colonial unrest and revolts. However, as my book demonstrates, there is no solid historical evidence substantiating these assumptions for the period preceding 1848. A brief recent book by Patricia Motylewski, while also stressing this theme, at least aims to give credit to the French abolitionists of the July Monarchy for preparing the way for emancipation, thus reducing in the process the role ascribed to Victor Schoelcher in many popular accounts.[2] Unfortunately, Motylewski's attempts to analyze the Société française pour l'abolition de l'esclavage fail dismally due to inadequate research. She bases her examination almost exclusively

[1] André Jean Tudesq, *Les grands notables en France (1840–1849): Etude historique d'une psychologie sociale* (2 vols.; Paris: Presses Universitaires de France, 1964), II, 834–51; Seymour Drescher, *Dilemmas of Democracy: Tocqueville and Modernization* (Pittsburgh: University of Pittsburgh Press, 1968), 151–95.
[2] David Rigoulet-Roze, "A propos d'une commémoration: L'Abolition de l'esclavage en 1848," *L'Homme: Revue française d'anthropologie*, no. 145 (1998): 127–36; Fabienne Federini, *L'Abolition de l'eslavage en 1848: Une lecture de Victor Schoelcher* (Paris: L'Harmattan, 1998); Patricia Motylewski, *La Société française pour l'abolition de l'eslavage, 1834–1850* (Paris: L'Harmattan, 1998).

on the printed works of the French abolition society, while totally ignoring the vast amount of material in the French colonial archives, French press, British abolitionist papers, and even the Schoelcher manuscripts, not to mention the entire panoply of English language secondary studies on the topic. The result is a poorly informed, highly limited, one-sided picture of the leading French anti-slavery formation. Therefore, the 150th anniversary of the ending of French slavery, like the 100th anniversary, has failed to produce a definitive study of the second French abolitionist movement.[3] This book is an attempt to remedy this situation. It provides the first detailed analysis in any language of the French anti-slavery lobby in the first half of the nineteenth century, but does not purport to be a study of French colonial slavery itself, something already extensively examined by scholars. Similarly, it does not attempt to cover the late nineteenth-century sequel to French colonial slavery, when France encountered the problem once again following its imperialistic conquests in Africa. That is a different story, and one already treated by Africanists.

In undertaking my research on the second French abolitionist movement I have proceeded by asking the question of why it took some fifteen years after the British decision to terminate slavery for French liberal governments to free the quarter of a million slaves in their plantation colonies of Guadeloupe, Martinique, Bourbon (Réunion), and Guiana. Answering this query has led me to center my analysis on the French abolitionist movement under the July Monarchy (1830–48), its structure, modus operandi, objectives, weaknesses, and achievements. This in turn has required an examination of planter interests that opposed emancipation and of government policy on all slavery and colonial issues. To explain the interaction between these different elements over time, and to show the progress, setbacks, fresh starts, and ultimate failures and achievements of French anti-slavery, I have found it preferable to adopt a largely chronological approach. I hope in this way to demonstrate the extreme complexities of an issue that could not be resolved until it was caught up in the vortex of the Revolution of 1848.

---

[3] The centennial of 1848 resulted especially in two books by Gaston Martin that were serious studies for their time, but are now dated: *L'Abolition de l'esclavage, 27 avril 1848* (Paris: Presses Universitaires de France, 1948) and *Histoire de l'esclavage dans les colonies françaises* (Paris: Presses Universitaires de France, 1948).

The results of some twenty years of research, this book attempts to break away from the standardized secondary accounts of French anti-slavery by basing its findings on a thorough examination of primary sources, most of which have so far been neglected by historians. In carrying out this research, the author has examined all of the rich documentation in the French colonial archives (Aix-en-Provence) concerning slavery and its abolition. This material makes it possible to fathom the official governmental view on the question, at the same time that it reveals colonial strategies for the defense of slavery. All of the extant port city press of Bordeaux, Nantes, and Le Havre have been read for the period 1830–48 because of the close connections their constituencies had with the colonies. So has much of the Parisian press, in an attempt to sound public, pro-colonial, and abolitionist opinion. Most important, all available French abolitionist papers and writings, and particularly those of the French abolition society, have been carefully scrutinized. This has made it possible to trace the complex development of French anti-slavery. Finally, French abolitionist correspondence with the British, largely unexploited by previous historians, has provided precious insights into the thoughts, aims, and procedures of French anti-slavery. All of this work on primary sources, when correlated with existing secondary source material, has enabled the author to put forth what he hopes will prove to be a comprehensive and definitive account of the French movement against colonial slavery in the first half of the nineteenth century.

I am grateful to Eric Jennings of the University of Toronto and David Eltis of Queen's University for having read the manuscript form of this book and for improving it with their suggestions. I wish to thank Mme Maïte Court-Isambert for sharing with me her knowledge of the French abolition society, and all the personnel of the Centre des Archives d'Outre-Mer (Aix-en-Provence) for their kind assistance over the many years I worked there. I am indebted to the *Revue française d'histoire d'outre-mer* and *French History* for permitting me to reproduce passages from my articles published with them. Finally, I could not have been able to undertake much of the research that made this book possible without the generous support of the Social Sciences and Humanities Research Council of Canada.

NAPOLEONIC AND
RESTORATION
ANTI-SLAVERY

The first French abolitionist movement centered around the Société des Amis des Noirs. Founded in early 1788 by the journalist Jacques Pierre Brissot and his associate Etienne Clavière, with the close collaboration of Count Honoré de Mirabeau, the Amis des Noirs was inspired by the humanitarianism and egalitarian currents of thought implicit in the eighteenth-century Enlightenment. It was also profoundly influenced from the moment of its inception by the British precedent. The Amis des Noirs was modeled upon the London Society for the Abolition of the Slave Trade, which had been formed in May 1787. Brissot, who had been in England in the autumn of that year, had become closely associated with the London anti-slave trade committee, and had been encouraged by it to form a similar group in France. The Amis des Noirs also followed the example of the British organization and, like it, made the strategic decision to direct its offensive against the slave trade specifically, rather than against the abolition of colonial slavery per se. Although the Amis opposed slavery in principle and favored its gradual elimination, they conformed to British reasoning that slavery would eventually disappear after the eradication of the slave traffic.[1] The British provided the Amis with

---

[1] A vast literature has been built up on French abolitionism during the Revolutionary period. For the above, and for the Amis des Nors in particular, see Daniel P. Resnick, "The Société des amis des Noirs and the Abolition of Slavery," *French Historical Studies* 7 (1972): 558–69; Valerie Quinney, "Decisions on Slavery, the Slave Trade and Civil Rights for Negroes in the Early French Revolution," *Journal of Negro History* 55 (1970): 117–30; Robert Stein, "The Revolution of 1789 and the Abolition of Slavery," *Canadian Journal of History* 17 (1982): 447–67; Françoise Thesée, "Autour de la Société des Amis des Noirs," *Présence africaine*, no. 125 (1983): 3–82; Robert Stein, *Léger Félicité Sonthonax: The Lost Sentinel of the Republic* (Cranbury, N.J.: Fairleigh

the necessary documents to attack the slave trade, disbursed subsidies to the French group, and even translated into French and distributed in France some thirty-four pamphlets against the slave traffic. The great British abolitionist Thomas Clarkson spent much time in France and was in frequent correspondence with the Amis des Noirs in an attempt to inspire and advance the French effort.[2] Even the seal of the Amis des Noirs was copied from the famous 1787 Wedgwood medallion of the British society; it depicted a kneeling chained slave, facing right, and stating "Ne suis-je pas ton frère?" (Am I not your brother?) rather than "Am I not a man and a brother?" British influence over French abolitionism began with the very first French anti-slave trade grouping. It also oriented French objectives toward slave trade repression rather than against slavery in general.

Besides Brissot, Clavière, and Mirabeau, other prominent members of the Amis des Noirs included the future revolutionary Abbé Henri Grégoire, the *philosophe* Antoine de Condorcet, and the hero of the American Revolution, the Marquis Marie Joseph Gilbert de Lafayette. The society, like later French abolitionist groupings, was elitist in character, and tended to center its activities in the legislative chambers. It avoided appeals to public opinion except through the published media, and never had more that 150 adherents. Besides attacking the slave trade, it became involved in the campaign for equal rights for what were then called "free persons of color" (*hommes de couleur libres*). Its interventions finally led to the law of April 4, 1792, that gave complete rights to these free blacks of mixed blood in the colonies.[3] However, as the Revolution advanced, society members gradually became sidetracked

Dickinson University Press, 1985); Yves Bénot, *La Révolution française et la fin des colonies* (Paris: La Découverte, 1988); David Geggus, "Racial Equality, Slavery, and Colonial Secession during the Constituent Assembly," *American Historical Review* 94 (1989): 1290–1308; Jean Tarrade, "Les colonies et les principes de 1789: Les assemblées révolutionnaires face au problème de l'esclavage," *Revue française d'histoire d'outre-Mer* 76 (1989): 9–34; and Marcel Dorigny, "Mirabeau et la Société des amis des Noirs: Quelles voies pour l'abolition de l'esclavage," *Les abolitions de l'esclavage de L. F. Son-thonax à V. Schoelcher: Actes du colloque international tenu à l'Université de Paris VIII les 3, 4 et 5 février 1994,* ed. *Marcel Dorigny* (Paris: Editions Unesco, 1995), 153–64.
[2] Lawrence C. Jennings, "The Interaction of French and British Antislavery, 1789–1848," *Proceedings of the Fifteenth Meeting of the French Colonial Historical Society, Martinique & Guadeloupe, May 1989* (Lanham, Md.: University Press of America, 1992), 81–2.
[3] Stein, "Revolution of 1789 and the Abolition of Slavery," 451; Geggus, "Racial Equality, Slavery," 1300–1303; Catherine Duprat, *"Pour l'amour de l'humanité": Le temps des philanthropes: La philanthropie parisienne des Lumières à la monarchie de Juillet* (Paris: Editions du C.T.H.S., 1993), 115–28, 179–85.

into more pressing issues of revolutionary politics. The Amis des Noirs was so closely connected to the Brissotin faction – also known as the Girondins – in the Legislative Assembly that when this group was proscribed by the Robespierrists in the spring of 1793, the society was dealt a mortal blow. Brissot and Clavière were guillotined; Condorcet committed suicide in prison; Lafayette surrendered to the Austrians; the other members of the group dispersed; and the society itself was eclipsed. The Amis des Noirs played no significant role in the first emancipation of France's nearly 700,000 colonial slaves by the Convention on February 4, 1794. This action was forced on the Republic by the slave revolt that had begun in 1791 in Saint-Domingue. Having lost control of the black population, commissioners of the Republic sent to the colony had issued decrees in August and September 1793 declaring the slaves free. In undertaking these moves they had hoped to rally blacks to the Republic and preserve French control over Saint-Domingue, for the colony was menaced by British and Spanish intervention once France had declared war upon these two powers in early 1793. The move by the Convention in February 1794 had simply formalized a fait accompli brought about by the Saint-Domingue slave uprising.

The first formation of the Amis des Noirs had effectively been stifled by the Terror. Due to the initiative of the inveterate abolitionist Abbé Grégoire, a small remnant of the Amis began to convene again as of 1796 under the name of the Société des Amis des Noirs et des Colonies. It exercised little influence, never united more than a small number of members, and was a mere shadow of its former self. Headed by the economist Jean Baptiste Say, and then the ex-Jacobin delegate to Saint-Domingue, Léger Félicité Sonthonnax, its main aims were to acclimatize blacks to their new-found freedom and to encourage their work under free labor. By the end of the 1790s its defense of the abolition of the slave trade and slavery was being undermined by a strengthening colonial lobby advocating coerced labor. The Amis des Noirs et des Colonies was finally suppressed in 1799 when Napoleon came to power.[4] Married to the Creole Josephine, and

---

[4] Daniel P. Resnick, "Political Economy and French Anti-Slavery: The Case of J.-B. Say," *Proceedings of the Third Annual Meeting of the Western Society for French History, 1975* (n.p.: Western Society for French History, 1976), 177–87; Duprat, *"Pour l'amour de l'humanité,"* 186–8; Ruth F. Necheles, *The Abbé Grégoire, 1787–1831: The Odyssey of an Egalitarian* (Westport, Conn.: Greenwood, 1971), 157–64.

favorable to colonial interests, Napoleon was no friend of freed blacks. Citing the economic needs of the colonies and the requirements of French overseas trade, Napoleon proceeded to reintroduce colonial slavery and the slave trade in 1802, at the same time that he undertook the reconquest of Saint-Domingue. He was unsuccessful in the latter, but did effectively rout out the last remnants of the first French abolitionist movement. It would be two decades before a society devoted to the ending of the slave trade and slavery in the French colonies would emerge once again within France.

With his draconian restrictions on the press, speech, meetings, and opposition groups, Bonaparte effectively stifled abolitionism in France from 1799 until his fall in 1814–15. Censorship prevented most abolitionist writings, or even publications on the colonies in general, from 1802 until 1817.[5] The failure by Bonaparte to reconquer Saint-Domingue, and the publicity given to massacres of whites perpetrated there, reduced sympathy for blacks in France. Proponents of slavery and the slave trade emerged victorious. Already in 1802–3 Pierre Victor Malouet and Bory de Saint-Venant wrote that slavery was required to force blacks to work and to maintain the security of colonial whites. The great Romantic writer François René de Chateaubriand argued in his *Génie du christianisme* (1802) that crimes by blacks in Saint-Domingue had erased any pity that might have existed for them. He and other animators of the officially sanctioned *Mercure de France* defended the reestablishment of slavery and the slave trade, while attacking at the same time the principles of the Enlightenment. Other works, such as the *Précis historique des derniers événements de la partie est de Saint-Domingue* (1811), by an army officer who had served in that colony, G. Guillermin, reinforced these themes and made a passionate plea for slavery as the only means for France to exploit tropical staple products.[6] Napoleonic officialdom gave full support to a whole series of publications promoting colonial interests while systematically blocking any organized abolitionist effort.

---

[5] Ibid., 177; David Geggus, "Haiti and the Abolitionists: Opinion, Propaganda and International Politics in Britain and France, 1804–1836," in David Richardson, ed., *Abolition and Its Aftermath: The Historical Context, 1790–1836* (London: Frank Cass, 1985), 117.

[6] Yves Bénot, *La démence coloniale sous Napoleon* (Paris: La Découverte, 1992), 186–94, 202–5.

In comparison with this wave of procolonial propaganda, abolitionist activity was reduced to a trickle. The liberal Ideologue review,
La Décade philosophique, littéraire et politique, directed among
others by J.-B. Say, was pro-black through 1801, but could make only
insinuations along these lines after Napoleon reestablished slavery in
1802.[7] Only Abbé Grégoire, a member of Napoleon's senate, dared go
beyond side remarks and innuendo in reiterating his principles in
print, though he too was prevented from making public statements on
the issues. In his *De la littérature des nègres*, written in 1808, Grégoire
stressed the unity of the human race, criticized the slave traffic, and
claimed that black violence in Saint-Domingue had been provoked by
the planters. Grégoire's publication of 1808 had been tolerated
because his old friend and minister of police under Napoleon, Joseph
Fouché, had protected him. But when Grégoire attempted to publish
another book in 1810 criticizing slavery, the authorities confiscated
and destroyed all copies of it. Even when Britain abolished the slave
trade in 1807, the French were unable to applaud this move. As one
author, Yves Bénot, has pointed out, Napoleonic repression had
caused French abolitionists to regress to the strategy of 1789 in clam-
oring first and foremost against the slave trade.[8] The British-inspired
tactic of attacking first of all the slave trade would continue to mark
French abolitionism throughout the Restoration that followed the
Napoleonic era.

When Napoleon faced defeat and abdicated in 1814, the restored
monarchy of Louis XVIII continued to scorn abolitionism, which it
identified with republicanism. The abolitionists were isolated and
accused by the new Ultraroyalists of being the allies of France's
conqueror, England. Because the abolitionists who still remained
(Grégoire, Lafayette, Benjamin Constant, baron Auguste de Staël-
Holstein, and the duc Victor de Broglie) had no popular support or
financial resources, they were indeed obliged to rely on the British
once again for documentation and funding. Madame Germaine de
Staël-Holstein – the famous daughter of Necker, mother of Auguste,
and mother-in-law of the duc de Broglie – helped circulate in France,

---

[7] Ibid., 234–50. On the Ideologues, see Emmet Kennedy, *A Philosophe in the Age of
Revolution: Destutt de Tracy and the Origins of "Ideology"* (Philadelphia: American
Philosophical Society, 1978).

[8] Necheles, *Abbé Grégoire*, 178, 181–4, 186; Bénot, *La démence coloniale*, 252–3.

for example, works by the noted British abolitionist William Wilberforce as of 1814.[9] Until her death in 1817, much of French anti-slave
trade sentiment was centered around her, her sons, son-in-law, and
former lover, Constant.[10] British abolitionists also visited France in
attempts to renew relations with their French colleagues and to persuade the nascent French regime to outlaw the slave trade. They
approved of the French abolitionist policy of concentrating attention
especially on the slave trade, but they were wary about encouraging
the French to form a new abolitionist organization because of the
opprobrium attached in France to the former republicans Grégoire
and Lafayette. As a result, French anti-slave trade sentiment prior to
1815 was limited to a few publications, such as the book by the liberal
economist Simonde de Sismondi issued in Geneva in 1814, *De l'in-
térêt de la France à l'égard de la traite des nègres*, arguing that the
slave traffic was not only inhuman but economically unsound.[11]

Although French abolitionists were encouraged when Napoleon
returned to power briefly for his "Hundred Days" in 1815 and proclaimed his intention of abolishing the slave trade, nothing came of
this. After the second Restoration restored Louis XVIII to power in
the summer of 1815, the plight of the abolitionists did not improve.
Louis XVIII's Ultra supporters launched again into an attack on the
abolitionists as radicals, and the latter remained totally ostracized.
Abolitionists could take some solace in the fact that Louis XVIII
now agreed to ban the slave trade, but he never applied the means to
eradicate it entirely. Moreover, any attack the abolitionists might have
launched against the principle of slavery was blunted by the fact that
France had lost most of its slave possessions during the Napoleonic
wars and did not repossess them until after the Restoration. Indeed,
the French colonies of Martinique and Guadeloupe were returned by
Britain only in 1814 and 1816, respectively, while Guiana remained
occupied by the Portuguese until late 1817. With few colonies, and
the menacing memory of Saint-Domingue dominating French minds,

[9] Serge Daget, "The Abolition of the Slave Trade by France: The Decisive Years
1826–1831," in Richardson, ed., *Abolition and Its Aftermath*, 141.
[10] Jean Michel Deveau, *La France aux temps des négriers* (Paris: France-Empire, 1994),
279.
[11] William B. Cohen, *The French Encounter with Africans: White Response to Blacks,
1530–1880* (Bloomington: Indiana University Press, 1980), 184–85.

the issue of slavery receded into the background in France. Grégoire stood nearly alone in courageously denouncing color distinctions in an article that he published in the non-influential *Chronique religieuse* in 1819.[12] No French organization advocating abolitionist principles would emerge in the first five years of the Restoration.

Grégoire and his handful of abolitionist associates remained concerned, however, about the continuation of the surreptitious French slave trade. The regulation that the Restoration had enacted under British pressure against the slave trade in 1814–1815 was too weak to deter some slave traders, and too haphazardly applied by French officials, who were so concerned with the economic recovery of the colonies that they often turned a blind eye toward slaving activities. Already in 1814–1815 some eighteen French ships were implicated in the slave trade.[13] Later measures of 1817–1818 against the slave trade also provided insufficiently dissuasive penalties. Moreover, Louis XVIII's regime was torn between its desires to strengthen its recently reclaimed colonies and to please the British, while at the same time not appearing dominated by the latter. Even when French officials ordered a closer surveillance of French ports and the African coast, the means for eradicating the slave traffic remained inadequate. Those French slave traders who nevertheless continued to ply the Atlantic were noticed by British observers, and reported upon by British abolitionists to their French associates.[14] Besides, the French learned about the continuing slave trade through a petition in 1820 by a French functionary in Senegal, Joseph Elzéar Morenas, who also established close ties with the British and Grégoire.[15] A leading British abolitionist, Zachary Macaulay – father of the famous historian – made trips to Paris, retained close contact with Grégoire, and channeled funds to France through him. Thus, following the death of Madame de Staël, Grégoire served as the chief intermediary between the London and

[12] Necheles, *Abbé Grégoire*, 196–203, 261.
[13] Serge Daget, *Répertoire des expéditions négrières françaises à la traite illégale* (Nantes: Centre de Recherches sur l'Histoire du Monde Atlantique, 1988), 1–18.
[14] Serge Daget, "L'abolition de la traite des noirs en France de 1814 à 1831," *Cahiers d'études africaines* 11 (1971): 22–30, 41; Yvan Debbasch, "Poésie et Traite: L'Opinion française sur le commerce négrier au début du XIXe siècle," *Revue française d'histoire d'outre-mer* 48 (1961): 316–7.
[15] Daget, "L'Abolition de la traite des noirs," 33–6; Daget, "J. E. Morenas à Paris: L'action abolitionniste, 1819–1821," *Bulletin de l'Institut fondamental d'Afrique Noire* 31 (1969): 875–85; Debbasch, "Poésie et Traite," 324–5.

Paris abolitionists, and had the means to hold sway over his French colleagues because of their utter dependence on British funding. The British encouraged Grégoire to publish anti-slave trade pamphlets and issue petitions, but the French group suffered from the effects of the Ultras' electoral victories in 1820, which led to new intimidating press laws. It was clear that the French abolitionists required some form of organization to be effective.[16]

By the early 1820s British anti-slave trade activists, led by Macaulay, were pressing abolitionists in France to create just such an organization against the illicit slave traffic. In the summer of 1821, Grégoire and Lafayette actually considered founding an anti-slave trade organization, but were deterred by the knowledge that leading liberals such as Broglie, Constant, and Auguste de Staël would prove reluctant to be openly associated with the anathematized Grégoire, accused by some of even being a regicide. Fortunately, a group of French Protestants proposed to form a philanthropic society similar to the benevolent associations that had developed in England to advance charitable works of all kinds, and not just anti-slave trade activities. Realizing, though, that any such French body must be nonsectarian and ecumenical to be effective, they turned to a group of important benevolent Catholics to head it. Most abolitionists joined it, but Grégoire, who as a former bishop and devout Catholic dared not associate too closely with Protestants, was effectively excluded from the new society. Though he retained contacts with the new group, Grégoire discretely remained outside its ranks and was reduced to producing an occasional article or booklet to vector his ideas about racial equality and the need to eliminate the slave trade. The British, however, would continue to exert considerable influence over the society throughout the 1820s by taking out membership in it, and by providing it with advice, documentation, and encouragement.[17]

Founded in a preliminary fashion in the summer of 1821, but organized definitively only on December 20 of that year when its first general assembly was held, the Société de la morale chrétienne was most active and important during the 1820s, though it continued to

[16] Necheles, *Abbé Grégoire*, 253–7.
[17] Ibid., 257–8, 261–4; Charles de Rémusat, *Mémoires de ma vie* (5 vols.; Paris: Plon, 1958–1967), II, 69; Paule Brasseur, "Libermann et l'abolition de l'esclavage," *Revue française d'histoire d'outre-mer* 73 (1986): 336.

exist in a diminished fashion until its final demise in 1860–1861.[18] According to police reports, its founders were the duc François Alexandre Frédéric de La Rochefoucauld-Liancourt – termed by the police "the banal patron of all philanthropies on earth" – the comte Alexandre de Laborde, the baron Joseph Marie Degérando, and the comte Charles Philibert de Lasteyrie du Saillant, all liberal Catholics. They were joined by several leading Protestants: Auguste de Staël, the pastor Goepp, the bookseller Jean Geoffroi Wurtz, and the highly influential clergyman and publicist Philippe Albert Stapfer. By the summer of 1823 its official membership stood at 255, but it rose to 332 by November 1824. Still, these same police reports stress the approximate nature of these official figures because subscribers could request that their names be withheld from membership lists.[19] After late 1824, participation seems to have stabilized, as a list for 1829–1830 shows it to have risen to only 388.[20] Technically, admittance to the Société required 25 francs in annual dues, nomination by two current adherents, and approval by two-thirds of attending members, though there is some evidence that anyone who requested entrance into the body and paid dues was in fact admitted. Nevertheless, membership was clearly dominated by the political, social, and religious elite. Adherents were solicited in both the provinces and foreign countries, and auxiliary societies were established in cities such as Bordeaux, Marseilles, Mulhouse, and Nimes – the latter two cities testifying to Protestant influence. Still, a large majority of members appear to have been Paris-based. There were a great many Protestants in the society, though claims of total Protestant dominance of the organization are exaggerated if a membership count and scrutiny of its leading officers is undertaken. Indeed, an examination of fifty-one leading members of the society mentioned in this study shows that only seventeen, or 33 percent, are identifiable as Protestants. When one notes, however, that Protestants constituted only approximately 2 percent of the total French population at the time, it is apparent that

---

[18] Rémusat, *Mémoirés*, II, 69; *Journal de la Société de la morale chrétienne*, vol. 1, 1822, p. 1. For an integral account of the society's anti-slavery stance, see Lawrence C. Jennings, "French Anti-Slavery under the Restoration: The Société de la morale chrétienne," *Revue française d'histoire d'outre-mer*, 81 (1994): 321–31.

[19] France, Archives Nationales, F7 6960, dossier 12024, Ministère de l'Intérieur, Direction de Police, reports dated Aug. 23, 1823, Aug. 31, 1824.

[20] *Journal de la Société de la morale chrétienne*, vol. 12, 1830, pp. 53–64.

Protestants did play a disproportionately large role in the society, as they did in many nineteenth-century French reform-minded or altruistic groups.

If the Société de la morale chrétienne was influential under the Restoration it was not because of its numbers, which in themselves fail to distinguish it from other associations of its time. It was through the importance of its members, who constituted a veritable Who's Who of the leaders of the liberal opposition in the 1820s and of the future governing elite of the July Monarchy that was to follow in 1830. Among the society's officers or committee members, in addition to the founders mentioned above, were individuals such as Broglie (who became its first president), Constant, Charles de Rémusat, baron Amable Guillaume Prosper Brugière de Barante, Charles Coquerel, comte Jean Denis Lanjuinais, Théobald Piscatory, Horace de Vielcastel, the Protestants François Guizot, Admiral Carel Henrik Verhuell, and Benjamin Sigismond Frossart (a former member of the Amis des Noirs), and the Protestant leader, Paul Henri Marron (president of the Reformed Church Consistory). Some of the other more noteworthy members were the comte Antoine Maurice d'Argout, Hippolyte Carnot (son of the revolutionary), François Delessert, Prosper Duvergier de Hauranne, baron Auguste d'Eichtal, comte Charles de Montalembert, Casimir Périer, General Horace Sébastiani, François Villemain, Adolphe Thiers, and the duc d'Orleans – the future King Louis Philippe – himself. Police reports dating from 1823–1824 noted that while the society had only three confirmed royalists in its ranks, it had eight peers, nine deputies from the extreme left, twelve professors, about the same number of lawyers, several editors, no priests, but many pastors.[21] Opposed to the government, and unable to implement its ideas legislatively, the organization was only occasionally effective in realizing its philanthropic agenda. It also had little popular support and deigned not appeal to public opinion because of its own elitist orientation. Nevertheless, by acting through the press, its own journal, petitions, pamphlet literature, and the back rooms of the legislative assemblies and government ministries, it exercised considerable moral and political sway during the last decade of the Restoration.

The Société de la morale chrétienne could be described as a liberal,

---

[21] Archives Nationales, F7 6960 (12024), Aug. 23, 1823, Aug. 31, 1824.

nondenominational philanthropic society, inspired by both universalist Enlightenment and religious principles, which devoted itself to advancing moral and social issues through education, propaganda, and political activism, while in the process indicting the government's retrograde social policies. In 1833 the Prefect of the Aude department quite aptly depicted it as an association where Catholics and Protestants met "on the terrain of confessional neutrality," for religious dogma was banned from its meetings.[22] Police observers were less generous in their analysis of a body which they categorized as neither Catholic nor Protestant, but as a "vast league formed by Protestants and liberals born Catholic" whose objective was "to de-Catholicize France and bring about the reign of a perfect religious tolerance formed upon the profession of a morality . . . stripped of all dogma."[23] Worse yet, according to these sources, the Morale chrétienne was "composed in general of former and new revolutionaries" who were trying to spread the principles of liberalism among "young people." Its "proposed aim" was the "improvement of the state of the unfortunate and of prisoners, and the amelioration of the human spirit through the propagation of the principles of the Scriptures," but its philanthropy was a mere "mantle with which it covered itself to escape from the view of the authorities" as it preached its "essentially political aim" which was "both anti-religious and anti-monarchical."[24] The point was that in the eyes of the authorities the society was "entirely composed of individuals devoted to the liberal cause," that it was associated with the "interests of a party," that of Guizot and the opposition. Police informers wondered "how much longer the Société could be tolerated without danger," whether its preachings were not "dangerous to the state."[25]

Despite the government's misgivings about the society as a front for the opposition, it survived untouched under the Restoration monarchy, probably due to its well-placed, moderate leadership, and its essentially esoteric nature. It shared the loose organization typical

[22] Pierre Genevray, "Gabriel Delessert, préfet, puis préfet de police, résistance en politique, apaisement dans les questions religieuses, 1834–1848," *Bulletin de la Société de l'histoire du Protestantisme français* 103 (1957), 15.
[23] Archives Nationales, F7 6960 (12024), Jan. 24, 1824.
[24] Ibid., Aug. 23, May 23, 1823, Aug. 31, 1824.
[25] Ibid., Jan. 24, March 16, 1824, Aug. 30, 1823, Aug. 31, 1824.

of associations of the time, being headed by an administrative council of thirty members which met monthly and was answerable in principle to a yearly general assembly.[26] The society's philanthropic works were managed by nine more or less active committees, among them an editorial committee for its journal, a committee for charity, a committee for the suppression of the death penalty, one for the repression of the lottery, another for improving prisons, yet another for assistance to the Greeks, and one for the abolition of the slave trade. Some of these bodies met weekly or monthly, others when convoked into session.[27] One of the most dynamic of these committees in the early years of the society was that on the slave trade, presided over by the energetic baron de Staël.

The slave trade committee of the Morale chrétienne played the leading role in French slave trade abolitionism in the 1820s. It sponsored an essay contest for the abolition of the illicit traffic, subsidized publications denouncing it, kept close relations with British abolitionists, and even supported a trip by de Staël to Nantes, where, in imitation of Thomas Clarkson's earlier visits to the slaving ports of Bristol and Liverpool, he gathered information on slaving activities. The society's initiatives probably sparked interventions against the slave traffic in the Chamber of Deputies by baron Jean Guillaume Hyde de Neuville (a former French minister to the United States) and Benjamin Constant, along with the long tirade on the subject by Broglie in the Chamber of Peers on March 28, 1822, that immortalized the Duke as the leading anti-slave trade proponent in France.[28] The sudden publicity given the slave trade question by Broglie's speech and the actions of the slave trade committee of the Morale chrétienne undoubtedly were connected with the decision of the then liberal-dominated Académie Française in 1822 to make the question

[26] On the similarity between the admittance practices and overall organization of the Société de la morale chrétienne and of other associations of the time, see Anne Martin-Frugier, "La formation des élites: Les 'conférences' sous la Restauration et la Monarchie de Juillet," *Revue d'histoire moderne et contemporaine* 36 (1989): 211–244.

[27] For the organization of the Society, see Archives Nationales, F7 6960 (12024), Aug. 31, 1824, and the first issue of the *Journal de la Société de la morale chrétienne*, vol. 1, 1822, pp. 1–16. On the group's position toward the Greeks, see Jean Dimakis, "La Société de la morale chrétienne et son action en faveur des Grecs lors de l'insurrection de 1831," *Balkan Studies* 7 (1966): 27–48.

[28] Daget, "The Abolition of the Slave Trade," 143–4; "L'Abolition de la traite des Noirs," 42–4, 46–7, 49; Debbasch, "Poésie et Traite," 326–7, 330.

of the abolition of the slave trade the subject of its poetry contest for 1823.[29] In the 1820s the Société de la morale chrétienne revived the slave trade abolition question and made an important contribution to advancing this agenda in France.[30]

In the 1820s, as earlier, French abolitionists followed the British tactic of concentrating primarily on undermining the slave trade. Indeed, in the early 1820s, important abolitionists such as Broglie and Duvergier de Hauranne believed that slavery was still considered too essential for the survival of the colonies to be attacked.[31] Their attitudes accurately reflected government policies toward slavery at this time. After all, comte Joseph de Villèle, president of the Council of Ministers under Louis XVIII and Charles X from 1822 to 1828, was himself an important colonial planter from Ile de Bourbon. When the Minister of the Navy and Colonies in 1821, Pierre Barthélémy, baron Portal d'Albaredès, heard that the Académie des Sciences et Belles Lettres de Lyon was opening an essay contest on how best to improve the situation of the colonies, he ordered the Prefect of the Rhône department to offer 1,500 francs toward the prize if the Lyon academy recognized the necessity of maintaining the status quo concerning slavery.[32] Still, the slave trade committee of the Société de la morale chrétienne demonstrated some concern about the slavery question as it dealt with what it considered to be the more important one of the slave trade. A thorough examination of the works of the Société de la morale chrétienne demonstrates the extent to which the slave trade committee under de Staël in the 1820s launched the movement for the second abolition of French colonial slavery.

Formed on April 8, 1822, at the instigation of a visiting English Quaker, Joseph Price, the slave trade committee of the society was composed at first of five members. Besides its president, de Staël, it included the deputy baron Jean Frédéric de Turckheim, the comte de Lasteyrie, pastor Marron, and the *négociant* (merchant) Vernes, but then rapidly expanded to include six others: baron Degérando, the

[29] Ibid., 311–2, 334–8.
[30] Serge Daget, "A Model of the French Abolitionist Movement and Its Variations," in Christine Bolt and Seymour Drescher, eds., *Anti-Slavery, Religion, and Reform: Essays in Memory of Roger Anstey* (Folkstone, Kent: Dawson, 1980), p. 72.
[31] Debbasch, "Poésie et Traite," 346.
[32] France, Archives Nationales, Centre des Archives d'Outre-Mer, Aix-en-Provence (hereafter cited as ANCAOM), Généralités 53 (472), Minister to Prefect, Nov. 5, 1821.

négociant Wilder, pastor Marck Wilks, the Protestant militant Charles Coquerel, the former deputy André Daniel Laffon-Ladabat, and the Catholic theologian Lhorente. Clearly, this early committee membership, which functioned during the most active phase of the committee, was heavily Protestant. From 1827 the duc de Broglie became its president and its numbers were stabilized at seventeen: Rémusat, de Staël, Lasteyrie, Laffon-Ladebat, Marron, Vernes, Coquerel, Wilks, Delessert, Jean Isidore Partarrieu-Lafosse, the lawyer Henri Dutrône (a future leader of the French abolition society), the marquis Félix Renouard de Sainte-Croix, the peers comte Marthe Camille Bachasson de Montalivet and the duc Napoleon Lannes de Montebello, the deputy Louis Guillaume Ternaux, and the former deputy Charles Guillaume Etienne. As of its formation in 1822 this committee attacked the problem of the slave trade, but during its very first meeting de Staël also declared that it would seek the "improvement of the state of blacks in diverse places around the globe." He was joined by Degérando, who emphasized that amelioration should be achieved primarily through the education of slave children.[33] From its very beginning, de Staël's group made it clear that it would also take the question of slavery under its purview.

By the second year of its existence the slave trade committee had clarified its stance and defined its objectives concerning slavery. Blacks, it was agreed, who were in no way inferior to whites, must be gradually prepared for their eventual freedom by instruction and moralization. Immediate emancipation would be dangerous and counterproductive, but a gradual process would achieve slave liberation without upheaval. Such an approach would also prevent another Saint-Domingue, undermine the slave trade, and actually improve colonial production because free labor would prove to be more profitable than the coerced variety. This latter point echoed the ideas of British liberal economists, and had obviously been influenced by writings of Liverpool abolitionists who had stressed in a pamphlet – reported upon by the French organization – the economic benefits of slave liberation. Showing a similar preoccupation with sustained slave labor, Coquerel proposed a model for gradual manumission through

[33] *Journal de la Société de la morale chrétienne*, vol. 1, 1822, pp. 66–7; 2nd series, vol. 6, 1834, p. 299.

progressive self-redemption by slaves, who would work certain days on their own and save up funds to purchase their freedom.[34] This approach to freeing the slaves would remain one of the options put forth by French abolitionists for the next twenty years. Already in 1823, then, the leadership of the society had become convinced that it was possible to "destroy the evil [of slavery] by degrees; we will begin by [pressing for] salutary regulations to improve the condition of blacks. Other measures will follow this first step, and within ten to twelve years this despicable system will be destroyed from top to bottom."[35] In espousing this approach to slave liberation, the French organization was aligning itself perfectly with the stance of British abolitionists who also believed at this time in the effectiveness of gradualism, rather than immediatism (or the advocacy of the immediate freeing of slaves), in arriving at the eradication of servitude in the colonies.[36]

After outlining its anti-slavery objectives, the Société de la morale chrétienne strove to attain them by means often supported by the British. In one of its annual reports the slave trade committee – which also began to refer to itself at times as the slavery committee – complained that its "slender pecuniary resources" limited its "means of action" in both slave trade and slavery matters to "gathering documents, stating facts, and enlightening public opinion and the government."[37] In reality, the committee was exaggerating its poverty, for its annual budget invariably showed a surplus, and it was able to offer substantial prizes in essay contests. More likely, the group's actions were limited by its elitist approach, and by government regulations on associations which made a public appeal and petitioning difficult, if

[34] Ibid., vol. 2, 1823, pp. 41–8, 51–4, 142–5.
[35] Report to the Société française pour l'abolition de l'esclavage by the duc Gaëtan de La Rochefoucauld-Liancourt on the early works of the Société de la morale chrétienne, *Journal de la Société de la morale chrétienne*, 2nd series, vol. 6, Dec. 1834, p. 304.
[36] On the process of gradualism versus immediatism, see the classic study by David Brion Davis, "The Emergence of Immediatism in British and American Antislavery Thought," *Mississippi Valley Historical Review*, 49 (1962): 209–230. On the British gradualist approach, see David Turley, *The Culture of English Antislavery, 1780–1860* (London: Routledge, 1991); William A. Green, *British Slave Emancipation: The Sugar Colonies and the Great Experiment, 1830–1865* (Oxford: Clarendon, 1976); and David Brion Davis, *The Problem of Slavery in the Age of Revolution, 1770–1823* (Ithaca: Cornell University Press, 1975).
[37] *Journal de la Société de la morale chrétienne*, vol. 7, 1826, p. 43.

not impossible. Be this as it may, the committee did undertake a concerted effort to publicize both slave trade and slavery issues. De Staël's group disseminated information on the state of slaves in France's colonies and the progress being made against servitude in Britain's tropical possessions by publishing relevant articles in the society's *Journal*, often resorting to British-supplied documentation in the process. The society noted that its British correspondents, William Allen, Joseph Price, General Macaulay, Zachary Macaulay, and Joseph Forster, had been particularly helpful in forwarding relevant information to Paris.[38] The society also subsidized the publication of at least one pamphlet of British-provided material against slavery, a sixty-four-page compilation of speeches by Thomas Fowell Buxton in favor of gradual emancipation, translated and introduced by Coquerel.[39] The aim of the society in emitting documentation of this kind was to demonstrate that "the black African race is as capable as the European one of being educated and civilized," and that emancipation would prove advantageous rather than inconvenient to all parties concerned.[40]

Besides publishing information on the slavery question, the Société de la morale chrétienne appealed to the government to adopt a program for eventual slave liberation, believing that where slave owners would not act they must be encouraged to do so by state intervention. Like its British equivalents after 1810, de Staël's group called for a general census of slaves, the elimination of barriers to manumission, according slaves free days to accumulate savings, and setting maximum prices for slave redemption. Such moves led the duc Gaëtan de La Rochefoucauld-Liancourt – who succeeded his father and became president of the society after Broglie stepped down – to claim that the Société de la morale chrétienne "supported the first measures for the amelioration of slavery" in French colonies.[41] The society even sponsored a contest with a prize of 1,500 francs for the best essay on the gradual elimination of slavery. Its proposed objective was to

---

[38] Ibid., vol. 3, 1824, pp. 127–8, 233; vol. 4, 1825, p. 10; vol. 5, 1825, pp. 108–121.

[39] J. [Thomas Fowell] Buxton, *Discours prononcé dans la Chambre des Communes d'Angleterre à l'appui de la motion pour l'adoucissement et l'extinction graduelle de l'esclavage dans les colonies anglaises* (Paris: Crapelet, 1824).

[40] *Journal de la Société de la morale chrétienne*, vol. 5, 1825, pp. 357–72; 2nd series, vol. 6, Dec. 1834, p. 308.

[41] Ibid., pp. 312–4.

demonstrate how "slaves could gradually be made salaried workers" and "how, by moral and religious education ... they could be brought gradually, but promptly, without danger for themselves and their present owners, to enjoy fully political and civil liberties."[42] This same measure of cautious concern about the rights of planters as well as slaves was echoed in reports by de Staël and Alphonse Mahul in which they emphasized that the master was also a man and that the brutalized slave was not ready to exercise complete freedom.[43] This attitude on the part of the society perfectly reflected the legalistic, moralistic, extremely timid gradualism that was predominant not only among British and French abolitionists in the 1820s, but which would mark much of French anti-slavery throughout the July Monarchy.

An examination of documentation emanating from the society shows that from 1822 to 1827 its slave trade/slavery committee had been one of its most active and prominent lobbying groups. Then, on November 11, 1827, August de Staël died. Though at the time he had already relinquished its presidency, de Staël had been the prime mover behind the anti-slave trade and slavery committee, and his passing was sorely felt. The committee's membership in 1828 remained at seventeen: Mahul, Carnot, vicomte Dejean, and the lawyers Edmond Blanc and François Isambert (later the leader of the Société française pour l'abolition de l'esclavage) replaced de Staël, Coquerel, Partarieu-Lafosse, Vernes, and Wilks, reducing considerably its Protestant element. But it lapsed into a state of lethargy and relative inactivity for the remainder of the Restoration. Following de Staël's death, the society's journal rarely published items on the slavery question, in marked contrast with the preceding years. As part of the society's annual report of 1829, Edouard Thayer (another future animator of the French abolition society) evoked de Staël's memory and avowed that "since such a precious assistance as his has been removed from us, the works of the committee [of the slave trade and slavery] have been much slowed down."[44] During the annual assemblies of 1828, 1830, and 1831 different committees made reports on their activities, but not the one on slave trade/slavery. In fact, the committee seems to have met but rarely following de Staël's demise, for as of 1828 it was

[42] Ibid., vol. 7, 1826, pp. 267–71.
[43] Ibid., vol. 7, 1826, p. 58; vol. 8, 1828, p. 129.
[44] Ibid., vol. 11, 1829, p. 160.

convoked only on special order, and not the first Monday of each month as in the past. The essay contest on gradual emancipation launched by the society in 1826 had never been concluded because of lack of interest, but in 1829 the committee somewhat grudgingly awarded the prize money jointly to the only two essays that had been submitted.[45] This was probably the most significant move on slavery by the committee between the death of de Staël and the Revolution of 1830. Quite clearly, the Société de la morale chrétienne was structurally weak, and overly dependent upon individual initiative. This dependence upon the input of influential individuals rather than the reduction of Protestant influence within the committee is the most likely explanation for the society's neglect of slavery after 1827. Following de Staël's passing from the scene, the society effectively tabled the slavery issue for the final two and a half years of the Restoration.

This inaction on slavery coincided with a general decline of the entire society by 1830. Rémusat, one of the leading figures within both the society and its slave trade/slavery committee, explained the situation as one in which members became distracted by the increased pace of political developments preceding July 1830 and consequently neglected philanthropic endeavors.[46] As a result, the society's journal shrank considerably in size prior to the July Revolution of 1830. With the advent of the Orleanist regime it temporarily took on a new name, *Archives philanthropiques*, and reduced even further its coverage of the society's works. The journal's concentration on humanitarian questions in other countries at this time provides additional evidence of the organization's lethargy and its neglect of French affairs. Apparently, the society's inaction in the early years of the July Monarchy was compounded by the fact that many of its members had assumed positions within the new Orleanist government after July 1830, and were too preoccupied with matters of power to devote much energy to charitable questions.[47] Never again would the society be as significant a body as it had been in the first few years of its existence. Rémusat even went so far as to assert that it had become a mere shadow of its former self, that it "existed only nominally after the Revolution of 1830."[48]

[45] Ibid., pp. 104, 153–70.
[46] Rémusat, *Mémoires*, II, 71.
[47] *Journal de la Société de la morale chrétienne*, 2nd series, vol. 9, 1836, pp. 188–9.
[48] Rémusat, *Mémoires*, II, 71.

Rémusat's claims can be misleading, however, for the Société de la morale chrétienne survived in atrophied form until 1860–1861. Indeed, an examination of its publications following the July Revolution shows that its committees covered most of the domains that it had treated before 1830, including slavery, albeit with reduced means, less determination, and diminished results. In the early to mid-1830s, when the July Monarchy itself was working to develop new colonial legislation, the society renewed in several ways its support for gradual slave emancipation. It continued to publicize cases of slave mistreatment, it organized a minor petition campaign, and, most important, it instituted a program to purchase the freedom of individual young female slaves whose offspring would subsequently be born free.[49] By the mid-1830s the organization's principal activity concerning slavery was this "redemption of Negresses."[50] As of the late 1830s the society, under the increased influence of its then president Gaëtan de La Rochefoucauld-Liancourt, slowly adapted a more radical position of denying indemnity to slave masters after emancipation, and even flirted at times with immediatism.[51] The point is, though, that by this time the Société de la morale chrétienne had yielded its leadership of the anti-slavery campaign to the Société française pour l'abolition de l'esclavage, and consequently displayed relatively little initiative in the emancipation question.

After the formation of the new anti-slavery organization in 1834, the Morale chrétienne rarely treated the slavery question. Moreover, its discussions or actions in the slavery sphere had few repercussions outside its own corridors. Seldom was the stance of the Morale chrétienne on slavery cited in the major organs of the French press, in debates within the legislative chambers, or in the proceedings and publications of other abolitionist groups. The society had become a marginal anti-slavery body, superseded by the larger, more specialized, and more influential Société française pour l'abolition de l'esclavage. In fact, many of the stalwarts of the Morale chrétienne, like Broglie, Isambert, de Laborde, Dutrône, Thayer, and La Rochefoucauld-Liancourt,

---

[49] *Archives philanthropiques*, vol. 1, 1830, p. 194; vol. 2, 1830, p. 69; *Journal de la Société de la morale chrétienne*, 2nd series, vol. 4, 1833, pp. 32–8; vol. 1, 1832, pp. 3–8, 16–18.
[50] Ibid., 2nd series, vol. 9, 1836, p. 194.
[51] Ibid., vol. 10, 1836, pp. 280–91; vol. 11, 1837, pp. 1–11; vol. 12, 1837, pp. 285–8; vol. 15, 1839, pp. 181–2.

played an important role in forming the new abolitionist society, as if they had come to realize the ineffectiveness of the Morale chrétienne by the early 1830s. And the heritage of the Société de la morale chrétienne continued to live on through its successor organization in the anti-slavery field. The Société française pour l'abolition de l'esclavage would not only borrow much of its initial leadership from its predecessor, but also its gradualist approach toward emancipation.

Indeed, social composition, ideology, and strategies differed little between French abolitionist formations of the Revolutionary period and those of the early 1830s. The ranks of the Amis des Noirs, of abolitionists under the Empire and early Restoration, and of the Morale chrétienne were all drawn from the same social, political, and intellectual elite, persons of noble or elevated status who had little confidence in the masses and who had great difficulty appealing to popular mobilization for the anti-slavery cause. Their methods were those of personal or legislative initiatives aimed at advancing their objectives through the action of governments to which they themselves often belonged. Their primary means of propagandizing was via the printed media, with the hope of persuading like-minded members of the upper classes to support their efforts. The revolutionary experience of the 1790s, if anything, had strengthened their class solidarity and confirmed their wariness of the people. Not only Girondin survivors, but their successor abolitionists under the Directory, Napoleonic, and Restoration regimes, saw the popular-based radical Revolution that had accomplished the first freeing of French colonial slaves as a period of instability, upheaval, and bloodshed that could be avoided only by restricting power to elite hands. Unlike their British anti-slavery brethren, they had much difficulty bringing themselves to resort to the tactics of popular appeal, mass mobilization, and large-scale petitioning of the sort that had swayed the British parliament to eradicate the slave trade and begin the process of undermining British colonial slavery. Furthermore, abolitionism had been so tied in with revolutionary radicalism and the bloodshed of Saint-Domingue that officialdom under both the Empire and Restoration associated advocates of anti-slavery with dreaded republicanism and terror. During the forty years following the first liberation of the slaves, French abolitionists both feared the populace and were themselves stigmatized for their populist tendencies by their fellow members of the ruling elite. The revolutionary tradition limited more than it advanced the anti-slavery cause in nineteenth-century France.

Unable to turn to the French populace for support, French opponents of the slave trade and slavery prior to the 1830s often turned to the British. The Amis des Noirs both before and after 1794, the cliques surrounding Madame de Staël and Grégoire, and finally the members of the Morale chrétienne all lacked the means to expand their activities. All were heavily dependent upon British abolitionists for funds, material, even concepts. In all probability, French anti-slave trade and anti-slavery groupings could not have developed to the point that they had without British inspiration and assistance. British support, however, carried with it drawbacks as well as advantages for French abolitionists both before and after 1830. It nourished French philanthropy, but also limited its influence and scope. Anti-British sentiment remained strong in France during the first three decades of the nineteenth century. Any formation close to the British, such as the abolitionists, would necessarily remain suspect in the eyes of many Frenchmen, not to mention French officialdom. The London–Paris anti-slavery axis probably alienated many Frenchmen from abolitionism. British support for French abolitionists limited the chances of anti-slavery becoming popular in France.

Both its elitist orientation and British inspiration influenced the concepts and tactics of French abolitionism from 1789 to 1830. All French abolitionists from Brissot to Auguste de Staël followed the British strategy of attacking first of all the slave trade before turning their attention to slavery itself. They, like the British, felt the slave trade to be the most visible and elementary of the two evils. They, again like the British, harbored the false assumption that eradicating the slave traffic would undermine slavery by curtailing its supply in the long run, and obliging masters to treat their subjects better in the short term. Only after the slave trade was eliminated would they concentrate their efforts entirely against slavery. Other principles animating French abolitionists, though, were determined as much by the times as by their friends across the Channel. Enlightenment universalist ideals inspired the French intellectual elite that led the struggle against the slave traffic and slavery from 1789 to 1830. The belief that all humanity possessed certain basic rights was prominent among the totality of French abolitionists. So was the conviction that the enslaved must be prepared and elevated before exercising their universalist rights. Whether they be British or French, abolitionists prior to 1830 were persuaded that true freedom entailed responsibilities, especially those of duty, orderliness, and work. Thus, French abolitionists from the Amis des Noirs through the Morale chrétienne stressed the need for gradually preparing slaves for freedom in order to avoid the disruptions and upheavals that had occurred in the 1790s. The coming of the July Monarchy changed many things, but after 1830 many of these same ideals, objectives, and strategies would continue to mark French anti-slavery.

In 1830, however, many observers believed a new era to be opening. A three-day revolution in July toppled the Restoration, and the last of the Bourbons, Charles X, fled to England. The duc d'Orléans was proclaimed King Louis Philippe. The new king, who had even been a member of the Jacobin club for a brief period during his youth, had an impeccable liberal background. He promised and produced change, being proclaimed King of the French rather than King of France. The tricolor flag was reintroduced, basic liberties were promised, and the electorate was expanded from 94,000 under Charles X to some 166,000, or 0.5 percent of the total population – though it would expand to nearly a quarter of a million by 1846. Because many of Charles X's supporters, the Legitimists, refused to cooperate with the new monarch, they were replaced in most functions by Orleanists, loyal to Louis Philippe.[52] The Orleanists were led by the liberal opposition leaders of the Restoration, Broglie, Guizot, Constant, Sébastiani, Villemain, Montalivet, Montebello, Casimir Périer, Adolphe Thiers. Many of them, who became future ministers in the new July Monarchy, had been members of the Société de la morale chrétienne, as had the King himself. It seemed as though a new page had been turned, that liberal causes, such as anti-slavery, would emerge victorious.

This faith in rapid change, however, failed to take into account the fact that these new leaders of the July Monarchy too were members of a landed, professional, commercial, or educated elite, the so-called

---

[52] On the Revolution of 1830 and the July Monarchy, see David Pinkney, *The French Revolution of 1830* (Princeton: Princeton University Press, 1972); John Merriman, ed., *1830 in France* (New York: New Viewpoints, 1975); and H.A.C. Collingham, *The July Monarchy: A Political History of France, 1830–1848* (London: Longman, 1988).

notables, who were of the same social groupings and political school as the previous ruling classes. They too feared popular participation in governmental affairs, were legalistic in their approach, and were conservative in their social orientation.[53] Their government too would be one of parliamentary maneuvers, shifting cliques, and cautious pragmatism. Louis Philippe himself fostered a fierce desire to rule behind the scenes, to play one faction off against the other, to strive for stability above all. As of 1840 he found the gifted political leader he required to rule for him, François Guizot, who based his dominance upon brilliant political skills and the ability to manipulate a majority strengthened by the presence of many placemen, or deputies rewarded for faithfulness by government offices. With its desire to avoid all reform and preserve the status quo at all costs, in many ways the Orleanist regime by the 1840s proved not that different from Restoration governments. This similarity would also be reflected in its policy toward colonial slavery.

---

[53] The classic study on this July Monarchy elite is André Jean Tudesq, *Les grands notables en France (1840–1849): Etude historique d'une psychologie sociale* (2 vols.; Paris: Presses Universitaires de France, 1964).

2

THE REVOLUTION
OF 1830 AND THE
COLONIES

Amidst this initial flurry of activity that marked the new regime in 1830, there were indications that the July Monarchy's reform measures would include the colonial domain. After all, the ruling elite of the new regime actually contained many members of the former liberal opposition who had criticized slavery and the slave trade, and even some of the leaders of the Société de la morale chrétienne. As of the autumn of 1830, Cyrille Bissette, the black activist who would become the most radical abolitionist under the July Monarchy, rejoiced to find some of his friends or associates in the Cabinet: Henry Gauthier, comte de Rigny, in the navy–colonial portfolio; Jacques Charles Dupont de l'Eure in the justice ministry; and baron Joseph Dominique Louis as justice minister.[1] The *Archives philanthropiques*, new organ of the Société de la morale chrétienne, expressed its confidence that this Orleanist administration would prove more willing than its legitimist predecessors to take measures to improve the plight of colonial slaves.[2] As if to confirm this expectation, *Le Courrier français* (Paris), a staunch opponent of Charles X and close to the new regime in the early 1830s, affirmed in August that the navy-colonial department was determined to bring about innovations in the colonial sphere.[3] Then, in reply to an interpolation by the marquis de Lafayette in the Chamber of Deputies on September 25, 1830, the then Minister

---

[1] Josette Fallope, *Esclaves et citoyens: Les Noirs de la Guadeloupe au XIXème siècle dans les processus de résistance et d'intégration, 1802–1910* (Basse-Terre: Société d'Histoire de la Guadeloupe, 1992), 247.
[2] *Archives philanthropiques*, vol. 2 (1830), p. 69.
[3] *Le Courrier francais*, August 26, 1830; Stella Pâme, "Cyrille Bissette, 1795–1858," doctorat de 3ème cycle, Université de Paris, 1978, p. 177.

of the Navy and Colonies, General Horace Sébastiani – another liberal and former *Morale chrétienne* adherent – announced his intention to implement soon reforms making free men of color equal before the law.[4] Overwhelmed as it might be in the summer of 1830 with formulating its internal and foreign policy, the Orleanist monarchy had apparently not forgotten the colonial issue. The colonial question remained a serious concern for the new regime as it had for all previous governments in the first half of the nineteenth century.

French colonies experienced mixed fortunes under both the Restoration and July Monarchy. French colonial commerce and the great Atlantic ports of Nantes and Bordeaux had never recovered from the crisis concomitant with the Revolutionary and Napoleonic eras and the revolt in Saint-Domingue. Prior to the Revolution, Saint-Domingue alone had produced 30 percent of world sugar in 1787, and the other French West Indian colonies an additional 13 percent, for a grand total of 43 percent. In 1788 France had imported a record 106,400 tons of sugar from the French West Indies in French ships alone, while in 1806 the entire French Empire imported only 29,450 tons on ships of any flag.[5] The loss of Saint-Domingue, the "pearl of the Antilles," along with the blockade or seizure of the other staple-producing French colonies during the almost continual period of warfare from 1793 to 1815, had been disastrous for French colonial establishments and their commerce with French ports.

Following the fall of Napoleon in 1814–1815, recovery was slow at first, for trade circuits were disrupted, and French colonial staples faced stiff competition from foreign producers. Martinique, Guadeloupe, and Bourbon restructured themselves to concentrate almost exclusively on sugar production to compensate for the loss of Saint-Domingue. This process required heavy investment, and it increased

---

[4] *Le Moniteur universel*, Sept. 27, 1830; Cyrille Bissette, *C.C.A. Bissette, homme de couleur de la Martinique, à un colon, sur l'émancipation civile et politique appliquée aux colonies françaises* (Paris: Imprimerie Gaultier-Laguionie, 1830), 26. Debates in the French Chamber of Peers and Chamber of Deputies were regularly inserted in the official newspaper, *Le Moniteur universel*, on the day following their actual occurrence (unless otherwise indicated).

[5] Seymour Drescher, *Econocide: British Slavery in the Era of Abolition* (Pittsburgh: University of Pittsburgh Press, 1977), 48, 129; Geggus, "Racial Equality, Slavery," 1291; Dale Tomich, *Slavery in the Circuit of Sugar: Martinique and the World Economy, 1830–1848* (Baltimore: Johns Hopkins University Press, 1990), 20.

colonial costs, especially because of manpower shortages due to restrictions on the slave trade. Restructuring and the high price of slaves obtained through the illicit traffic also drove up colonial indebtedness. Problems were exacerbated by the fact that French colonial sugar proved unable to compete on the world market. Some protective tariffs were introduced already in 1814, but it was not until 1822 that the colonial lobby succeeded in persuading the Ultras to pass high tariffs that practically excluded foreign sugar from the French market. Under this artificial protection, French colonial sugar producers experienced a steady increase in fortunes in the late 1820s.[6]

As of 1830 the situation of the colonies had improved markedly. The latter part of the 1820s were known as the golden age of sugar production in the West Indies. French imports from the colonies and the number of ships involved in colonial trade doubled between 1816 and 1829. One-third of indebted planters were able to reach solvency by the time of the July Revolution.[7] The colonial system was consolidated and strengthened in the process. As one recent historian has remarked, at the outset of the July Monarchy, the colonies had become an "indispensable component of the power and richness of France" in the eyes "of a majority of those in power" in Paris.[8]

To be sure, French plantation economies suffered some setbacks even under the July Monarchy. Though indebtedness diminished by the early 1830s, it began to increase again following 1835. After 1837, Martinique even experienced a permanent balance of trade deficit with the mother country.[9] Most of the economic problems facing the colonies from the mid-1830s on were due to the decline in sugar prices and to decreased demand for colonial sugar caused by the increased competition from metropolitan-grown beet sugar, because

---

[6] Ibid., 33–4, 43–6; Francis Démier, "Esclavage, économie coloniale et choix de développement français durant la première industrialisation, 1802–1840," in Les abolitions de d'esclavage, 273–81; Jacques Fiérain, Les raffineries de sucre des ports français, XIXe – au début du XXe siècle (New York: Arno, 1977), 55; Fallope, Esclaves et ciyoyens, 71.

[7] Ibid., 73–5; Tomich, Slavery in the Circuit, 41–2; Christian Schnakenbourg, Histoire de l'industrie sucrière en Guadeloupe aux XIXe et XXe siècles, vol. 1: La crise du système esclavagiste, 1835–1847 (Paris: L'Harmattan, 1980), 140–41; Démier, "Esclavage," 282.

[8] Ibid., 283.

[9] Schnakenbourg, Historie de l'industrie sucrière, 123; Tomich, Slavery in the Circuit, 108–9.

the same protective tariffs that sheltered cane sugar encouraged beet production in France.[10] Other colonial difficulties arose from the usurious lending rates – a minimum of 16 percent – levied on the planters by local middlemen or metropolitan merchants who could not foreclose on plantations for which there were few buyers, and who resorted to offsetting investment losses through high interest payments.[11] Finally, the menace of eventual slave liberation weighed upon the colonies, decreasing slave and plantation prices and discouraging further investments. In Guadeloupe, for instance, plantation values declined approximately 50 percent between the mid-1820s and late 1830s, and another 50 percent by 1848.[12] The result was a constant flow of complaints to Paris by planters who simultaneously demanded economic relief measures and the retention of the slave system upon which their continued viability depended. In the process, the *colons* also became increasingly dependent upon the export-generated revenue derived from their sugar monoculture.

Throughout the July Monarchy, sugar accounted for 92 and 90 percent, respectively, of the total French imports from the two leading slave colonies of Guadeloupe and Martinique. As of the Restoration, Bourbon too had become a significant producer of sugar cane. Despite the increased competition of beet sugar, from 1837 to 1848 France imported an annual average of 84,371 tons of sugar from its four colonies of Guadeloupe, Martinique, Bourbon, and Guiana. Though this was slightly less than the approximately 88,000 tons imported into France annually from French holdings between 1785–1790, when France still had Saint-Domingue and was the world leader in sugar production, it nevertheless constituted an important factor in French commerce. Moreover, in some individual years, such as 1845, sugar imports into France from French colonies surpassed the pre-Revolutionary average, attaining 102,000 at this particular time – or nearly as much as the exceptional amount of 1787.[13] To be

---

[10] See Chapter 5.

[11] Schnakenbourg, *Historie de l'industrie sucrière*, 125–30; Tomich, *Slavery in the Circuit*, 114–22.

[12] Ibid., 110; Schnakenbourg, *Historie de l'industrie sucrière*, 130, 184–5. For slave prices, see Chapter 9.

[13] France, Administration des douanes, *Tableau décennal du commerce de la France avec ses colonies et les puissances étrangères, 1837–1846* (Paris: Imprimerie Nationale, 1848), 150; Schnakenbourg, *Historie de l'industrie sucrière*, 141; Jean Tarrade, *Le*

sure, overall French colonial staple production had fallen from pre-Revolutionary levels. In 1788, Saint-Domingue alone had produced 86,300 tons of sugar, and the other French West Indian holdings an additional 38,900, or 125,200 tons altogether.[14] But a good proportion of this was sold on world markets, unlike under the July Monarchy when inflated prices of French produced colonial sugar restricted it largely to the French market. Then, too, the considerable pre-Revolutionary French colonial production of coffee, cocoa, and cotton had dwindled to a mere trickle, as a sugar monoculture set in in French tropical possessions after 1815. The point is, then, that French colonies had diminished somewhat from the prosperous multi-staple producing entities they had been during the *ancien régime*, but they still remained vital colonial possessions in the 1830s and 1840s, especially as suppliers of sugar. For the last ten years of the July Monarchy, France was drawing nearly as much sugar from its colonial establishment as it had at the end of the *ancien régime*. Under the July Monarchy metropolitan authorities and the *colon* oligarchy deemed the colonial system as a valuable asset that France must retain. Both the plantocracy and the government also believed that France could preserve its colonial holdings only through prolonging the structure of coerced labor upon which they depended. Even the abolitionists conceded the economic importance of the colonies, and hoped to end slavery through measures that would not undermine their viability.

Although the colonial problem was already on the agenda of the new government in the summer and autumn of 1830, there was no question at the time of implementing drastic measures such as liberating the approximately 270,000 French colonial slaves residing in Guadeloupe, Martinique, Bourbon, and Guiana.[15] Prior to the

---

commerce colonial de la France á la fin de l'Ancien Régime; L'évolution du régime de l'Exclusif de 1763 à 1789 (2 vols.; Paris: Presses Universitaires de France, 1972), II, 747; Fierain, *Les raffineries*, 54.

[14] Drescher, *Econocide*, 48.

[15] While the number of French colonial slaves diminished by approximately 20,000 before 1848, it seems that, after the ending of the surreptitious slave trade, slave births and deaths remained relatively equal, and that most of the decrease in slave population was due to manumissions. See, for example, Schnakenbourg, *Historie de l'industrie sucrière*, 49; Fallope, *Esclaves et citoyens*, 96; and Tomich, *Slavery in the Circuit*, 83–4. It should be noted too that Senegal, with its relatively small slave population almost entirely Moslem, its nonplantation economy, and its African form of domestic rather than staple-producing slavery, was not considered one of the four regular French slave colonies by

decision by Great Britain in 1833 to take the initiative in slave emancipation, French liberal and philanthropic circles still concentrated
their efforts on denouncing the illicit slave trade and improving the
status of the *hommes de couleur libres*. Even individuals who would
later emerge as abolitionist leaders were now preoccupied with the
situation of freed persons of color in the colonies. Ever since 1828 a
number of free persons of mixed race residing in Paris, headed by
Bissette, had been working together for the interests of their people.
Receiving some encouragement and limited financial support from
their fellow free blacks in Martinique and Guadeloupe, three of them
assumed the title of "mandatories of the men of color" and claimed
to represent unofficially their fellow men. In effect, committees were
formed by *hommes de couleur libres* in 1831–1832 in both Martinique and Guadeloupe to support their mandatories in Paris.[16] And,
despite pressure from colonial representatives, mixed race leaders in
Martinique steadily refused to repudiate their support for Bissette.[17]
Bissette emerged as the foremost *mandataire* because of his ability to
expand upon his reputation as a martyr to colonial injustice. As a
merchant in Fort-de-France in 1824, he had been arrested with other
free black acquaintances, branded, and exiled from Martinique on
trumped-up charges of subversion. Defended in French courts by the
brilliant young lawyer François Isambert – also a future abolitionist
leader – the case of the branded exiles received considerable publicity
and became known as the "Bissette affair." Bissette's close associate,
Louis Fabien, who had suffered similar treatment at the hands of
the *colons*, emerged as the other mandatory of Martinique, while
Mondésir Richard assumed similar status for Guadeloupe.

In Paris the three mandatories argued that free blacks had been so
excluded from colonial affairs by the white colonials that the latter's

French officialdom throughout the July Monarchy. None of the discussions or decisions
concerning slavery in the corridors of French power had Senegal in mind or referred to
this holding. Only in the late 1840s did the government begin to take Senegal (at the
time little more than scattered posts and settlements around Gorée and Saint-Louis) into
consideration as it realized that a global solution to the French slavery problem must be
considered.

[16] Fallope, *Esclaves et citoyens*, 280–1.
[17] Elborg Forster and Robert Forster, eds., *Sugar and Slavery, Family and Race: The Letters
and Diary of Pierre Dessalles, Planter in Martinique, 1808–1856* (Baltimore: Johns
Hopkins University Press, 1996), 82, letter of Dessalles to his brother Charles, Jan. 7,
1832.

representatives in Paris, the colonial delegates, had no right to act on their behalf. The three challenged colonial authority, and operated by petitioning the government, eliciting support from liberal French politicians, and producing dozens of pamphlets or newspaper articles. Bissette alone, for example, lent his name on some twenty-one brochures between 1828 and 1834 in favor of the cause of mixed bloods in the colonies.[18] Besides publicizing the regrettable implications of the "Bissette affair," the mandatories denounced other instances of colonial injustice, and berated the retrograde nature of colonial government. They especially called for equal political rights for free blacks, their right to inherit, and their integration into white schools, jobs, and society in general.[19] Though they might also denounce colonial cruelty or injustice toward slaves in the process, immediately after the Revolution of 1830 the mandatories continued focusing their efforts upon obtaining equal civil and political rights for free persons of color. Only in 1831–1832 would Bissette expand his vistas by drawing up a program for improving the plight of slaves.

In the period immediately following the July Revolution, the Orleanist regime also decided to concentrate its priorities in the colonial sphere on regulating the position of free persons of color and redefining the relationship of the colonies to metropolitan France. It was natural for navy-colonial administrators to continue in the line of moderate reforms of colonial legislation begun already in the last years of the Restoration. By an ordonnance of February 9, 1827, the Paris government had brought administrative reform to Martinique by creating such institutions as the Private Council (to advise the governor), the *Ordonnateur* (colonial treasurer), and Director of the Interior, innovations which were consequently extended to Guadeloupe,

---

[18] See Lawrence C. Jennings, "Cyrille Bissette, Radical Black French Abolitionist," *French History* 9 (1995): 48–66. For excellent accounts of the "Bissette affair," see Pâme, "Cyrille Bissette," 66–133, and her entry, "L'Affaire Bissette (1823–1830)," in *L'Historial Antillais* (5 vols.; Fort-de-France, Dajani, 1980–1981), III, 222–39; Françoise Thésée, *Le général Donzelot à Martinique: Vers la fin de l'Ancien Régime colonial, 1818–1826* (Paris: Karthala, 1997): 147–84. An adequate treatment in English is available in Melvin D. Kennedy, "The Bissette Affair and the French Colonial Question," *Journal of Negro History* 45 (1960): 1–10.

[19] See, for example, C.C.A. Bissette, *Pétition des hommes de couleur de la Martinique, déportés aux colonies étrangères par Général Donzelot en décembre 1823 et janvier 1824* (Paris: E. Duverger, 1828); and Bissette, *C.C.A. Bissette … à un colon, sur l'émancipation civile et politique appliquée aux colonies françaises* (Paris: Ledoyen, 1830).

Bourbon, and Guiana. Then, by an ordonnance of September 24, 1828, alterations were introduced in the colonial judiciary, although some were rescinded the following year in response to colonial complaints.[20] Indeed, in 1828 and 1829 the Restoration had asked the opinion of the colonies on its moves, a measure which was now repeated on August 31, 1830, with a circular to the colonial governors, informing them of the administration's intention to introduce more innovations, and requesting colonial reaction to them. Subsequently, on September 7, Paris issued an ordonnance stipulating that henceforth legal acts concerning both blacks and whites would be entered on the same registers in the colonies. Even earlier, on August 23, the government decreed that in the future, colonial representatives would be appointed by their respective colonial legislatures, the General Councils (*Conseils généraux*). On the same date the July Monarchy created a "commission on colonial legislation" to elaborate reforms.[21] This twelve-man body contained several philanthropists connected with the Société de la morale chrétienne, or sympathetic to blacks: the comte d'Argout, Isambert, and Victor Destutt de Tracy. With the government seemingly prepared to pass a law to encourage slave manumission, and the commission staffed with well-known problack activists, it appeared by the autumn of 1830 that a series of meaningful colonial reforms would soon be implemented.[22]

In the course of its debates in late 1830, the commission considered whether the colonies should send full-fledged deputies to Paris, or simply delegates as their representatives. The government itself hesitated over this decision before expressing its preference for the latter. The commission regularly consulted with Bissette and Fabien, who took every opportunity to extol the principle of equality between free persons of mixed blood and whites. Perhaps because of their influence, or that of the problack elements within its ranks, on January 28, 1831, the commission submitted to the navy-colonial office its draft of a bill proposing full civil and political rights for free persons of color. The government now hesitated, however, about accepting such

---

[20] Pâme, "Cyrille Bissette," 151–160.

[21] Christian Schefer, *L'Algérie et l'évolution de la colonisation française: La politique coloniale de la Monarchie de Juillet* (Paris: Champion, 1928), 67–71.

[22] Cyrille Bissette, *Examen rapide des deux projets de loi relatifs aux colonies, adressé à la Chambre des députés* (Paris: d'Everat, 1833), 3–4.

a far-reaching proposal, which the *colons* claimed would destabilize the colonies. After consulting the planters, who objected vociferously to the idea, Paris decided to await the arrival of the colonially appointed delegates before acting. Instead, to appease the commission and the colored mandatories, it simply issued on February 24, 1831, an ordonnance which permitted free blacks to inherit from whites and which annulled all colonial regulations restricting full exercise of civil rights. Then on March 1 it made a move to encourage slave manumissions by suppressing taxes levied heretofore upon the act of freeing a slave, thus correcting a situation which had left many blacks free de facto but not de jure, the so-called *patronnés*. The Orleanist government was adopting a piecemeal rather than comprehensive approach to colonial reforms, something it would continue to do for most of its duration.[23] For the first time, too, the July Monarchy displayed another tendency that would mark its entire policy toward the slavery and colonial questions. Faced with opposition from the colonies, it adopted a cautious approach concerning the status of blacks. Rather than going too far, it preferred hardly moving at all in deference to *colon* interests. Its colonial policy, especially at first, did not differ that much from that of the Restoration which had preceded it. A regime that at first had appeared potentially progressive on the colonial front was in fact nearly as conservative as the preceding government.

In the meantime, on February 22, 1831, the chambers approved a law which provided for the imprisonment of French slave traders along with the seizure of their ships, the first effective anti-slave trade legislation France had implemented in the nineteenth century. In the spring of 1831 the July Monarchy also completed negotiations with Great Britain for the first of two treaties for the mutual right of search of suspected slavers off the slave coasts. Together, these measures practically ended the covert French slave trade which had brought some 77,300 slaves to the French Caribbean between 1814 and 1831.[24] Part of the general foreign policy rapprochement between

---

[23] Schefer, *L'Algérie*, 70–74.

[24] Serge Daget, *La traite des Noirs: Bastilles négrières et velléités abolitionnistes* (Evreux: Ouest-France Université, 1990), 204–6, 246; David Eltis, *Economic Growth and the Ending of the Transatlantic Slave Trade* (New York: Oxford University Press, 1987), 246. Between 1832 and the abolition of slavery in 1848 only fourteen French ships engaged in or were suspected of being involved in the slave trade, and even some of these were probably indirect participants in the slave traffic by simply transporting to the

Paris and London that marked the early 1830s, the mutual search treaty was ratified on November 30, 1831, but the King alluded to its conclusion in his discourse from the throne opening the second session of the Chamber of Deputies and Chamber of Peers on July 23. In the meantime, too, a minor slave uprising had occurred in Martinique, leading to the execution of some twenty slaves.[25] The King, however, made no mention in his speech of this uprising or of colonial developments concerning reforms. Believing that this silence indicated government procrastination on colonial matters, Tracy, an abolitionist member of the now disbanded commission on colonial legislation, spoke up in the Chamber of Deputies on September 6, 1831, to introduce formally the commission's own recommendations, now shelved by the administration. Tracy's proposal called for facilitating the manumission process by declaring legally free all those blacks who had been de facto liberated, the *patronnés*, along with those who had served in the military, or who had been born of a free mother; it also stipulated that such freedmen should enjoy full civil and political rights. Taken aback by this initiative, the navy-colonial minister, once again the comte de Rigny, defused the issue by requesting its adjournment on the basis that the government would soon present its own legislation on manumission.[26] In a scenario that would be repeated many times during the July Monarchy, the administration had been forced to take face-saving action of some kind to counter an abolitionist initiative.

On October 27, 1831, Rigny submitted in the Deputies a bill calling for civil and political rights for every person born free in the colonies, along with the abrogation of any law or decree contrary to this. However, the proposed law also stipulated that freed slaves would benefit from this legislation only ten years after their manumission, provided

African coast goods destined for the purchase of slaves (Daget, *Répertoire*, 549–55). For a discussion of indirect French participation in the slave trade, see Lawrence C. Jennings, "French Policy towards Trading with African and Brazilian Slave Merchants, 1840–1853," *Journal of African History* 4 (1976): 515–28.

[25] *Le Moniteur universel*, July 24, 1831. On the slave uprising in Martinique, see Dale W. Tomich, "'Liberté ou mort': Republicanism and Slave Revolt in Martinique, February 1831," *History Workshop* 29(1990): 85–91.

[26] *Le Moniteur universel*, Sept. 7, 11, 1831; Cyrille Bissette, *Observations sur les projets de lois coloniales, présentés à la Chambre des députés* (Paris: Impr. A. Mie, 1832), 5–6, 17–22; Bissette, *Examen rapide des deux projets de loi relatifs aux colonies, adressé à la Chambre des députés* (Paris: Impr. d'Everat, 1833), 4.

that they could read and write – something unlikely for most slaves. It stated too that political rights would be granted "under the conditions prescribed by the laws," a vague phrase that could lead to the perpetuation of the colonial status quo. Then Rigny returned to the chambers on December 16 with another bill reworking the legislative structure of the colonies by abolishing the *Conseils généraux* and replacing them with *Conseils coloniaux* (Colonial Councils) to be chosen by electors who qualified by paying high taxes (*cens*), just as in metropolitan France. In fact, voting qualifications were set at such high tax rates as to disenfranchise effectively most free persons of color.[27] The bill also stipulated that the Colonial Councils would appoint delegates to represent them in Paris. Both of these proposals had been influenced by intense lobbying from *colon* and free black advocates. According to Bissette, the Minister of the Navy and Colonies had originally planned to remain silent about political rights for *hommes de couleur libres*, and had agreed to include them in the legislation only after the intervention of the mandatories. Even here, however, the minister had angered Bissette and Fabien by insisting that there be a waiting period of ten years for all the newly liberated. Colonial representatives, for their part, had written a firm letter to the minister, insisting that high property qualifications be confirmed for colonial electors. They had even suggested that if this were not the case, whites would boycott the entire legislative process.[28] Neither the planters nor the free persons of mixed race were satisfied with the concessions made to the other side. Caught in the middle, and not enthusiastic about reform of any kind, the government began to reconsider the entire matter.

Things became more complicated still for the government when a commission of the lower house, appointed to examine the two bills, attempted to amend them drastically. A report made in the Deputies on April 13, 1832, by Nicolas Ferdinand Marie Louis Joseph Martin, called Martin du Nord – a liberal and future minister of justice – was supported by the abolitionist Hippolyte Passy. It recommended

[27] Qualifications were set at 400 francs for Martinique and Guadeloupe, 300F for Bourbon, and 200F for Guiana. Very few free persons of color could qualify as electors or candidates at these rates, especially since the latter were required to pay double these amounts (Bissette, *Observations sur les projets*, 40).

[28] Ibid., 14–24, 43, 51.

lowering the *cens* for electors, along with granting complete freedom immediately to the *patronnés*. With prime minister Casimir Périer dying of cholera, and the legislative session closing in just eleven days, the administration preferred tabling both bills. As an interim measure it extended the life of the *Conseils généraux* and sent them the proposed reforms for their advice. It also issued an ordonnance on July 18, 1832, extending the judicial rights of the de facto liberated, and encouraging the colonies to treat them in every way as free persons.[29] The government was once again consulting widely, biding its time, and promulgating only minor reforms. Only in late 1832 and early 1833 would it reintroduce its colonial legislation.

In effect, Paris had taken advantage of the ending of the legislative session of 1832 to rid itself of the bothersome Martin–Passy commission recommendations, because everything still on the legislative docket was wiped away by the adjournment of the chambers. On December 28, 1832, Rigny presented to the Chamber of Peers – appointed by the monarch and more conservative and procolonial than the elected Deputies – the same proposal he had submitted to the lower house the previous legislative year on civil–political rights for free persons of color and the reorganization of the colonies. Duly approved by the Peers in early March 1833, the legislation was then handed on to the Deputies, where it was debated in late April. Bissette criticized the draft of the law in another of his pamphlets, and Passy intervened in the debate on April 20 to request that the tax requirement for voting in the colonies be lowered.[30] But all of this was to little avail, for the law passed by a large majority, and the King promulgated it into law already on April 24, 1833.

The colonies now had their constitutional law, with *Conseils coloniaux* to vote on local matters and colonial delegates appointed by the latter to represent them in France. Still, most real powers remained with the metropolitan government and its colonial representative, the governor, who proposed the budget, had total initiative in legislative

---

[29] *Le Moniteur universel*, April 14, 1832; Bissette, *Examen rapide des deux projets*, 4; Schefer, *L'Algérie*, 94–5; Augustin Cochin, *L'Abolition de l'esclavage* (1861; rpt., Fort-de-France: Désormeaux, 1979), 36.

[30] *Le Moniteur universel*, April 21, 23, 1833; Cyrille Bissette, *Note sur le projet de loi relatif au régime legislatif des colonies* (Paris: Impr. Dupont & Laguionie, 1833); Pâme, 209.

matters, and retained the right to decree by ordonnances on issues relating to slavery, trade, education, and the press. The law of April 24, 1833, also gave *hommes de couleur libres* theoretical equality in civil and political affairs, though the high *cens* eliminated nearly all of them from the political scene. No sooner was the so-called colonial constitution activated than the French government showed a willingness to exercise its power over slavery by promulgating an ordonnance of April 30, 1833, abolishing branding and mutilation of slaves, and another in early August calling for a slave census.[31] Then too, on March 22 France had ratified a second slave trade repression treaty with Great Britain to strengthen the one of 1831 by providing for the arrest of ships equipped for the trade even if carrying no slaves at the time.[32] With the colonial constitution and slave trade issues settled in the spring of 1833, both the French government and the abolitionists could increasingly turn their attention to slavery.

The main French abolitionist organization of the time, the Société de la morale chrétienne, had never forgotten slavery, even though the eradication of the slave trade had always remained its first priority. The society's president, La Rochefoucauld-Liancourt, used the occasion of its annual meeting held on April 18, 1833, to speak of the changing French mentality toward slavery and to express his hopes that the government would "search with more ardor than ever for means to arrive at [the] abolition of slavery."[33] The mandatories of the free of mixed race, and especially their chief spokesman Bissette, also became increasingly interested in the plight of slaves within a year after the July Revolution. Indeed, Bissette was apparently moved at first by the parallels he perceived between mistreatment by colonials of both free and enslaved blacks.[34] In brochures published in 1831, Bissette and Fabien had already condemned cruelty toward slaves

---

[31] Schefer, *L'Algérie*, 107–19; Cochin, *L' Abolition*, 36.

[32] For more detail on the right of search conventions of 1831 and 1833, see Daget, *La traite des Noirs*, 242–4, and especially Daget, *La répression de la traite des Noirs au XIXe siècle: L'Action des croisières françaises sur les côtes occidentales de l'Afrique (1817–1850)* (Paris: Karthala, 1997), 414–38. On French opinion on this and subsequent Franco–British cooperation to eradicate the slave trade, see Lawrence C. Jennings, "The French Press and Great Britian's Campaign against the Slave Trade," *Revue française d'histoire d'outre-mer* 67 (1980): 5–24.

[33] *Journal de la Société de la morale chrétienne*, vol. 3, 2nd series, no. 1, Jan.–June 1833, pp. 187–91.

[34] Bissette, *C.C.A. Bissette … à un colon*, 11.

and the savage *colon* repression of the 1831 Martinique uprising.[35] By 1831 Bissette had even developed a program for improving the situation of slaves. Declaring that "slavery is not a natural state," Bissette suggested that special magistrates be instituted to oversee the moral development of slaves. He also proposed that slaves be freed from the whip, and that they be given the right to purchase their liberty.[36] This tendency to concentrate on the slavery question would become more marked after 1833 when freed blacks were granted at least a semblance of rights and Bissette could focus his attention on those still in bondage.

In 1832 Bissette and his colleagues reminded the government that, now that rights were being given to free blacks, slaves were "'men' also" who must be prepared for eventual liberty so that the "monstrous abuse of slavery could not remain an eternal fact on earth." Thus, they admonished, it was imperative to draft legislation for the amelioration of slaves.[37] Not only Bissette, but his mandatory colleagues too were making the transition from advocates of free blacks to defenders of slaves. But by the spring of 1833 they and the Société de la morale chrétienne did not stand alone in this role. The future abolitonist leader Victor Schoelcher published a book in 1833, one of his first studies on slavery, in which he attempted to show the evils of servitude, demonstrate that blacks were equal to whites, argue that they should be liberated in forty to sixty years, and suggest safeguards for their protection in the meantime.[38] Moreover, the Protestant weekly *Le Semeur* (Paris), which had close links with the Morale chrétienne in the early 1830s, was opposed to slavery from the very moment of the weekly's appearance in 1831. And in 1832 the *Semeur* declared its intention to fight incessantly against slavery until the moment of its abolition, making it at this point in time probably the

---

[35] Cyrille Bissette and Louis Fabien, *Demande en grâce pour Adèle, jeune esclave de la Martinique condamnée à la peine de fouet pour avoir chanté la Parisienne* (Paris: Impr. August Mie, [1831]).

[36] Cyrille Bissette, *Mémoire au Ministre de la Marine et des Colonies, et à la Commission de législation coloniale sur les améliorations legislatives et organiques à apporter au régime des colonies françaises* (Paris: Impr. A. Mie, 1831), 40–47.

[37] See, for example, Cyrille Bissette, Louis Fabien, and Mondésir Richard, *Pétition à la Chambre des députés, relative à l'amélioration du sort des esclaves aux colonies* (Paris: Impr. P. Dupont & Laguionie, [1832]), pp. 2, 10.

[38] Victor Schoelcher, *De l'esclavage des noirs et de la législation coloniale* (Paris: Paulin, 1833).

most radical anti-slavery advocate, even though it had as yet no clear-cut emancipation program.[39] Furthermore, during the debate on the colonial laws in the Chamber of Deputies in April 1833, some legislators requested measures to restrict the mistreatment of slaves by their masters.[40] Two or three years after the July Revolution, slavery was becoming an item of humanitarian attention in France, just as it was already in Great Britain.

In the spring of 1833 anti-slavery forces in Britain were about to achieve their greatest victory, a development which would have profound repercussions in France. British emancipationism had been revived after 1830 by the growing abolitionist belief in the ineffectiveness of any gradual approach to slave liberation and by the formation in 1831 of a more radical anti-slavery organization, the Agency Committee, pledged to immediatism, or immediate slave liberation. The Reform Bill of 1832 also prepared the terrain for emancipation by bringing into Parliament a group of young members determined to end slavery. As of 1832–1833, British anti-slavery fervor, working through massive popular lecture and petition campaigns, had won over public opinion and swayed the government.[41] Some French observers were fully aware of these developments. The virulently pro-slavery Le Journal du Havre (Le Havre) strove to dissuade its readers

[39] Le Semeur, June 13, Oct. 10, 1832.

[40] Le Moniteur universel, April 21, 23, 1833; Schefer, L'Algérie, 119.

[41] Some of the most noteworthy of the many important recent publications treating British anti-slavery and its achievement of slave liberation in the 1830s are the works by: David Turley; William Green; Robin Blackburn, The Overthrow of Colonial Slavery, 1776–1848 (London: Verso, 1988); Seymour Drescher, Capitalism and Antislavery: British Popular Mobilization in Comparative Perspective (New York: Oxford University Press, 1987); David Brion Davis, Slavery and Human Progress (Oxford: Oxford University Press, 1984); Michael Craton, "Slave Culture, Resistance and the Achievement of Emancipation in the British West Indies, 1783–1836," in James Walvin, ed., Slavery and British Society 1776–1846 (London: Macmillan, 1982), 100–122; Drescher, "Public Opinion and the Destruction of British Slavery," in ibid., 22–48; James Walvin, "The Propaganda of Anti-Slavery," in ibid., 49–68; Walvin, "The Public Campaign in England Against Slavery, 1787–1834," in David Eltis and James Walvin, eds., The Abolition of the Atlantic Slave Trade: Origins and Effects in Africa and the Americas (Madison: University of Wisconsin Press, 1981), 63–79; Walvin, "The Rise of British Popular Sentiment for Abolition, 1787–1832," in Christine Bolt and Seymour Drescher, eds., Anti-Slavery, Religion and Reform: Essays in Memory of Roger Anstey (Folkstone, Kent: Dawson, 1980), 149–62; Roger Anstey, "The Pattern of British Abolitionism in the Eighteenth and Nineteenth Centuries," in ibid., 19–42; and Howard Temperley, British Anti-slavery, 1830–1870 (Columbia: University of South Carolina Press, 1972).

from imitating the British anti-slavery movement.[42] The abolitionist *Le Semeur*, on the contrary, asked why a petition campaign of the British kind could not be undertaken in France.[43] The Société de la morale chrétienne, always close to British philanthropy, attempted to model its campaign of 1832 to raise funds for manumitting female slaves on the British example, for it had been highly impressed by British success both in propagating and subsidizing the anti-slavery message.[44] Nevertheless, French opinion, and the press in particular, tended for the most part to remain ignorant of, or uninterested in, anti-slave trade and slavery matters in England prior to 1834.[45] No doubt French observers believed that British abolitionism was experiencing just another phase of the gradualist movement against slavery begun already in 1823, and that emancipation was still far from realization. Judging from the dearth of documents on the topic in the French navy-colonial archives, it appears that French officials, though engaged in active negotiations with Britain over the slave trade issue at this time, were also largely indifferent toward the British anti-slavery campaign until its first significant successes in the spring of 1833.[46]

News from the British press, reproduced by the *Moniteur universel*, that an abolition bill was being debated in the House of Commons in March 1833, suddenly startled the French navy-colonial department into action.[47] Minister Rigny informed the French ambassador in London, the famous Prince Charles Maurice de Talleyrand-Perigord, that his government had "the greatest interest in discovering exactly what" was occurring on the British emancipation front because "France's [tropical] colonies closely touch everywhere upon England's." France especially feared that "violent perturbations" in British holdings would have "repercussions ... immediately in French possessions."[48] When it became clear two months later that Britain would liberate

---

[42] Dec. 21, 1831. For more information on the Le Havre press as a bastion of anti-slavery, see Lawrence C. Jennings, "La presse havraise et l'esclavage," *Revue historique*, 272 (1984): 45–71.

[43] Feb. 29, 1832.

[44] *Journal de la société de la morale chrétienne*, vol. 1, 2nd series, no. 3, Jan.–June 1832, pp. 18–20.

[45] For further information, see Jennings, "The French Press ... against the Slave Trade."

[46] See Lawrence C. Jennings, *French Reaction to British Slave Emancipation* (Baton Rouge: Louisiana State University Press, 1988), 9–26.

[47] *Le Moniteur universel*, March 11, 1833.

[48] ANCAOM, Généralités 206 (1513), Minister to Ambassador, March 13, 1833.

its colonial slaves in the near future, Rigny informed his four governors in the Caribbean and on Bourbon of his conviction that abolition, "which will be so grave for England's colonies, could not be without importance for those that France possesses." He especially feared that when Britain freed its slaves, "*provocateurs* or even emissaries will attempt ... to disrupt the peace of our slave establishments." Rigny admonished his governors to be vigilant within their own colonies, observant of developments in the nearby British ones, and ready to repress any disturbances that might occur. He also informed them that the French navy-colonial department intended to consult the newly formed colonial councils of Martinique, Guadeloupe, Bourbon, and Guiana as to what measures could be taken to improve the position of slaves.[49] France's initial reaction to impending British emancipation was one of surprise, caution, and apprehension. With no intention to imitate the British action, the July Monarchy's first concern was to shield its own possessions from negative repercussions.

This became increasingly apparent after the British Parliament debated the emancipation bill, approved it, and passed it into law in late August 1833. The measure proposed to compensate slave owners with the enormous sum of £20 million, and to free all slaves as of August 1, 1834, although adults would continue to be subjected to a period of apprenticeship for four to six years before obtaining complete freedom. Because apprenticeship still entailed blacks working for their masters without wages, it was soon denounced by abolitionists as nothing more than prolonged, if ameliorated, slavery.[50] As far as the French were concerned, the fact that actual emancipation would not come into effect immediately in British tropical colonies gave Paris time to study and reflect upon its own path of action. No sooner were the fundamentals of British policy laid down in late August 1833 than Rigny emitted an internal memorandum on August 25, 1833, stating that France "wishes to remain a quiet spectator to the grave measures that England has decided to take for slave liberation."

[49] Ibid., Correspondance Générale, Colonies françaises, 1833, Minister to governors, May 24, 1833.
[50] The Bill of 1833 is reproduced in Edith F. Hurwitz, *Politics and the Public Conscience: Slave Emancipation and the Abolition Movement in Britain* (London: Allen & Unwin, 1973), 158–73.

He added, however, that for France to be able "to maintain this attitude and shield French colonies from the peril of similar situations, it is necessary ... to enter frankly and broadly into the path of ameliorations."[51] France seemed poised to renew and reinforce its slave amelioration policy in reply to the British initiative of slave liberation.

French intentions were reiterated and elaborated upon in an internal navy-colonial office memo, drawn up for the Director of the Colonies, Edmé Jean Fileau de Saint-Hilaire – who held the position as second in command to the minister from 1825 to 1842 – explaining possible options vis-à-vis the British situation. The document pointed out that British authorities in freeing their slaves "had been forced to yield" to religious-inspired movements that had won over public opinion. However, it added, "in France, while the great mass of the population is little concerned with the colonial regime, protests against slavery only have reverberations within the circle of philosophical discussions, and our government remains ... almost free in its choices." Though the British Parliament was prepared to pay a huge sum in reparations to slave owners, the French chambers would not "be eager to impose on the state a heavy monetary burden to satisfy a few publicists." Moreover, the tranquillity in the French colonies enabled "the real friends of humanity to wait for time to bring about the most durable improvements in the condition of blacks." Many slaves had already been manumitted since 1830, the note pointed out, so perhaps the introduction of *rachat* (or self-redemption, the right of slaves to purchase their own freedom) would suffice and eliminate slavery slowly. In any case, the memo concluded that "everything tends to coincide in determining the French government to persevere in the line of conduct it has adopted for the last three years ... and await, as a simple spectator, but with the necessary precaution for the preservation of public order, the result of the great experience that is taking place in the English colonies."

An addendum to the memo repeated the argument that "in France, where very few people know what the colonies are, or concern themselves with the fate of the slaves," the legislature "would not decide to increase the public debt in favor of the *colons*, for whom, it must be

---

[51] France, Archives Nationales, Papiers Guizot (hereafter cited as Guizot Papers), 43AP40, position paper by the Director of the Colonies for the Minister of the Navy and Colonies, dated Dec. 21, 1836, citing an earlier document of Aug. 25, 1833.

said, the country has very little sympathy, only to satisfy morally a few philanthropists."[52] Between August and December 1833 the French government had apparently softened its position on reforms, arriving at the conclusion that it would be possible to end slavery in a very long-term perspective simply by encouraging manumissions through such measures as self-redemption.[53] These memos also introduced themes concerning government policy that would recur throughout the entirety of the July Monarchy, such as the idea that France could not afford to pay the requisite indemnity to slave holders, that it was necessary to await the complete result of British emancipation, that the administration must follow the gradualist path toward eventual slave liberation, and that the French abolitionists had disdainfully little political influence. In late 1833 the French government felt little compulsion to act forcefully in the face of impending British emancipation, because of the moribund state of French anti-slavery. Despite the suggestion made by Rigny at the end of August 1833, no new reforms were seriously considered for French slaves until after renewed abolitionist pressure in 1835. The administration did, however, take contingency measures in the colonies to preclude any possibility of serious slave unrest.

An uprising of free persons of color in Grande Anse, Martinique – sparked by a minor altercation between a white and a mixed blood – broke out over Christmas 1833, but was of short duration. It led, however, to the execution of fifteen blacks and the trial of 117 more.[54] These difficulties in Martinique may have combined with concerns about developments in the British Caribbean in underlining the need to strengthen security in France's tropical possessions. Fearing

[52] ANCAOM, Gén. 206 (1513), memo for the Director of the Colonies – perhaps by his important assistant Henri Joseph Mestro – dated Dec. 27, 1833.

[53] These attitudes perhaps reflect the large number of manumissions that had occurred since 1831 when the tax on registering an act of freeing a slave was removed, and many de facto liberated became officially free. In his position paper prepared for the Council of Ministers and dated Dec. 21, 1836, Saint-Hilaire revealed that since 1831, some 29,058 slaves had been officially liberated, though 17,000 of these were *patronnés*, those who had actually been freed by their masters earlier, but whose libeation became official only after the tax on the process had been rescinded (Guizot Papers, 42AP40).

[54] On the Grande Anse affair, see Cyrille Bissette, *Polémique sur les évènements de la Grande Anse* (Paris: Impr. J. S. Cordier, 1834); Louis Fabien, *Appel aux amis de l'humanité contre un épouvantable arrêt* (Paris: Impr. Dezauche, 1834); *La Revue des colonies*, July 1834, pp. 8–16; Sept. 1834, pp. 9–13, 23–4.

particularly that unrest might spread from the British West Indies to nearby French holdings, the July Monarchy took measures to dispatch additional ships to the Antilles naval station and to increase garrisons in all four French slave colonies. Statistics on military movements are incomplete, but it seems that by 1836 there were 3,883 infantry, marines, and artillery troops evenly divided between Martinique and Guadeloupe, along with nearly 200 gendarmes in the two colonies, and 10,811 militiamen. In 1837, Bourbon could muster 811 troops plus 6,593 militiamen, while Guiana had 337 militiamen in 1836 and 737 troops by 1838. Among the militiamen in Bourbon, some 24 percent were free colored, while in Guiana the free blacks constituted 41 percent of the total, for in French colonies the authorities had always relied on the free blacks to repress slave uprisings such as the one of Carbet, Martinique, of 1822 in which even Bissette had answered the call to arms.[55] For Bourbon, the 811 troops stationed there in 1837 had increased by 144 over the previous year. In fact, the number of troops in Bourbon augmented dramatically between 1840 (816) and 1841 (1,492), reaching an all-time high of 1,802 plus 72 gendarmes in 1846. Likewise, Guiana's troop contingent reached its apex of 954 in 1842, but then was allowed to descend into the 700–800 range for the mid-1840s. These statistics may reflect the fact that troop increases to the French colonies during the early 1840s probably corresponded to rising tension with Britain as much as to internal security needs. Similarly, for Guadeloupe, troops numbered 1,962 in 1838, 2,958 in 1841, and reached a peak of 3,025 in 1842, before descending to only 1,211 in 1847. Statistics for Martinique are incomplete, but in 1843 the number of troops there did total 2,329. Besides these regular army members, the number of gendarmes remained consistently around 100 for the three largest French colonies as of the late 1830s.[56] Different statistics, published by L'Abolitioniste français [sic], indicate that colonial garrisons increased overall from 5,425 in

[55] *Notices statistiques sur les colonies françaises* (Paris: Impr. Royale, 1837–1838), Part I, pp. 79, 81, 192, 194; Part II, pp. 65–6, 207, 209. In referring to these same statistics, Blackburn, *The Overthrow* (p. 485), came up with "6,000 troops, backed up by 5,000 — 6,000 members of the militia" for Martinique and Guadeloupe alone. Concerning the Carbet uprising, see Françoise Thésée, "La révolte des esclaves du Carbet à la Martinique (oct.–nov. 1822)," *Revue française d'histoire d'outre–mer* 80 (1993): 551–84.
[56] ANCAOM, Corr. Gén., Série géographique, Guadeloupe 278, Martinique 232, Guyane 140, Réunion 131, population tables for 1830–1847.

1836 to 8,356 in 1841.[57] Similarly, a well-informed French abolitionist, Jean Baptiste Rouvellat de Cussac, who was in the Antilles at the time, wrote that in 1838 there had been approximately 6,000 troops in the French colonies, but that by 1845 the number had risen to over 9,000. He added – borrowing a strategy employed by British abolitionists – that France should be concerned by the 1,200 to 1,500 soldiers who had perished through disease while serving in the colonies. Moreover, as the famous abolitionist Victor Schoelcher remarked, France was spending some six and a half million francs per year to cover the costs of such large garrisons – not to mention additional sums for the upkeep of its West Indian fleet.[58] This relatively high number of troops, gendarmes, and militiamen, no matter what their raison d'être, probably contributed to preserving stability in all the French colonies. French colonial slaves and free persons of color carried out no uprisings or revolts between 1833 and 1848. While there might be some connection between the Grande Anse episode and the initial decision to send added troops to the colonies, the affair did not lead Paris to implement further colonial reforms at a time when its attention was fixed upon the British scene.

Uncertain about the direction of British emancipation or its implications for France's possessions, the French government established a policy of actively seeking information on British colonial developments. One of its first moves was to note and summarize articles published on the question in the French press. Judging from an index in the French colonial archives, between 1833 and January 1836 officials analyzed some 104 newspaper articles – a list which was far from complete – appearing in French newspapers on the British slave colonies. The navy-colonial minister also requested that French representatives in London forward British dailies to Paris so that his office could scrutinize them, for in reality most French journalistic entries on British developments were lifted from London publications in the first place. It soon became apparent to French officials, nevertheless,

---

[57] L'Abolitioniste français, Jan.–Feb. 1844, p. 16. In the mid-nineteenth century the French word abolitionniste was still spelled in the English fashion, with only one "n."

[58] Jean Baptiste Rouvellat de Cussac, A Messieurs les membres de la Chambre des députés. Quelques observations sur le projet de loi relatif à l'esclavage dans les colonies (Paris: Pagnerre, 1845), 14, Victor Schoelcher, Histoire de l'esclavage pendant les deux dernières années (2 vols.; Paris: Pagnerre, 1847), I, 489–90, 496.

that press reports of any kind were incomplete and unreliable. There-fore, French authorities instituted a parallel source of information-gathering by sending observers to the British colonies. The process apparently began in the summer of 1833 when the governor of Mar-tinique, Admiral Jean Henri Joseph Dupotet, after receiving Rigny's request of May 24 for more information on the British West Indies, sent a naval captain and his vessel to nearby Saint Lucia to gather intelligence. By the summer of 1835 the then Minister of the Navy and Colonies, Admiral Guy, baron Duperré, concluded that these official French missions to British holdings provided the best source of infor-mation, and sanctioned the practice.[59] A register in the French colo-nial archives lists some thirty-nine such missions between 1833 and 1841. Though the reports of these many observers varied in length, astuteness, and reliability, they actually provided a massive amount of information on the situation in British tropical colonies.[60] This process enabled the French government to keep abreast of the British colonial situation and to assure its critics that it was well informed. In reality, though, it had no reason to worry about French abolitionist pressure before 1835.

Surprisingly enough, the British decision in mid-1833 to abolish colonial slavery the following year elicited little more reaction from French abolitionist spokesmen than had the British anti-slavery cam-paign of 1831–1833. Once again French comments were exceedingly sparse. The important liberal daily *Le Constitutionnel* (Paris) made perhaps the most emphatic statement when it hailed the British eman-cipation project as a "great measure" which was also of relevance to France.[61] Jean Charles Léonard de Sismondi, a noted liberal economist,

[59] See Jennings, *French Reaction*, 28–31.
[60] Ibid., 31–49. For detailed accounts of the activities of two exemplary French observers, Captain Marie Jean François Layrle and Jean Marie Eugène d'Arvoy, see, respectively, Lawrence C. Jennings, "French Perceptions of British Slave Emancipation: A French Observer's Views on the post-Emancipation British Caribbean," *French Colonial Stud-ies*, 3 (1979): 72–85; and Jennings, "Réflexions d'un observateur sur l'émancipation des esclaves britanniques à l'île Maurice," *Revue d'histoire moderne et contemporaine*, 29 (1982): 462–470. For English translations of some of these reports, see David L. Gobert and Jerome S. Handler, eds. and trans., "Barbados in the Apprenticeship Period: The Report of a French Colonial Official," *Journal of the Barbados Museum and Historical Society*, 36 (1980): 108–28; and Gobert and Handler, eds. and trans., "Barbados in the Post-Apprenticeship Period: The Observations of a French Naval Officer," *Journal of the Barbados Museum and Historical Society* 35 (1978): 243–66; 36 (1979): 4–15.
[61] July 9, 1833.

gave a more mitigated evaluation of the British move, praising its just nature, but criticizing its hastiness.[62] And the *Journal de la morale chrétienne* greeted the British decision in a general sense as "a great question of justice and humanity."[63] But, as a whole, French abolitionists tended to ignore or underestimate this British measure which had not as yet gone into effect. Perhaps this silence also reflects upon the underdevelopment and inactivity of abolitionist forces in their entirety in France during the early 1830s.

In Great Britain in the early 1830s emancipationism was at its height and on the eve of achieving its great accomplishment of slave liberation. This was not, however, the case in France. Despite the liberal and reformist atmosphere prevalent in the early years of the July Monarchy, the Orleanist regime made few moves on the slavery front. Its primary concern was to end the illicit slave trade, reform colonial institutions, and regularize the position of the free of mixed race. Only after the implementation of effective legislation against the slave trade, the granting of rights to free persons of color, and the British decision to emancipate in 1833 did French authorities realize the need to act on the slavery question. It was the latter development especially that shook the French administration out of its lethargy. Still, the French government's first measures were hesitant, tentative, and inadequate. Paris decided to observe the evolution of the British emancipation process and take only those moves necessary to prevent unrest in the colonies. Faced with no abolitionist or public pressure in France, the July Monarchy procrastinated, as it would so often in the future too. Not only was the new regime essentially conservative in its colonial policies, but the navy-colonial department that was in charge of the slavery dossiers had not been transformed by the Revolution of 1830. Although regimes and ministers changed, Saint-Hilaire and other high functionaries who administered and often formulated policies remained largely the same. After 1830, as before, France opted for a cautious stance of piecemeal adjustments and ameliorations on the colonial scene without significant reforms.

Much the same could be said about the position of French abolitionists concerning the slavery question during this same time period.

---

[62] *La Revue mensuelle d'économie politique* (Paris), Dec. 1833.
[63] Vol. 4, 2nd series, no. 5, p. 254.

Bissette and his fellow mandatories remained preoccupied with denouncing injustices toward the *hommes de couleur libres*, and were just beginning to focus their attention on the slaves. Other future French abolitionist leaders, such as Schoelcher, would not emerge as important anti-slavery advocates until the late 1830s or early 1840s. Even the Société de la morale chrétienne was interested more in other philanthropic topics, such as adopting orphans or militating in favor of prison reform or the elimination of the death penalty, than in slavery. Indeed, this society, the leading abolitionist organ under the Restoration, was in a state of decomposition, a far cry from its former days of glory. *Le Semeur*, itself silent on the 1833 British decision to free the slaves, uttered the opinion that the morale chrétienne group "has been dying since the July Revolution, despite the efforts of its president, hardly aided by a small number of members."[64] In 1833 no other organization had as yet emerged to take its place. If French anti-slavery remained largely impassive to the British decision to emancipate, it was essentially because of its own undermanned, leaderless, disorganized, and unfocused state. French abolitionists might occasionally query the government in publications or the legislature, but they had as yet no overall organization or program. Because of weak abolitionist pressure, the government felt no overwhelming concern about British developments, and had been able to abide by its approach of piecemeal minor reforms to the colonial system. It would take the implementation of British slave emancipation in the summer of 1834 to stimulate the French abolitionist movement, force it to organize, and furnish it with a mission. Prior to 1834 abolitionism was still in its infancy in France.

[64] April 24, 1833.

3

FORMATION OF THE
FRENCH ABOLITION
SOCIETY

The official ending of slavery in the British colonies on August 1,
1834, accelerated the tempo of emancipationism in France. French
anti-slavery reaction to the implementation of British slave liberation
was more enthusiastic and widespread than a year earlier with the
mere passage of the emancipation bill. Amongst the French press, the
Journal de la Société de la morale chrétienne greeted August 1 as "a
new era," while once again *Le Constitutionnel* praised this "great
measure of colonial regeneration."[1] This time, though, their enthusiasm was also shared by other newspapers. *Le Semeur* proclaimed that
August 1 would "begin a new era for an entire race of men," and the
moderately republican *Le National* (Paris) hailed "this noble example
which is occurring peacefully and without disorders."[2] For its part, *Le
Courrier français* referred to "this great measure" which the British
government had triumphantly prepared and achieved. Even *Le Sémaphore de Marseille*, a port city daily with an open mind on slavery at
the time, spoke of "this grand measure carried out without shock"
despite "sinister prediction " to the contrary by *colons*.[3] All of these
newspapers suggested that British emancipation was being implemented smoothly and peacefully, thus contradicting predictions by
the government and planters that disorders and disruptions would
inevitably accompany the British act. Furthermore, in their eyes the
British initiative was worthy of emulation by other countries such as

---

[1] *Journal de la Société de la morale chrétienne*, vol. 6, 2nd series, July 1834, p. 45; *Le Constitutionnel*, Oct. 22, 1834.
[2] *Le Semeur*, July 23, 1834; *Le National*, Aug. 12, 1834.
[3] *Le Courrier français*, Sept. 8, 1834; *Le Sémaphore de Marseille*, Sept. 20, 1834.

France. From their very first articles on British slave liberation, the liberal French press was intimating that the British move was not only a noteworthy humanitarian accomplishment, but an example that should be followed by France.

Another journal also rejoiced over the British achievement. As if to anticipate the British emancipation act, Bissette and his cohorts launched the opening issue of what would become the first French abolitionist periodical run by blacks, *La Revue des colonies* (Paris). Constantly plagued by financial difficulties, up until now the mandatories of the free persons of color had been obliged to limit their publications to the pamphlet or brochure format. They now decided to put out a monthly review – though it would be forced to suspend publication on several occasions after 1837 because of recurrent debt – that would develop into one of the leading French anti-slavery organs until the summer of 1842, when it finally folded. Although Bissette controlled the review and served as its principal editor, he was assisted by Fabien and Richard, at least in its early period. A close examination of its pages over the years shows that it boasted correspondents in several of the colonies, and that it regularly published articles by such white abolitionists as the lawyer Adolphe Gatine, the banished Guadeloupe magistrate Xavier Tanc, and the former colonial priests C. Dougoujan and E. Goubert, who had been expelled from Guadeloupe and Martinique, respectively. These expatriate colonials provided firsthand, moving indictments of slavery. However, throughout most of the review's existence, Bissette seems to have written, directed, and edited it almost single-handedly. The periodical was viewed as the personal fief of Bissette both by his critics in the plantocracy and by his supporters, such as the famous mixed-blood novelist Alexandre Dumas, who wrote in 1838 to associate himself with the ideals of the review and its leading editor. Though the *Revue*'s influence was curtailed by its limited readership – its subscribers numbered a mere 250 in 1840 – its devotion to the abolitionist cause was demonstrated by the fact that colonial authorities did everything possible to impede its circulation within their jurisdictions. The *Revue des colonies* would prove to be the nemesis of French planters, especially of those in Martinique, whom Bissette never forgave during the course of the July Monarchy for his branding and expulsion under the

Restoration, and whom he steadily covered with his invective.[4] But in its opening issues the *Revue* was far from the fiery radical abolitionist advocate it would later become.

In the very first number of the review, a prospectus published in July 1834, Bissette explained his conviction that philanthropy could be propagated effectively only through the press, because petitions and interpellations in the legislative chambers were often ignored by the authorities. He proclaimed that the *Revue's* principles were those of the Enlightenment and the Declaration of Rights of 1789, and that his publication would not cease to expose the oppression meted out in the colonies to free persons of color and slaves alike. Bissette also stressed that the precept of liberty necessitated the abolition of slavery. However, it was only in his second issue, August 1834, that Bissette employed the British precedent to offer an impassioned plea for emancipation. He began by enthusiastically hailing "the admirable bill" that had freed British colonial slaves, this "work entirely of philanthropy and justice, of liberty and conciliation together." He then cited this "good example" to emphasize that emancipation was "an urgent necessity" for French possessions because *colons* "are walking on a volcano!" It was imperative, he insisted, to "look into immediately the means by which abolition could be accomplished as gently as possible," for otherwise the slaves would eventually revolt. Bissette's monthly was not as yet advocating immediate and outright emancipation, but it had been spurred by the British precedent into seizing upon the abolitionist issue. In its August 1834 issue the *Revue* also announced that a "society for the abolition of slavery" had been founded under the direction of "members of the Chamber of Deputies."[5]

The formation of the Société française pour l'abolition de l'esclavage coincided with and was a direct result of British slave emancipation. In its issue appearing in mid-August, the *Journal de la Société de la morale chrétienne* too proclaimed that an abolitionist society had

---

[4] See Jennings, "Bissette," 54–66. Bissette reconciled himself with the planters only after the Revolution of 1848 brought the establishment of the republic, and led Bissette to ally himself with the plantocracy in order to be elected deputy in Martinique, campaigning against his arch-enemy Schoelcher (Pâme, "Cyrille Bissette," 315–320; Nelly Schmidt, *Victor Schoelcher et l'abolition de l'esclavage* (Paris: Fayard, 1994), 124–9).

[5] *La Revue des colonies*, July 1834, no. 1, pp. 1–13; Aug. 1834, no. 2, pp. 3–5, 17–19.

just been created in Paris "for the purpose of taking such measures as are required to imitate the example of England to arrive at the general emancipation of slaves."[6] In its following number this periodical also specified that this "Society for the abolition of slavery" had been "formed in the midst of the Chamber of Deputies." It pointed out that during the initial meeting of the new group on August 15, the duc de Broglie, former president of the Société de la morale chrétienne, had been appointed to preside over it because of his leadership in the battle against the slave trade under the Restoration. In reality, Broglie had undoubtedly been chosen to head the society because of his high status within the doctrinaire Orleanist ruling clique. He had been minister of public instruction under the Jacques Laffitte Cabinet in 1830, and minister in charge of religious affairs and then foreign minister in the administration headed by General Nicolas Jean de Dieu Soult, duc de Dalmatie, between 1832 and 1834. Furthermore, in 1835 Broglie would become once again foreign minister, combined this time with the role of head of government as President of the Council of Ministers, or prime minister. In effect, he was the dominant political figure of the period 1832–1836. Two other high-placed Orleanist liberals, Passy and Odilon Barrot, were named vice-presidents, while Isambert and the influential Orleanist comte Louis Joseph Alexandre de Laborde – a former aide-de-camp of Louis Philippe – became secretaries. The first administrative duties of the new society had also been decided upon during the opening meeting of August 15. Passy was charged with drawing up the agenda of the society; Isambert was entrusted with listing proposed changes to existing colonial legislation; and La Rochefoucauld-Liancourt – president of the Société de la morale chrétienne in the 1830s – agreed to do a report on the preceding anti-slavery activity of the Morale chrétienne.[7]

Formed within the antechambers of the lower house, and often holding meetings there, the Société française pour l'abolition de l'esclavage was so closely tied to legislative schedules that, when the chambers adjourned in late August, the society followed suit. It would renew its activities in early December 1834 when the chambers were reconvened once again. It seems that its members, "who belong

6 *Journal de la Société de la morale chrétienne*, vol. 6, 2nd series, no. 1, July 1834, p. 49.
7 Ibid., vol. 6, 2nd series, no. 2, Aug. 1834, pp. 114–15.

for the most part to the two chambers, dispersed into the departments during the time when legislative works were interrupted and had to await their return before constituting definitely the Society."[8] Throughout its existence the Société française pour l'abolition de l'esclavage would routinely suspend its sittings between legislative sessions, leaving just a correspondence committee, animated usually by Isambert, to handle urgent matters. Being constituted by members of the ruling elite might have been advantageous for an organization that would operate by attempting to influence the government to decree emancipation. It certainly enabled the body to exist and operate under a regime in which laws against associations technically forbade societies of this kind. Still, by being closely bound to the legislative calendar, the society also suffered constantly from a lack of continuity, steadfastness, and momentum in its activities. Consequently, it was never as well organized, persistent, or committed to the cause as the British abolitionists.

The Société française pour l'abolition de l'esclavage reconvened once again at the beginning of December, when its deputy and peer membership returned to Paris for the start of the new legislative session. The society, in fact, would carry on a hectic pace of activity in its first months as it worked out its program, drafted its constitution, held open hearings to gather information, and planned its future course of action. Its opening agenda was once again heavily inspired by the British example. A prestigious British abolitionist delegation was in the French capital already on November 22. On that day Zachary Macaulay, John Scoble, and James Cooper attended the appeals court hearing for blacks condemned for the Grande Anse affair, a proceeding in which the well-known abolitionist lawyers Gatine and Adolphe Crémieux – both society members, and the latter a member of the Provisional Government of 1848 – led the defense.[9] Then, the very first working meeting of the Société française pour l'abolition de l'esclavage on December 3 was devoted entirely to listening to these three emissaries of the Universal Abolition Society (formerly the Agency Committee) explain the path followed by their

[8] Ibid., no. 6, Dec. 1834, p. 294; *Le Semeur*, Dec. 10, 1834. These same phrases were employed by both newspapers, though *Le Semeur* appeared earlier in the month and was therefore the original source of this statement.

[9] *Revue des colonies*, no. 6, Dec. 1834, pp. 25–35.

country in ending slavery and smoothly implementing the emancipation bill. The prospectus of the Société française, drawn up by Passy, and approved by society members during their next meeting on December 15, also demonstrated the imprint of British influence. It opened with a denunciation of slavery as a violation of Christian charity, before citing the British example to show how bondage could be eliminated only when well-intentioned men "came together to work in concert" toward this aim. During the December 15 meeting also the French group decided to employ the time-tested English abolitionist strategy of petitioning the two French legislative chambers for abolition.[10] There was such a preponderant role played by British delegates and concepts in the first sessions of the French abolition society in December 1834 that there can be no doubt about the profound cross-Channel influence on the formation of the leading French anti-slavery organization.

The prospectus also defined the society's aims, outlined its organizational structure, and listed its early membership. It indicates that the Société française pour l'abolition de l'esclavage intended to work for the amelioration of slaves and for their "progressive" liberation. Amelioration signified that the society would strive not only to improve the plight of the slave but also to "enlighten his intelligence and prepare him for a liberty that will be useful and profitable for all the inhabitants of the colonies." Progressive liberation meant gradually staged emancipation achieved in a cautious fashion. The prospectus stressed, therefore, that slave liberation must be an act of "prudence" as well as of humanity, that the society did not favor precipitous actions, and that it hoped to prevent any difficulties from accompanying emancipation. It called for persons of all political persuasions to rally to the new organization, and it assured them that it intended to sound differing opinions on the emancipation issue. The message of this first publication of the Société française was that circumspection would be the watchword of the French group.[11] In this sense the French organization was breaking sharply with the British

---

[10] *Prospectus de la Société française pour l'abolition de l'esclavage (Programme de la Société)* (Paris: Impr. E. Duverger, 1835), 12. For transformations in the structure of the British abolitionist movement, and the internationalist perspective of the new Universal Abolition Society, see Temperley, *British Antislavery*, xii, 25–6.

[11] *Prospectus ... de la Société*, 6–8, 11.

model of general, rapid emancipation at a specific date, be it followed by a transition period like apprenticeship or not. The society remained wedded to French anti-slavery antecedents of the pre-1830 period and to the gradualist British abolitionist approach of the 1820s, not to its immediatism of the 1830s. Despite the admonitions of Macaulay and other British abolitionists, the Société française was committed to a carefully prepared long-term process, rather than to the immediate eradication of slavery. Indeed, immediatism still had no part in the French abolitionist discourse of 1834.

The statutes of the Société française pour l'abolition de l'esclavage also reflected this cautious, conservative approach. They stipulated that the twenty-seven founding members would control the society, with new members having to be introduced by two of the original founders. Annual membership dues were set at a minimum of twenty-five francs (at the time there were approximately five francs to a dollar), a goodly sum when the standard daily wage of French workers was two francs.[12] Funds accumulated in this manner would be used to carry out inquiries and subsidize the society's publications. All members of the body could attend meetings and vote, but the vote of nonfounders would simply be consultative. The founders would also constitute the Central Commission. Affairs would be handled by this commission and by special commissions, named by the central one, for particular tasks; new members while on such commissions would also have an official vote in society matters. The very structure of the French abolition society assured that its membership would be restrictive, its leadership oligarchic. The society seemed to be openly discouraging new members. Run by a small clique dominated by legislators, this could not be an open organization seeking mass support along the lines of the British model. It would operate largely as an appendage of the Chamber of Deputies and seek to employ the legislative process to achieve its goals.[13]

By its very structure, then, the French abolition society was destined to remain a small, elitist body. While its membership varied somewhat throughout the July Monarchy, all indications are that it

---

[12] For the average wage of workers under the July Monarchy, see Fernand Braudel and Ernest Labrousse, *Histoire économique et sociale de la France* (4 vols.; Paris: Presses Universitaires de France, 1976–1982), vol. 3, part 2, pp. 775–8.

[13] *Prospectus ... de la Société*, 11.

probably never had more than a hundred or so different adherents during its fourteen-year life-span. Although no accurate list of total membership exists for the society, a careful examination of existing lists, all dated between 1834 and 1842, indicates 89 names of individuals having belonged at one time or another to the Société française pour l'abolition de l'esclavage (see table). Historians have been able to identify with certainty only three other confirmed members of this body (Victor Schoelcher, the radical editor Laurent Antoine Pagnerre, and Joseph France), bringing the number to 92.[14] It is probable that the three members not on the above-mentioned lists joined after 1842. Although the names of other famous early nineteenth-century personages have been bantered about as belonging to the Société française – Louis Blanc, Godefroy Cavaignac, Louis Antoine Garnier-Pagès, Victor Hugo, Alexandre Auguste Ledru-Rollin, Edgar Quinet, Eugène Sue[15] – there is no evidence to substantiate these allegations. Yearly membership appears to have fluctuated between 40 and 70. For instance, by mid-1835 the total number reached 58; by 1836 it had even grown to 68. There is no evidence that it ever attained this number again. And active participation in the society must have been considerably less than this. The latest document that we have mentioning membership numbers dates from 1842, and simply lists adherents of the society present at and absent from an important banquet held by the organization in Paris. Extrapolating from this list gives a total of merely 40. Moreover, of these 40, 16 were still founding members, and eight others were early members who had joined before mid-1835. All indications are, then, that this was a very static, exclusivist group, one which did not readily expand or renew itself.

An examination of the backgrounds and affiliations of society members (given in the table) makes it possible to create a rudimentary prosopography of the identifiable adherents to this group. Politically, the Société française was clearly dominated by the governing elite. Of its 92 certifiable members, 52, or fully 56 percent, were deputies or peers. Among its membership were some of the leading figures of

[14] Motylewski (*La Société*, p. 84) has pointed out that Pagnerre's personal papers show his adherence to the society. Schmidt (*Victor Schoelcher*, 64) certifies that Schoelcher was a member, and that he presented France for membership.

[15] Motylewski, *La Société*, 11, 84; Janine Alexandre-Debray, *Victor Schoelcher, ou la mysteque d'un athée* (Paris: Perrin, 1983), 104.

Identifiable Membership of the Société française
pour l'abolition de l'esclavage

Abby. Voyager

Appert, B., baron. Functionary, member Morale Chrétienne

Baillehanche, de. Army officer, author

Barrot,* Odilon. Deputy, judge, leader of left opposition.

Beaumont, Gustave, comte de. Deputy, lawyer, liberal, companion of Tocqueville, moderate opposition

Béranger* [de la Drôme], Alphonse Marc Marcellin Thomas. Peer, liberal

Berville,* Albin de. Deputy, lawyer, liberal, member Morale chrétienne, Freemason

Billiard, Auguste. Former prefect, former resident of Ile de Bourbon

Biard, A. Morale chrétienne

Bonnin, François Urbain Céleste. Deputy, lawyer, liberal, dynastic opposition

Broglie,* Victor, duc de. Peer, minister, premier, Orleanist mainstay, illustrious family, Morale chrétienne, married to Protestant

Bureaux de Puzy, Maurice Poivre. Deputy, former prefect, liberal opposition

Carnot,* Lazare Hippolyte. Deputy, dynastic opposition, son of the revolutionary, Saint-Simonian, Morale chrétienne, Freemason

Cerclet, Antoine. Functionary, journalist, former Carbonari, leading Saint-Simonian, Morale chrétienne

Chambolle, François Adolphe. Deputy, journalist, dynastic opposition

Chapuy de Montlaville, Benoît Marie Louis Alceste, baron. Deputy, left opposition, Morale chrétienne

Corcelles, François de. Deputy, liberal opposition, former Carbonari, Morale chrétienne

Cordier, Joseph Louis Etienne. Deputy, administrator, left opposition

Courtois, Armand. Toulouse banker, Protestant

Courtois, Louis. Toulouse banker, Protestant

Courtois, Franck. Toulouse banker, Protestant

Crémieux, Isaac Adolphe. Deputy, lawyer, left opposition, Jewish, Freemason

Delespaul, Adolphe Clément Joseph. Deputy, magistrate, liberal opposition

Doublet de Boisthibault. Lawyer in Chartres, Morale chrétienne

Desjobert,* Amédé. Deputy, left opposition, agronomist, laissez-faire economist

Degérando,* Joseph Marie, baron. Peer, administrator, former Bonapartist, Morale chrétienne

Dessailly

Dugabé, Charles Casimir. Deputy, lawyer, Legitimist then staunch Guizot supporter

Dufau, Armand. Man of letters, Morale chrétienne

Durosier, Jean Théodore, baron de. Deputy, landowner, progovernment

Dutrône,* Henri. Lawyer, Morale chrétienne

Faure, Pascal Joseph. Deputy, moderate opposition

Feline

Férussac, André, baron de. Deputy, naturalist, army officer, progovernment

France, Joseph. Army officer, former colonial gendarme

Ganneron, Auguste Victor Hippolyte. Deputy, banker, merchant, progovernment

Gatine, Adolphe. Lawyer, former
magistrate in colonies
Golbery,* Marie Philippe, Aimé de.
Deputy, lawyer, center-left, then
Guizot supporter
Godde. Learned societies member
Guerin, V. Former Guadeloupe lawyer
Guilleminot, Armand Charles, comte.
Peer, general, ambassador, govern-
ment supporter
Hain
Harcourt, François Eugène Gabriel,
duc d'. Deputy then peer, ambas-
sador, progovernment, laissez-faire
liberal
Isambert,* François. Deputy, lawyer,
famous jurist, left opposition,
Morale chrétienne, Freemason
Isambert, Alfred. Lawyer, son of
François, above
Jay, Antoine. Deputy, lawyer, writer,
journalist, former Bonapartist,
Orleanist, Morale chrétienne,
Freemason
Laborde,* Louis Joseph Alexandre,
comte de. Deputy, army officer,
administrator, former slave owner
in Saint-Domingue, close to Louis
Philippe, Freemason
Lacrosse,* Bertrand Théobold Joseph,
baron de. Deputy, dynastic left.
Lafayette,* Georges, marquis de.
Deputy, liberal opposition, son
of revolutionary hero, Morale
chrétienne, Freemason
Laisné de Villevêque,* Gabriel Jacques.
Deputy, merchant, Orleanist
Languinais, Victor. Deputy, center left,
Morale chrétienne
Lamartine,* Alphonse de. Deputy,
poet, diplomat, ministerial then
liberal opposition, Morale
chrétienne

Larochefoucauld-Liancourt,* Frédéric
Gäetan, duc de. Deputy, philanthropist, liberal, Morale chrétienne
president
Las Cases, Emmanuel, comte de.
Deputy, diplomat, pro-Guizot, son
of Napoleon's consort on Sainte-
Helena, Morale chrétienne,
Freemason
Lasteyrie, Ferdinand Charles Léon,
comte de. Deputy, dynastic oppo-
sition, nephew of Tracy, Morale
chrétienne
Lasteyrie, Jules, marquis. Deputy,
moderate opposition, brother-in-
law of Rémusat
Leyraud, André. Deputy, center left
Lherminier, Eugène. Jurist, educator,
journalist, Orleanist, Morale
chrétienne
Lucas, Charles. Functionary
Lutheroth,* Henri. Lawyer, Protes-
tant, Morale chrétienne
Macaulay, Zachary. Honorary presi-
dent, British abolitionist leader,
Protestant
Marchal, Pierre François. Deputy,
lawyer, left opposition
Matter. Functionary, educator
Montalembert, Charles Forbes, comte
de. Peer, liberal Catholic leader,
family holdings in West Indies,
Morale chrétienne
Montrol,* François Mongin de.
Journalist, liberal
Mornay, Auguste Joseph Christophe
Jules, marquis de. Deputy, army
officer, left opposition
O'Connor, Arthur Condorcet. Gen-
eral, publicist, liberal, Protestant,
exiled Irish reformist leader, married
to daughter of Condorcet
O'Connor, Daniel

Pagnerre, Laurent Antoine. Editor of abolitionist writings, lawyer, republican, Freemason

Passy,* Hippolyte Philibert. Deputy then peer, minister, political economist, center left

Pinet. Lawyer, Morale chrétienne.

Réal, Félix. Deputy, liberal opposition, then ministerial, lawyer

Rémusat,* Charles, comte de. Deputy, minister, ministerial then moderate opposition, Morale chrétienne

Ricord, D.

Roger* [du Loiret], Jacques François, baron. Deputy, liberal Legitimist, former administrator in Senegal, Freemason

Roger [du Nord], Edouard Leon, comte de. Deputy, former diplomat, ministerial then center-left opposition

Sade,* François Xavier, comte de. Deputy, dynastic opposition

Saint-Albin, Marie Philibert Hortensius, Rousselin de Corbeau, comte de. Deputy, lawyer, dynastic opposition

Saint-Albin. Probably relative of Marie, above

Saint-Antoine, Hippolyte Daniel de. Doctor, proprietor in West Indies, Morale chrétienne

Saint-Horrant

Sainte-Croix,* Félix Renouard, marquis de. Proprietor in West Indies, Morale chrétienne

Salverte,* Eusèbe Baconnière de. Deputy, lawyer, left opposition

Schoelcher, Victor. Republican, Freemason, merchant

Teste, Jean Baptiste. Deputy then peer, minister, lawyer, ministerial, implicated in venality scandal in 1847

Thayer,* Amédée William. Banker, lawyer, American parentage, co-owner of plantation in Martinique, Protestant, Morale chrétienne

Thayer,* Edouard James. Banker, lawyer, brother of above, probable colonial proprietor, Protestant, Morale chrétienne

Thivier. Son-in-law of Isambert

Thibault. Morale chrétienne

Tocqueville, Alexis de. Deputy, political theorist, historian, lawyer, moderate opposition, Morale chrétienne

Tracy,* Alexandre César Victor Destutt, marquis de. Deputy, son of the Ideologue, moderate opposition

Verhuel,* Carrel Henrik. Peer, former Dutch officer and Bonapartist, Protestant, Morale chrétienne

---

* Indicates founding member.

Source: This table is built upon membership lists dated 1835, 1836, 1837, 1838, and 1842, found in various Société française pour l'abolition de l'esclavage publications. No lists are available after 1842, but it is unlikely that many abolitionists joined the society after this date. Besides the names listed here, the most likely prospects are the deputies Ledru-Rollin, Beugnot, and Paul de Gasparin, along with Caillet, Rouvellat de Cussac, and Wilks. Biographical information is drawn from several standard sources, but especially A. Robert and G. Cougny, *Dictionnaire des parlementaires français* (5 vols.; Paris: Bourloton, 1889–1891) for members of the legislature. Supplemental information is culled from biographical dictionaries, secondary works, as well as abolitionist and government papers. Other insights were kindly provided by Madame Maïté Court-Isambert.

the July Monarchy: Barrot, Beaumont, Broglie, Harcourt, Laborde, Passy, Rémusat, Tracy, and Tocqueville. Most of the highest officials of the organization (President Broglie, Vice-President and then President Tracy, Vice-President Passy, Secretary Laborde), were either very close personally to the King, or ministerial material. This undoubtedly explains why the society could exist, and operate within certain clearly defined boundaries, despite government laws prohibiting most association. Nevertheless, aside from much of its leadership, a good proportion of its total membership was of liberal persuasion. Although it is difficult to establish exact political affiliations under a regime in which political parties did not exist and in which political alliances fluctuated regularly, it is apparent that many legislative members of the society can be classified as belonging to the moderate, liberal, center left, or left dynastic opposition, in contrast to the centrist or conservative Cabinets that held power under the Orleanist monarchy. The composition of the Société française, then, was overwhelmingly loyal to the dynasty, and establishment-oriented, but with marked liberal, even opposition, tendencies vis-à-vis the King's Cabinets. This Orleanist liberalism is also witnessed by the massive transfer between Société de la morale chrétienne and abolition society membership. Some 33 adherents to the new abolitionist grouping, or an impressive 36 percent of the total, had been or continued to be affiliated with the Morale chrétienne. The liberal, philanthropic, Christian, universalist principles of the two organizations merged, as did their adherents.

The Société française pour l'abolition de l'esclavage also displayed the religious, political, and social structure typical of the upper strata of the *notable*-dominated July Monarchy. The number of Protestants within the abolition society was considerably less than in the Morale chrétienne. Even including its honorary British president Macaulay, Protestants accounted for only 9 percent of the total, and most of these were not legislative members. Still, this percentage was more than the national average, and two of the society's most active supporters, Amédée Thayer and Lutheroth, were Protestants. There were relatively few identifiable Freemasons among its members. Although ten members of the society (or 11%) were masons, the only two dominant figures were Isambert and baron Roger du Loiret. Schoelcher probably joined the Société française late, and he was never active in it; Bissette, while a lodge member, was not affiliated with the society. Though Isambert, Bissette, and Schoelcher were the leaders of French anti-slavery under the July Monarchy, it would be an exaggeration to argue that nineteenth-century French abolitionism was dominated by Freemasons.[16] As for occupations, a good portion of society members, 29 percent, were lawyers, jurists, or magistrates. This, indeed, is a minimum, for an even greater number may have had legal training. Still others were active or former administrators, a few of them, per- haps, even being among the famous placemen of Guizot in the 1840s, who were given government salaried positions – deputies and peers remained unpaid under the July Monarchy and were all people of sub- stance – in exchange for votes. Some of the lawyers and functionaries had served in the colonies. In fact, some eleven adherents – not count- ing Macaulay – or 12 percent, were actual or former residents or land owners in the colonies, or individuals who had close family connec- tions to the colonial system. Though most of these members with colonial backgrounds were advocates of gradual emancipation, four (Roger du Loiret, Gatine, and the Thayer brothers) would emerge as immediatist abolitionists by the 1840s. The French abolition society, then, did have a small core of followers who could give firsthand testi- mony on slavery in the tropics. In terms of social background, a great many members were nobles or members of the Chamber of Peers. Ducs, comtes, barons, marquis, and peers numbered 29, or 32 percent, not to mention other nobles, such as Lamartine and Tocqueville, who chose not to flaunt their aristocratic lineage. The society's political and social composition reflected its highly elitist, legalistic, hierarchi- cal orientation concerning the emancipation question. It would oppose servitude out of liberal, humanitarian, altruistic principles. It would not resort to extraparliamentary, antigovernment, or popular based strategies in its cautious confrontation with slavery. It could hardly be expected to create a vast organizational network, appeal for massive public support, or readily change its tactics as its British brethren had done in their successful campaign against servitude.

Membership in the French abolition society was quite limited at first, and it appears that much of its leadership and planning was the work of an even smaller group. For example, the principles of the

---

[16] Tudesq, *Les grands notables*, II, 835.

society, as outlined in the prospectus, were drawn up by Passy, sent to Isambert for changes and additions, and then rubber-stamped by the membership on December 15.[17] For the first few months, however, meetings tended to center around the gathering of information and evidence, and to be quite open to different participants. After its first two sessions devoted largely to organizational matters, on December 22 the society examined the question of emancipation during the French Revolution. Following this, the body listened on January 5, 1835, to La Rochefoucauld-Liancourt deliver his long report on the past anti-slavery activity of the Société de la morale chrétienne. The president of the Morale chrétienne showed how this forerunner to the abolition society had evolved from an anti-slave trade stance to one of requesting slave amelioration to its final position of encouraging *rachat*. He also intimated that the Société française pour l'abolition de l'esclavage would be carrying out the work of his group if it could succeed in changing the condition of slaves. At a time when the Morale chrétienne was diminishing its anti-slavery activities, it seemed to be passing the emancipationist torch on to the new abolition society, itself heavily stocked with members of the earlier organization.[18] Indeed, it is this relay of anti-slavery activity from one body to the next that best explains the massive immigration of past and present members of the morale chrétienne into the French abolition society.

Subsequently, in a series of meetings at a frequency of approximately three per month, the society heard a succession of anti-slavery spokesmen describe conditions under several slave regimes. Gustave de Beaumont, friend of Alexis de Tocqueville and a leading member of the society in the 1830s, spoke on January 12, 1835, about his recent voyage to the United States, and of the preference given in Maryland to free over slave labor. Auguste Billiard, a former prefect and resident of Ile de Bourbon who like Beaumont joined the society by June 1835, reported during the January 26 meeting on attitudes in his Indian Ocean isle toward emancipation. To receive perspectives on the other French staple-producing colonies, the society listened on March 2 to Fabien and Persegol – a nonmember but ex-president of the royal

---

[17] Letter from Passy to Isambert, Oct. 29, 1834, kindly made available to the author by Madame Maïté Court-Isambert.

[18] *Prospectus ... de la Société*, 12; *La Revue des colonies*, no. 9, March 1835, pp. 25–36.

court of French Guiana – about slavery and the possibility of ending it in their colonies. And on March 12 founding member the marquis de Sainte-Croix, a proprietor in Martinique who was author of a work on statistics in that colony, spoke on the poor material condition of slaves in his island.[19] In the tradition of the British abolitionist bodies that had preceded theirs, members of the French abolition society were attempting to become as well briefed on the slavery question as possible. Drawn in the most part from the two houses of the French legislature, members of the society planned to operate as any responsible legislative committee would, by gathering all possible information, weighing it carefully, and then making an informed and persuasive recommendation to sway the government. The society's rational, parliamentary approach to the slavery question witnessed once again its commitment to a cautious, gradual, long-term solution rather than rapid moves toward emancipation.

British evidence on colonial developments also continued to be a focus of interest for the French abolition society. In February 1835 the organization produced its second publication, following the prospectus, by influential member François Mongin de Montrol on the consequences of emancipation in the British colonies. Once again a member of the Société française was citing the beneficial effects of British slave liberation to inspire French emulation.[20] Concerning society meetings, the entire session of March 23 was devoted to examining British data on the efficiency of free labor in Puerto Rico. Then, a week later Macaulay returned to Paris to present the abolitionist leader Thomas Buxton's report on free blacks in Haiti.[21] The British emancipation experience may not have totally dominated the French abolitionist debate in the spring of 1835, but it certainly continued to play a significant role in it.

These early meetings of the Société française pour l'abolition de

---

[19] *Prospectus ... de la Société*, 12–13. When speaking of Sainte-Croix, whom it described as owner of one of the best sugar establishments on Martinique, the pro-slavery *Le Moniteur du commerce* (Paris) asked whether he too might not have used the whip when he himself managed his estates before his conversion to philanthropy (*Le Moniteur du commerce*, Feb. 20, 1835).

[20] François Mongin de Montrol, *Des colonies anglaises, depuis l'émancipation des esclaves, et de l'influence de cette émancipation sur les colonies françaises* (Paris: Impr. E. Duverger, 1835).

[21] *Prospectus ... de la Société*, 14.

l'esclavage were not only marked by their wide range of subject matter, but also by their openness to differing points of view. Following its commitment in its prospectus to entertain a variety of opinions on the emancipation question, the society even took the initiative to invite defenders of slavery to address it. La Rochefoucauld-Liancourt made overtures to a former colonial delegate of Guadeloupe, Alexandre Foignet, to speak to the society, evidently because he believed Foignet to be a liberal *colon* close to his own opinion that slavery should be eliminated gradually after due preparation. When Foignet appeared before the society during its January 19 meeting, he offered the sort of presentation that should have been expected from a colonial apologist. He began by conceding that slavery was doomed in the long run, but then switched to the argument that slaves were far too uncivilized to be freed soon, and that to do so would bring disaster and barbarism to the colonies. Instead, he insisted, it was necessary to prepare them gradually, through "wise and slow methods," such as offering them religious instruction, teaching them to save, and encouraging them to marry. He even suggested that slaves were not badly off materially, and that manumission was in itself slowly eliminating servitude.[22] His message was a typical plantocratic one: emancipation should be postponed as long as possible, if not suspended ad infinitum. He also stressed the need for a generous indemnity for the slave owners, something that certain abolitionists were reluctant to concede. Apparently, Foignet even dared argue against the right of the French abolitionist society to exist, a remark which, according to Bissette's review, caused great hilarity among society members. Besides, Foignet carried the affront so far as to go public with his statements and publish his presentation in pamphlet form. Once all this came out into the open, Bissette joined the fray to lambaste Foignet's arguments as "the summary of sophisms and errors by which the *colons* defend their detestable domination."[23]

Fortunately for the abolitionists, they were able to save face by presenting as a rejoinder to Foignet a writing completed at this time by the Marquis de Sainte-Croix – himself a *colon*, albeit one of the rare abolitionist ones – which emphasized that France could not act fast

[22] *Journal de la société de la morale chrétienne*, vol. 7, 2nd series, Jan.–June 1835, pp. 2–15; *Le Semeur*, Feb. 25, 1835.
[23] *La Revue des colonies*, no. 8, Feb. 1835, p. 44; no. 9, March 1835, pp. 47–8.

enough to follow the British example.[24] Sainte-Croix also delivered a speech before the Société française, contradicting all the points made by Foignet. But the latter returned to the charge and took the entire matter before the press. Foignet published a letter on March 23, stating that the French abolition society was torn by divisions and that many of its adherents agreed with him that emancipation was impracticable at this time. This obliged Sainte-Croix to issue another rebuttal to Foignet, this time in the *Revue des colonies*, asserting that he and his fellow members of the society had "a single aim, to arrive by all legal and moral means at the abolition of slavery."[25] Foignet and his colonial backers had obviously intended to drive a wedge between the moderate and progressive members within the new abolitionist society, and thereby divide and weaken it. After all, the objectives of the Société française pour l'abolition de l'esclavage amounted, in the eyes of the pro-slavers, to "a signal of death for the colonies."[26] Altogether, Foignet's repeated interventions had brought negative publicity to the abolitionists, and amounted to a considerable embarrassment for the new society. It also taught the Société française that it should not confide in and trust the *colons*. The corridors of the society would not be open to colonial advocates in the future.

After its unfortunate encounter with Foignet, the French abolitionist society returned to its format in which various members made presentations on the slavery question. On May 4 it was the turn of Isambert to speak on the situation in Martinique and Guadeloupe. He was followed a week later by Guérin, a former lawyer in Guadeloupe, who stressed "the unfortunate state of slaves" and their urgent need for freedom.[27] As *Le Semeur* perspicaciously pointed out, after having gathered evidence for some time already, by late spring the French abolitionist society was also beginning to consider different plans for abolition.[28] Thus, on April 20, member Odilon Barrot, a leader of the left-center opposition under the July Monarchy, spoke about the views on emancipation of the recently deceased free trade economist

---

[24] *Journal de la société de la morale chrétienne*, vol. 7, 2nd series, Jan.–June 1835, pp. 15–20; *Le Semeur*, Feb. 25, 1835.

[25] *La Revue des colonies*, no. 9, March 1835, pp. 29–33; no. 10, April 1835, pp. 40–45.

[26] ANCAOM, Gén. 156 (1299), Colonial Council of Guadeloupe, 1835 session, statement by Gérard.

[27] *Prospectus ... de la Société*, 14–15.

[28] April 29, 1835.

Jean Baptiste Say; on May 4, baron Jacques François Roger (known as Roger du Loiret), a stalwart member of the society and a former administrator in Senegal, presented a plan containing a substitute for the standard indemnity planters claimed to be their due; and on June 1 and 8, Sainte-Croix and Billiard discussed proposals in which only a third of any indemnity would be provided in cash. Other members of the society had also devised their own plans for slave liberation. Isambert, Guérin, and Gabriel Jacques Laisné de Villevêque all developed independent projects calling for gradual emancipation through different variations of *rachat*. Montrol had come up with a gradualist idea similar to those of Sainte-Croix and Billiard, while Lutheroth called for ending slavery five years after 1836. The French abolition society had generated a whole series of individual approaches to eliminating bondage, without adopting any particular one. Its first year was among its most active ones, but it was also indicative of the society's difficulty in establishing a common ground or consensus among its diverse membership. By late June too, the 1835 legislative session was approaching its end. The Société française pour l'abolition de l'esclavage held its last meeting of the year on June 15, when the group delegated all powers to a committee of correspondence, and adjourned its sitting. For the next six months its affairs would be in the hands of Billiard, Armand Dufau, Lazare Hippolyte Carnot (son of the revolutionary), Sainte-Croix, the treasurer Amédée Thayer, and the secretary Isambert, with the latter probably handling most matters.[29] Its activities did not cease entirely during this six-month interim, but it seems to have lost momentum, and to have accomplished little of a concrete nature during the intersession period.

One of the issues that French abolitionists and *colons* had raised in 1835 was that of an indemnity for slave owners. This raises the question of what constituted a just indemnity in the minds of all protagonists in the slavery debate. The benchmark against which all estimates were measured was the British precedent. The British, adamant like the French about the inviolability of property, had set an example in granting 20 million pounds, or 500 million francs, as total compensation

---

[29] *Prospectus ... de la Société*, 14–16; *La Revue des colonies*, no. 12, June 1835, pp. 7–13; 2nd year, no. 3, Sept. 1835, pp. 97–102. For views on the early abolitionist career of Say, see Resnick, "Political Economy and French Anti-Slavery: The Case of J.-B. Say," 177–86.

to colonial slave owners. This sum was so large that most British observers at the time had been shocked by the unexpected liberality of the British Parliament. French Director of the Colonies Saint-Hilaire calculated in late 1833 that a proportional indemnity to the British one would amount to 180 million francs to free all of France's then 285,000 colonial slaves, or approximately 643 francs for every man, woman, and child. The disbursement of such a significant sum, he believed, would be highly unlikely by any French administration as long as French public opinion did not force the authorities to act.[30]

In reality, though, no one sum was ever agreed upon as adequate or acceptable by government, abolitionists, and *colons*, either among themselves or with their antagonists. Some members of the abolition society might advocate granting planters only a reduced indemnity for their slaves, but almost all French abolitionists agreed with the government and colonial establishment that compensation of some kind was absolutely essential. Rare were the abolitionists like Bissette who argued that the slaves, not the masters, should be indemnified. Even other future radical abolitionists, like Schoelcher, believed in the need for compensation of some sort, though Schoelcher shared in the common trait of indecision in fixing an exact sum: in 1842 he suggested the excessive amount of 1,000 francs per slave, but by 1847 he calculated that 750 francs, or a total sum of 140 million, would be adequate.[31] Planters, especially, steadily exaggerated their demands to render them unacceptable. Already by the mid-1830s the plantocracy was insisting that masters should be compensated not only for slaves but for the totality of their property, because the latter supposedly would become useless without coerced labor. Subsequently, their demands always ranged between the exorbitant sums of 150 and 300 million francs, amounts which they realized the July Monarchy would never appropriate to resolve the slavery question. Even the Broglie commission of the early 1840s was so solicitous of planter welfare that it estimated slave values at their highest point and suggested the ludicrous sum of 1,200 francs per slave, or a total of 300 million, as just compensation. From this time on colonial spokesmen tended to coopt this sum as their minimum requirement simply because they

[30] ANCAOM, Gén. 206 (1513), memo for the Director of the Colonies, Dec. 27, 1833.
[31] Schmidt, *Vitor Schoelcher*, 94, 120.

knew it unobtainable. The point is, though, that even the government never decided upon what would constitute an appropriate indemnity. No definite amount was ever settled upon because the July Monarchy never approached the point on the road to emancipation at which it would have to resolve such essential matters. As for the abolitionists, neither in 1835 nor later did they make concerted efforts to call the government to task over this, or to obviate the need for an indemnity by insisting that none should be paid. Most French abolitionists, like the government, did not believe that the time had yet come to free the slaves.

In late 1835 abolitionist activity was winding down. In the meantime, however, other important developments had occurred on the anti-slavery front. In March 1835 the duc de Broglie, head of the Société française pour l'abolition de l'esclavage, was asked to form the government and assume the position of President of the Council of Ministers. The society immediately chose a delegation comprised of the peer and Protestant Admiral Carel Verhuel (Broglie's wife, after all, was Protestant), the deputies Passy and La Rochefoucauld-Liancourt, and the authors Sainte-Croix and Beaumont to congratulate the duke on his appointment. Broglie reciprocated by issuing a letter to Passy on April 14 that amounted to government authorization of the society.[32] The fact that the leader of the French abolition society would now also be prime minister certainly delighted anti-slavery forces and raised expectations among them. Lord Brougham, speaking at a large abolitionist assembly in London attended by Beaumont, exclaimed that he knew Broglie and that the latter "would not let three months go by without proposing measures concerning the abolition of slavery."[33] Those British and French emancipationists who placed high hopes in the appointment of Broglie, however, would soon come to realize that the accretions of power would transform many a French abolitionist, be he Broglie, Rémusat, or François Guizot, into cautious statesmen. In less than three months Broglie's administration revealed what it really intended to do concerning the slavery question.

There had been no interpellations of the government by abolitionists within the French chambers during the 1834 session. Indeed, only

[32] *Prospectus ... de la Société*, 14–15; *La Revue des colonies*, no. 9, March 1835, p. 48; no. 10, April 1835, p. 39.
[33] *Prospectus ... de la Société*, 15; *Le National*, June 15, 1835.

Isambert had made even an oblique mention of the slavery question in the 1834 legislature.[34] The navy-colonial department was well aware, though, that members of the new-found society would seize the first opportunity to question the Cabinet in the lower house during the 1835 session. Accordingly, it prepared a strategy paper to this effect already on March 18, as soon as Broglie was nominated first minister.[35] The slavery question arose for the first time in the 1835 session when a petition calling for abolition, drawn up by the Société française in December 1834 and signed by Lutheroth and seventeen other inhabitants of Paris – the low number of signers indicating a total lack of network for gathering petitions along British lines – was reported upon and debated in the Chamber of Peers on February 24, 1835. Interestingly enough, at this time, before he had become prime minister, Broglie spoke in favor of slave liberation by arguing that the British example had demonstrated its feasibility.[36] Therefore, after Broglie came to power the abolitionists were anxious to put the question directly to one of their own. When the navy-colonial minister, Admiral Victor Guy baron Duperré, presented a request to the Chamber of Deputies on April 22–23 for additional funding for colonial garrisons in light of British emancipation, the abolitionists seized the occasion to question the government on the slavery issue. In a well-orchestrated effort, six members of the abolition society joined in the debate: Isambert, Laborde, Alphonse de Lamartine (the famous poet), Passy, Tracy, and Eusèbe Salverte.[37] All of them followed Broglie's example and cited the British precedent as proof that slavery could be ended without disorder, though some, like Laborde, emphasized the caution with which Britain had preceded, while others, like Passy, underlined its overall rapidity. Isambert made the most impassioned plea for emancipation, and Tracy exclaimed that if the government did not introduce an abolition bill he would do so himself.

After the debate was well advanced Broglie finally stepped forward

---

[34] *Le Moniteur universel*, May 9, 1834.
[35] ANCAOM, Gén. 156 (1299), "Question de l'émancipation des esclaves," by Saint-Hilarie, March 18, 1835.
[36] *Prospectus ... de la Société*, 16; *Le Moniteur universel*, Feb. 25, 1835; ANCAOM, Gén. 156 (1299), report by Duperré for Council of Ministers, March 1835.
[37] Société française pour l'abolition de l'esclavage, *Analyse de la discussion de la Chambre des Députés et de la Chambre des Pairs relative à l'émancipation des esclaves, par M. F. de Montrol (Troisième Publication)* (Paris: Impr. Paul Dupont, 1835), pp. 1, 25.

to the tribunal to employ a rhetoric different from the one he had advanced two months earlier, at a time when he was only president of the abolition society. Broglie began by announcing that his personal sentiments on the slavery question were well known, but that he now had to speak as French prime minister. He then avowed that slavery was not a priority with the government. Since his administration had come to power six weeks earlier it had not as yet had time even to discuss colonial servitude. Broglie insisted, though, that with the English experiment not yet complete, France, as a slave-possessing nation, "must be preoccupied with calming tempers rather than agitating them." Broglie was convinced that "the government ... must impose upon itself the greatest reserve; that its work at the present time, its natural role, is to wait, to observe, to gather facts, information, and to meditate upon them." The July Monarchy would "gather all information" possible, "reflect," and "make decisions only with complete knowledge of the facts." Broglie was supported by navy-colonial minister Duperré, who recited verbatim the arguments against rapid emancipation outlined in Saint-Hilaire's note of March 18. Duperré was adamant that, "before launching itself into ... these new paths," France must "prepare the population" of its colonies "by practical lessons of religion, morality, and civilization.... This is what the government is already doing, and will not cease to continue doing." The garrison funding bill put forth by the government was passed by a vote of 240 to 51 in the deputies, and by an even greater margin, 85 to 2, in the peers the following month.[38] The Cabinet, even under Broglie, had proved inflexible on the slavery issue.

Throughout the late spring debates of 1835, nevertheless, the French abolition society, government, and plantocracy had all clearly enunciated their positions on the emancipation question. Despite Broglie's appointment, the government's stance on slavery was closer to that of the proslavers than to that of even the most moderate abolitionists. The administration's policy, in fact, had not evolved appreciably since the first pronouncement of Minister of the Navy and Colonies Rigny in the summer of 1833, despite the fact that the head of the French abolition society was now also first minister. Duperré's statements in the course of the debate indicate that Broglie, like the

---

[38] *Le Moniteur universel*, April 23, 24, June 16, 1835.

minister, was undoubtedly following the lead of high-placed public servants within the French colonial office, and especially of Saint-Hilaire, who had shaped much of French colonial policy since the Restoration. In this sense, French slavery policies had already become institutionalized early under the July Monarchy. Moreover, as the republican-oriented *Le National* pointed out, in France the prime minister, "servant above all to the royal will," could not impose his own opinions on government policy without losing his portfolio.[39] As of the mid-1830s it had become evident to some astute observers that Broglie, as president of the council, could not oppose the will of King Louis Philippe, who throughout the July Monarchy would prove reluctant to liberate French colonial slaves. The basically static nature of French policy toward the slavery question was becoming explicit already by 1835.

Broglie's performance as prime minister received a chilly reception in most liberal circles. *Le Temps* (Paris) and *Le Constitutionnel* asserted that, as could be expected from a first minister, Broglie had been evasive on the slavery issue.[40] *Le Semeur* attempted to put the best possible face on things by reasoning that, "despite the accommodations with which he had been obliged to explain things in the chamber," Broglie had "made his opinion prevail within the council" of ministers.[41] Other anti-slavery organs were less sanguine in their evaluations. *Le National* remarked with sarcasm that the government under Broglie had no time for "the interests of the colonies and the liberty of blacks." After noting the dual presidency of Broglie, *Le Courrier français* suggested ironically that the duke had displayed a "double conscience of statesman and philanthropist."[42] More acerbic yet were the words uttered by *Le Journal du commerce* (Paris), a liberal newspaper until 1836, to the effect that Broglie had displayed "Jesuitical doctrinairism" in the chamber, a take-off on the fact that the duke was one of the leaders of the "doctrinaire" Orleanist faction. Bissette, in reproducing these terms in his review, associated himself with them.[43]

---

[39] Aug. 15, 1835.

[40] *Le Temps*, April 23, 1835; *Le Constitutionnel*, April 23, 1835.

[41] April 29, 1835.

[42] *Le National*, April 23, 1835; *Le Courrier français*, April 23, 1835.

[43] *Le Journal du commerce*, April 24, 1835; *La Revue des colonies*, no. 12, June 1835, pp. 30–31.

The disappointment of some abolitionists with the July Monarchy's slavery policy was manifest already in the early stages of the newly organized second French anti-slavery movement.

In the autumn of 1834 Bissette's *Revue des colonies* continued along the same lines as it had in its first two issues. The black emancipationist carried on his vendetta against Martinique planters, denounced again the inhuman treatment of slaves, and repeated his warnings that France must free its slaves, as Britain had, or risk slave uprisings more serious that the Grande Anse affair. He also began developing other themes, such as denouncing British apprenticeship as "a sort of bastard state between slavery and enfranchisement" or calling for the fusion of whites and blacks in the colonies.[44] In his attacks on apprenticeship, Bissette proved closely attuned to British abolitionists, who also soon came to denounce this intermediary state as no better that slavery.[45] As of late 1834, however, Bissette was concentrating more than ever on French slave emancipation. He now began to turn away from the thesis that slaves might free themselves to other hypotheses, such as the then current credo among economic liberals that slavery impeded progress and prosperity. In this sense he cited such diverse authorities as David Hume, Benjamin Franklin, and Say about the superiority of free over slave labor; he also reprinted an article on this topic by Jerome Adolphe Blanqui, a well-known French economist and elder brother of the revolutionary Louis Auguste Blanqui.[46] Still, throughout 1834 and into 1835 Bissette had not distinguished himself as basically different from the French abolition society. Both held the premise that abolition should be prepared for and implemented as soon as possible, the implication being that slaves could be freed only after proper preparation to assume the responsibilities of liberty.

During this period too, Bissette retained his informal ties to the Société française pour l'abolition de l'esclavage and its members. Isambert, Bissette's lawyer and defender in the 1820s, refused to collaborate with or become a silent partner in the *Revue des colonies*

---

[44] Ibid., no. 4, Oct. 1834, pp. 6–7; no 6, Dec. 1834, pp. 3–7.

[45] See Green, *British Slave Emancipation*, 129–162; Izhak Gross, "Parliament and the Abolition of Negro Apprenticeship, 1835–1838," *English Historical Review* 96 (1981): 560–76; Alex Tyrrell, "The 'Moral Radical Party' and the Anglo-Jamaican Campaign for the Abolition of the Negro Apprenticeship System," *English Historical Review* 99 (1984): 135–44.

[46] *La Revue des colonies*, no. 7, Jan. 1835; pp. 3–14; no. 8, Feb. 1835, pp. 36–9.

when it first appeared, because of what he described as the verbal "violence of its editorship." Still, in an early issue of his monthly, Bissette referred to his former benefactor as a defender of the oppressed.[47] Similarly, Bissette was laudatory of French abolition society members, including its president, during the early stages of this organization's existence. Adherents to the society, in his eyes, were "elevated spirits, generous hearts, in a word, elite men" and "honorable philanthropists." Broglie, Bissette intoned, was "the grandson-in-law of Necker" – the duke had married the daughter of Madame de Staël, whose father was the pre-Revolutionary banker and reformer Jacques Necker, who had himself questioned slavery – and was ensconced "in the first rank of the faithful and enlightened friends of the blacks."[48] Bissette's cooperation with the Société française seemed close at first. It is highly likely that Bissette, along with Fabien, had testified at French abolition society meetings, and worked hand in hand with the organization throughout early 1835.

In the spring of 1835, however, Bissette's words reflect a change in orientation. At the same time that he reprinted the phrase about Broglie's Jesuitism, Bissette specified that of all the individual emancipation plans put forth by members of the abolition society, the one he favored least was Isambert's, even though it was similar to those of several of the latter's colleagues. And Bissette added that, while the society should be congratulated for taking the initiative in formulating anti-slavery proposals, its projects had often been "timid and insufficient."[49] A gap was growing between Bissette and the society – which never asked the black abolitionist to join its ranks – because of the latter's pronouncedly cautious approach to the emancipation issue. Navy-colonial minister Duperré's request for armed reinforcements for the colonies persuaded Bissette that the French government did not envisage freeing the slaves in the near future. Bissette, in fact, shared the opinion of the radical Parisian newspaper, *Le Bon Sens*, that Paris should be sending an emancipation law rather than additional bayonets to the French colonies.[50] By this time too Bissette had

[47] Jennings, "Bissette," 57; *Revue des colonies*, no. 6, Dec. 1834, p. 47.
[48] Ibid., no. 8, Feb. 1835, p. 30.
[49] Ibid., no. 12, June 1835, pp. 8–10.
[50] Ibid., no. 9, March 1835, p. 3. The *Bon Sens* was cited by Bissette, but the issue in question of the newspaper itself is no longer extant.

become convinced that the real aim of the colonists was to delay emancipation indefinitely, an idea he believed was shared by the French navy-colonial office.[51] Therefore, in the April 1835 issue of the *Revue* Bissette decided to strike off on his own. The black abolitionist declared that political, religious, and humanitarian factors militated against a cautious approach to the slave liberation question. Slaves should be freed immediately and completely. Once liberated, they could then be educated and inculcated with the work ethic that Bissette, like all French abolitionists of the time, valued highly.[52] In reversing the accepted process of first preparing and then freeing slaves, Bissette had emerged as the first French immediatist abolitionist. He had also widened the gulf between himself and the French abolition society, not to mention between himself, the government, and the planters. By the end of its first year of existence, French abolitionism was beginning to separate into two different currents, while the government and pro-slavers were following a third.

In the summer of 1834 British colonial slave emancipation had precipitated the organization of French anti-slavery forces. The emergence of the Société française pour l'abolition de l'esclavage was a crucial development, for France now had a body with the potential to lead the struggle against servitude. This society, like its predecessors from the Revolution through the Restoration, displayed its universalist principles and its deep indebtedness to the British. The Société française was significant too because, animated by the great *notables* who dominated the July Monarchy, it could operate through government corridors, especially the chambers, to stir the regime to action. But its potential source of strength was also its weakness. Already by the end of its first year of activity it was apparent that this organization, functioning as a practical appendage of the legislative chambers to which most of its members belonged, necessarily approached the emancipation question with staidness, legality, and caution.[53] Like earlier anti-slavery formations, it was an elitist group that dared not

[51] Jennings, "Bissette," 58; *Revue des colonies*, no. 6, Dec. 1834, p. 5.

[52] Ibid., no. 10, April 1835, pp. 3–4.

[53] Other reform movements under the July Monarchy, such as the attempt to limit and restrict child labor, suffered also from an elitist, cautious, parliamentary approach. See Lee-Shai Weissbach, *Child Labor Reform in Nineteenth-Century France: Assuring the Future Harvest* (Baton Rouge: Louisiana State University Press, 1989), esp. 59–61.

appeal to the populace, and which preferred sketching out a program calling for thorough preparation of slaves, ameliorative measures to improve their plight, but only a gradual emancipation process that would provide for the rights of planters as much as for those of the enslaved. In its first parliamentary joust with the government, headed ironically at the time by the abolitionist society's own president, it became clear that it could challenge and embarrass the authorities, but not oblige them to make significant moves. The government, for its part, had already displayed its tendency to follow the conservative colonial policy it had elaborated during the early years of the monarchy's existence, coopting if necessary any abolitionist leader that entered its ranks, while persevering in its policy of watchful waiting.

By the end of the first year it was also apparent how individualist and tentative French abolitionists tended to be. They now had an organization to air their demands, but the latter remained largely undefined, a tendency that would persist throughout most of 1830s and 1840s. Already in its first session the French abolition society had showed its proclivity not only to stress the gathering of information above all, but to let individual members expound ad infinitum their own doctrines. Dominated by a group of prominent thinkers and politicians, abolitionists tended to be prima donnas rather than organization men. Already in 1835, members of the Société française pour l'abolition de l'esclavage had a penchant for putting forth individual solutions to the slavery question rather than formulating common policies acceptable to all. Just as the July Monarchy had no fixed parties of the modern kind but constantly fluctuating political formations, the abolition society could not establish a common approach to the slavery question beyond desiring its gradual solution, accompanied by all the guarantees necessary to assure order and the preservation of property. One should not forget that this was a regime more frightened by the revolutionary tradition than stimulated by it, and a monarchy threatened in the early 1830s by instability from both Legitimists and republicans.[54] Orleanists more than abolitionists, society members insisted on stability and caution in all matters.

---

[54] Standard histories of the July Monarchy, like the one by Collingham, provide an excellent account of the destabilizing events of the regime's first five years.

Then too, already in the first year of its existence, the French anti-slavery movement was being slowly fractured between gradualists, who remained within the Société française, and the immediatists, few in number as yet, but who could not suffer their company. The black Bissette was among the first abolitionists to read correctly the lesson of the British emancipation process and to come to realize that gradualism would not work, and that it was playing into the hands of a circumspect government and of a colonial establishment that was banking on postponing slave liberation as long as possible. Unfortunately, this fissuring of abolitionist ranks would continue for most of the July Monarchy and necessarily weaken them. Gradualism too would predominate within the French abolitionist movement for over a decade. Faced with a government and plantocracy determined to advance even more slowly down the path toward eventual slave liberation, French anti-slavery would be limited for the remainder of the 1830s to provoking its adversaries within parliamentary channels.

4

PROCRASTINATIONS, CONSULTATIONS, AND INTERPELLATIONS

At the same time that abolitionist forces were forming their ranks in 1834–1835, the colonial establishment was organizing its efforts in defense of slavery. The *conseil colonial* in each colony was dominated by the large landowners, who from the time of the Restoration had been primarily engaged in sugar production. Plantocratic elements controlled not only the elective colonial legislatures, but also the courts and local administrations. In Paris, however, the colonial general staff was centered in the Council of Delegates. The legislation of April 1833 had authorized the colonial councils of the most populated colonies, Guadeloupe, Martinique, and Bourbon, to elect two representatives each, and Guiana one. These highly paid emissaries of the *colons* met frequently in their council in the capital, deciding upon strategy and tactics by a majority decision of delegates present. Some of the delegates were themselves planters and thus slave owners, such as Favard for Guiana, E. de Jabrun in Guadeloupe, or Amédée Cools Desnoyers of Bourbon. Jabrun, for example, possessed 154 slaves on a medium-sized plantation, and was one of the most astute and forward-looking planters in the French West Indies.[1] Still, the most effective lobbyists were inevitably those who had important connections with Paris officialdom. Because the delegates were accredited only to the navy-colonial ministry, and not to the chambers, the best placed lobbyists were those recruited among eloquent members of the two chambers, for one of the characteristics of the legislative system of the July Monarchy was that legislators could hold different positions simultaneously. Thus, the most influential delegates of the mid-1830s

[1] Tomich, *Slavery in the Circuit*, 100, 148, 190.

were the deputies Mauguin and Dupin, the latter being promoted to the peerage in 1837. Such powerful spokesmen were enticed to the colonial cause by exhorbitant salaries of 20,000–25,000 francs annually, and their appointments at times brought about rapid political volte-faces. Before becoming a colonial delegate François Mauguin had been a well-known liberal of republican orientation, a defender of the oppressed, an advocate of the Polish cause, and an opponent of slavery. Baron Charles Dupin, another liberal, had actually been nominated but not confirmed for the position of Minister of the Navy and Colonies in late 1834, due to the influence exercised by his brother, André Marie Jean Jacques Dupin, President of the Chamber of Deputies from 1832 to 1840, a liberal economist and confidant of the King.[2] Charles Dupin remained a leader of the movement for the reform of child labor under the July Monarchy, but the generous salary he received from the colonists transformed him into an indubitable proslaver.[3] These articulate spokesmen not only pleaded the colonial case in the French chambers, but regularly met with the minister and leading functionaries of the navy-colonial department, not to mention the King. The delegates exercised such prestige and sway that Bissette believed that "the minister of the navy cedes to the intrigues of the colonial coterie seated in Paris," which was "all powerful within the navy[-colonial] office by some strange influence." Bissette was equally convinced that "Saint-Hilaire and his consorts" within the Directory of the Colonies – the office which, according to him, was the real architect of French colonial policy – were under the "perfidious influence" of the delegates.[4] Regardless of whether Bissette was correct in his accusations, they reflect the fact that under the July Monarchy the delegates were perceived as carrying tremendous political weight.

The activities of the delegates were far-flung, stretching well beyond lobbying in parliamentary and ministerial corridors. They were provided with huge slush funds from the colonial councils which, in turn, it was believed, obtained these monies with surreptitious taxes levied on the annual sugar harvests. With these resources the delegates

[2] *La Revue des colonies*, no. 6, Dec. 1834, pp. 36–39; no. 9, March 1835, pp. 20–22.
[3] Weissbach (*Child Labor Reform*, 65) has termed Charles Dupin "one of the most important champions of child labor reform France would ever see."
[4] *La Revue des colonies*, no. 8, Feb. 1835, p. 7; no. 12, June 1835, p. 41.

attempted to purchase favor by holding lavish dinners, and probably even by offering under-the-table gifts. They certainly disbursed hundreds of thousands of francs to influence, or even buy, newspapers and editors. As a result, the Council of Delegates had a formidable weapon in the printed media, for it could publish an infinite number of newspaper articles, brochures, and books.[5] And the delegates were mounting an efficient campaign against abolition already in 1835.

According to the governor of Guadeloupe, Admiral René Arnous Dessaulsay, Mauguin had been elected delegate by the colonial council of his colony because he was thought to be "capable of opposing with great success Isambert and other orators, enemies of the current colonial system."[6] Mauguin and his colleagues immediately adopted a two-pronged approach of acting in government circles and through the press to defend slavery. Or, as General Ambert, president of the Colonial Council of Guadeloupe, put it, the aim of the delegates should be "a double action of enlightening the authorities and directing public opinion."[7] Part of the success of the *colons* in achieving these objectives was due to a realistic new strategy adopted by the plantocracy in the 1830s.

Under the July Monarchy, a handful of diehard defenders of slavery still had recourse to the classical economic and strategic arguments of their predecessors. As during the Revolutionary, Napoleonic, and Restoration periods, some irrepressible colonial advocates continued to contend that the existence of the colonies depended on slavery, that French trade was reliant upon the colonies, and that the navy was tributary to both. The Chamber of Commerce of Nantes, for example, enunciated ideas echoing a different era when it predicted that emancipation would destroy the colonies, and that this in turn "would bring the rapid ruin of our maritime commerce, the decadence of our merchant marine, and the annihilation of our navy."[8] The staunch

---

[5] For a repertory of the ways in which the delegates influenced the press, the large number of newspapers that they inspired, and the impressive list of newspapers that they paid off, see Lawrence C. Jennings, "Slavery and the Venality of the July Monarchy Press," *French Historical Studies* 17 (1992): 957–78.

[6] ANCAOM, Guadeloupe 193 (1176), Governor to Minister, May 25, 1834.

[7] France, Bibliothèque Nationale, Papiers Schoelcher, MSS, n. a. f. 3632 (henceforth referred to as Schoelcher Papers), President of Colonial Council of Guadeloupe to Guadeloupe delegates, Jan. 8, 1835.

[8] Archives départementales de la Loire-Atlantique, Chambre de Commerce de Nantes, 6 JJ

proslavery *Le Journal du Havre*, voice of another leading sugar port, uttered similar sentiments. According to this organ, slavery was the mainstay of the colonies, which were indispensable for French maritime commerce, the merchant marine, and the navy.[9] However, language of this kind was rare in French colonial circles after the mid-1830s. The essential tactic of the *colons* already at this time was to accept emancipation in principle, but postpone it as long as possible and pose impossible conditions for its accomplishment. When intervening in the deputies' debate on April 22, 1835, Mauguin conceded that slavery could not be justified, but insisted that slaves were far from being prepared for freedom, and that this would require a slow process of amelioration over many years. Knowing also that the French administration was little inclined to pay out a large indemnity to slave owners, he asked whether France was ready to set aside 150 to 200 million francs for this, and whether such substantial sums could not be better spent for improvements to the infrastructure within France itself. His colleague Dupin supported him with the argument that all social progress must be achieved with necessary prudence, that it was essential to begin by preparing the slaves, and that everything should be accomplished "with calm, with leisure, with security."[10] Mauguin, as president of the delegates in the mid-1830s, confirmed this stance in a letter to the minister shortly thereafter. He admitted that emancipation was "only a question of time," but once again he stressed that a generous indemnity must be paid. Mauguin, like other colonial apologists, insisted that the notion of indemnity for confiscation of property was ensconced in French law, thus underlining the principle of the sacredness of property so dear to the July Monarchy notables. In his opinion too, the entire emancipation measure had to be prepared with "sufficient caution and prudence," and could have only "a very distant conclusion."[11] The colonial delegates

---

79*, letter to Guizot, president of the commission of the Chamber of Deputies charged with the examination of the proposal of Mr. Passy on the abolition of slavery, May 2, 1838.

[9] September 14, 27, 1831. By the late 1830s Le Havre had actually become the leading port dealing with the colonies of Guadeloupe and Martinique. See Jennings, "La presse havraise et l'esclavage," 66–71.

[10] *Le Moniteur universel*, April 23, 1835.

[11] ANCAOM, Gén. 156 (1299), President of the Council of Delegates to Minister, June 18, 1835. The assimilation of slavery with property rights was a common assumption of

were presenting a solid case for preventing emancipation by shelving the issue. Faced with the inescapable baggage of liberty inherent in the heritage of the Enlightenment and Revolutionary period, French plantocrats accepted the principle of slave liberation but prevaricated and attempted to postpone it indefinitely. In so doing, they effectively deflected the egalitarian challenge of the abolitionists, and isolated the latter by aligning themselves with a government that also wished to proceed slowly on the emancipation question. Much of the colonial success in confronting the forces of anti-slavery could be attributed to the brilliant *colon* delaying strategy. Unlike their equivalents in the American South, French planters chose to defend slavery tactically rather than in principle.

The delegates also worked diligently already in the mid-1830s at putting forth their message through the media. Probably at the instigation of their representatives in Paris, the Guadeloupe colonial council took the lead in 1835 by despatching 30,000 francs to their delegates to subsidize newspapers. The Guadeloupe colonial legislature had come to the conviction that the best means of influencing public opinion with "the aid of the press" was through advances to existing journals. It also intended to purchase a printing press to facilitate the publication of brochures. The island hoped that the other French colonies would take note of and imitate its actions.[12] Although at first the efforts of the delegates to insert articles in the daily press appear to have been stymied, Bernard Adolphe Granier de Cassagnac – Bissette's arch-enemy whom he qualified already at this time as "stupid" – published blatant apologies for the slave system and justifications for the status quo in two important reviews, the *Revue de Paris* and *Revue des deux mondes*, periodicals with a common owner.[13] We now know that Granier de Cassagnac received 6,000 francs from the Guadeloupe

ruling classes in the first half of the nineteenth century. See Seymour Drescher, "Public Opinion and the Destruction of British Colonial Slavery," 44; and Stanley L. Engerman, "Some Considerations Relating to the Property Rights in Man," *Journal of Economic History* 33 (1973): 43–65.
[12] Schoelcher Papers, n. a. f. 3632, President of the Colonial Council of Guadeloupe to Guadeloupe delegates, Jan. 8, 1835.
[13] *La Revue des colonies*, 2nd year, no. 4, Oct. 1835, pp. 145–65; 2nd year, no. 5, Nov. 1835, pp. 193–210. For information on Granier de Cassagnac, whom Karen Offen terms a "notoriously controversial" person (p. 11), see her book, *Paul de Cassagnac and the Authoritarian Tradition in the Nineteenth Century* (New York: Garland, 1991).

delegates for his efforts between 1835 and 1837.[14] It is also likely that until the spring of 1836 the colonies were subsidizing the short-lived daily *Le Moniteur du commerce* (Paris), a fervently colonial organ under the inveterate defender of slavery Théodore Lechevalier, later editor of two other colonial journals, *Le Globe* (Paris) and *Le Courrier du Havre* (Le Havre).[15] Bissette, for one, referred to *Le Moniteur du commerce* as the "semi-official newspaper of the delegates of the colonial aristocracy."[16] Then, in late 1836 the plantocracy changed strategies somewhat and purchased outright a liberal daily, which up until this time had opposed servitude. The delegates bought *Le Journal du commerce* (later *Le Commerce*, Paris), and Mauguin openly became its director. Although Mauguin guaranteed its readers that his acquisition of the paper would not change its political orientation, its next article on the emancipation question uttered the colonial line that the slave must be civilized before being liberated, "being made a man before being made a citizen."[17] Documentation in the navy-colonial archives indicates that in 1836 the two islands of Guadeloupe and Martinique disbursed 118,000 francs for the purchase and operation of this newspaper alone.[18] And in 1837 a second colonial-oriented newspaper appeared in Paris, *L'Outre-mer*, run by Granier de Cassagnac, which would become transformed into *Le Globe* in 1840, an organ again highly subsidized by the *colons*.

Newspapers under colonial influence all contained remarkably similar defenses of slavery. *Le Journal du Havre*, for example, like procolonial Parisian organs, stressed the sanctity of slave property, the necessity of an adequate indemnity, and the need to civilize slaves before liberating them.[19] All of this indicates a well-coordinated effort by the colonial lobby, centered in the delegates, to preserve slavery. The delegates had launched themselves into their long and costly attempts to sell slavery through the press, a process which would absorb even larger sums in the 1840s.[20] The colonists had convinced themselves that their press campaign, along with lobbying the government, was

[14] *Le Moniteur universel*, March 7, 1841.
[15] For more on Théodore Lechevalier, see Jennings, "La presse havraise et l'esclavage," 65.
[16] *La Revue des colonies*, 2nd year, no. 8, Feb. 1836, p. 351.
[17] *Le Journal du commerce*, Feb. 21, May 26, 1836.
[18] ANCAOM, Gén. 271 (1853), report of the Director of the Colonies [1839].
[19] *Le Journal du Havre*, April 24, 1835.
[20] See Jennings, "Venality."

the best means of preserving their interests and countering the actions of the new-found abolitionist movement.

Many of the arguments put forth by colonial defenders of servitude were bound to strike a common chord with a French government itself unanxious to abandon slavery. French officials, like the *colons*, believed that slavery could not be abolished without an indemnity, that the slaves were not prepared for freedom, and that the entire emancipation process must be slow and gradual. The formation of the French abolition society and the appointment of its president as prime minister had made colonists fearful that the French government had its own agenda for slave liberation and might be contemplating rapid emancipation.[21] The Minister of the Navy and Colonies immediately reassured colonial representatives that his administration was sensitive to colonial needs, and that they were mistaken in assuming that the government's preoccupation with the slavery question was due to anything other than the pressure of abolitionist interpellations in the chambers.[22] Indeed, the spring and summer of 1835 saw a whole series of consultations between the delegates and colonial department officials as the latter formulated policy in close collaboration with the former.

The first inclination of Minister Duperré, after the legislative debates of April 22–23, had been to contact immediately the colonial councils about the question of emancipation, convoking them into special meetings if necessary, but the delegates convinced the minister that this might destabilize the colonies by giving the impression that abolition was imminent. As a result, the governors were ordered to put the slavery question before the colonial councils only during their next regular legislative session, beginning in May 1836, thus deferring the process for a year.[23] To calm colonial qualms the government assured the delegates that it intended "to submit this grave question to the test of time and experience." It also confided to colonial representatives in Paris that it hoped circumstances would not oblige it

---

[21] ANCAOM, Gén. 156 (1299), "Question de l'émancipation des esclaves," by Saint-Hilaire, March 18, 1835; President of Council of Delegates to Minister, June 18, 1835; Governor of Martinique to Minister, July 15, 1835.

[22] Ibid., Minister to Delegates, July 21, 1835; Minister to Governors, Sept. 11, 1835.

[23] Guizot Papers, 42AP40, position paper by Saint-Hilaire, Dec. 21, 1836; ANCAOM, Gén. 156 (1299), Minister to Governors, Aug. 1, 1835.

to abolish slavery "until the end of 1841 at least," giving it a year to digest the outcome of British apprenticeship.[24] Then, in the autumn of 1835 the navy-colonial department, probably through the urgings of Broglie, drew up two proposals aimed at increasing the number of manumissions by introducing *pécule* (peculium) and *rachat*. Again it discussed these drafts with the delegates before sending them to the governors of France's four slave colonies on February 23, 1836, with instructions to air them before the colonial councils during their May meetings.[25] This desire by the government to act with the cooperation of the Council of Delegates went well beyond the stipulations of the law of April 24, 1833, which held that Paris could pass ordonnances on colonial matters only after consultations with the colonial councils or their delegates. In the entire process the authorities not only consulted with colonial representatives, but confided their inner intentions and plans to them. The navy-colonial department even entertained the hope that the colonies would assist in the emancipation matter by formulating constructive proposals of their own which the government could then use to draft laws to submit for adoption in the chambers. The naive and vain hope by the government that the colonies would cooperate in a slow-moving solution to the slave liberation question did not disappear until at least the mid-1840s, limiting and stultifying government initiatives. Bissette had not been far from the truth in his claims of *colon* influence on French navy-colonial officials. Their positions were so close that at times cooperation replaced mere consultation between them.

Despite its cautious predispositions, the course of government policy-making in 1835 indicates that anti-slavery activity had had some effect after all. Abolitionist interventions in the legislative chambers in April 1835 had brought a subtle change in the government's position on slavery. Until this time the July Monarchy had only really contemplated a policy of slow preparation of slaves while waiting for the outcome of apprenticeship in British possessions. This is the course of action that Rigny, Duperré, even Broglie had articulated in internal

---

[24] Ibid., Saint-Hilaire's note for the minister, June 5, 1835; Minister to Delegates, June 9, 1835.

[25] Ibid., Corr. Gén. 187, Minister to Delegates, Sept. 29, 1835; Guizot Papers, 42AP40, position paper by Saint-Hilaire, Dec. 21, 1836; *La Revue des colonies*, 2nd year, no. 2, Sept. 1835, pp. 97–101.

circulars or parliamentary debates. However, already in the spring of 1835 the navy-colonial office, faced with an anti-slavery prime minister and abolitionist interpellations in the lower house, decided to formulate plans for gradual emancipation at the same time as it continued ameliorative efforts. While stressing that watchful waiting was still the preferred stance of the government, an internal colonial department document queried whether this would be possible in light of the formation of the Société française pour l'abolition de l'esclavage. It conjectured that most moderate abolitionists were prepared to accept the government's projects for carefully preparing the slaves before considering liberation, but that there were also pressures caused by numerous publications, by discussions within Protestant and Catholic circles, and by "the pressure in the capital of English sectarians whose mission is to obtain the universal extinction of slavery." Besides, it noted – in an apparent reference to Bissette and friends – there were those "who obey to, almost exclusively, their prejudices, if not to say enmity, against the colonial regime and especially the *colons*." Interpellations could be expected every year in the future, and they, or any series of unforeseen developments, could oblige the government to emancipate the slaves. If none of these suppositions proved true, the government could "fortify itself in its path of observation and meditation" and wait until 1841 when English apprenticeship could be evaluated. But if any of these possibilities became reality, it was necessary to prepare contingency plans for emancipation, even if these were to be of a gradual nature and acceptable to the *colons*. These ideas, broached by Saint-Hilaire within the colonial office already in March 1835, were elaborated upon, discussed with the colonial delegates, and then approved by the Cabinet after the April chamber debates. The navy-colonial minister was emphatic that "the active zeal of the society formed in Paris for the abolition of slavery" required something more that "an inert waiting."[26] Under the external pressure of the abolitionists, and perhaps the internal influence of Broglie, the navy-colonial office was beginning to think seriously about the possibility of emancipation.

The Société française pour l'abolition de l'esclavage resumed its

[26] ANCAOM, Gén. 156 (1299), note for the Minister by Saint-Hilaire, June 5, 1835; Minister to Governors, April 1, 1835; Guizot Papers, 42AP40, note for the minister by Saint-Hilaire, Dec. 21, 1836.

meetings on January 4, 1836, determined to continue its strategy of combating the proslavers and pressing the government. During the preceding six months some society members, back in their provincial constituencies, had pressed their General Councils – departmental consultative and administrative legislatures, similar to the colonial councils – to request slave liberation. In particular, Tracy, Isambert, and Roger had convinced the General Councils of the Allier, Eure et Loire, and Loiret, respectively, to emit statements favorable to emancipation.[27] Still, this was far from a resounding success, for only five out of eight-six department councils overall had responded. At the very moment that the French abolition society reconvened, one of its members, the liberal deputy François de Corcelles, presented in the Parisian newspaper *Le Droit* two rebuttals to insulting articles that Granier de Cassagnac had published the previous autumn.[28] Then, once the society reopened its regular sessions, its activities expanded markedly. In January 1836 Macaulay continued to play an important role within the group, as if to justify the government's concern about "the presence of English sectarians" within the French abolitionist structure. He intervened in several meetings, presented the society with two of his works showing the advantages of free over slave labor in the British colonies, and was named honorary president of the Société française pour l'abolition de l'esclavage.[29] It is quite likely that Macaulay was acting as liaison between the British and French anti-slavery organizations, and that the British were subsidizing the French editions of five of Macaulay's works in an attempt to convince France to follow the British example.[30]

Most of the French abolition society's actions in early 1836, how-ever, were in anticipation of interpellating the government in the chambers. During the January 11 meeting of the organization, Passy announced that he and Tracy had drafted a three-point emancipation proposal for submission to the Chamber of Deputies. It called for freeing the slaves on January 1, 1840, the preparatory measures necessary for this, and the financial means to permit it. The society briefly

---

[27] *4ème Publication*, 41; *La Revue des colonies*, 2nd year, no. 8, Feb. 1836, pp. 351–6.
[28] Ibid., 2nd year, Jan. 1836, pp. 295–6; *Le Moniteur du commerce*, Jan. 13, 1836; *Le Semeur*, Jan. 20, 1836; *4ème Publication*, p. 53.
[29] Ibid., pp. 42–4; *La Revue des colonies*, 2nd year, no. 7, Jan. 1836, pp. 324–7.
[30] See Jennings, *French Reaction*, 94–5.

adopted this approach, only to amend it during its February 15 meeting to stress that slave liberation should proceed with "prudence,
equity, and precautions." Besides, the society now stipulated in its
draft that masters be indemnified, and that "regulations to assure
work during several years" be passed.[31] Such an amendment indicates
second thoughts by many moderate or conservative members of the
French group, and divisions in its ranks as how best to proceed
toward its eventual aims. It also suggests that at this point in time the
moderates and conservatives were dominant, for a concrete plan for
relatively rapid emancipation was in effect being shelved by the
society.

In the meantime too, the Cabinet headed by Broglie – a haughty,
aloof, and condescending *doctrinaire* who had had difficulties working with Louis-Philippe – fell from power in early February 1836, and
the president of the French abolition society became a simple member
of the Chamber of Peers once again. Nevertheless, in the new government, headed by Adolphe Thiers, the society's vice-president, Passy,
assumed the position of minister of commerce. What the anti-slavery
body had lost on one hand in the ministerial shuffling it had gained on
the other, for Passy was perhaps the most radical abolitionist in the
entire organization, the one singled out by delegate Dupin as the only
society member seemingly prepared to accept immediate emancipation in the mid-1830s.[32] Still, the Société française felt compelled to
alter its tactics in light of this change in government. At its meeting of
February 29, 1836, its members voted to "suspend all proposals to the
Chamber of Deputies in order to allow the Cabinet time to become
seated." In the process, it rescinded the Passy–Tracy proposal for the
submission of a definite emancipation plan. Perhaps the fall from
power of Broglie had convinced society members that such a project
would now have little chance of success anyway. Instead, when the bill
for supplemental colonial credits came before the deputies, society
members would simply "ask for explications on the Cabinet's
thoughts concerning emancipation."[33] The French abolition society's
propensity to cooperate and work with the government, rather than

---

[31] *4ème Publication*, 42, 45.
[32] Statement by Dupin in the Chamber of Deputies debate of April 23, 1835 (*Le Moniteur universel*, April 24, 1835).
[33] *4ème Publication*, 45.

firmly challenge it, was manifest. Deferring to parliamentary niceties had robbed the group of an opportunity to press its objectives, and had permitted further delay on the slavery question.

Given the abolition society's retreat on the issue, the outcome of its interpellation in the chambers was predictable. On March 9, 1836, society member Roger du Loiret inquired what the government had done so far concerning emancipation. Navy-colonial minister Duperré – who had survived the Cabinet changes – replied that his administration was gathering all possible information on slave liberation, and that the colonial councils were being asked to debate this, along with the *pécule* and *rachat* options, that very spring. As soon as Paris received the advice of the colonies, he assured the assembly that, "the government will follow up on this"; in the meantime it was considering every means to ameliorate the position of the slaves.[34] These assurances quieted society members for the time being, but obviously did not satisfy them entirely. Some 159 free persons of color of Martinique, most of them town dwellers, had drawn up petitions for emancipation – probably at the instigation of their mandatories – for the legislature and submitted them to the French abolition society for sponsorship. During its meeting of April 11 the organization decided that Broglie would present the Martinique petitions in the Chamber of Peers, for "this step by the president of the society will serve as a reply to those rumors spread in the colonies on the supposed change of opinion of the noble duke."[35] Concurrently, some members of the Société de la morale chrétienne, who also belonged to the abolition society – Lutheroth, Corcelles, Carnot, and Eugène Lherminier – submitted a petition to the upper house in favor of emancipation on behalf of the Morale chrétienne. When the two petitions were reported on before the peers on May 7, two members of the abolition society, former Bonapartist Admiral Verhuell and liberal Catholic Count Charles Montalembert, stepped up to the tribune to argue for gradual emancipation.[36] Determined to push the matter further, other members of the Société française pour l'abolition de l'esclavage decided to return to the attack during the discussion in the lower house of the regular navy-colonial budget later in May.

---

[34] *Le Moniteur universel*, March 10, 1836.
[35] *4ème Publication*, 48–49.
[36] *Le Moniteur universel*, May 8, 1836.

On May 23 Larochefoucauld-Liancourt launched into a veritable attack on Duperré for wishing to cooperate with the *colons* in effecting emancipation when it was well known that colonial councils always refused any meaningful moves toward slave liberation. He accused the government of adopting a "system of deception" in trying to satisfy both colonials and abolitionists by facilitating the manumission of some slaves while maintaining slavery. When the debate resumed on May 25 the great poet Lamartine stood up to make his usual eloquent, but contradictory and ultimately moderate appeal, against slavery, one which expressed concern for the masters as well as the slaves. Isambert, who followed, made a more pointed critique of the system of status quo that the government had espoused, while pleading at the same time for serious measures to prepare slaves for freedom. Both Isambert and Tracy, who appeared next at the tribune, agreed with Lamartine that slaves could not be moralized under slavery, but Tracy issued the most urgent plea of all for rapid emancipation. After Charles Dupin vouched for the good intentions of slave owners and urged prudence, Duperré was obliged to take the floor once more to defend his government's good faith. He repeated his arguments of March about the necessity of preparing gradually for emancipation, and waiting on the advice of the colonial councils. However, he now added that "emancipation is the constant object of [his administration's] meditations." Under pressure from the abolitionists, Duperré even exaggerated the facts by claiming that his office had prepared plans not only for *rachat* and *pécule*, but also for freeing upon birth all children born of slaves.[37]

The Director of the Colonies later admitted in an internal governmental note that Duperré's claim had not been true. The idea of preparing to free newborn slave children had simply been bruited in the halls of the colonial office, and had just been mentioned in passing in one unofficial memo. Only after his statement to the deputies on May 25 did Duperré feel the necessity of masking his misrepresentation by requesting the colonial governors on June 7 to seek the advice of the colonial councils, or at least of some of their members, about this possibility, even though he realized that their legislative sessions would probably be closed by the time his dispatch

---

[37] Ibid., May 23–24, 26, 1836.

arrived.[38] The government also gave added credence to its amelio-ration program by issuing two new ordonnances in May 1836. One followed up on earlier decrees of 1791, 1824, and 1832, assuring that any slave brought to France would be automatically freed; the other facilitated manumissions by regulating the naming of freed slaves.[39] Nevertheless, both of these ordonnances, as Saint-Hilaire admitted, "though useful, had not advanced by one step the questions of eman-cipation."[40] The government's proposals were still limited to amelio-ration, preparation, and manumission, rather than emancipation, and would remain so for the remainder of the regime. Furthermore, many of the measures that the administration was taking, or claiming to be taking, constituted replies to abolitionist pressures.

After the May 1836 parliamentary debates, Isambert, as secretary of the Société française, met in early June with Director of the Colonies Saint-Hilaire. The latter assured him that his office was "sincerely abolitionist" to the point where it was "sharply attacked by the colonial party." The director also indicated that his department would "implement its abolitionist intentions" in three years; that an intermediary system like British apprenticeship was "worthless"; and that "it is necessary to look after the interests of the treasury," because "France would never consent to give 200 million francs to the colo-nies to redeem 260,000 slaves." Concerning the latter statement, the government itself was seemingly exaggerating the amount of any proposed indemnity whenever it wished to demonstrate the impossi-bility of effecting slave liberation. Saint-Hilaire then terminated the exchange by guaranteeing Isambert that before the next session of the chambers the government would prepare more effective measures toward emancipation than the two May ordonnances.[41] This inter-view probably reassured the society about the government's stance at a time when French abolitionists saw their opponents in the colonies

---

[38] Guizot Papers, 42AP40, note by Saint-Hilaire, Dec. 21, 1836; ANCAOM, Corr. Gén. 188, Minister to Governors, June 7, 1836.

[39] *Le Moniteur universel*, May 26, 1836; ANCAOM, Corr. Gén. 188, Minister to gover-nors, May 10, 1836. For a discussion of the principle that touching metropolitan French soil freed slaves under the *ancien régime*, see Sue Peabody, *"There Are No Slaves in France": The Political Culture of Race and Slavery in the Ancien Regime* (New York: Oxford Univerity Press, 1996).

[40] *4ème Publication*, 52.

[41] Ibid.

weakened by divisions in their own ranks. Indeed, in its meeting of May 30, the society had concluded that, while the colonies appeared to "prefer the system of temporization and gradual emancipation that the ministry seems to have adopted," the colonial delegates probably favored a "collective emancipation with large indemnity." Moreover, the abolitionists believed colonial spokesmen to be haunted by the fear that any indemnity paid for slaves would be undermined by gradual emancipation plans.[42]

In the spring of 1836 there was reason for the abolitionists to suspect that the colonial camp was experiencing second thoughts about wholeheartedly espousing temporization when this could diminish the indemnity that the planters believed to be their eventual due. In any emancipation scenario, the slave holders demanded above all a generous monetary compensation for what they considered to be their "just and sacred" property rights.[43] Bissette noticed how the colonials had a "fixation" with this problem in the spring of 1836.[44] Proslavers should have been reassured by Duperré's guarantees in the summer of 1835, that the July Monarchy would never emancipate without an adequate indemnity, although he, like other administrators, never did specify what such an indemnity would be.[45] Still, despite these official assurances, the *colons* were well aware that a few abolitionists, most notably Montrol, Passy, and Bissette, did not believe that slave owners had the right to an indemnity. Bissette even went so far as to argue that if any indemnity were to be paid, it should go to the slaves rather than their owners.[46] The fact that so few other abolitionists agreed with him on this point shows once again the innate conservatism of most of the French anti-slavery movement in the 1830s. However, the very existence of thoughts along this line was a subject of great concern for the plantocracy.

Not only was the principle of an indemnity under attack in certain abolitionist circles, but some colonial spokesmen had come to fear that the government itself might be reneging on, or at least circumscribing, its own commitment. Quite simply, in the eyes of perceptive

---

[42] Ibid., 51.

[43] Forster and Forster, *Sugar and Slavery*, 140. The words "just and sacred" were employed by Martinique planter Pierre Dessalles.

[44] *La Revue des colonies*, 2nd year, no. 12, June 1836, pp. 551–52.

[45] ANCAOM, Corr. Gén. 187, Minister to Governors, Aug. 1, 1835.

[46] *La Revue des colonies*, no. 12, June 1835, pp. 11–12; 2nd year, no. 1, July 1835, p. 7.

colonial advocates, delaying tactics were a double-edged sword. They could put off emancipation for many years, but such actions could also diminish the number and value of slaves, and thus undercut indemnification in the long run. This appears to have been the opinion, for example, of the two delegates of Bourbon, Jacques Sully-Brunet and Conil. According to reports, they wrote from Paris to suggest to their constituents in Bourbon that it might be best to agree now to conditions for slave liberation within a few years, accompanied by a sufficient indemnity, rather than waiting for time to diminish and perhaps even eliminate such a reimbursement.[47] We now know that there was some basis for their concern. Saint-Hilaire himself believed that over the years the price of slaves might decline, permitting the state to disburse less to the planters for freeing their chattel property.[48] And Saint-Hilaire, while insisting that "a just indemnity" must accompany any emancipation plan, admitted that *pécule* and *rachat* "truthfully would be a means of diminishing the number of slaves without the state having to make any pecuniary sacrifices."[49] Colonial suspicions were correct that government circles contemplated the possibility of reducing the indemnity by prolonging the emancipation process.

Colonial defenders were confronted with a real dilemma over the indemnity issue in the spring of 1836. However, they did not hesitate long in seeing where their true interests lay. Faced with the alternatives of a long-term solution of retaining their forced labor while procrastinating and lobbying steadily for just compensation, or a short-term outcome of slave liberation with just compensation, the *colons* quickly made their choice. They would reject outright *pécule*, *rachat*, and the freeing of children, take their chances with a declining indemnity, and opt for the maintenance of the status quo pure and simple.

In early June 1836, when Isambert reported on his discussions with Saint-Hilaire to his colleagues, the French abolition society was still uncertain about the stances of the government and *colons*. It did realize, though, that its interventions in the chamber had had some effect in advancing the debate on the slavery issue and forcing the government into movement. With the legislative session rapidly approaching its end, however, the society made plans during its last meetings for its

[47] Ibid., 2nd year, no. 8, Feb. 1836, pp. 410–411.
[48] ANCAOM, Gén. 156 (1299), note for the minister by Saint-Hilaire, June 5, 1835.
[49] Guizot Papers, 42AP40, note by Saint-Hilaire, Dec. 21, 1836.

next annual parliamentary encounter with the government. On May 30, 1836, the abolitionists decided to follow up on the initiative that a handful of members had already taken the previous year to involve provincial opinion in the debate by appealing to the *conseils généraux*. In an attempt to convince more than just five of them to express their wishes for emancipation, it planned to draft a letter to all eighty-six departmental bodies to persuade them that freeing the slaves was both a humanitarian issue and one of national interest. Because society members believed that the principle of emancipation was now an established one, and that all that remained was to "decide upon its means of execution," Lamartine volunteered to draft a slave liberation plan for the next parliamentary session. He suggested that he could present the plan to the society after it reconvened; the proposal could be discussed and altered as necessary, and then supported unanimously by all members of the group seated in the lower house. After entrusting Lamartine with following through on his proposal, the society suspended its meetings on June 6. It implemented its standard procedure of appointing a special committee to assist its secretary, Isambert, with handling correspondence and publications during the parliamentary intersession. This time the guiding committee would consist of Montrol, Billiard, Dufau, Lainé de Villevêque, Lamartine, Macaulay, Victor Ambroise Lanjuinais, and Hippolyte Daniel de Saint-Anthoine.[50] Once again the Société française pour l'abolition de l'esclavage greatly reduced its activities for six months until the opening of the next parliamentary session, squandering any impetus that it might have built up during the session of 1836. By correlating its sessions to the legislative calendar, the French abolition society was displaying much less dedication and determination than its British counterparts ten years earlier.

While the abolition society went into dormancy, anti-slavery initiative was left in the hands of Bissette and a few independents. All along, Bissette had been continuing his attack on the "colonial aristocracy" and voicing calls for immediate emancipation. In the summer of 1835 he had outlined his own plan for slave liberation. According to the black abolitionist, the government should free the slaves without

---

[50] *4ème Publication*, pp. 50–53. It is likely that these individuals were chosen to assist the secretary simply because they would be available in Paris at least part of the time between parliamentary sessions.

consulting or indemnifying the *colons*; the freedmen should be given full rights, but have their salaries fixed by Paris; and young ex-slaves should be submitted to compulsory civic and religious instruction.[51] In subsequent issues he went on to denounce any intermediary system, to refer to the colonial delegates as paid purveyors of lies, and to single out those of Bourbon for their "stupid diatribes."[52] Bissette's bluntness in denouncing his colonial opponents departed from the norms of polite early nineteenth-century journalism, and probably contributed to deepening the gap between him and members of the Société française pour l'abolition de l'esclavage. Moreover, Bissette's analyses typically bounded between optimism and pessimism, his hopes at times gaining the ascendancy over his basic realism. He had the impression that the May 1836 chamber discussions marked a turning point because no one had attempted to defend the principle of slavery. But at the same time he warned the Société française not to sleep on its laurels, for the *colons* were attempting to postpone emancipation.[53] As the *Revue* entered its third year of publication, Bissette also changed tactics somewhat, and began stressing improvements that could be made for slaves while awaiting their liberation. This amounted to an admission on his part that, despite his efforts, slave liberation would not be immediate. For example, he made an impassioned appeal for the end of the whip as a first concrete step toward freeing the slaves. Always generous with advice, he also pointed out the need for French abolitionism to "descend into the masses," along British lines, if it wished to "popularize its principles."[54] All of this made Bissette the bugbear of the colonial coterie. When a minor confrontation occurred between free persons of color and planters on Bourbon, the colonial council of that island moved to ban the *Revue*, that "infamous journal," along with *Le Semeur*.[55] The latter publication, for its part, was less caustic than Bissette's journal, and it only occasionally seized upon the slavery problem. Still, its Christian-based critique of bondage had also seriously perturbed the plantocracy.

---

[51] *La Revue des colonies*, 2nd year, no. 1, July 1835, pp. 3–14.
[52] Ibid., 2nd year, no. 4, Oct. 1835, pp. 145–65; no. 7, Jan. 1836, pp. 289–91; 3rd year, no. 2, Aug. 1836, pp. 56–60.
[53] Ibid., 2nd year, no. 10, April 1836, p. 60; no. 11, May 1836, pp. 481–4.
[54] Ibid., 3rd year, no. 4, Oct. 1836, pp. 145–6; no. 5, Nov. 1836, p. 224.
[55] Ibid., 3rd year, no. 3, Sept. 1836, pp. 105–111, 117–122.

In the summer of 1836, however, all eyes were on the colonial councils, rather than the abolitionists, as reports on colonial deliberations over *pécule*, *rachat*, and emancipation in general began to reach Paris. Although abolitionists had been skeptical for the most part, the government had actually entertained some hopes for bona fide colonial cooperation in implementing these processes. After all, the colonial council of Martinique during its 1835 session had even accepted in principle the idea of peculium and self-redemption, much to the government's satisfaction.[56] As a result, no one in the navy-colonial department could have predicted the extent to which the colonial legislatures would now rebuff its proposals.

Concerning emancipation itself, the Guadeloupe colonial council predicted that such a move would be a veritable "scourge"; according to the legislatures of Guiana and Bourbon, it would bring ruin. Martinique's council postulated that freeing the slaves was in the interest of no one, and that for the slave in particular it would "substitute laziness and brutishness for the benefits of civilization," a classical proslaver argument. All the colonies insisted that any emancipation measure must commence with the indemnification of masters for their slave property. Martinique and Guiana even carried this assertion further, insisting that all colonial property (slaves, lands, and installations) must be reimbursed because slave liberation would undermine the plantation system entirely.

The colonial councils were equally unanimous in rejecting *pécule* and *rachat*. As the governor of Bourbon reported, legalized savings and personal redemption were particularly objectionable because they seemed to presage piecemeal attacks upon slavery without the indispensable guarantees of indemnity and order. The *colons* interpreted both of these moves quite correctly as "emancipation without indemnity" from Paris. As for the freeing of newborn slave children, this, they argued, would divide offspring from their parents and undercut the family spirit that was essential to inculcate in slaves in long-term preparation for freedom. In truth, what they really feared was the elimination of their future labor supply without adequate compensation, and the truncating of the slave system. Instead of all of these disruptions, what was required, according to the plantocracy,

---

[56] ANCAOM, Gén. 156 (1299), Minister to Governor of Martinique, Sept. 11, 1835.

was continued preparation for slaves, through religious education in particular. More priests were needed to civilize the blacks, and especially, as the Guadeloupe colonial council explained, to teach them "the dangers of laziness," for "liberty must be the reward of work, good services, and good conduct." The legislature of Bourbon uttered what seemed to be the consensus of all the colonies when it encouraged France to "persevere in the prudent slowness that the government has declared to be its rule of conduct." According to the proslavers, the best approach was that of "waiting and observation" first enunciated by Paris in 1833. All the colonies even put forth the specious argument that the mainland had no right to regulate by ordonnance such things as *pécule* and *rachat* because under the law of April 23, 1833, matters of this kind fell within the colonial legislative domain.[57] Such unanimity of reply was encouraged by the colonies communicating with each other over the issues in question.[58] Any discrepancy in position or hesitancy on the part of the different colonies had disappeared once the government had put the emancipation issue before them. The Council of Delegates had apparently forged a common front among the colonies on the slavery problem. They had rallied to the ideas of the most reprobate defenders of slavery, such as Granier de Cassagnac, in demanding the maintenance of the status quo combined with a few cosmetic ameliorations.

The response of the colonial councils to the government's overtures caused dismay, though little surprise, in abolitionist circles. The *Semeur* expressed its profound disappointment in "the most blind fanaticism" of the *colons*. As soon as the first reports arrived in Paris in August the Société française pour l'abolition de l'esclavage observed that they "foretell a formal resistance to all progress on the emancipation question." The *Courrier français* agreed with this assessment, adding that the colonies obviously wished to postpone slave liberation indefinitely.[59] The navy-colonial office itself now became fully

---

[57] Ibid., analysis of debates of Colonial Council of Bourbon, Feb. 1836; Colonial Council of Guiana, June 22, 1836; analysis of votes, Colonial Council of Martinique, 4th session, 1836; Governor of Guadeloupe to Minister, Sept. 1836; Governor of Bourbon to Minister, Dec. 3, 1836; Guizot Papers, 42AP40, note by Saint-Hilaire, Dec. 21, 1836.

[58] Schoelcher Papers, n. a. f. 3632, f. 91, President of Colonial Council of Guiana to President of Colonial Council of Martinique, July 2, 1836.

[59] *Le Semeur*, Dec. 21, 1836; *4ème Publication*, 54; *Le Courrier français*, Nov. 6, 1836.

aware that the *colons* had opted for "a system of absolute delaying action."[60] Any illusions the colonial department might have entertained of the colonies cooperating in the emancipation process should have been dashed.

As the government awaited replies from all of the colonial councils, it actually anticipated one of their suggestions. In the summer of 1836 the navy-colonial ministry took initial measures to foster the spread of Christianity among blacks in the West Indies. In a letter to the governors of Martinique and Guadeloupe, the minister ordered them to encourage their respective colonial councils to provide funding for additional priests. He also stressed the need to combine primary and religious education so as to "add work habits to moral and religious precepts."[61] Despite these suggestions from Paris, there was little likelihood of the colonies acting on their own on meaningful ameliorative measures. Still, the government's move demonstrated a concern it shared with the planters for gradual preparatory action for slaves, such as employing religion for moralizing blacks and indoctrinating them with the work ethic. It also indicated that the government was anxious to claim at least a semblance of ameliorative measures when it faced off with the abolitionists again during the upcoming legislative session of 1837.

The French abolition society resumed its sittings in December 1836 when the legislative chambers were recalled. In the meantime it had received a setback when Passy lost his ministerial portfolio in September 1836, as the Thiers cabinet was replaced by that of comte Louis Mathieu de Molé. For the first time the society would face a legislative session without one of its own in an important ministerial position. Also, despite the renewed efforts of the abolitionists, a mere eight out of eighty-six departmental general councils had expressed the desire for emancipation during the winter of 1836, an increase of only three over the previous year.[62] This high abstention rate might be attributed in part at least to the fact that the Council of Delegates had sent out its own letter to the departmental councils to counter that of the abolitionists by reminding them of the "necessity not to precipitate

[60] Guizot Papers, 42AP40, note by Saint-Hilaire, Dec. 21, 1836.
[61] ANCAOM, Corr. Gén. 188, Minister to Governors of Martinique and Guadeloupe, Aug. 19, 1836.
[62] *Le Semeur*, Dec. 21, 1836.

the emancipation measure."[63] Still, French anti-slavery must have been disappointed with these meager results. The abolitionist appeal to public opinion in the mid-1830s, whether it be through petitions or the departmental councils, was ineffective. Unlike in Britain, French opinion remained distant from the slavery question.

Despite these setbacks, or perhaps because of them, the Société française redoubled its efforts in early 1837. Nothing apparently came of Lamartine's proposed emancipation plan. Evidently, the abolitionists decided to give the government another chance to introduce its own program leading to emancipation. The society did decide, though, to alter its stategy, follow the advice of both the British and dissidents like Bissette, and appeal to a wider public. The group, which until now had met in the parliamentary quaestor chambers or the dwellings of individual members, obtained permission of the Prefect of Paris, through the intermediary of its member the duc d'Harcourt, to use one of the salons of the Hôtel de Ville (city hall). In addition, the right to hold a public meeting, forbidden under the July Monarchy, was requested of the Minister of the Interior, the Count Adrien Etienne Pierre de Gasparin, father of the abolitionist Agénor de Gasparin.

Judging from the society's later record, a "public meeting" probably implied appealing to a select group of *notables* who would be admitted by invitation only, or who would be obliged to pay an entrance fee, rather than a popular meeting open to all as in the British model. Still, this move indicated that the Société française was aware of the need to expand its recruitment and support, at least among the privileged classes. In March 1837 the minister authorized the meetings of the society in general, but couched his approval in terms discouraging any innovations.[64] This meant that the government was prepared to continue tolerating the existence of the society, but unwilling to permit it to expand its format. Given this stance by the authorities, there is no evidence that the public meeting, scheduled for April, and with the duc de Broglie himself presiding, ever took place. The society's practice of publishing brief minutes of its meetings ceased after the end of 1836, suggesting that it was either embarrassed

---

[63] ANCAOM, Gén. 156 (1301), Sully Brunet and Jabrun to Presidents of the *Conseils Généraux*, Aug. 25, 1836.

[64] *La Revue des colonies*, 3rd year, no. 8, Feb. 1837, p. 331; *Le Semeur*, March 8, 1837.

at the prospect of publicizing further its internal divisions, or that it was facing financial restraints. But an important public meeting of this kind would have attracted the attentions of the press, and no pro-abolitionist organs made mention of such an event ever having occurred. The proposed meeting was probably aborted because of government pressure or the uneasiness of conservative members of the society itself who were wary of deviating from parliamentary procedures. And this was not the last time that the July Monarchy would discourage the Société française from opening up its meetings and appealing to a larger segment of the French public. Shaken by republican demonstrations in Paris and uprisings in Lyon, Broglie-dominated Cabinets had reinforced anti-association laws in 1834 and introduced draconian press restrictions in 1835. The Société française, composed of this same ruling class, obviously shared these fears of radical republicanism and remained disinclined to open its ranks to the general public. Nevertheless, what efforts it had undertaken to expand its following were dashed by the government. The French abolition society was obliged to restrict its activities to the political arena.

By the spring of 1837 too the French abolition society was preparing for its annual interpellation of the administration during the presentation of the naval budget. That matters did not augur well for anti-slavery became apparent on March 11, when the lower house tabled a report on a petition by a Martinique planter, Vitalis, which had called for slave liberation on terms highly favorable to the slave holders and with an inflated indemnity of 230 million francs. On this occasion François Guizot, Minister of Public Instruction and a friend of Broglie, spoke up briefly on behalf of the Molé Cabinet. Even before this, Guizot had been the butt of abolitionist criticism for his silence on the slavery problem. The French abolition society had expressed its regrets already in 1836 that someone "so highly placed" in government circles, and also president of the philanthropic Protestant biblical society, should have taken no part in anti-slavery activities. Guizot's intervention in the chambers on March 11 justified the society's suspicions of his noncommitment to its cause. He claimed that the government favored emancipation in principle, but that it was still examining the situation, aided by the colonial delegates. He asserted too that time and patience were necessary, and that a premature discussion would compromise future government proposals.[65] Then, any ambiguity that might have existed as to exactly what the Molé administration intended to propose for the slavery question was lifted when Tracy questioned the navy-colonial minister, Admiral Claude Charles Marie de Campe de Rosamel, in the Chamber of Deputies on June 6, 1837.

The position paper authored by Saint-Hilaire in late December 1836 outlined the policy the government now proclaimed it would follow. France, Saint-Hilaire postulated, could not afford to abolish slavery and must wait at least until 1841 to judge British colonial consequences of emancipation. In the meantime the government should continue "in the constant path of examination and observation," though it might continue its attempts to convince the colonial councils to cooperate on *rachat* and *pécule*.[66] The navy-colonial minister himself appears to have singled out this latter point for further exploration, for he suggested to Molé in February 1837 the possibility of turning to the colonial councils once more before preparing any government legislation on peculium and self-redemption.[67] Any initiatives along these latter lines seem to have been postponed, however, for Rosamel followed Guizot's cautious approach when replying to Tracy's query as to whether the Cabinet intended to "act soon" on the emancipation question. Rosamel began by stating that, although he opposed slavery, he doubted that the assembly was prepared to disburse 271 million francs to free France's 271,555 colonial slaves at a rate of 1,000 francs per head – again an arbitrarily set, excessively high rate. Thus, he argued, it was imperative to gather more information, wait for the outcome of British apprenticeship, and prepare the slaves. In sum, he intoned, "I believe that it is best to wait." First minister Molé also stepped up to the podium to specify that the government's task should involve satisfying all interests and rights, those of the slaves and *colons*; therefore "it is necessary to advance slowly, gradually, with prudence and discernment." According to the prime minister, the administration still did not possess adequate information to enable it to act, but would by next year's session, when it could make proposals to the chambers. Finally, Molé seemed to disapprove

[65] *4ème Publication*, 52; *Le Moniteur universel*, March 12, 1837; *La Presse* (Paris), March 13, 1837.
[66] Guizot Papers, 42AP40, note by Saint-Hilaire, Dec. 21, 1836.
[67] ANCAOM, Corr. Gén. 189, Minister to Molé, Feb. 15, 1837.

entirely of the idea of giving slaves the right to redeem themselves, arguing that this would just add to the approximately 30,000 blacks rapidly manumitted since 1830 who "weigh upon our three colonies" with their idleness.[68] The Molé administration had dispelled any doubts that might have existed about where it stood on the slavery question. Molé also displayed his disapproval of what he viewed as the disruptive force of abolitionism when writing a diplomatic dispatch to the French ambassador in Washington in 1838, for he congratulated the Americans on having tabled their emancipation question.[69] With no abolitionist in the Cabinet, and Molé known to be more pliant than Broglie to the will of the King, the government had reverted to the cautious approach that had originated in 1833 and that fell in line perfectly with the colonial position of postponing any real action leading to slave liberation. Even increased manumissions through *rachat* seemed to have been rejected by the Molé government.

The abolitionists in the lower house bewailed the apparent retreat by the government in the face of planter resistance. Isambert suggested that the Cabinet lacked "good will," while Tracy denounced the government's "unbelievable shortage of foresight and its obstinacy in postponing from year to year the solution of this question."[70] Abolitionist supporters in the press were even more forthright in castigating the administration. *Le Courrier français* charged that after years of pretending to have concern for the slaves, "the government is weakening in face of colonial passions" and concluding that slave liberation was primarily a financial question. All of its previous "maneuvers were only intended to drag out the issue."[71] The abolitionists finally had accurately gauged the attitude of the July Monarchy on the emancipation question. The government might be pushed into face-saving action and meaningless gestures, but it could not be counted on to take concrete and consistent measures toward slave liberation.

The years 1835–1837 had clarified the positions of both the planters and government while edifying the French abolition society. Planter cohesion had suffered somewhat in 1836 when *colon* leaders had hesitated over the indemnity issue, but as a whole the colonial

[68] *Le Moniteur universel*, June 7, 1837.
[69] Drescher, *Dilemmas of Democracy*, 170.
[70] *Le Moniteur universel*, June 7, 1837.
[71] *Le Courrier français*, June 7, 1837.

lobby had devised an infallible political strategy already in the mid-1830s. The French plantocracy would not defend slavery in principle, but simply strive to postpone emancipation indefinitely. This tactic was all the more successful because it could appeal to very cautious abolitionists at the same time that it dovetailed with French government intentions on the slavery question. This period had also witnessed marked regression in the stance of the July Monarchy on the emancipation issue. In early 1835 the government had responded to anti-slavery pressure in the chambers by offering to go beyond its policy of "inert waiting" on the slavery scene first formulated in 1833. Convinced that action of some kind was required in light of British slave liberation and the formation of the Société française pour l'abolition de l'esclavage, it had for the first time progressed beyond promises of preparing slaves, going so far as to outline an actual program for encouraging individual slave liberations through *rachat* and *pécule*. By the early summer of 1837, however, French authorities had formally retreated on this front and returned to their position of watchful waiting. In the process they had demonstrated not only their affinity to plantocratic aims and strategies, but their propensity to cave in to *colon* pressure. Either the government no longer feared abolitionist interpellations because of the inability of anti-slavery forces to move beyond their institutional approach to emancipation, or the successive Cabinets themselves felt less urgency on the issue and reverted to their natural inertia when faced with a potentially costly project. Perhaps too the internal pressure applied subtly by first Broglie and then Passy within the Council of Ministers had been the real source of whatever movement had occurred within official French slavery policy. Such an influence could have been brought to bear between March 1835 and September 1836, when these two abolitionists were in the Cabinet, a time when the government loosened up its approach, but it certainly ceased by 1837 when the Molé ministry came to power. After Molé assumed office, the government demonstrated its firmness by preventing the Société française from opening up its meetings to a larger audience and expanding its support even within the upper layers of French society. From this time on it became apparent that French abolitionism would have difficulty expanding, not only because of its own anti-popular tendencies, but also because the Orleanist regime would not permit it. By 1837 the static position of French authorities on the slavery issue was increasingly evident.

In the mid-1830s French anti-slavery was also being defined. The Société française pour l'abolition de l'esclavage was more liberal than its predecessor in that it was willing to expand its influence to the elite outside the corridors of power, but it lacked the cohesion of the planters and the resolution of the authorities. Its membership was rich in individual ideas, but poor in extracting concrete proposals from them. Specific projects put forth by Passy–Tracy and Lamartine could not retain the adherence of a majority of society members. If there was any consensus among society members, it was that emancipation must proceed slowly, and with full regards for planter rights. But even here there was no unanimity. Within the Société française Passy, Tracy, and Isambert hoped to move rapidly toward emancipation; the two former, along with the generally moderate Montrol, also opposed granting an indemnity to planters. Throughout its existence, one of the basic weaknesses of the Société française pour l'abolition de l'esclavage was that it could not muster unity and firmness among its members, whose individual stances on slavery also constantly wavered and changed. This pattern was developing already in its early years. So too was the tendency for any radicals, like Bissette, who insisted upon a rapid repression of slavery, to find little room within the main French abolitionist organization. This body, with no real determined policy of its own, had been reduced to acting within parliamentary circles, where forceful individuals could take the initiative on certain issues dear to them. Moreover, the abolitionist tactic of encouraging movement by interpellating the government had had little real success. It could assuage abolitionist consciences, rally anti-slavery troops, and seriously annoy, even embarrass, the government and the planters. But it alone could not bring marked change. French anti-slavery forces were now back to square one. Unable to obtain progress through legislative interpellations alone, they would now be obliged to forge some specific plans for slave liberation.

5

ABOLITIONIST PROPOSALS AND PARLIAMENTARY COMMISSIONS

Faced with an administration determined to temporize on the slavery question, the Société française pour l'abolition de d'esclavage resolved to appeal to those avenues of French public opinion still open to it. One of its last activities before adjourning in the summer of 1837 was to open a contest with a prize of 1,000 francs, funded by the estate of the Abbé Grégoire, for the best essay on how to extirpate racial prejudice.[1] Its other major effort was to try to win over more support from the *Conseils généraux*. In a long, rambling letter to all the departmental councils in the summer of 1837, the society requested their adherence to emancipation on both humanitarian and economic grounds. The group also reminded these bodies that Molé's promise for detailed emancipation proposals in 1838 was "very vague," and that "its realization could again be adjourned if public opinion does not require it."[2] At this point at least, the French abolition society displayed little faith in the government's pledge to act on the slavery front.

The Société française's appeal to the provinces met with more success this time than previously. Twelve different general councils made replies, though some only favored preparatory measures for gradual slave liberation. Still, an examination of their statements indicates that most councils really acted not because of an effective abolitionist appeal, but once again at the instigation of individual abolitionists from particular departments. Isambert had moved the Eure-et-Loir to action; Tracy the Allier; Rémusat the Haute-Garonne; Roger the Loiret; Larochefoucauld-Liancourt the Cher; comte Xavier de Sade the

[1] *Le Semeur*, July 26, 1837.
[2] Société française pour l'abolition de l'esclavage, *No. 5. Année 1837* (Paris: Duverger, 1837), 3–6.

Aisne; André Layraud the Creuse; Adolphe Clément Joseph Delespaul the Nord; Lamartine the Saône-et-Loire; and a nonmember of the society, but a local abolitionist, Laurant de Saverdun, the Ariège. Only two departmental council votes, that of the Seine-et-Marne and Vendée, cannot be traced directly to the pressure of local abolitionist notables.[3] The French abolition society had proven efficient in publicizing its efforts and in mobilizing some of its adherents to lobby in their respective provinces. But its results were still meager, and certainly did not reflect an outpouring of public opinion. The government's refusal to allow public meetings effectually blocked access to mass support on the British scale, even if members of the society had been willing to pursue such initiatives. The society must also have felt itself more isolated on the anti-slavery front at this time. Bissette, always strapped for funds, suspended the publication of his *Revue* for a year from the summer of 1837; when it resumed in 1838 it would appear on an intermittent basis until it finally folded for good because of financial reasons in 1842.[4]

As the Société française pour l'abolition de l'esclavage struggled to put across its message in the summer of 1837, *colons* and government dug into their respective positions and showed little sign of movement. As during the previous summer and autumn, the colonies provided a steady flow of negative feedback on the proposals submitted to them by the government. These reports led Jean Guillaume Jubelin, newly appointed governor of Guadeloupe – who had served already under the Restoration as governor of Guiana – to reflect upon the disposition of his subjects. According to Jubelin, known himself as being sympathetic to the colonies, "the government should not wait to receive from the colonies a favorable opinion on any detailed measure proposed in view of the emancipation of slaves, nor to see any plan spring from the colonial assemblies for implementing such a work." He also confided that "nothing has been done yet for the amelioration of the slave population." If anything, he indicated, the situation had regressed over the last dozen years.[5] If the government still harbored

---

[3] Société française pour l'abolition de l'esclavage, *No. 6. Année 1838* (Paris: Duverger, 1838), 3–7; *Journal de la Société de la morale chrétienne*, 2nd series, vol. 12, no. 1, July–Dec. 1837, pp. 150–2.

[4] See Jennings, "Bissette," 54–5.

[5] ANCAOM, Corr. Gén., Guad. 84, Governor to Minister, Sept. 11, 1837.

illusions as to where the colonies stood on slavery and its reform, it was once again fully apprised of what could be expected from colonial quarters.

Some evidence suggests that this same tendency to inertia, if not regression, was also being reinforced in government circles at this time. Statements emanating from colonial delegates must be taken with caution, for these officials often attempted to emphasize their importance and effectiveness. However, reports by delegates which were not refuted or challenged by government authorities can be assumed to have some basis in fact. This is the case with a revealing dispatch from Charles Dupin, president of the Council of Delegates in Paris, to General Ambert, president of the Colonial Council of Guadeloupe, a copy of which ended up in the hands of the navy-colonial department without receiving any marginal comment or denial of the kind that was customary when blatantly false or objectionable material reached this office. Dupin informed his superiors that he had had an audience with King Louis Philippe and that he was pleased with "the reassuring words of the head of state." The King, Dupin recounted, had authorized him to report that:

The King wishes to be a firm and enlightened protector for the colonies and their present social state [meaning the slave system]; he wishes to remain the guardian of your rights, your fortunes, and your security. His superior mind will not be misled by any vain utopia. He knows the colonies which he has visited; he appreciates their interests of which he has never lost sight; he sympathizes with their sufferings which he keenly hopes will be relieved. Therefore, do not fear in the future any abrupt, unexpected, inopportune, or disastrous measure: in his wisdom the King will not permit such things.[6]

Historians are now aware that Louis Philippe constantly endeavored to exercise power behind the scenes throughout the July Monarchy. While he only fully achieved his objective after 1840 under the Soult-Guizot administrations, already in the late 1830s comte Molé was prepared to follow the King's directives. This could explain Molé's tabling of the plans for *rachat, pécule,* and the freeing of slave children that his government had inherited from earlier Cabinets containing

[6] Ibid., Gén. 161 (1323), Dupin to Ambert, Dec. 26, 1837.

abolitionists. King Louis Philippe's penchant for the *juste milieu*, his notorious desire to satisfy everyone, and his determination to preserve the status quo at any cost were perhaps the determining factors obliging many Cabinets – especially those without an abolitionist voice and led by obedient figures – to demur on the slave liberation question.

Faced with an impasse on the emancipation scene, the French abolition society met for the first time in six months on December 27, 1837.[7] In anticipation of the legislative session of 1838, it once again plotted its strategies. Cognizant of the government's immobility on the slavery issue, Vice-President Passy wrote to Molé to ask whether his ministry would honor its commitment to present an emancipation-related proposal in the upcoming session. When Molé admitted that his administration did not intend to act after all on the emancipation scene in 1838 – as the abolitionists had suspected – the society resolved to take matters into its own hands and no longer just interpellate the government. On February 9, 1838, early in the legislative agenda, Passy presented a motion for a bill in the Chamber of Deputies. It called for freeing all slave children born after the promulgation of the law, with an indemnity of 50 francs per year accorded the master for ten years. It also provided for the institutionalization of peculium and self-redemption, along with a clause encouraging marriage by reducing the redemption price for married slaves by one-third. When the motion was discussed in the lower house on February 15, Passy explained that he would have preferred leaving the matter in the hands of the Cabinet, but that its immobility had compelled him to propose a law similar to the government's own previously stated intentions.[8]

In introducing his bill in the chambers, Passy admitted that it was not perfect, and that he would have preferred a more rapid approach to slave liberation. However, he had felt obliged to present a project that could gain wide support within French parliament and have the best chance of passing. Slavery, he argued, was condemned by Christian principles and contrary to the rights of man; the English emancipation experience had also proven it unnecessary for colonial staples production. Passy was supported by Laborde, who agreed that the

[7] *Le Semeur*, Jan. 3, 1838.
[8] *Le Moniteur universel*, Feb. 10, 16, 1838.

British example had shown it possible "to conciliate cultivation, richness, and well-being with liberty," though he emphasized more than his colleague the need for adequately indemnifying masters for their property. Lamartine also joined in to stress the need for following Britain, providing an adequate indemnity to the *colons*, and ending "these temporizations" that marked government policy.

The abolitionists were opposed by Pierre Antoine Berryer, Legitimist leader in the lower house and deputy of the port city of Marseille who systematically defended slavery under the July Monarchy, and Mauguin, speaking for the delegates. Throughout the July Monarchy, Legitimist forces regularly supported the planters' cause, presenting themselves as the defenders of the colonies and navy that depended on colonial trade.[9] Berryer insisted that the Passy motion was premature, and that emancipation would not only destroy French colonial establishments, but hurt French commerce, which, he claimed, shipped one-tenth of total French exports to the colonies.[10] Mauguin underlined the willingness of colonists to emancipate if reimbursed for their slaves and lands – the typical colonial tactic of posing impossible conditions for cooperation. Still, it was navy-colonial minister Rosamel who led the charge against the Passy proposal. He requested that the chambers refuse to take it into consideration and instead accord the government an opportunity to present its own plans "when the time comes." According to Rosamel, the colonies were already faced with economic difficulties which the Passy motion would aggravate by failing to provide adequate indemnification. Besides, he argued, the slaves were not prepared for liberation; *pécule* and *rachat* would undermine masters' authority; and planter rights, as important as those of the slaves, must be protected. Molé seconded Rosamel on all of these allegations, and pointed out too that the British experiment was still inconclusive. Once again, *colons* and government were united in rejecting abolitionist demands. Once again, the government had avowed that in its mind the property rights of masters predominated over the basic rights of slaves.

[9] Tudesq, *Les grands notables*, II, 843.
[10] A more accurate calculation shows that trade with French slave colonies constituted only between 5 and 7 percent of total French foreign trade during the 1830s and 1840s (Seymour Drescher, *Capitalism and Antislavery: British Mobilization in Comparative Perspective* (New York: Oxford University Press, 1987), 139).

Fortunately for the abolitionists, Guizot, no longer a member of the Cabinet and now an opponent of Molé, intervened to request that the chambers take the Passy proposal into consideration because it was necessary to continue discussing and examining the slavery question. This enabled Passy to support Guizot's rationale, even suggesting that putting the proposition before a parliamentary commission would assist the government by enlightening it and providing it with opinions other than those of the *colons*. In the end, the chamber voted by an immense majority to take the motion into consideration and appoint a legislative commission to examine it.[11] The debate of February 15 had given both sides of the issue another occasion to elucidate their positions. It showed that the abolitionists were still quite moderate in their demands, but that they had for the first time made a concrete proposal of their own to the French parliament, even if it only amounted to what the government itself seemed prepared to concede when Broglie and Passy had been in the Cabinet. Concerted abolitionist support for the Passy proposal in the lower house indicated that his initiative emanated from the French abolition society as a whole. The vote to consider officially the Passy motion also constituted a significant step in the emancipation problem, for it implicated the legislature directly and proved the lower house desirous of finding a solution to it.

The vote of the Chamber of Deputies constituted a victory for the anti-slavery cause. The elective chamber had actually opposed the Cabinet's wishes on the slavery issue, giving what one abolitionist newspaper called a rude shock to the administration. The daily also pointed out, though, that Passy's gradualist demand had not gone far enough, and that the vice-president of the Société française should have instead proposed a plan for general slave emancipation within a decade.[12] Other anti-slavery spokesmen, nevertheless, were pleased that the lower house had encouraged the administration to act in some manner on the slave liberation front.[13] Then, when the parliamentary commission was named to examine the Passy motion, it gave further reason for satisfaction to the abolitionist camp. Of its nine members, only two, Berryer and Jean François Xavier Croissant, were

[11] *Le Moniteur universel*, Feb. 16, 1838.
[12] *Le Constitutionnel*, Feb. 15, 16, 1838.
[13] *Le Semeur*, Feb. 21, 1838.

defenders of slavery. Five belonged to the Société française pour l'abolition de l'esclavage: Isambert, Laborde, Passy, baron Roger du Loiret, and Rémusat. Two others, Guizot and Joseph Henri Galos of the Gironde, were considered to be opponents of slavery by the *Journal de la société de la morale chrétienne*.[14] Guizot became president of the body and Isambert its secretary. Rémusat was charged with writing its report. With the parliamentary commission stacked with abolitionists, the Rémusat report was bound to be favorable to the anti-slavery effort.

The Guizot–Rémusat commission met nine times between February 26 and April 24, 1838. It heard testimony not only from its own members, but from the prime minister, navy-colonial minister, colonial office officials, and the colonial delegates.[15] Rémusat's report was presented in the lower house on June 18, shortly before the end of the parliamentary session and the dissolution of the legislature. As a result, it could not be discussed during the 1838 session. Indeed, the dissolution of the chambers removed it entirely from the parliamentary agenda and made it officially a dead letter. However, the Rémusat report was published by the French abolition society, and widely commented upon by the press. Its recommendations, therefore, remained pertinent, and became the basis for discussions by the abolitionists, government, and plantocracy for the remainder of 1838.

In investigating the Passy proposal, the Guizot–Rémusat commission had examined the entire slavery and emancipation questions. Early on in the report, the commission attempted to chide the administration into action by noting that its "good intentions have been evident, its good thoughts numerous, but this is not enough, and we must remind the government that its role is one of resolution and action. It has meditated, but it has done little."[16] The commission also warned the colonies that their rejection up until now of all ameliorative or preparatory measures had diminished the colonial councils in the eyes of metropolitan France to the point where some people were

---

[14] 2nd series, vol. 13, no. 1, Jan.–June 1838, pp. 102–108.

[15] ANCAOM, Gén. 161 (1322), minutes of the commission on the Passy proposal.

[16] Société française pour l'abolition de l'esclavage, No. 9. *Rapport fait au nom de la commission chargée de l'examen de la proposition de M. Passy sur le sort des esclaves dans les colonies françaises, par M. de Rémusat, député de la Haute-Garonne* (Paris: A. Henry, 1838), p. 37.

questioning the utility of consulting these bodies in the future. In out-lining its own principles, it applauded the Passy initiative, which it believed would lead slowly and surely to emancipation. Nevertheless, it stressed that the commission had attempted to consider all interests involved and to come to a balanced conclusion. And it announced that the majority of its members preferred mass emancipation to the pro-gressive Passy system of liberating slave children, though any general move must be preceded by adequate preparation of slaves and indem-nification of their masters. As a result, the commission did not recom-mend the partial and gradualist approach of Passy, but a policy of waiting to act upon slavery until 1840 when the British experience could be fully judged, combined with the active preparation of slaves for liberation in the meantime. More precisely, it recommended that the state immediately undertake preparatory measures and provide funding for them; that ordonnances be introduced to encourage marriage and institutionalize peculium and self-redemption; and that government inspectors be appointed to overlook this process. It added in passing that colonial objections to *rachat* and *pécule* were largely chimerical. Finally, throughout the latter part of the report it stressed the weakness of existing religious structures in the colonies, particu-larly those concerning religious education of slaves.[17]

The religious structure of the French colonies under the July Mon-archy was still suffering from the setbacks it had received during the era of the French Revolution and Napoleonic period. The religious orders, responsible for ministering to the slaves under the *ancien régime*, had been decimated during the Revolutionary era. Some of France's colonies had been lost entirely to British or allied occupation. In the interval the religious and teaching orders had disappeared, while the number of ecclesiastics had plummeted. The Congrégation du Saint-Esprit, charged with forming colonial priests from the begin-ning of the eighteenth century, had ceased to exist during the Revolu-tion. Only in 1817 did Louis XVIII renew its mandate of providing ecclesiastics for the colonies, but even then the supply of candidates was inadequate. During the Restoration some Christian Brothers, and Sisters of Saint Joseph of Cluny, had been dispatched to the colonies for teaching purposes, but they served mostly whites, and sometimes

---

[17] Ibid., 3–6, 36, 52–69.

persons of color. The contingent of priests sent to the colonies during the Restoration had increased their totally inadequate numbers only slightly.[18] The Rémusat report underlined the dearth of curates still prevalent in the 1830s. As of 1838, it noted, there were only 88 priests in the four French slave colonies: 33 in Martinique, 29 in Guadeloupe, 19 in Bourbon, and seven in Guiana. This amounted to less than one ecclesiastic per 4,000 persons in the French colonies, whereas in Jamaica in 1834 there had been one for every 2,000, in Antigua one for 1,000.[19] Moreover, the few priests in the French holdings operated in towns, not on the plantations. They, even more than the teaching orders, ministered almost exclusively to whites, rarely to the *hommes de couleur libres*, almost never to slaves. Many of the priests lacked a missionary calling, were too preoccupied with administrative matters to leave their churches, and were discouraged by the planters from caring for rural slaves. Thus, attempts to moralize French colonial slaves through religion had been "almost entirely abandoned since 1793."[20] Until the late 1830s, the colonial clergy had little interest in abolitionism, held a negative attitude toward slaves, and shared in colonist fears about disorders caused by any change in the status of blacks. One Martinique priest, abbé Poncelet, captured these concerns when writing in 1836 to the head of his order in Paris about the anti-slavery movement: "Let us hope that these ideas of general emancipation do not bring trouble" to the tranquility that was reigning in his island.[21] As the Rémusat commission report indicated, in its present state the Church in the colonies could not serve as an agency for slave amelioration.

Colonial spokesmen such as Mauguin, when speaking in the chambers, also blamed the government for failing to take adequate

---

[18] Philippe Delisle, *Renouveau missionnaire et société esclavagiste: La Martinique, 1815–1848* (Paris: Publisud, 1997), 37–41; Geneviève Lecuir-Nemo, "Femmes et vocation missionnaire, permanence des congrégations feminines au Sénégal de 1819 à 1960: Adaption ou Mutations? Impact et insertion," 2 vols., doctorat, Paris I, 1994–95, I, 65; Claude Prudhomme, *Histoire religieuse de la Réunion* (Paris: Karthala, 1984), 28, 33, 44–56; Seymour Drescher, "Two Variants of Anti-Slavery: Religious Organization and Social Mobilization in Britain and France, 1780–1870," in Bolt and Drescher, eds., *Anti-Slavery, Religion, and Reform: Essays in Memory of Roger Anstey*, 49.

[19] No. 9 (Rémusat report), 59–60.

[20] Ibid., 51.

[21] Philippe Delisle, "Eglise et esclavage dans les vieilles colonies françaises au XIXe siècle," *Revue d'histoire de religieuse de la France* 84 (1998): 55–7.

religious measures to moralize the slaves.[22] Abolitionists, though, viewed the situation in an entirely different light. Abbé Orsini, a former priest in Guadeloupe, testified before the Société française pour l'abolition de l'esclavage that masters would not give slaves time to attend services and had in effect forbidden religious instruction for them.[23] Passy and Isambert both affirmed before the Guizot–Rémusat commission that not only were the slaves given no time from their work for religious practices, but that masters feared ideas of liberty and equality that religion might inspire in their charges.[24] It was well known that the few priests like Orsini who propagated liberal Christian principles were expelled from the colonies. Within the confidentiality of the Guizot–Rémusat hearings, colonial apologists admitted that they harbored other than Christian aims in advocating religious education for blacks. De Cools, delegate of Bourbon, suggested that religious instruction represented the best means of inculcating in slaves the idea that work was honorable. Jabrun, one of the leading planters of Guadeloupe as well as its delegate, regretted that "the clergy does not minister to the blacks" because, "if in the name of God, one preaches work to them, this recommendation is much more powerful than that of the master." Prime minister Molé agreed that priests must be closely regulated in the colonies so that they would not preach subversive ideas to slaves. Under these conditions, he pledged that his government would associate itself to any request by the commission to the chambers for religious and educational funding for slaves.[25] Though they had different views as to its objectives, there was a consensus among government, *colons*, and abolitionists that measures of some kind must be taken to encourage religious instruction in the colonies.

The Rémusat report amounted to a call for concrete measures to prepare for emancipation rather than an endorsement of the Passy proposal for a partial and progressive approach. It was recognized as such by *Le Semeur*, which appreciated its vision of a complete elimination of slavery rather than a drawn-out, partial liberation process.

---

[22] *Le Moniteur universel*, Feb. 16, 1838. Mauguin spoke in these terms during the Passy proposal debate.
[23] *4ème Publication*, 49.
[24] ANCAOM, Gén. 161 (1322), minutes of the commission on the Passy proposal.
[25] Ibid.

However, a different pro-abolitionist organ, *Le Siècle*, was critical of it as concentrating on preparatory actions and condoning "an adjournment" of slave liberation.[26] Conversely, advocates of a cautious, long-term approach to emancipation applauded the Rémusat report for these very reasons.[27] The government, which had assumed an immobile stance on the slavery question for over a year, was once again piqued into action by this report just as in the past it had been aroused by abolitionist interpellations in the lower house.

Another factor also shook the French government out of its lethargy in the summer of 1838. Reports reached Paris that apprenticeship for all former British slaves would be cut short and terminated on August 1, 1838, rather than 1840. All of the French government's projections about the desirability of waiting until after 1840 and the ending of apprenticeship to judge the final outcome of British slave liberation were now undercut by this development. Logically, the French government could be called upon to act on the slavery issue immediately. This unsettling eventuality combined with pressure from the Rémusat report's recommendations to cause a flurry of action in the French colonial office in mid-1838. At first the navy-colonial ministry seemed prepared only to consult the colonial councils about means for encouraging slave marriages; it did not even contemplate bringing up the questions of *pécule* and *rachat* again.[28] However, this constituted such a timid response to the current circumstances that Henri Joseph Mestro, chief assistant to Saint-Hilaire, questioned the tendency to "remain with crossed arms for nine more months," and asked whether it was not "best to take as a legislative basis as of now, the ... resolutions proposed [by the Rémusat report] and act immediately, rather than continuing to deliberate." Either his superior or the minister replied on the bottom of the note: "*Act* does not seem to be in the mind of the government" (emphasis in original). Instead, the matter should be taken before the Cabinet.[29] After consulting with the council of ministers, and taking into consideration the British

---

[26] *Le Semeur*, Sept. 19, 1838; *Le Siècle*, July 29, 1838.

[27] Excerpt from *Le Censeur* (Paris), a short-lived legislative review, pp. 157–160, July 1838, in ANCAOM, Gén. 161 (1323).

[28] Ibid., Gén. 161 (1322), internal navy-colonial department note addressed to Mestro, dated June 25.

[29] Ibid., note in the hand of Mestro, dated July 11.

decision to terminate apprenticeship on August 1, 1838, the navy-colonial ministry decided upon a more complex and cautious course of action.

The French colonial office realized that the Rémusat report would be brought up by the abolitionists early in the next session. Internal departmental memos indicate that the foremost objective of the navy-colonial ministry was to reject proposals made in the chambers in order to keep all initiative on the slavery issue out of the hands of the legislature and within its own grasp. Therefore, it planned to parry any abolitionist thrust by claiming that the administration itself was preparing to carry out as soon as possible all feasible ameliorative measures. Because the government as yet possessed no strategy for slave liberation, though, any abolitionist pressure to emancipate in light of British developments would have to be met with repetitions of assurances that the government intended to realize slave liberation eventually.[30] It was in this sense that the minister wrote to the four colonial governors on August 21, 1838, informing them of the administration's intentions and asking them to consult the colonial councils on certain questions. Paris wished to hear the opinion of the colonial legislatures on moralizing slaves, encouraging marriages, establishing savings banks to encourage peculium, and the possibility of freeing government-owned colonial slaves. The *colons* should also be informed that the government planned to issue ordonnances enforcing previous decrees on the census of slaves and their manumission. The minister mentioned in passing that his administration hoped to legalize *pécule* and *rachat* sooner or later, despite colonial objections, and was simply waiting for the opportune time. In a draft but not the actual dispatch, the minister avowed that the real intent of his moves was to constitute "effective rebuttals to the propositions enumerated in the [Rémusat] report."[31] Measures such as *rachat* and the freeing of newborn slaves had actually been tabled, as moderate as they might be, to be replaced by far more vague and ineffective proposals. Under the July Monarchy peculium and self-redemption would not be legislated upon until 1845; the freeing of slave children would remain a dead issue until 1847 at least. Once again the government

---

[30] Ibid., drafts in the hands of Mestro and Saint-Hilaire for the council of ministers, dated July 23, 1838.

[31] Ibid., Corr. Gén. 190 and Gén. 174 (1389), Minister to Governors, Aug. 21, 1838.

was following its strategy of offering the minimum necessary in the way of reform promises to head off abolitionist demands.

Despite the retreat of the government and the softening of its already weak reform package, the colonial councils reacted as might be expected. They joined in rejecting in toto the suggestions emanating from Paris. They denounced any measures leading to emancipation as inevitably undermining the colonies. They unanimously expressed their preference for general emancipation with an adequate indemnity, knowing full well that such a scenario was out of the question for the present time. Martinique's legislature asked simply to be left alone and not bothered by projects that would do no good while antagonizing the master–slave relationship. French Guiana's body even refused to discuss any question concerning slavery until after an indemnity had been voted in the French parliament.[32] The colonies were as intent on rejecting all proposals from the government as the administration was determined to refuse those of parliamentary commissions dominated by abolitionists. Colonial defenders realized that they could act with impunity because it was impossible for the government to meet their one demand of a generous indemnity. The French administration, for its part, was willing to countenance behavior of this kind by colonial councils because its own position on the slavery question approximated that of the *colons*.

Two of the colonies, Martinique and Guadeloupe, had commented in their replies to the government that what French staple-producing establishments really needed was relief from poor sugar prices and lower taxes on cane sugar imported into France. Governor Jubelin of Guadeloupe suggested in his dispatches to Paris that if his colony showed little moderation, and even made "violent attacks" against government moves concerning emancipation, it was because of its "state of suffering" brought on by the fall in sugar prices. Therefore, if France wished its colonies to consider seriously reforms such as those put forth by Passy, they should be "accompanied by some favorable measures on the sugar question."[33] Both the abolitionists and

---

[32] Ibid., Gén. 171 (1376), Governor of Martinique to Minister, Nov. 14, 1838; Corr. Gén., Guadeloupe 85, Governor to Minister, Nov. 26, Dec. 29, 1838; Gén. 161 (1323), Governor of Guiana to Minister, Dec. 4, 1838; Governor of Bourbon to Minister, April 13, 1839.

[33] Ibid., Gén. 171 (1376), Governor of Martinique to Minister, Nov. 14, 1838; Corr. Gén., Guadeloupe 85, Governor of Guadeloupe to Minister, Oct. 20, Dec. 29, 1838.

government were aware of the congruence between the sugar and emancipation issues. Several abolitionists displayed a willingness to make concessions to the colonies in the form of reduced taxes on cane sugar in exchange for colonial flexibility on the slavery issue. Lamartine became one of the leading proponents of lowering taxes on cane sugar, a move which ingratiated him with colonial advocates, who proclaimed him favorable to the colonies.[34] Even Bissette's review congratulated the administration for its actions in 1836 to lower sugar duties and thus alleviate economic suffering in the colonies to the point where *colons* could consider liberalizing the slave system.[35] The government, for its part, was willing since 1833 to cede in certain ways to cane sugar producer demands for more equitable taxation between cane and beet sugar. Thus, the navy-colonial ministry viewed the law of July 26, 1837, taxing beet sugar, as a move favorable to the colonies.[36] In fact, this was the first time that France had taxed the young sugar beet industry, marking an important initial step in the battle between beet and cane sugar that had been engaged already in the late years of the Restoration.

To assist in the revival of the French colonies after their return to France at the beginning of the Restoration, the regimes of Louis XVIII and Charles X had not only adopted an ambivalent attitude toward the clandestine slave trade, but had encouraged the development of the cane sugar industry. Protectionist as a whole, the Restoration had placed a series of taxes on foreign-produced cane sugar, culminating in the almost prohibitive ones of 1822 and 1826. The latter practically excluded foreign sugars from France.[37] At the same time as it taxed French colonial cane sugar, it also stimulated the production of the latter with subsidies and drawbacks to facilitate its reexportation from France. As a result, cane sugar production in French colonies shot up from 17 million kilograms in 1817 to 52 million in 1822, and protected French cane sugar prices reached their height in the late 1820s, when sugar grown in Martinique and Guadeloupe sold for twice the

[34] *Le Moniteur universel*, May 26, 1836; Schoelcher Papers, n. a. f. 3632, A. de Saint-Priest, director of *La Revue du XIX`eme siècle*, to Colonial Council of Martinique, Nov. 8, 1840.

[35] *La Revue des colonies*, 3rd year, no. 6, Dec. 1836, pp. 232–39.

[36] ANCAOM, Gén. 161 (1323), Minister to President of the Council of Delegates, Oct. 5, 1838.

[37] Fiérain, *Les raffineries*, 55.

price as in Puerto Rico. Consequently, the French colonies thrived and reached what has been called their golden years of the nineteenth century, with sugar becoming almost a monoculture. In Guadeloupe, for example, sugar cultivation spread from 18,700 hectares in 1817 to 26,200 in 1834; the number of sugar plantations rose from 389 in 1816 to 620 by 1835. By 1832 colonial sugar exports to France, 82,200 metric tons, reached almost the average annual exports for the pre-Revolutionary period of 1785–1790, when they had stood at 88,000 tons.[38] These same encouragements, however, also stimulated the French beet sugar industry and provided increased competition for cane sugar. Sugar beet growers turned out only 3 million kilograms in 1828, but nearly 50 million by 1836, when beet sugar, still untaxed, satisfied one third of internal French demand. The result was a glut in French sugar markets and falling prices in the 1830s and 1840s. French consumption of sugar increased steadily under the Restoration and during the early years of the July Monarchy, but in 1834 for the first time consumption fell behind the total amount of sugar exported from the French colonies, 83 million to 87 million tons. Prices for French West Indian sugar dropped by 11 percent from 1832 to 1834, and 20–25 percent by 1837. In Guadeloupe alone raw sugar prices declined from 58 francs per 100 kilogram to 32 francs in 1839. To make matters worse, the July Monarchy, much more open to free trade ideas than the Restoration, decreased taxes on foreign grown sugar in 1833 and increased them on French colonial sugar by 10 percent in 1834 in an obvious attempt to increase government revenues.[39]

By the late 1830s, the French cane sugar industry faced a major crisis. The administration did not wish to decrease colonial sugar taxes, which varied from 38.5 to 120 francs per 100 kilos according to quality, because it depended upon the revenue generated by them. Instead, it began seriously contemplating taxing beet sugar, whose production between 1821 and 1836 spread from 58 to 400 factories situated in 36 different French departments, though concentrated in the North. The

---

[38] See Chapter 2.
[39] Cochin, *L'Abolition*, 164–66, 400; E. Boizard and H. Tardieu, *Histoire de la législation des sucres (1664–1891)* (Paris: Impr. Dubreuil, 1891), 21–23, 31; Christian Louis-Joseph, "La Monarchie de Juillet et la guerre des deux sucres," in *Historial Antillais*, III, 353–4; Schnakenbourg, *Histoire de l'industrie sucrière*, 140–42; Fallope, *Esclaves et citoyens*, 253; Fiérain, *Les raffineries*, 57–8.

government considered such a tax already in 1832, and proposed one in 1834, only to have it rejected by the chambers. By 1836 the situation had become so menacing for cane producers that a government commission predicted that if something were not done soon, beet would eventually replace cane sugar entirely, threatening in the process the very existence of the French colonies and gravely perturbing French commerce and the port cities. Subsequently, in 1837 the Molé Cabinet proposed a tax of 15 percent on beet sugar, which, after being amended to defer its implementation until 1838–1839, passed in both houses and was proclaimed on July 26, 1837.

In the long run this measure had its desired effect, decreasing drastically the number of beet manufacturers and concentrating them almost entirely in the North after 1839. It also drove sugar beet production down by 1840–1841 to pre-1835 levels. Still, in the short term the new tax exacerbated the crisis. Beet producers rushed to dump their product on the market before the tax went into effect. At the same time colonial cane growers enjoyed a bumper crop in 1838, for in the 1830s planters reacted to rising costs and falling prices by producing more. Prices now fell precipitously due to overproduction. The average price of ordinary sugar on the Le Havre market declined from 75 francs for 50 kilos for 1819–1828, to 68 for 1829–1836, to 52 at one point in late 1837, before rebounding to 60 francs.[40] Colonial spokesmen shrieked that the colonies were foundering, and that in such conditions they could not contemplate further moves towards emancipation.

Sugar crisis or not, the abolitionists demanded some progress on the emancipation scene. As of the summer of 1838 Bissette's *Revue des colonies* reappeared briefly to join in the anti-slavery chorus once again. Its author reacted favorably to the Rémusat report, which he termed "a remarkable and complete work." The *Revue* also rejoiced about a second event marking the abolitionist calendar in the autumn of 1838: Isambert had been awarded a medal by a delegation of persons of color in Paris. This perhaps reflected the close ties that Isambert had established with free black lawyers in the colonies, many of whom even stayed at his home when visiting Paris. Any differences

---

[40] Boizard and Tardieu, *Histoire de la législation des sucres*, 29, 31–35, 40–46, 49–52; Tomich, *Slavery in the Circuit of Sugar*, 45, 108–9.

that Bissette might have had with Isambert seemed resolved at least temporarily, for the *Revue* used the occasion of the medal ceremony to hail "the zeal, the perseverance and the disinterestedness" of Isambert, whose name "shined brilliantly" as a defender of blacks.[41] Another independent abolitionist also made his mark when the Protestant doctrinaire Orleanist, Agénor de Gasparin, published his first important book on the slavery question.[42] At this point in his career Gasparin espoused the gradualist approach to slave liberation, advocating a system of self-redemption whereby the slave would slowly purchase his own freedom. Widely reviewed in the press, Gasparin's *Esclavage et traite* gave added weight to the struggle to impose at least a gradualist solution to the slavery problem upon the colonies and government.

The Société française pour l'abolition de l'esclavage was less successful in some of its endeavors in 1838. First, it suffered the loss of its honorary president Zachary Macaulay, and offered in his memory a eulogy which enumerated his contribution to the anti-slavery cause. With Macaulay's passing, an important intermediary between the French and British movements had been removed from the scene.[43] Second, the society's committee administering the Abbé Grégoire prize examined four entries, but put off making an award because of supposed faults with all of them. Third, the society faced the unpleasant task of admitting that one of its noteworthy members, Emmanuel Las Cases, son of Napoleon's companion at Saint Helena, had abandoned the anti-slavery cause after a diplomatic mission to the Caribbean in 1837. Las Cases had succumbed to the all too typical syndrome of visiting the colonies, being well received there, and falling under the charms of colonial hospitality. As a result, he had returned to France as a defender of the *colons*.[44] Finally, the society's

---

[41] *La Revue des colonies*, 5th year, no. 1, July 1838, pp. 3–5; no. 6, Dec. 1838, pp. 182–92. Information on the ties between Isambert and free colonial blacks has been kindly provided by Madame Maïté Court-Isambert.

[42] *Esclavage et traite* (Paris: Joubert, 1838).

[43] Jennings, *French Reaction*, 94–5, 102. Although Macaulay's reputation as a leading anti-slave trade activist has recently been impugned (Eltis, *Economic Growth and ... Slave Trade*, 110–11), there is no doubt about the important role he played in the early years of the French abolition society.

[44] Société française pour l'abolition de l'esclavage, *No. 8. Année 1838* (Paris: Hingray, 1838), 25–7, 41–8.

efforts to extract favorable statements from the departmental *Conseils généraux* regressed in 1838, for only nine replied positively. The French colonial office duly noted this abolitionist setback. As Mestro remarked on a confidential document, nine out of 86 departments "is not very many."[45] The government did not seem displeased with the failure of the French abolition society to garner more support for the anti-slavery cause from *notable* opinion in the provinces.

Still, the government also had reason for concern in late 1838. It feared that the termination of British apprenticeship could give an unforeseen impulse to the French emancipation process. Rosamel's letter to his governors on August 21 ended with a statement showing his department's uncertainty about the situation now that apprenticeship had ended prematurely. It is possible, he explained, "that the question raised by the [Rémusat] report will become magnified in 1839 as a result of what is going to happen in the English colonies, and that the [French] government will be compelled by the force of things to become immediately preoccupied, no longer with preparatory measures for emancipation, but with the very application of this great measure to our possessions." He added that if this were to prove to be the case, he would not elaborate on what his administration might do, but he could assure the governors that "the King's ministers will not in any way deviate from the conservative principles that one of my predecessors has already expressed and that guarantee colonists *indemnity and security*" (emphasis in original). In an earlier draft of the dispatch the minister revealed the factor that most worried his office. He ordered his governors to "report to me frequently and faithfully the influence that the proclamation of definitive liberty for all the blacks in the English colonies could have on the spirit of the slave population" in French holdings.[46] Such a statement strongly suggests that French authorities feared that the news of complete British slave liberation could cause sizable disruptions or even revolts in French colonial possessions. Indeed, such an avowal implies that a major slave revolt might have been the only factor forcing the French July Monarchy to free rapidly its colonial slaves.

In the 1830s the memory of the Saint-Domingue slave revolt of the

---

[45] ANCAOM, Gén. 156 (1301), note for the Director of the Colonies, Nov. 25, 1838.
[46] Ibid., Gén. 174 (1389) and Corr. Gén. 190, Minister to Governors, Aug. 21, 1838.

1790s was still alive in France. Negative references to Saint-Domingue were especially prevalent in the discourse of French colonial spokesmen, who remained prepared to muster every possible demonic vision in their campaign against slave liberation. Contrariwise, as might be expected from those advocating emancipation, French abolitionists rarely made mention of Saint-Domingue. When they wished to remind the government that the price of procrastination could be revolt by French slaves, they quite naturally preferred citing the British colonial slave revolts of Barbados in 1816, Demerara in 1823, or, most often, of Jamaica in 1831–1832. It is noteworthy, though, that the French abolition society's prospectus, written by Passy in 1834, referred to French remembrances of Saint-Domingue as one of the leading reasons causing France to lag behind Britain in anti-slavery activity until that point in time.[47] However, the negative consequences of Saint-Domingue upon the French abolitionist movement from the mid-1830s on should not be exaggerated.[48] It is far too facile to overemphasize the effects of Saint-Domingue on French consciousness and overlook far more important and complex elements hindering French anti-slavery. In the late 1830s and especially in the 1840s, all evidence indicates that this memory had faded considerably. References to Saint-Domingue declined markedly after the British experience showed that emancipation could be achieved without violence.[49] As for the *colons*, the French government listened closely to the colonists in most matters, and was extremely solicitous of their well-being. But it apparently paid little attention to statements such as those made by Mauguin in the chambers that Saint-Domingue alone should warn France against acting too precipitously on the slavery question.[50] Among the multitude of documents in the French colonial archives treating slavery in the French colonies or its abolition, whether they be in the hand of the minister himself, the Director of the Colonies, or some lesser functionary, there are exceptionally few references to the example of Saint-Domingue. There is little evidence that this late eighteenth-century

[47] *Prospectus*, 6–8.
[48] This is the case with the study by Serge Daget, "Les mots esclave, nègre, Noir, et les jugements de valeur sur la traite negrière dans la littérature abolitionniste française de 1770 à 1845," *Revue française d'histoire d'outre-mer*, 60 (1973): 534.
[49] See Jennings, *French Reaction*, 24–5.
[50] *Le Moniteur universel*, Feb. 16, 1838.

slave revolt directly influenced French government policy in the latter part of the 1830s or the 1840s prior to 1848. As the correspondence of the navy-colonial minister in the summer of 1838 showed, it was not the precedent of Saint-Domingue but the situation in the neighboring British colonies that led French officials to fear troubles in French slave establishments.

There is a growing corpus of historical literature on how blacks in the English colonies contributed to their own liberation.[51] Some attempts have been made to apply this theory also to the French colonial scene in the first half of the nineteenth century.[52] In French colonies as elsewhere under slavery there was a considerable amount of passive resistance by slaves, along with cases of open insubordination or resistance against individual masters or the system as a whole. French slaves resisted passively by toiling as little as possible or disrupting work patterns. More overt instances of resistance took the form of poisonings, barn burnings, fleeing plantations (*marronnage*), or open confrontations with the *colons*.[53] Although all of this was disconcerting to French colonial authorities and the planters, there is little evidence that this interfered with production on a measurable scale or undermined the viability of the French slave system. As mentioned previously, there had been small revolts at Saint-Pierre

[51] Two noteworthy studies are by Michael Craton, *Testing the Chains: Resistance to Slavery in the British West Indies* (Ithaca: Cornell University Press, 1982), and Richard Hart, *Slaves Who Abolished Slavery* (2 vols.; Mona, Jamaica: Institute of Social and Economic Research, University of the West Indies, 1980–1985).

[52] See Nelly Schmidt, *L'Engrenage de la Liberté: Caraïbes – XIXe Siècle* (Aix-en-Provence: Publications de l'Université de Provence, 1995), pp. 27–9; and Bernard Moitt, "Slave Resistance in Guadeloupe and Martinique, 1791–1848," *Journal of Caribbean History* 25 (1991): 136–59. A totally exaggerated version of this theme, quite widespread among popular literature commemorating the 1998 sesquicentennial of French slave liberation, is offered in the brief article by Rigoulet-Roze, "A propos d'une commemoration." After stressing how the slaves of Saint-Domingue had freed themselves, this author refers to the Bissette affair of the 1820s and the minor uprisings of 1831 and 1833 in Martinique, before jumping directly to the events of 1848, as if an anti-slavery movement had never existed under the Restoration and July Monarchy.

[53] See the excellent study by Fallope, *Esclaves et citoyens*, for a detailed discussion of the different forms of slave resistance (pp. 304–309). See also Schnakenbourg, *Histoire de l'industrie sucrière*, 104, 109–118; Tomich, *Slavery in the Circuit*, 250–8; and Sudel Fuma, *L'Esclavagisme à la Réunion, 1794–1848* (Paris: L'Harmattan, 1992), 65–72. A recent publication has shed light upon the maroon phenomenon during the last years of slavery in Guadeloupe; see the *Cahier de marronnage du Moule (1845–1848)* (Basse-Terre: Société d'Histoire de la Guadeloupe, 1996).

(Martinique) in 1831 and at Grand-Anse in 1833, but no noteworthy incidents followed these for the remainder of the July Monarchy. Moreover, even these troubles of the early 1830s were minor events compared with the Jamaican slave revolt of 1831–1832. When *hommes de couleur libres* spoke to slaves in Martinique about the possibility of rapid emancipation, or when an American merchant-man captain spread rumors in Guiana that the French government had acted to abolish servitude, perfect tranquility continued to prevail among the French colonial slave population.[54] Only after news of impending slave liberation reached Martinique and Guadeloupe in the spring of 1848 did uprisings oblige colonial officials to proclaim immediate freedom. Until the initiative for slave liberation came from Paris in early 1848, French slaves did not carry out actions of the kind feared by the navy-colonial ministry in the summer of 1838 that could have forced the hand of the government.

One historian has suggested that no slave uprisings occurred in French colonial possessions after 1833 because from this point on determined slaves could obtain freedom by escaping to nearby British colonies.[55] Once emancipation was declared for British holdings, some French slaves did flee to British establishments. However, the total number of escapees probably did not amount to many more than 2,000 for the fifteen years preceding the ending of French servitude in 1848.[56] The departure of these fugitive slaves could indeed have acted as a safety valve, removing from the scene the most rebellious elements. As a whole, the French colonies remained remarkably calm during all stages of British emancipation and French preparatory measures. Perhaps due to the increased security moves taken as of the mid-1830s, French slaves did not revolt. As has been demonstrated in the American context, French colonial slaves were undoubtedly wise enough to recognize that it was not in their interest to risk their lives in confronting overwhelming planter power.[57] Except for a few rare instances, such as the one reflected in the draft dispatch of August 21,

---

[54] ANCAOM, Gén. 161 (1350), memoire by Governor C. A. Duval d'Ailly for Captain Mathieu, his successor in Martinique, Dec. 1844; Gén. 171 (1379), Governor of Guiana to Minister, Aug. 10, 1843.

[55] Schnakenbourg, *Histoire de l'industrie sucrière*, 108–9, 113.

[56] Jennings, *French Reaction*, 20–22.

[57] See Eugene D. Genovese, *Roll, Jordan, Roll: The World the Slaves Made* (New York: Pantheon, 1974), 587–96.

1838, the French navy-colonial office seemed unpreoccupied with the possibility of uprisings. The dearth of references to possible slave revolts within policy statements, notes, or dispatches preserved in the French colonial archives indicates that the government was not highly concerned with such eventualities. During the time of the French Revolution and the Saint-Domingue uprising, slaves had acted to liberate themselves, but in France under the July Monarchy the power to emancipate remained in the hands of Paris. At times abolitionists might brandish the threat of slave uprisings as the natural consequence of inaction on the emancipation front, but the government – which alone could decree slave liberation – never took these threats seriously. Government authorities were much more anxious about the machinations of the abolitionists than of the slaves. As the legislative session of 1839 opened, they prepared for the onslaught of embarrassing questions from the anti-slavery ranks in the chambers.

The French navy-colonial office expected the abolitionists to place the Rémusat report on the agenda of the Chamber of Deputies immediately after the opening of the 1839 session.[58] However, the abolitionists did so only on June 12. Perhaps they were deterred from acting earlier by news that arrived in the mainland in early 1839 of the devastating earthquake that had shaken Martinique, or by ministerial instability that brought one cabinet change in late March and yet another in mid-May. More likely, the abolitionists were waiting for the government to introduce its own program, for word of its intention to request special funding for religious education of slaves was discussed by the press early in the year. Be this as it may, Tracy finally rose in the lower house on June 12 to reintroduce purely and simply the Passy proposal of the previous year rather than the Rémusat report on it.

Tracy explained his action by pointing out that the French colonial department had at one time advocated *rachat* along with the freeing of slave children, as outlined in the Passy project, and that he wished to conform abolitionist efforts as much as possible with the inner thoughts of the government. Tracy now felt confident that something could be done along these lines because the mid-May Cabinet shuffle had returned to the navy-colonial portfolio Admiral Duperré,

---

[58] ANCAOM, Gén. 161 (1322), note, Direction of the Colonies, Dec. 1838.

someone who "inspires ... the most complete confidence." More significant, it had also returned to the council of ministers a leading anti-slavery advocate, the vice-president of the Société française, Passy, now appointed finance minister. Passy actually took the floor to support Tracy and argue that it was necessary to seize the chambers once again with the emancipation problem and require "a new examination of the question."[59] The French abolition society knew that the government was prepared to propose ameliorative measures as requested by Rémusat. It wished to keep the emancipation issue on the agenda too now that Passy was in the Cabinet to champion it. Indeed, Tracy had been obliged to take the initiative on the legislative floor because Passy was now a member of the Cabinet. Both obviously hoped to convince the government to retreat from its retrograde policies of 1837–1838 and revive gradualist measures along the lines of *rachat* and the freeing of children.

Faced with Tracy's proposal, the administration strove to avoid having to commit itself to even moderate abolitionist moves. Duperré therefore informed the chamber that his government had already acceded to abolitionist wishes by introducing new reforms along the lines suggested by the Rémusat commission the previous year.[60] In reality, though, the government's measures fell far short of those suggested by the Rémusat report. On the one hand, the navy-colonial office hoped to "neutralize the proposals" put forth in the legislature by the abolitionists. On the other hand, it was frustrated by the colonial rejection of any plan altering the status quo.[61] It also felt bound to follow strictly the provisions of the law of April 1833 and implement only those changes approved by the delegates or colonial councils. The delegates, when consulted, had had no objections to Paris acting to tighten up on previous ordonnances for carrying out a slave census and regulating manumissions. Accordingly, the government had promulgated new decrees on these matters. The minister also announced his intention to request 650,000 francs in the budget of 1840 for sending out additional priests and members of the teaching orders to the colonies. Finally, he pledged to prepare shortly ordonnances encouraging marriages among slaves along with other

[59] *Le Moniteur universel*, June 13, 1839.
[60] Ibid.
[61] ANCAOM, Gén. 161 (1323), Minister to Governor of Martinique, Jan. 4, 1839.

ameliorations.[62] Caught between the obstructionism of the plantocracy and the demands of the abolitionists in the chambers, the government was limiting itself to minor, innocuous moves that would
neither alienate nor please anyone. The intransigent colonial organ
L'Outre-mer, run by Théodore Lechevalier in the pay of the delegates,
denounced even these half-hearted moves.[63] Likewise, several members of the Société française pour l'abolition de l'esclavage wrote in
protest to the navy-colonial minister, proclaiming that with reforms
of this kind, "it will take nearly a century to attain emancipation."[64]
Dilatory steps like these by the government probably also encouraged
the next parliamentary commission to go beyond emphasizing preparatory moves as the Guizot–Rémusat commission had done.

When the Chamber of Deputies duly took into consideration the
Tracy motion and appointed a commission to examine it, this body
was once again dominated by abolitionists. Of its nine members, six
belonged to the French abolition society: Barrot, Roger du Loiret,
Sade, Rémusat, Charles Casimir Dugabé, and Tocqueville, the latter
acting as reporter. Tocqueville's report pointed out that there seemed
to be a consensus, as the colonial council of Guadeloupe had itself
admitted on December 26, 1838, that "emancipation is henceforth
an inevitable fact." The only disagreement was as to when and how an
emancipation bill should be implemented. The Tocqueville commission believed that, while slaves must be prepared for freedom, it was
impossible for this to occur under slavery, for "to try to give a slave the
opinions, habits, and mores of a free man is to condemn him to remain
a slave forever." Therefore the commission rejected the Passy–Tracy
concept of progressive emancipation in favor of the idea of general or
simultaneous liberation of all slaves at a future date. It proposed that
during the 1841 session a law be introduced in parliament setting
the future date for freeing the slaves from their masters in exchange
for an indemnity. In turn, slaves would be handed over to the state so
that they could be inculcated with "laborious and virile habits of liberty." During this intermediary stage the state would become the tutor
of blacks, who would be paid a salary by the *colons*, part of which

[62] Ibid., Gén. 161 (1322), Note by the Direction of the Colonies for the Council of Ministers, Dec. 1838.
[63] Cited by *Le Semeur*, March 27, 1839.
[64] Société française pour l'abolition de l'esclavage, *No. 13* (Paris: Hingray, 1839), 51–9.

would be recuperated by the state to pay back the original cost of the indemnity. It was hoped that the colonies would adhere to such an arrangement because their spokesmen had reiterated during testimony before the commission that they preferred general emancipation with indemnity and preparation of slaves to piecemeal approaches.[65] In effect the Tocqueville commission had agreed with the Rémusat report that there should be a general rather than progressive emancipation. It had also espoused the concept of the Passy and Tracy proposals that preparatory measures were insufficient and that a definite emancipation plan must be drawn up. Moreover, its recommendations constituted a serious attempt to circumvent the problem of an indemnity by arranging for the slaves themselves to reimburse government coffers. Once again a parliamentary body was pressuring the government to act. This time it was much more specific in its demands, calling for a plan that would bring simultaneous freedom for all slaves from their masters followed by regimentation from the state. Under the Tocqueville proposal the government would play the central role in implementing this entire process.

The Tocqueville report, completed in late July 1839, was sent to the navy-colonial minister only in early August.[66] It appeared so late in the parliamentary session that there was not even enough time to print it up and present it to the lower house before the adjournment of the chambers. By the autumn of 1839, when the report was made public through the press, it became clear, however, that the colonies were no more prepared to accept the Tocqueville approach than earlier amelioration or emancipation plans. Charles Dupin, speaking for the delegates, attacked the report and argued that slaves were not yet ready for freedom.[67] The colonial council of Martinique was wary of it because it had not considered indemnity as a colonial right and therefore seemed to challenge the idea of slaves being property.[68] The plantocratic organ *Outre-mer* remarked that the parliament should

---

[65] ANCAOM, Gén. 171 (1376), report of the commission examining the Tracy proposal, July 23, 1839. An English version of the report has been published in Seymour Drescher, ed., *Tocqueville and Beaumont on Social Reform* (New York: Harper 1968), 137–173. The best study of Tocqueville's role in French anti-slavery remains Drescher's *Dilemmas of Democracy*, in particular pp. 171–92.

[66] ANCAOM, Gén. 171 (1376), Tocqueville to Minister, Aug. 3, 1839.

[67] Ibid., Dupin to Minister, Dec. 20, 1839.

[68] Ibid., Corr. Gén., Guadeloupe 86, Governor to Minister, Dec. 7, 1839.

desist from interfering in colonial affairs and let the government, in combination with the colonial legislatures, decide when to abolish slavery.[69] Despite what the Tocqueville commission had been led to believe, the colonies seemed as determined as ever to combat any project altering the status quo. To the contrary, anti-slavery newspapers like *Le Constitutionnel* hailed "the beautiful work of Mr. Tocqueville" as an important step on the road to emancipation.[70]

Aside from the Tocqueville report, French abolitionism experienced mixed results in other slavery-related developments in 1839. On the one hand, the Académie des Sciences morales et politiques in Paris sponsored a contest in an attempt to find a means of emancipation which could prepare slaves for liberty while guaranteeing an indemnity and sustained labor to the planters. This proposal incurred the wrath of delegates Eimar Jabrun and de Cools, who insisted that such a question should not be brought before the public but left to the realm of government prerogatives. On the other hand, a committee of the Société française pour l'abolition de l'esclavage examined four new essays submitted for the Grégoire prize, and again decided to postpone any award until the following year. Efforts by the society had evidently not been successful in stirring up public consciousness and conjuring up a plethora of anti-slavery works.

The abolition society was pleased, though, with the apostolic letter promulgated by Pope Gregory XVI on December 3, 1839, in which the Holy See criticized the capturing and mistreatment of slaves.[71] Up until now the Church establishment and almost all priests had appeared to be tolerant of servitude. The French abolition society had itself lamented the fact that the French episcopate tended to oppose emancipation. In a session of the society in 1836 one member even "complained about the little support ... obtained from the Catholic clergy."[72] That the pope's declaration did not fundamentally change the attitude of the French Catholic establishment toward slavery is shown by the fact that as late as 1846 the Seminaire du Saint-Esprit in Paris, which trained priests for service in the colonies, defended its

---

[69] *L'Outre-mer*, Sept. 30–Oct. 3, 1839.

[70] Nov. 16, 1839.

[71] *No. 13*, 3–9, 32–5; Société française pour l'abolition de l'esclavage, *No. 15* (Paris: E. Duverger, 1840), 1–8.

[72] *4ème Publication*, 44, 52.

stance of accepting slavery as in line with the general teachings of the Church at the time. Indeed, it was not until 1965 that the Church in the Second Vatican Council directly denounced slavery.[73] Still, the pronouncement of Gregory XVI gave abolitionists exaggerated hopes that the Church might become active in the emancipation question and pressure its ecclesiastics to condemn slavery. It probably did encourage a few colonial priests to question, even criticize slavery. Dedicating his work to the Pope, abbé Pierre Paul Castelli, who had been forced to resign as apostolic prefect of Martinique (leader of the clergy of the island) in 1839 because of planter pressures, wrote a pamphlet in 1844 calling for gradual emancipation well prepared by religious instruction. Edouard Goubert, a defrocked priest who married a Creole after being chased from Martinique, wrote a booklet in 1840 advocating immediate emancipation. Two other colonial ecclesiastics, Alexandre Monnet of Bourbon and Casimir Dugoujon of Guadeloupe, would also come out in favor of immediatism by the 1840s.[74] The papal pronouncement of 1839 not only whetted abolitionist hopes but facilitated a handful of colonial priests joining abolitionist ranks by the 1840s.

In the autumn of 1839, however, most activity on the slavery front was concentrated in French government circles. As had been the case a year earlier, opinion was divided within the administration on how best to proceed on the emancipation question. During the 1839 vote on the 1840 budget, the chambers had approved a request for 650,000 francs by the navy-colonial department for improving the moral and religious instruction of slaves. The colonial delegates, Dupin disclosed, had interpreted the funding of these measures as simply "an explicit sanction of a system of trials and temporization."[75] By late 1839 the navy-colonial office had decided exactly how these funds should be used. Of the total sum, 400,000 would go to increasing the colonial clergy, 200,000 for primary education through the teaching orders, and 50,000 for government inspection. A further breakdown

---

[73] John Francis Maxwell, *Slavery and the Catholic Church: The History of Catholic Teaching Concerning the Moral Legitimacy of the Institution of Slavery* (Chicester: Barry Rose, 1975), 10–11, 73–4, 111–2.

[74] Delisle, "Eglise et esclavage," 65–8. For more information on Monnet, see Prudhomme, *Histoire religieuse*, 79–81; for Dugoujon, see Chapter 8.

[75] ANCAOM, Gén. 161 (1323), President of the Council of Delegates to Minister, Dec. 20, 1839.

of these accounts indicates that 50,000 was designated for the Seminaire du Saint-Esprit in Paris for training additional priests, 150,000 to pay for these new ecclesiastics, and 200,000 for the construction of chapels. With the latter costing approximately 15,000 each, this would translate into between two and four new chapels for each colony in 1840. The administration also hoped to send out 16 priests to Guadeloupe, 11 to Martinique, seven to Bourbon, and two to Guiana. Besides, a contest would be opened offering a prize medal worth 1,500 francs for the best model for a special catechism for blacks. The idea would be "to turn the black into both a citizen and a Christian." More specifically, the aim of the catechism would be "especially to combat and destroy the prejudices that prevent blacks from understanding the necessity and the morality of work." This notion of a prize contest for the drafting of such a spiritual guide had been the express idea of King Louis Philippe.[76] The monarch demonstrated once again his profound interest in the most minute detail concerning the slavery question. The government as a whole had endorsed the recommendation of the Rémusat report and finally produced a concrete project for moralizing blacks through religion.[77]

Besides these practical preparatory and ameliorative moves, the government was also making contingency plans of a much graver nature. Early feedback obtained by the abolitionists concerning the government's intentions seemed encouraging for the anti-slavery cause. Isambert wrote to John Scoble, Secretary of the British and Foreign Anti-Slavery Society in London, that he had spoken to Passy, still a member of the Cabinet, about the administration's plans. Isambert reported that the primary impediment to emancipation rested in the chambers' hesitancy to "vote a large subsidy of 120–150 million" francs for an indemnity when the French colonies remained in "such a precarious [economic] condition." Then too, the sentiment still prevailed among officialdom that freed blacks would not work, and would even rapidly revolt against their former masters, this latter point being "the personal feeling of the King of the French." Nevertheless, Passy informed Isambert that "far from combating the conclusions of

[76] Ibid., Corr. Gén. 191, Minister to Governors, Dec. 24, 1839; Gén. 187 (1450), draft of an ordonnance for ameliorations dated Nov. 6, 1839.
[77] Ibid., Corr. Gén. 192, Minister of the Navy and Colonies to Minister of Justice and Ecclesiastical Affairs, Nov. 22, 1839.

the Report of Mr. Tocqueville, the Cabinet would support them."
There would be no formal, British-type apprenticeship, but the government would take over the policing of the slaves, the masters retaining
no power over them.[78] Although some reservations still existed among
the governing elite, especially on the part of the King, the abolitionists
had reason to believe that the French government was prepared to
adopt the slave liberation process outlined in the Tocqueville report.

French colonial office documents confirm this inclination toward
emancipation in government circles during the autumn of 1839 and
the beginning of 1840. The colonial department noted that the delegates had informed their office that the planters would accept emancipation if they were guaranteed an indemnity and maintenance of
work – perhaps the government did not realize, however, the extent
to which such a claim was part and parcel of the colonial delegates'
tactic of demanding what they deemed impossible to achieve. Moreover, the colonial councils had proclaimed their preference for general
rather than progressive or partial emancipation. Furthermore, the
government wished to put an end to the debates in the Chamber of
Deputies that had occurred for some years now over this issue. Therefore, colonial department officials mused that, if the lower house were
to adopt the Tocqueville report recommendations in its 1840 session,
"there is no reason for the government not to enter spontaneously
into the paths traced therein and that lead to the social transformation
that England has just concluded in its colonies." During the debate on
Tocqueville's recommendations in the chambers, the government
would "declare that it adheres to the conclusions of this report and
that it is undertaking dispositions to present in the 1841 session a
draft bill destined to cease slavery in our colonies." In conjuncture
with this measure the government would try to alter the import taxes
on cane sugar as much as possible in favor of the colonies. More
important still, the Director of the Colonies expressed the conviction
that "to try to bring about emancipation with the cooperation of the
colonial councils would be to try the impossible; their cooperation
could never be obtained." Thus, he suggested to the minister that the
colonial councils be abolished and replaced with general councils on

---

[78] Bodleian Library, Oxford, Rhodes House Anti-Slavery Papers (hereafter referred to as
Rhodes House Anti-Slavery Papers), MS Brit. Emp. S22, G103, Isambert to Scoble, Nov.
8, 1839.

the departmental model that had no control over local budgets. In their place, the colonies would be offered deputies in the French lower house. In all respects there would be "a total assimilation of the colonies." In the meantime, special councils would be formed, composed of the governor and other high administrators in each colony, to elaborate concrete suggestions on how emancipation could be implemented.[79] In the summer of 1839 the French parliament had already passed a law controlling the amount of secret funds colonial councils could employ to influence public opinion, limiting in effect the prerogatives of these councils.[80] Paris now contemplated their outright elimination. The French colonial office was proposing nothing less than a revolution in colonial–metropolitan relations. The administrative structure put in place in 1833 and the institution of slavery would both be overturned if the colonial department's plans were implemented.

When Saint-Hilaire presented these recommendations to navy-colonial minister Duperré in early 1840, he was told to wait with restructuring of any kind until after the Chamber of Deputies debate on the Tocqueville report actually took place. This suggests that the minister, aware of the discussions within the Council of Ministers and the attitude of the King, was more wary by this time than his subordinates in the colonial office about the wisdom of implementing wide-ranging reforms unless forced to do so by the chambers. Still, in two separate meetings of November 15 and December 16, 1839, the Council of Ministers had debated and approved the principle of accepting the points made by the Tocqueville report. In mid-December the Cabinet had resolved upon the minister proposing the course of action approved in its November and December meetings when the lower chamber opened debate on the Tocqueville recommendations in its 1840 session; Duperré would commit himself to presenting a law in the 1841 session based upon the conclusions of the Tocqueville report. It would encompass four basic points: "general and simultaneous emancipation," the payment of an indemnity to the slave owners, the gradual reimbursement of this indemnity from slave salaries, and the maintenance of work by blacks under government supervision. The French government would not relinquish its responsibilities to either

---

[79] ANCAOM, Gén. 171 (1376), note dated Nov. 5/Dec. 16, 1839; note for the minister, Jan. 16/18, 1840.

[80] Ibid., Gén. 271 (1853), law of Aug. 3, 1839.

the *colons* or slaves, for "France wishes to work to make civilized societies in its colonies and not hordes of savages."[81] At the end of 1839 the French government was prepared to accept the ideas of the Tocqueville commission, free the slaves from their masters, and itself assume the role of overseeing the newly liberated blacks. Legislative opposition to disbursing large sums for an indemnity could be overcome by recuperating these outlays slowly from the salaries of the ex-slaves. The colonies would receive indemnity, security, and labor. The abolitionists' wishes would be fulfilled and the slaves liberated. A French Cabinet containing an important abolitionist, Passy, had finally decided to act on freeing the colonial slaves.

Over the previous two and a half years the abolitionists had improved considerably their parliamentary strategies. They had progressed from merely interpellating ministers to submitting actual proposals for slave liberation. Anti-slavery pressure in the Chamber of Deputies led to the calling of parliamentary commissions in 1838 and 1839, the first one formed against the wishes of the administration. The taking into consideration of both abolitionist motions also demonstrated support for the anti-slavery cause within the lower house of the legislature, though public opinion in general – as witnessed by the dormancy of the departmental general councils – remained tepid at best to the abolitionist appeal. Nevertheless, the reports issued by the two parliamentary commissions and other ponderables shook the government out of the period of torpor that had seen it regress on the slavery question in 1837 to the point where it had even withdrawn from consideration the gradualist emancipation approach of the freeing of slave children along with the granting of self-redemption. If in early 1839 the government hoped to stymie abolitionist advances simply by proposing the first meaningful ameliorative measures aimed at preparing slaves for freedom, by late 1839 and early 1840 the situation had changed. The government, containing the determined abolitionist Passy, now felt vulnerable to parliamentary pressures to the point where it seemed prepared to accept the Tocqueville commission recommendation of indemnifying the *colons*, freeing the slaves, placing them under government tutelage, and obliging them to repay the

---

[81] Ibid., Gén. 171 (1376), note dated Nov. 5/Dec. 16, 1839; note for the minister, Jan. 16/18, 1840.

administration for their liberty. While such an arrangement was still tentative, there appeared to be a real possibility that French colonial slaves would be emancipated in the early 1840s. The influential French abolitionist Passy, serving within the Cabinet and working behind the scenes within the corridors of power, had almost certainly played a key role in weakening government opposition to emancipation.

Still, there were certain disquieting signs also present at the end of the 1830s. The *colons*, for one thing, remained as adamantly opposed as ever to any settlement of the slavery question. The navy-colonial ministers and the King, if not their subordinates in the colonial department, remained attuned and sympathetic to colonial demands. For another, the abolitionists themselves continued to demonstrate lack of unity and steadfastness in their anti-slavery campaign. In 1838 Passy introduced a gradualist emancipation proposal in the legislature, but an abolitionist-dominated parliamentary commission, including Passy himself, rejected the original proposal for one enunciated by the more moderate abolitionist Rémusat in which emphasis was placed on preparation for an eventual emancipation. Then, in 1839, when Passy had entered the Cabinet, the abolitionist Tracy reintroduced under his own name the Passy proposal, rather than recommendations of the Rémusat commission. This time, the abolitionist-dominated legislative commission rejected the Passy–Tracy plan and promoted one put forth by its reporter Tocqueville in favor of emancipation in the near future with the government adopting a mediative role between master and slave. All of these moves indicate the extent to which individuals, rather than mutually agreed upon programs, dominated the French abolitionist scene. Throughout the July Monarchy members of the French abolitionist society would hesitate and waver in their own positions on slavery, and never define a firm and decided position on the emancipation issue until the very eve of the Revolution of 1848. The best hope of abolitionists impacting upon Orleanist policy remained in the personal action of specific individuals, such as Passy, within Cabinet corridors. Passy's presence in the Council of Ministers, and the conclusion of British slave liberation, had apparently swayed the government, though, in late 1839 and early 1840. At no time under the July Monarchy would France come closer to legislating the elimination of slavery. It appeared that only the reticence of the King could delay the process.

François Isambert
(Cliché Bibliothèque nationale de France, Paris).

Cyrille Bissette
(Cliché Bibliothèque nationale de France, Paris).

Victor Schoelcher
(Cliché Bibliothèque nationale de France, Paris).

Maître ... moi pouvoir plus travailler ti canne! ... pendant que ti français manger li sucre de li Betterave, moi avoir engraissi, moi pouvoir plus bougis de tout

"News": "Master ... me can no more work di cane ... while di French eat beet sugar, me got fat, me no more can move" (pro-slavery propaganda by Honoré Daumier) (Cliché Bibliothèque nationale de France, Paris).

Pauvre Négresse! qui languis dans la captivité & pleures sur ton Enfant malade, quoique personne ne te voie, Dieu te voit; quoique personne n'ait pitié de tes peines, Dieu a pitié de toi. élève ta voix, ô femme malheureuse et délaissée! Appelle ton Dieu du milieu de tes chaines, car très certainement il t'entendra.

Anti-slavery propaganda: "Poor Negress! You who languish in captivity and weep over your sick child, though no one sees you, God sees you; though no one pities your suffering, God pities you. Raise up your voice, unfortunate and abandoned woman! Amid your chains, call upon your God, for He most certainly will hear you" (Cliché Bibliothèque nationale de France, Paris).

Duc de Broglie
(Cliché Bibliothèque nationale de France, Paris).

Freeing the slaves in the island of Réunion, December 20, 1848: "Let me engrave upon your hearts our motto: God, France, and Work!" (Sandra Garriga, Commissar of the Republic) (Cliché Bibliothèque nationale de France, Paris).

6

STALEMATE
AND REGRESSION

In early 1840 the French government undertook several initiatives that seemed to support its intention to advance toward emancipation. On January 5, 1840, it issued an ordonnance regulating the expenditure of the 650,000 francs in ameliorative funds allotted to the navy-colonial budget by the legislature in 1839. This decree implemented the July Monarchy's first substantial preparatory measures for slaves by providing for the building of chapels and the sending of additional priests.[1] A month earlier the Minister of Justice and Ecclesiastical Affairs, Jean Baptiste Teste, himself a moderate member of the French abolition society, had sent out a letter to the bishops and archbishops of France requesting that more priests be recruited for colonial service as a prerequisite for slave liberation. This action in turn elicited an impassioned pastoral missive by Archbishop de Bonald of Lyon, appealing for ecclesiastics to volunteer to evangelize colonial blacks and transform them into Christians. These developments gave the impression that the Catholic Church, following the Pope's encouragement in 1839, might finally become more actively involved in the abolition question.

The government took other steps to prepare the colonies for the transformation from a slave-based to a liberal economy. On April 10, 1840, the navy-colonial minister introduced into the Chamber of Peers – less favorable to emancipation than the lower house – legislation lifting the ban on the legal expropriation of indebted colonial property in the three French Caribbean colonies that had been granted

---

[1] ANCAOM, Gén. 187 (1450), Minister of the Navy and Colonies, Report to the King, January 5, 1840.

these exemptions during the Restoration as a means of protecting planters from their creditors. Removing this restriction was now judged essential by most economists to prepare for emancipation by eliminating highly ineffective planters and attracting new capital to the Antilles; colonial spokesmen certainly viewed such a move as a step on the road to slave liberation. Finally, in the spring of 1840 the Cabinet also proposed in the Chamber of Deputies a bill aimed at propping up the colonial sugar industry and improving the economic plight of the colonies.[2] The law of July 4, 1840, in its amended form increased beet sugar taxes more than those on cane sugar, and was viewed as the first move toward the equalization of taxation on the two sugars.[3] In many ways the government seemed to be making the necessary preparations for following through on the measures approved by the Cabinet in November and December 1839 for accepting the slave liberation plan recommended by the Tocqueville report.

Well aware of the administration's inclination toward emancipation because of Passy's role in the Cabinet, the French abolition society reconvened at the very beginning of 1840, just before the opening session of the chambers. Anticipating further debate in the legislature on the implementation of emancipation, the group first discussed the success of abolition in the British colonies, and raised the theoretical question of whether or not an indemnity should be paid to the *colons*. The society concluded almost unanimously that indemnification was not due the planters as a right, because no person could justly claim property over another. Still, it agreed that slave owners should be given compensation "as a measure of justice and equity." Members of the Société française remained distant from the thesis of Bissette and the handful of other radical abolitionists that no indemnity was due the planters. The society also made the strategic decision that, as soon as the lower house met, Laborde would reintroduce the Tracy motion. At the same time the organization would make known its support for the conclusions of the Tocqueville report. Then too, Barrot in the deputies and Broglie in the peers would deposit a petition

---

[2] Société française pour l'abolition de l'esclavage, *No. 17* (Paris: Hingray, 1840), 50, 60–61, 77–9, 86–93.
[3] Boizard and Tardieu, *Historie de la législation des sucres*, 61–3; Louis-Joseph, "La monarchie," 353.

signed by all nonlegislative members of the society – an avowal that the society was still unable to garner petition signatures outside its own midst. This document would request emancipation on the basis of religious and humanitarian principles, but it would also contain an admonition that the spirit of liberty emanating from British colonies would cause a "terrible catastrophe" in French possessions if moves toward slave liberation were not taken.[4] All of these measures indicate that the Société française intended to provoke the government to act quickly on the slavery issue. Early in the parliamentary session, on January 16, 1840, Laborde, supported by other society members, seized the occasion to request the reconsideration of the question. The lower house immediately voted to do so, and put the item on the legislative calendar for the spring.[5]

In awaiting the parliamentary debate, the Société française pour l'abolition de l'esclavage publicized its efforts to renew ties with British abolitionism. The formation of the British and Foreign Anti-Slavery Society in 1839 marked a refocusing of British attempts to press for international suppression of slavery and the slave trade once apprenticeship had ended and British colonial blacks had achieved full freedom.[6] In early February 1840 three British anti-slavery leaders, Scoble, William Alexander, and James Whitehorne, arrived in Paris "to tighten the bonds that existed already between the two societies." In two successive meetings held in the quaestor chambers of the lower house, the two formations exchanged greetings and the British provided their French colleagues with documentation requested by Isambert on the success of British emancipation. The second of these meetings took the form of a banquet in honor of the English on February 1, at which twenty-one French legislators and thirteen other members of the society attended. After toasts and speeches by both sides, Lamartine caught the attention of the press by his praise for "the generous efforts of England," along with his prediction that "within three years there will be no longer a single slave" in French possessions. Lamartine also stood out for his insistence that masters be given an indemnity, and that slaves be prepared for freedom and work under an apprenticeship system controlled by the government,

---

[4] *L'Espérance* (Paris), Jan. 4, 1840.
[5] *Le Moniteur universel*, Jan. 17, 1840.
[6] Temperley, *British Antislavery*, 62–6; Turley, *Culture of English Antislavery*, 77–8.

terms similar to the package that Tocqueville had proposed. This brought a rejoinder from Scoble that apprenticeship of any kind must be avoided and that the French government should not pick up and wield the whip abandoned by the planters. The visit of the British delegation ended with a promise by the French to attend an international anti-slavery conference in London in June 1840.[7] The British and French groups had renewed their contacts, but divisions remained between the British approach of immediatism and the tendency of most French abolitionists, like Lamartine, to advocate a much more conservative and gradualist means of attaining the eradication of slavery. Immediatists, still only a small fraction of the French anti-slavery movement, had until now exerted little influence within the French abolition society.

At a meeting of the Société française pour l'abolition de l'esclavage on March 18, 1840, Isambert presented a detailed report, no doubt based on his analysis of the documentation brought by the British, on the improved status of British colonial blacks after emancipation.[8] The society was still employing its tactic of citing the British example to try to convince Frenchmen of the feasibility of emancipation. But by this time a new portent of impending difficulties for abolitionism had already emerged upon the French political scene. The government headed by Marshal Soult, in which Passy had played an active role, fell in February 1840. It was replaced on March 1 by one presided over by Thiers, with Admiral Albin Reine Roussin holding the navy-colonial portfolio. The only abolitionist in the new council of ministers was the very moderate Rémusat, serving as Minister of the Interior. As so often occurred with Cabinet changes in July Monarchy France, these circumstances posed a whole new set of imponderables for French anti-slavery, so dependent upon functioning within government channels. In a meeting of the abolition society on April 15, its members attempted to fathom the implications of the new appointments. The introduction of the bill on forced expropriations of indebted colonial property seemed to suggest impending slave liberation.

---

[7] *Le Temps*, Feb. 12, 1840; *Le Courrier français*, Feb. 13, 1840; No. 17, 3–9; Société française pour l'abolition de l'esclavage, No. 16. *Banquet offert à la députation de la Société centrale britannique pour l'abolition universelle de l'esclavage, 10 février 1840* (Paris: Hingray, 1840), 2–13.

[8] *Le Courrier français*, March 20, 1840; *Le Temps*, March 21, 1840.

The abolitionists were also encouraged by rumors that the new administration would appoint a special commission on the slavery question. The general assumption was that this commission would "finally occupy itself with the preparation of a draft law for the next session" on emancipation.[9] These indications, combined with the knowledge that the Soult Cabinet had seemed prepared to implement the recommendations of the Tocqueville report, provided a source of optimism within the French abolitionist community.

Already at the beginning of 1840, however, there was other more disquieting evidence as to what the government might do. Isambert made a revealing assessment of the situation in a letter that he addressed to J. H. Tredgold, secretary of the British and Foreign Anti-Slavery Society with which French abolitionist leaders now opened a regular correspondence. According to Isambert, who now had imme-diatist sentiments and who was probably kept informed by Passy, "the present ministers are not opposed to us; but the King, who has so much influence with the government, is anxious that the question should be adjourned." Isambert understood that in the forthcoming chamber debates the Cabinet would not defend slavery, but that "an indefinite adjournment" of emancipation "will be rigorously main-tained." He also prophesied that "if we are beaten here, I would not answer for it but that emancipation may be postponed for 8 or 10 years." Because Isambert believed that King Louis Philippe could be swayed by British pressure, though, he suggested that it might be wise "to announce in all the newspapers under your influence that the only obstacle to the emancipation of the Blacks is the will of the King of the French."[10] The leader of the French abolition society clearly believed the King to be the chief impediment to slave liberation. These pes-simistic predictions, moreover, were made even before the Cabinet change removed Passy from his portfolio and brought a less sympa-thetic set of ministers to power. It is noteworthy also that from this time to the end of the July Monarchy no radical abolitionist like Passy or Tracy ever obtained a ministerial appointment – which required the sanction of the monarch. Because French abolitionism depended so much on influencing Cabinet decisions, this augured poorly for the

---

[9] Ibid., April 16, 1840.
[10] Rhodes House Anti-Slavery Papers, G103, Isambert to Tredgold, Jan. 18, 1840.

future success of the anti-slavery movement. From 1840 on the government could and did stymie French abolitionism by refusing access to the corridors of power of any of its more radical elements.

Indications of what the future held came when the French king accorded an interview to a delegation of three British abolitionists on May 8, 1840, after the Thiers administration had been formed. At this time Louis Philippe spoke of the need for "a prompt amelioration" in the condition of the slaves and the necessity of "an intermediary stage" to prepare them for freedom.[11] Quite revealingly, the King made no mention of a forthcoming government proposal for emancipation, and his reference to ameliorations suggested that the policy of French governments since the mid-1830s would remain intact. Isambert, unknowingly, had been correct in his predictions. Emancipation would be postponed "8 to 10 years," and would only occur when the Revolution of 1848 overthrew the July Monarchy of King Louis Philippe.

Still, the abolitionists hoped to prod once again the administration into action by raising the question in the legislature. The government, to the contrary, aimed to retain its initiative on the slavery question and "proceed with calm and prudence," just as the British colonial office had done between 1823 and the early 1830s.[12] No formal debate on the slavery issue had begun when the government introduced its new sugar bill in the lower house on May 5, 1840. In the course of the debates that followed Thiers mentioned that emancipation was "a grave measure which must be taken with prudence." When Tocqueville intervened on May 13 to request further explanations from the prime minister, Thiers clarified his administration's new policy on the slavery question. His Cabinet, he pointed out, had given the matter serious consideration and debate before deciding to name a government "commission composed of several members of the two chambers to examine this grave subject and prepare a work which will ultimately be submitted to the deliberations of the two chambers."[13] By forming a government-appointed commission, rather than permitting the chamber of deputies to create another legislative investigative body to examine the matter, Thiers had effectively removed the issue from parliamentary purview and undercut abolitionist plans

[11] No. 17, 79–81.
[12] ANCAOM, Gén. 171 (1376), note by Saint-Hilaire, Jan. 6, 1840.
[13] *Le Moniteur universel*, May 9, 14, 1840.

to discuss the Tracy and Rémusat proposals in the lower house. He had also resorted to the typical ploy of tabling an issue by referring it once again to a committee. Thiers's actions corresponded exactly to what Isambert had predicted concerning the King's desire to "adjourn indefinitely" the emancipation question.

Although the government had some difficulty recruiting participants for the new commission, a royal ordonnance of May 25, 1840, officially formed the body. When ultimately constituted, it drew seven deputies from the elective lower house: Passy, Sade, Tracy, Tocqueville, André Elysée Reynard, François Bignon, and Jacques Henri Wustemberg. From the Chamber of Peers came Broglie, the marquis Charles Louis Gaston d'Audiffret, and Pellegrin Louis Edouard Rossi. Admiral Mackau and Director of the Colonies Saint-Hilaire were added on from the administration. Mestro was appointed secretary, acting as a mere scribe who did not participate directly in the discussions. The government had attempted to represent diverse interests on the commission. There were six abolitionists: the first four mentioned deputies, plus Rossi and Broglie. They covered the entire spectrum of French anti-slavery, from the radical Passy to the very moderate Broglie. Port city interests, with their assumed procolonial tendencies, were well represented with Reynard from Marseille, Bignon from Nantes, and Wustemberg from Bordeaux. Thus, colonial sympathizers, including navy-colonial officials and d'Audiffret, also numbered six, a balance which the government had undoubtedly established to assure no dominance by abolitionists as had occurred in previous parliamentary commissions. Broglie was named president.[14] Almost immediately the commission came to be known as the Broglie commission.

Initial abolitionist reaction to the formation of a special commission was favorable, especially when Broglie, still president of the abolition society, was appointed to head it. The general assumption in abolitionist circles was that the Broglie commission would simply build upon the Tocqueville commission report and concentrate upon drawing up an emancipation act for presentation during the next parliamentary session.[15] However, the report that minister Roussin

---

[14] ANCAOM, Gén. 171 (1379), Report to the King, May 26, 1840; *No. 17, 96.*
[15] *Le Semeur*, June 10, 1840; *L'Espérance*, August 29, 1840. Documents show that Broglie remained president of the abolition society at least until 1842. There is no evidence to

submitted to the King – and also made public – on the formation of the commission pointedly indicated that the task of the body would be to look into "affairs relative to slavery" and "the political constitution of the colonies" in general.[16] Because such a mandate differed significantly from just drafting an emancipation law, Roger du Loiret of the abolitionist society requested explanations from the minister during the discussion of the navy-colonial budget in the Chamber of Deputies. As Roger pointed out, after having originally applauded the formation of the commission, he and his colleagues had become concerned about the "general" and "vague" instructions given its members. Abolitionists had not expected the commission to become involved in a simple discussion of slavery and of the legislation of 1833 governing the colonies. More perturbing still was the fact that Roussin's report negated the intentions of the previous Cabinet and seemed, as Roger declared, "to have been calculated to avoid the expression or even the thought of the abolition of slavery." Roussin frankly replied that the objective of the commission was to study the slavery question "because slavery is a fact, [and] emancipation is not yet a fact." Moreover, the minister insisted, slavery must be thoroughly examined with "great circumspection" as an integral part of the entire political and social structure of the colonies.[17]

Once aware of the government's real intentions, disappointment was manifest in abolitionist circles. Isambert accurately analyzed the new Cabinet's position in a letter submitted to the anti-slavery *Le Siècle*. According to the animator of the Société française, the remarks uttered by the new administration indicated that it "did not wish to proceed rapidly towards emancipation."[18] Preoccupied with the beginning of the Egyptian crisis of 1840 that would soon lead to a serious war threat for France from Great Britain supported by the rest of Europe, the King, with the accord of the Thiers government, had undoubtedly decided to seize the opportunity and place the emancipation question on the back burner.[19] Thiers, generally uninterested in

substantiate the claim of one author that Lamartine assumed the presidency in 1840 (Alexandre-Debray, *Victor Schoelcher*, 104).

[16] ANCAOM, Gén. 171 (1379), Report to the King, May 26, 1840.

[17] *Le Moniteur universel*, June 8–9, 1840.

[18] *Le Siècle*, May 26, 1840.

[19] For background on the Egyptian or Eastern crisis, see M. S. Anderson, *The Eastern Question, 1774–1923* (London: Macmillan, 1966).

the colonial situation outside Algeria – whose conquest he steadily supported because of this territory's trade connections with his home city of Marseille – was obviously allowing the King more of a free hand with slavery policy than had been the case under the Soult Cabinet in which Passy had been influential.[20] Besides, as a son of Marseille, a city that had important commercial ties with the slave colonies too, Thiers himself probably favored maintaining the social–economic status quo in the plantation colonies. Nevertheless, the King was most likely behind this volte-face in French policy, to which Thiers merely acquiesced. After all, Isambert had surmised that there would be "an indefinite adjournment" of the emancipation question already in January 1840, nearly two months before Thiers assumed office.

The intention to postpone slave liberation became increasingly evident as the public came to realize the scope of the Broglie commission's task and the slowness of its proceedings. The Broglie commission met only five times in 1840, between June 4 and 18. It agreed that the moment had come to remove the uncertainty weighing upon French colonies by determining how and when slave liberation should take place. It insisted that any emancipation operation must be accompanied by a "reasonable, sufficient indemnity" and by "an intermediary regime between slavery and liberty" in which slaves would be prepared morally and religiously for freedom. In both of these latter points the commission immediately distanced itself from radical abolitionism and associated itself with the cautious approach of the government. The commission also decided that it did not as yet possess adequate information on which to base a recommendation, so Broglie requested all possible documentation from the navy-colonial department. Then too, the body agreed with the government that it could not discuss emancipation without investigating at the same time the entire colonial administrative and economic structure. The commission concluded that a series of questions on three possible modes of emancipation should be submitted to the colonial governors for their opinions: (1) the Tracy proposal of partial and progressive emancipation through *rachat* and the freeing of newborn slaves, (2) the Tocqueville system of simultaneous emancipation with the state

[20] On Their's position on the colonies, see J. P. T. Bury and R. P. Tombs, *Thiers, 1797–1877: A Political Life* (London: Allen & Unwin, 1986), 89, 268. The Thiers papers, held by the French Bibliothèque Nationale, afford no insight into his ideas on slavery.

serving as tutor to the slaves for an indeterminate period, and (3) the English procedure of simultaneous emancipation followed by apprenticeship.[21] The Broglie commission would not just work up an emancipation proposal for presentation to the chambers in 1841, as the previous government had been prepared to do in late 1839. The new entity was committed to drawing up a plan for eventually freeing the slaves, but its primary function was to carry out a much more extensive examination of the entire colonial question than the two parliamentary commissions that had preceded it. Such a thorough approach would necessarily take time. After making its requests to the minister, the Broglie commission proceeded to adjourn until the end of the year, for most of its participants were members of the two houses that were themselves entering the intersession period. Besides, it could not hope to receive replies from the colonial governors until the end of the year. The very nature of the commission's inquiry dictated the postponement of the entire process for at least a year.

The requests and recommendations of the Broglie Commission went to the navy-colonial department for consideration in the late spring of 1840. The commission had suggested that its questions be put only to the governors, because its abolitionist members were wary of the obstructionist tactics of the colonial councils and wished to avoid airing any emancipation project before them again. Minister Roussin concluded that the governors should examine the Broglie commission recommendations with the assistance of the special councils that the Soult government had envisaged creating in 1839. However, the navy-colonial office went beyond simply creating these new bodies. Although it was as aware as the abolitionists of the inflexibility of the colonial councils on any measure altering the status quo, it decided that the colonial councils should be given a chance to redeem themselves. Thus, it concluded that the Broglie commission's questions should be submitted to the governors, special councils, and colonial councils, though it suggested that the governors could call new elections for the latter if necessary to make them more amenable. It is

---

[21] ANCAOM, Gén. 171 (1378), Broglie to Minister, June 19, 1840; Ministère de la Marine et des Colonies, *Commission instituée par décision royale du 26 mai 1840 pour l'examen des questions relatives à l'esclavage et à la constitution politiques des colonies* (2 vols.; Paris: Imprimerie Royale 1840–1843) (henceforth referred to as Broglie Commission, Minutes or Report), vol. 2, part 1, pp. 1–112.

interesting to note also that before Roussin took the Broglie proposals, rewritten by Saint-Hilaire, before the Cabinet for approval, he
struck out a phrase by the Director of the Colonies affirming that the
"formal intention of [the] government is to occupy itself as much as
possible with the abolition of slavery."[22] Quite clearly, this was no
longer the case. The contrast between the position of the new Cabinet
and that of its predecessor in late 1839 on the emancipation question
is manifest. The July Monarchy was backing away from any commitment to slave liberation whatsoever. The new government evidently
was not displeased with a more complicated process of consultation
that would probably require a second year, putting off to 1842 at the
earliest any substantive discussion of the slavery issue within the
Broglie commission. The task of the Broglie commission was not to
implement emancipation as the abolitionists had hoped, but to study
the question ad infinitum.

In early 1840, Isambert had displayed considerable perspicacity in
evaluating his country's stance on emancipation. Over the summer,
though, he and his colleagues changed their tone somewhat, at least in
public statements. When Isambert led a small French delegation to the
World Anti-Slavery Convention organized by the British in London in
late June, he informed his audience that France would probably opt
for the Tocqueville system of "complete and mass emancipation."[23]
Similarly, the French abolition society sent a letter to London, signed
by de Laborde and Laisné de Villevêque, assuring the British of "the
favourable progress that public opinion is making in France toward
the prompt abolition of slavery."[24] These statements reflect a wavering of French abolitionist opinion, patriotic attempts to shield French
honor when dealing with the British, or efforts to force the French
government's hand through public announcements. It is noteworthy,
though, that Isambert had great difficulty putting together a delegation to accompany him to England. Guizot did embellish his abolitionist blazon by attending the convention unofficially as French
ambassador to London.[25] Many French abolitionists, however, might

---

[22] ANCAOM, Gén. 171 (1378), Report to the Council of Ministers, June 23, 1840; Gén.
184 (1441), Minister to Governors, July 18, 1840.
[23] *British and Foreign Anti-Slavery Reporter* (London), July 1, 1840; *Le Siècle*, June 30, 1840.
[24] *British and Foreign Anti-Slavery Reporter*, July 15, 1840.
[25] See Jennings, *French Response*, 99–100.

have had an inkling of the storm that would soon arise between France and Britain over the Egyptian question, and have chosen not to associate themselves too closely with their British brethren at this time.

In the early autumn of 1840, Bissette and Isambert again found some reason for optimism when communicating with the British. In the late 1830s Bissette had been eclipsed as a leading spokesman for French anti-slavery when he was obliged to interrupt the regular publication of his *Revue des colonies* and subsequently issue it only sporadically. Even when his periodical did reappear, Bissette often seemed to be distant from mainstream abolitionism and increasingly preoccupied with his personal pet peeves with the *colons*. The determined black abolitionist would make a comeback, however, as of the mid-1840s when immediatism began to emerge as a viable alternative to gradualism in France. Already in 1840, though, Bissette made an attempt to overcome his financial difficulties and continue his publications by appealing to the new British abolitionist formation. He began making a series of obsequious and demeaning requests for sums large and small from the British. In the process he obtained relatively little assistance, gradually alienated his benefactors, and ultimately gave credence to those planters who claimed French anti-slavery to be in the pay of the British. In part of his correspondence with the British and Foreign Anti-Slavery Society in September 1840, Bissette contended "that the French government is thinking seriously of the abolition of slavery"; he added that it was preparing a plan to submit to the chambers when they opened in 1841.[26] Perhaps Bissette was exaggerating French abolitionist progress to please the British, or he was just repeating the optimistic predictions circulating in anti-slavery circles about the Broglie commission's intentions of rapidly producing an emancipation bill. Bissette might also have been trying to extract funding from the British by suggesting that the time was ripe to sponsor French abolitionists like himself.

More significant is the mixed message that Isambert sent the British in the autumn of 1840. He noted that the French government was increasing the number of gendarmes sent to the tropical colonies and

---

[26] Rhodes House Anti-Slavery Papers, C13/113, Bissette to Scoble, Sept. 28, 1840; Jennings, "Bissette," 55.

that the war minister, General Amédée Louis Despans Cubières, had remarked that this measure was "to prepare the surveillance which the abolition of slavery shall compel." While such a statement in itself might seem promising, Isambert avowed that he did not know when or whether the Broglie commission would resume its sittings. He especially bemoaned the breakdown of the Anglo-French entente and the fact that, with "national opinion ... so sensibly wounded ... it is impossible now for any French abolitionist to invoke the authority of the example of Great Britain in favour of emancipation."[27] The entente that had marked British–French relations in the 1830s and that had permitted abolitionists on the two sides of the Channel to fraternize openly had broken down entirely in July 1840 over French support for Mohamet Ali of Egypt. By the summer French newspapers were replete with bellicose phrases. Such developments could have only negative repercussions on Franco–British anti-slavery cooperation. French faith in the British example of slave liberation would be further undermined in early 1842 when another dispute, this time over slave trade repression methods, compounded ill relations between the French and British. French abolitionists had always cited the success of British emancipation as an example worthy of imitation. An important element in the French abolitionist argument against servitude was weakened considerably by growing Anglophobia in France. The close association between French and British anti-slavery was also weakening French abolitionism under these circumstances. Equally disquieting was the fact that the French government became so preoccupied with the diplomatic arena that the slavery question, never high on its agenda, slipped inexorably down its list of priorities. In the early 1840s the French government had every reason to put the slavery issue on hold.

French abolitionism, though, did not give up hope, at least not yet. The beginning of 1841 and the opening of the legislative session coincided with renewed activity in both the French abolition society and the Broglie commission. The Société française pour l'abolition de

---

[27] Rhodes House Anti-Slavery Papers, G103, Isambert to Tredgold, Oct. 28, 1840. Paris sent its first contingents of gendarmes to Guiana and Bourbon, 41 and 100, respectively, as of 1841. Although there are no statistics for Guadeloupe and Martinique, it can be assumed that these islands received as many gendarmes as Bourbon (ANCAOM, Corr. Gén., S.G. Guyane 140; Corr. Gén. S.G. Réunion 131).

l'esclavage concentrated its efforts on two major fronts. First, in its meeting of February 10, it decided to try to influence the discussions within the Broglie commission by submitting to it a resolution in favor of emancipation. Much of the society's sessions of March 24, April 21, and May 5 were devoted to debating this motion, discussions which afford insight into the group's thought at the time.

In its final form the society's motion recommended that there be no indemnity in principle for slave owners, for the possession of one human being by another could not be recognized. Besides, the society held that in the long run free labor would prove more productive than the coerced variety, and hence more advantageous to sugar magnates. Therefore, in the short term, slave holders should be given compensation only to cover their immediate losses. This coincided with earlier feelings within the Société française that slave owners had no rights in principle to an indemnity, but that they should nevertheless be given one as a measure of equity. The most salient section of the society's proposal, however, was a four-point draft law that it hoped the commission would adopt. One of these points was the above-mentioned concept of limited indemnity for slave owners. The most important one, though, was the call for the abolition of slavery in the near future, with emancipation being implemented six months after the promulgation of the decree. A third item was the recommendation that regulations be introduced to repress vagabondage after emancipation, while the final one was that measures be taken to assure the moral and religious education of the black population in preparation for their liberation.[28] In some ways, the Société française seemed, in effect, to be advocating the idea of British-style simultaneous emancipation in the near future. Point four of the proposal shows that this was not really immediatism, though, but a thinly veiled gradual approach which entailed general and not progressive or partial methods. The resolution constituted above all an appeal to Broglie commission members to get back on track and to concentrate on the drafting of an emancipation law. At the same time the abolition society was attempting to facilitate the great transformation by eliminating the need for a large indemnity, the leading impediment to freeing the slaves. In the process the society was also expressing disappointment with a government

[28] Société française pour l'abolition de l'esclavage, *No. 19* (Paris: Hingray, 1842), 58–65.

that constantly postponed the date for introducing legislation eliminating bondage.

The French abolition society also concentrated on another tactic in
early 1841 to advance the anti-slavery cause. It hoped to raise up what
Lamartine referred to as "holy anger and indignation" by stressing
abject cases of slave abuse still occurring in the French colonies despite
supposedly ameliorative measures. The abolitionists devoted their
entire meeting of February 22 to discussing their strategy for interpellating the government along these lines. One of the society's members,
baron Bertrand Théobald Joseph Lacrosse, was charged with questioning the navy-colonial minister about Lucie, a slave in Guadeloupe
who had been sequestered in a frightful dungeon for twenty-two
months. In the lower house in early March, he put the question to the
new minister, Duperré, once again.[29] Indeed, the Thiers government
had fallen over the Egyptian crisis in October 1840, lessening French
differences with Britain and its European allies. The new Cabinet was
headed again by Marshal Soult. In reality, though, it was Guizot,
recalled from his ambassadorship in London to become foreign minister, who acted as effective leader of the government under the Soult
administration and the dominant figure in French politics until the
Revolution of 1848. A sometime abolitionist, albeit a very moderate
one at best, was playing a significant role in the French Council of
Ministers once again.

When Lacrosse intervened on March 5, 1841, in the lower house
to cite the mistreatment of French slaves, Duperré deflected the issue
by promising to investigate the matter and apply current laws preventing such occurrences in the future. Passy, though, seized the occasion to turn parliamentary attention to the Broglie commission. He
did this by unleashing a bitter attack on the Thiers government's
actions toward this body, of which Passy himself was a member.
Passy claimed not only that the Thiers administration had failed to
support the commission properly, but that its navy-colonial minister
had gone against the express wishes of the commission by consulting
the colonial councils after all. Furthermore, Passy charged that the
Thiers administration had paid for a trip by Granier de Cassagnac to
Guadeloupe which Cassagnac had used to denounce the moderate

[29] Ibid., 55–7.

delegate Jabrun and obtain his own election in his place. Rémusat, who had been a member of the Thiers Cabinet, intervened in turn to defend his personal conduct by arguing that none of this had been approved by the Council of Ministers in his presence. This was only a half-truth, for documents show that the issue of sounding out the colonial councils, if not of Cassagnac's trip, had indeed gone before the Cabinet for approval. Still, the net result of this heated debate was to reinforce general belief in the duplicity of Thiers and Roussin, who seemed to have acted on their own concerning the slavery question. Guizot was obliged to take the floor to calm matters by insisting that his own administration took the Broglie commission and its two objectives seriously. He also pledged to act upon the commission's resolutions on emancipation and the political reorganization of the colonies as soon as they were forthcoming.[30] Guizot's intervention kept Passy from resigning from the Broglie commission, and gave the body some credence once again. Nevertheless, the entire episode confirmed that the Thiers government had acted against the wishes of the commission rather than in cooperation with it. Abolitionist hopes that the Broglie commission would speedily resolve the slavery question were evaporating.

By late 1840 the navy-colonial minister had not as yet received the advice of the colonial councils on the three plans circulated by the Broglie commission. As a result, it was decided that the commission would be convoked to discuss only possible changes in the political constitution of the colonies, not the slavery question. It and subcommittees designated by it met only briefly, from December 22, 1840, to May 12, 1841. Most of its deliberations centered around the issue of how the colonies should be represented in France. The commission concluded that the system of delegates should be abolished and replaced with direct colonial representation in the chamber of deputies.[31] The government, however, was hesitant to act along these lines, for it judged such a system difficult to implement as long as servitude existed in the colonies. Moreover, it was loathe to touch upon any aspect of the delicate problem of parliamentary reform in metropolitan France, an issue which the King and his Cabinet wished

---

[30] *Le Moniteur universel*, March 7, 1841; ANCAOM, Gén. 171 (1377), Report for the Council of Ministers, June 3, 1840.
[31] Broglie Commission Minutes, vol. 2, part 2, pp. 1–171.

to avoid above all else in the 1840s, as the regime became ensconced in a posture of immobility in face of growing demands for change.[32] As for the Broglie commission, it was simply marking time in the spring of 1841.

At this moment, though, the government did take some measures to placate the abolitionists and project a semblance of activity on the colonial front. By an ordonnance of April 12, 1841, it finally put into effect the law of August 3, 1839, limiting disbursement by the colonial councils of secret funds to influence the press. In the meantime it was revealed that the colonies had allocated 518,207 francs in secret funds along these lines between 1835 and 1838 alone. The colonial practice of purchasing the press continued, but was rendered more difficult by this legislation.[33] The government also took other moves intended to rein in on the colonies. In June 1841 the administration pushed through parliament a law reducing the taxing prerogatives of the colonial councils, a step that was interpreted as making these colonial legislative bodies more similar to their departmental equivalents in mainland France. Then too, the government ordered the dissolution of the colonial council of Guadeloupe in order to revoke immediately the appointment of the implacable Granier de Cassagnac as delegate. The Guadeloupe legislature duly responded by appointing more moderate figures to represent it in Paris. Finally, in the autumn of 1841, Duperré implemented his promise made to the Chamber of Deputies that spring by outlawing dungeons on plantations and limiting the disciplinary powers of masters.[34] All of these actions, along with Guizot's pledges in the Chamber of Deputies, sent mixed messages to the abolitionists by indicating that the government was still committed to certain preparatory measures anticipating emancipation, even if it was procrastinating in its handling of the Broglie commission.

Immediately after the intervention by Passy that had incriminated the Thiers administration, Isambert had echoed abolitionist disappointment with this same Cabinet. Thiers, he reported to London, had

---

[32] The Collingham book (pp. 289–302, 385–406) affords an excellent discussion of these internal developments.

[33] For more detail on the government's attempts to limit colonial abuses of this kind, see Jennings, "Slavery and Venality," 963.

[34] Rhodes House Anti-Slavery Papers, G103, Isambert to Tredgold, June 22, 1841; *British and Foreign Anti-Slavery Reporter*, June 30, July 28, 1841; *L'Abolitioniste* [sic] *français* (Paris), Jan.–Feb. 1844, pp. 6–9.

been "acting treacherously." It appeared that Thiers "had, with the concurrence of his colleagues and contrary to the wishes of the Count de Rémusat, our worthy and faithful colleague ... indirectly endeavoured to throw obstacles in the way of the [Broglie] commission." Isambert's kind remarks concerning Rémusat show that radical French anti-slavery leaders were still not prepared to admit that moderates within their midst like Rémusat, Broglie, and Guizot could not be counted on to press hard for emancipation when exercising positions of power. Instead, Isambert expressed to the British his confidence that the French abolition society's attack in the chambers on the issue of cruelty to slaves was having good effect on French opinion and was delivering "a final blow" to servitude. He also entertained the hope that the general situation concerning emancipation could improve because "Guizot ... is favourable to us." The secretary of the Société française believed that Guizot would "give a new impulse to the colonial commission presided over by the Duke de Broglie which has done nothing for eight months but ask questions." Guizot, Isambert recounted, had promised to support the commission, and appeared to be the same abolitionist who had spoken up a year earlier at the World Anti-Slavery Convention in London.[35] Guizot's emergence as the head of government appeared momentarily to lift spirits and provide new sources of optimism in French anti-slavery circles.

Others besides Isambert expressed faith in Guizot's abolitionist principles shortly after the latter's ascension to power. Thomas Clarkson, the aging hero of British anti-slavery, addressed a letter to the French foreign minister on January 18, 1841, thanking his administration for having avoided war and imploring him "to use your high influence with the French Cabinet to put an end to slavery." Guizot replied graciously on March 12, informing the British that "to concur in the abolition of slavery in our colonies" would afford him as much "honour and happiness" as preserving the peace. He also raised British hopes by stating: "It is our intention therefore before the end of the present session to present the outline of a law which will lay the

---

[35] Rhodes House Anti-Slavery Papers, G103, Isambert to Tredgold, Feb. 26, March 8, 1841; Ibid., Minutes of the British and Foreign Anti-Slavery Society, March 12, 1841; *British and Foreign Anti-Slavery Reporter*, March 10, 24, 1841.

foundation for this great measure" of emancipation.[36] In exchanging cross-Channel niceties, Guizot was certainly alluding to the law his government would pass in the late spring to reduce the powers of the colonial councils and thus, in a way, prepare the terrain for eventual emancipation. Still, this exchange undoubtedly raised Guizot's abolitionist credit in London. All too soon both French and British anti-slavery activists would come to realize that the erstwhile moderate abolitionist Guizot would prove as tentative as other previous Cabinet leaders in advancing anti-slavery aims.

As late as mid-May 1841 Isambert expressed his satisfaction with the laws passed by the Soult–Guizot government limiting colonial powers. French abolitionist expectations were strong, he reported to his British colleagues, that "the present Cabinet will present to the chamber, at their next session, the law of emancipation; and Mr. Guizot, it is hoped, will not fail in the duty imposed upon him."[37] Perhaps such buoyancy reflected yet another attempt by Isambert to emphasize his society's effectiveness, please his British correspondents, or convince them to apply pressure on the French administration. Indeed, bursts of patriotic optimism seemed to be a trait marking French anti-slavery correspondents with the British, for Schoelcher also waxed eloquent about "the holy cause of slaves" making rapid progress in his homeland when writing to Thomas Clarkson in 1843.[38] Interestingly enough, *Le Semeur* had also interpreted Duperré's introduction of the law diminishing the colonial council's taxing power as indicative of the administration's intention to issue an emancipation bill in the next parliamentary session.[39] In all probability, however, this represented yet another moment of optimism in French anti-slavery ranks faced with a government that was emitting a variety of messages on the slavery front.

There were other causes for encouragement among French abolitionists in 1841. In June the Société française pour l'abolition de l'esclavage received the visit of two British abolitionist dignitaries,

---

[36] Rhodes House Anti-Slavery Papers, Minute Books, Clarkson to Guizot, Jan. 18, 1841; Guizot to Clarkson, March 12, 1841.

[37] Ibid., G103, Isambert to Tredgold, May 18, 1841; *British and Foreign Anti-Slavery Reporter*, June 2, 1841.

[38] Nelly Schmidt, ed., *La correspondance de Victor Schoelcher* (Paris: Maisonneuve et Larose, 1995), 339.

[39] *Le Semeur*, July 7, 1841.

Joseph and Josiah Forster, bringing a resolution requesting France to adopt "complete and unconditional emancipation."[40] Then too, in the spring *L'Espérance*, a Protestant biweekly founded in 1839, became a radical abolitionist organ. It began to advocate the British example and to call upon Frenchmen to write, petition, and stir up public opinion against slavery.[41] For the time being such an appeal had little effect, but it was a precursor of a development that would take firmer root amidst French abolitionist forces by the mid-1840s. Not to be outdone by a Protestant newspaper, in late 1841 *L'Univers* (Paris), the noted Catholic daily soon to be taken over by Louis Veuillot, unleashed a sharp attack against slavery and those parties that defended it. This organ too exclaimed that "it is no longer possible to adjourn" anti-slavery legislation.[42] Finally, Schoelcher made his entrance as an important player on the French anti-slavery scene in 1841 when excerpts from his forthcoming book, *Des colonies françaises: Abolition immédiate de l'esclavage*, began appearing in the liberal French press.[43] Already in 1840 Schoelcher had published a book that had been refused the Grégoire prize by the French abolition society, *Abolition de l'esclavage: Examen critique du préjugé contre la couleur des Africains et des sangs-mêlés*. It had marked Schoelcher's emergence as an immediatist, for it had called emphatically for rapid emancipation. However, it had not received much publicity, apart from a laudatory review by Bissette, later Schoelcher's bitter enemy.[44] Now, in the autumn of 1841, shortly after his return from a fact-finding mission to the West Indies that had confirmed his faith in immediatism,[45] Schoelcher's excerpts fit in perfectly with the tactic adopted by the abolition society of highlighting the continued horrors of slavery. As *Le Siècle* remarked, his piece was an appeal against the inhumanity of slavery and a striking reply to those who wished to postpone emancipation.[46] With the appearance of *Des colonies françaises*, Schoelcher

[40] *British and Foreign Anti-Slavery Reporter*, June 30, 1841.
[41] March 8, 1841.
[42] Nov. 30, Dec. 4, 1841.
[43] *Des colonies françaises. Abolition immédiate de l'esclavage* (Paris: Pagnerre, 1842).
[44] *L'Abolition de l'esclavage: Examen critique du préjugé contre la couleur des Africains et des sangs-mêlés* (Paris: Pagnerre, 1842); *La Revue des colonies*, 7th year, no. 3, Sept. 1840, pp. 81–5.
[45] Schmidt, *La correspondance*, 113.
[46] *Le Siècle*, Oct. 27, 1841; *L'Espérance*, Nov. 12, 26, 1841.

stood out as one of the leading immediatists among French abolitionists. The unyielding attitude of the colonies and the tergiversations of the government on the slavery issue were turning an increasing number of French anti-slavery advocates away from the gradualist approach to slave liberation. This tendency would grow in the mid-1840s as the government's stalling became increasingly apparent.

By the autumn of 1841 Isambert's enthusiasm about the possibility of a breakthrough in the matter of imminent emancipation had waned considerably. Despite the reassuring words by Guizot in the spring, the Broglie commission had met only briefly that year. Archival documentation shows that reports of the colonial and special councils had arrived in Paris by early February 1841. However, they had been withheld from the Broglie commission, and were submitted to that body only when it reconvened again nearly twelve months later.[47] The Broglie commission had been put on hold by the Soult–Guizot government. When Isambert wrote to Scoble in October about the situation in France his mood was somber. He reported that an anti-slavery law undoubtedly would not be introduced in the French chambers in 1842. Even if it were, it would probably take more than one session to adopt and implement it, for the government had too much respect for colonial pressure and was always prepared to temporize.[48]

Isambert was more pessimistic still by the end of the year. On December 11, 1841, the government added Louis Jean Jubelin, former governor of Guiana and Guadeloupe, and a notorious colonial apologist, to the Broglie commission, breaking the original balance between abolitionists and colonial supports and giving a majority on that body to the latter. *Le Constitutionnel* denounced the move as evidence of the retrograde attitude of the Soult–Guizot Cabinet on the slavery question. Such a development, the newspaper charged, reinforced the "resistance party" and showed the new administration to be no better than the Thiers Cabinet.[49] From Broglie in the mid-1830s to Guizot in the 1840s, French heads of government reigned in any anti-slavery convictions they might have had as a price for holding office. Isambert sent a clipping of this article to the British with the

---

[47] ANCAOM, Gén. 184 (1441), Résumé of the advice of the Special Councils and Colonial Councils, Feb. 7, 1841.

[48] Rhodes House Anti-Slavery Papers, G103, Isambert to Scoble, Oct. 2, 1841.

[49] Dec. 19, 1841.

remark that he was now more certain than ever that no emancipation bill would be forthcoming in 1842, because the government was weakening abolitionist influence on the Broglie commission by adding Jubelin.[50] Indeed, Jubelin was a Creole who had expressed in confidential dispatches his "affection for this country [Guadeloupe]" and for a colonial society in which "perhaps, nowhere, man ... has more well-being and less privations."[51] As Bissette remarked, Jubelin "shared in all the caste prejudices" of the colonial society to which he belonged.[52] Using Isambert's correspondence as the basis for its column, the British abolitionist organ correctly assessed Jubelin's appointment as a decision by the Guizot-dominated Cabinet not "to arrive at a solution of the [slavery] question." It then went on to accuse French authorities of having postponed the sittings of the Broglie commission, of having withheld documents that should have been submitted to it, and of wishing to adjourn the emancipation issue.[53] Anti-slavery elements on both sides of the Channel were becoming increasingly aware that the Orleanist government, be it under the aegis of Thiers or Guizot, intended to continue pursuing its policy of procrastination.

French emancipationism had reached new heights in late 1839, when it appeared that the July Monarchy was prepared to accept the slave abolition plan advocated by the Tocqueville Commission. The government at the time was finally ceding to steady abolitionist pressure applied since the mid-1830s. Abolitionists had improved their tactics by introducing proposals that resulted in parliamentary reports capable of gaining widespread support in the lower house. The inside work of Passy within the Cabinet had probably also weakened government opposition to progress in this matter. Indeed, in late 1839 it seemed that a breakthrough on the abolition front was imminent. However, from 1840 the situation rapidly deteriorated for the friends of the slaves. The Egyptian crisis brought to power a new Council of Ministers headed by Thiers and without any radical abolitionists. It also distracted government attention from the slavery problem. The Thiers administration ceded to royal pressure and put the colonial

[50] Rhodes House Anti-Slavery Papers, G103, Isambert to Tredgold, Dec. 19, 1841.
[51] ANCAOM, Corr. Gén., Guadeloupe 86, Governor Jubelin to Minister, Dec. 2, 1839.
[52] *La Revue des colonies*, 8the year, no. 5, Nov. 1841, pp. 211–215.
[53] *British and Foreign Anti-Slavery Reporter*, Dec. 29, 1841.

situation on hold by appointing a royal commission to investigate again not only the slavery question but a possible reorganization of the colonies. With its balance between abolitionists and colonial defenders, the Broglie commission could not propose a radical solution to the slavery problem. The Orleanist regime had, in effect, chosen to investigate to death the emancipation option. It had opted to perpetuate French colonial slavery.

For their part, abolitionists, who had been successful in the late 1830s in presenting plans before parliament and sparking the formation of favorable legislative committees, regressed after 1840 to their mid-1830s stance of simply interpellating the government in the chambers, even if they did so with more indignation. The abolition society also demonstrated in its proposal of 1841 to the Broglie commission that it still favored adequate preparation for slaves and an indemnification of some kind for their masters. Radical, immediatist-oriented anti-slavery was beginning to sprout in some circles after 1840, but not within the Société française pour l'abolition de l'esclavage. Nevertheless, in some ways by 1841 slow recovery seemed to be occurring in abolitionist fortunes. The war scare of 1840 ended when Thiers was toppled from power and replaced by a new Cabinet dominated by Guizot. The latter, unlike Thiers, did have abolitionist antecedents. He also assuaged abolitionists with soothing promises. This gave initial hope to anti-slavery elements, even if the Guizot government too seemed to be stalling the proceedings of the Broglie commission by late in the year. More ominously, Guizot's pledges did not prevent the appointment of Jubelin to the Broglie commission, a move that gave the balance of power to colonial defenders and precluded any recommendation for a rapid solution to the emancipation question by this body. By the early 1840s abolitionist fortunes were experiencing a typical pattern of promising advances quickly negated by disappointing regressions. Still, abolitionists could envisage altering their tactics in 1842 and applying renewed pressure on the administration. Little did they know, however, that the next two years would bring renewed crisis and further setbacks for the anti-slavery cause.

7

CRISIS AND
FURTHER SETBACKS

Faced with the government's stonewalling attitude, in early 1842 the Société française pour l'abolition de l'esclavage made a conscious decision once again to attempt to alter its tactics. When it opened its 1842 session, the society began by concluding some unfinished business by awarding its long-awaited Grégoire prize to S. L'Instant, a person of color from Haiti, for a book that he had published in 1841 but that had made little public impact. In the process, the abolition society had refused the prize to Schoelcher for his *Abolition de l'esclavage* on the grounds that the latter had advocated immediate emancipation but had not treated directly the required theme of racial prejudice. Schoelcher reacted poorly to this decision and the entire incident underlined the continuing chasm between the gradualist abolition society and the more radical advocates of immediatism.[1] Schoelcher was so annoyed over this matter that in a private letter he denounced the inaction of the Société française and the aloof, exclusivist nature of two of its leaders, Passy and Lamartine.[2] Schoelcher ended up by joining the society – probably, though, only after 1842 – attending many of its sessions and cooperating with it on some issues, but he was never a mainstay within it, finding it too conservative, and preferring to act on his own.[3] Ironically too, this was the last time the society held the Grégoire prize competition, marked by an embarrassingly low

---

[1] L'Instant's book was: *Essai sur les moyens d'extirper les préjugés des blancs contre la couleur des Africains et des sangs-mêlés* (Paris: Pagnerre, 1841). For Schoelcher's reaction, see his *Abolition de l'esclavage*, 7–16.
[2] Schmidt, *La correspondance*, 91–2. Schoelcher wrote his remarks on Sept. 22, 1839, to his good friend Ernest Legouvé, writer, poet, and dramatist.
[3] Schmidt, *Victor Schoelcher*, 64.

participation and success rate. In early 1842 also the French abolition society acted to encourage the formation of auxiliary bodies in the provinces, though this move does not appear to have proved fruitful at the time.[4] Organized French anti-slavery was still Paris-centered and limited in scope.

The decision to open up to the provinces, though, falls in line with the general efforts by the Société française to reorient its approach to the emancipation problem in early 1842, to reach out to a larger public, and to make a concerted attempt to win over popular opinion. Society members knew all too well that it was the mobilization of public sentiment that had enabled the British abolitionists to press successfully for emancipation in the early 1830s. Restrained by government legislation forbidding public meetings and by its own elitist reticence to appeal to the masses, the French abolition society had been unsuccessful in its limited attempt in 1837 to break out of these restrictions and expand its influence.[5] Now society members decided to take another more forceful step in this direction. The group was aware of the publicity generated by its banquet for the English delegation in 1840, and impressed by the large anti-slavery convention held in London that year. Besides, French legislative elections were scheduled for the summer, and the abolitionists hoped to make the slavery question an electoral issue. Therefore, in the society's first meeting of 1842, on January 5, Barrot proposed the holding of a large public assembly to which a British delegation would be invited to attend. The organization even considered planning an international convention on the British model, but realized that this could not be carried out in time to have the desired effect upon the 1842 legislative elections. Accordingly, the Société française tentatively set the date for its public meeting for late February or early March, and inquired as to which week would be most convenient for the British. The decision by the society to go beyond "closed door meetings" constituted a determined attempt by French abolitionists to borrow a page from the British and break out of the temporizing syndrome that the government had imposed upon the emancipation process in France. It also indicated that the Anglophobia associated with the Egyptian crisis of 1840 had

[4] No. 19, 72, 77–82.
[5] See Chapter 4.

abated sufficiently for French abolitionists to resort once again to British strategies.

When Isambert informed London, on behalf of the society, about his organization's intentions, the British "rejoiced" and formed a thirteen-member delegation to attend the Paris meeting, eventually set for March 7.[6] On February 23 the French abolition society requested from the prefect of police the required permission to rent a hall for a "public meeting" under the presidency of the influential and highly respectable Broglie. Once again, the meeting would be not nearly as "public" as British anti-slavery assemblies, for attendance would be by invitation only, and participants would require formal recognition by the president before being able to speak. It does appear, though, that the planned public meeting of 1842 would have been larger than the one envisaged in 1837. This, then, was an attempt to increase participation beyond that of society members and a few select guests, while still remaining somewhat restrictive. It was undoubtedly felt that such a tactic could skirt restrictions on mass assemblies and perhaps placate officialdom to the point where such a meeting would be permitted.

In 1842, as in 1837, however, this initiative was too much for the authorities to accept. On February 28 the under-secretary of state at the ministry of the interior informed Broglie that the police feared trouble at such a gathering. Broglie immediately called upon the Minister of the Interior, Tanneguy Duchâtel, who informed him that police reports foresaw "150 to 200 troublemakers" disrupting the meeting with shouts of "down with the English." Duchâtel assured Broglie than any disorders could be quelled, but asked whether it might not be best to cancel the assembly. Broglie refused to accept the hint, and departed, telling Duchâtel that he would leave his ministry to carry out its responsibilities. This brought a prompt written reply from Duchâtel on March 1 that it was not desirable to hold a public meeting. Society members, who understood all too well the language of those in power, interpreted this as an outright ban, and immediately canceled the entire affair. Because the British were already en route to France, though, it was decided to hold a simple banquet – permitted under French laws – in their honor on March 9.[7]

---

[6] No. 19, 66–7; Rhodes House Anti-Slavery Papers, Jan. 11, Feb. 25, 28, 1842.
[7] No. 19, 67–9.

When informed of these developments, one British abolitionist, Sturge, angrily returned home, refusing to participate in such a sham.[8] The other members of what had become a large British delegation – twenty-four altogether, according to one report – exchanged friendly toasts with their French colleagues.[9] In fact, though, the July Monarchy had forcefully reminded the French abolition society that it might be willing to tolerate its existence, despite the law against associations, but only on the condition that the society continue to operate as an elitist appendage of the legislative assemblies. The government was not prepared to permit it to contravene the laws against public meetings. Moreover, this time the government's refusal, unlike in 1837, was a formal and public one. The administration had destroyed any aspirations the society might have had of transforming itself into a group capable of winning popular backing and stirring up national opinion through meetings on the British model. In the process the government had also dashed abolitionist hopes to translate additional exposure of anti-slavery ideas into an election plank to help abolitionist candidates in the 1842 elections. Anti-slavery themes remained totally removed from every election campaign under the July Monarchy.[10] The support of public opinion had been the key to the success of British abolitionists in the early 1830s. As of 1842 it was apparent that French anti-slavery could not have recourse to public meetings to activate such opinion. Only later in the 1840s would French abolitionists concentrate on petitioning as a means of tapping public sentiment refused to it through meetings. For the time being, however, the government had delivered a severe blow to the French abolition society, seriously restricting the effectiveness of this troublesome if influential lobby group by limiting the scope of its operations.

French abolitionists fully understood the message that they had received from the authorities. As Le Constitutionnel pointed out, pro-colonial troublemakers could have and should have been repressed by the forces of order; in reality, the government was ceding to the demands of the colonial party for the preservation of the status quo. Le Semeur wrote in the same vein, going so far as to accuse the delegate Jollivet and Granier de Cassagnac of Le Globe of having recruited

[8] Temperley, British Antislavery, 186.
[9] Annales de l'Institut d'Afrique (Paris), no. 3, March 1842; No. 19, 32–54.
[10] Drescher, Capitalism and Antislavery, 56.

ruffians in preparation for the disruption of the abolitionist meeting. The real sense of the government's actions was best captured, though, by *Le Siècle*, when it exclaimed that the administration had now dropped "its mask of philanthropy." Or, as *Le National* put it even more bluntly, "in fact Mr. Guizot cares little about the negroes."[11] Leaders of the French abolition society viewed the government's decision in the same light. Isambert reported to the British: "If the government had not prevented our society from holding its public meeting, if it had not succeeded in shutting us up within closed doors," the Société française could have hoped to win over popular opinion as the English had in their victory over slavery. The government "wished to gain time by prohibiting our communications with the public.... It has succeeded.... Mr. Guizot has been able to adjourn the preparation of the project of law [for freeing the slaves] for several sessions. We know where the obstacle is."[12] The last phrase was certainly an oblique reference to the King, who often overshadowed Guizot's moves. In the process, Isambert had correctly analyzed the government's intention to defer as much as possible the emancipation issue.

Isambert was equally disheartened by other circumstances surrounding the slavery question in early 1842. In discussing parliamentary developments he exclaimed: "The French chamber closed its session of 1842 in full reaction against emancipation." The secretary of the abolition society recounted to the British that the law on forced expropriation of colonial property in the West Indies, a measure that was viewed by many as a necessary preparatory step toward slave liberation, had passed by a vast majority in the Chamber of Peers, generally considered favorable to the colonies. However, the government had allowed it to die in the Chamber of Deputies by not presenting it for discussion. In like fashion, the law to reduce the powers of the colonial councils had been approved by a commission of the lower house, but "Mr. Guizot himself abandoned it" on May 20. Isambert went on to explain that: "If Mr. Guizot was [sic] really devoted to the

[11] *Le Constitutionnel*, March 6, 1842; *Le Semeur*, March 9, 1842; *Le Siècle*, March 3, 1842; *Le National*, March 3, 1842. Bissette also charged that Granier de Cassagnac's *Le Globe* had intrigued to persuade the Minister of the Interior of possible trouble if a public meeting were to be held (*La Revue des colonies*, 8th year, no. 9, March 1842, pp. 337–49).

[12] Rhodes House Anti-Slavery Papers, G103, Isambert to Scoble, May 9, 1842; *British and Foreign Anti-Slavery Reporter*, June 1, 1842.

cause of emancipation, he ought to have pressed the question in the chamber, and to have supported with firmness the two colonial laws." Besides, "he ought to have urged the commission presided over by the Duke de Broglie to terminate its labours." Instead, Isambert related, just when Broglie was in the process of presenting his final report, the commission was adjourned for the remainder of the year. In conclusion, he observed: "It is thus shown that our government only desires to gain time in order to disembarrass itself of [the slavery] question."[13] The Société française was fully aware of the July Monarchy's intention of shelving the emancipation issue.

By the summer of 1842, Isambert was uttering predictions of doom and gloom for the French abolitionist cause. In a confidential letter to Scoble he voiced his opinion that: "The affairs of abolition go very badly in France." He feared that in the present circumstances the completion of the Broglie commission report might be postponed indefinitely. He explained too that efforts to render anti-slavery an electoral issue had backfired for the abolitionists. Even though emancipationist issues had not constituted a part of abolitionist candidates' platforms, Isambert reported that in the summer elections "Mr. Passy, vice-president of our society, nearly lost his seat in parliament." Isambert himself, Tracy, and other abolitionists had "run the same risk in consequence of our zeal for the abolitionist cause, not for that cause itself, but because the vulgar confound it with the right of search." In the face of new developments in 1842, just being identified with anti-slavery was enough to reduce one's electoral appeal. Because of the emergence of the right of search crisis, Isambert predicted that: "We are threatened with an indefinite adjournment of the [emancipation] question" in France.[14]

The right of search controversy between France and Great Britain erupted upon the scene in late 1841 and early 1842, reaching a fever pitch in the spring of that year. The right of naval cruisers of both nations to stop and search each other's merchant ships in certain zones off Africa and the West Indies was an intrinsic provision of the Anglo–French anti-slave trade agreements of 1831 and 1833 that had

---

[13] Rhodes House Anti-Slavery Papers, G103, Isambert to Reverand J. H. Hinton, April 3, 1842; *British and Foreign Anti-Slavery Reporter*, June 15, 1842. Hinton was editor of the *Reporter*.

[14] Rhodes House Anti-Slavery Papers, G103, Isambert to Scoble, Aug. 1, 1842.

eliminated by and large the remnant of the illegal French slave trade. Actions carried out previously under the clauses of these treaties had received few negative comments by the French press of the 1830s, which was largely indifferent to the entire process. Indeed, as long as the Anglo–French diplomatic entente of the 1830s endured, French opinion tended to approve of mutual search procedures.[15] All of this changed, however, after the Egyptian crisis of 1840 destroyed the entente and threatened to plunge France into war with Britain. The fall of Thiers and the ascension of Guizot ended the war threat, but the yielding of the new administration to British demands humiliated France, and revived rabid Anglophobia in most of the French population. Amidst this atmosphere of deep animosity toward Britain, Frenchmen suddenly became aware of the right of search. British seizures of French merchantmen such as the *Sénégambie* and *Marabout* as suspected traders off the African coast in 1840 and 1841, respectively, began to receive considerable publicity in press articles, accompanied by charges that Britain was attempting to disrupt growing French trade with Africa. By a quirk of fate, these accusations of arbitrariness by the British navy broke in France at the very moment that word arrived of a new multination slave trade repression treaty initialed in London on December 20, 1841. This agreement extended even further the conditions and zones under which mutual search could be effected. The French press, and then the chambers, began vociferously denouncing British actions as self-serving and entirely nonhumanitarian, as confounding slave trade repression with discouragement for French maritime commerce. Starting with the French port city newspapers and then spreading rapidly to Parisian organs, the right of search controversy and its concomitant reinforcement of Anglophobia became the most important item in much of the press in early 1842.[16] Unfortunately for French anti-slavery, the slave trade

---

[15] For a discussion of the reaction of the French press to slave trade repression measures in the 1830s and 1840s, see Lawrence C. Jennings, "The French Press and Great Britain's Campaign," 5–24. For details on the right of search in the 1830s, see Serge Daget, "France, Repression of the Illegal Slave Trade, and England, 1817–1850," in David Eltis and James Walvin, eds., *The Abolition of the Atlantic Slave Trade: Origins and Effects in Europe, Africa and the Americas* (Madison: University of Wisconsin Press, 1981), 193–217; and Daget, *La répression de la traite*, 438–79.

[16] For a detailed account of the right of search imbroglio, see Lawrence C. Jennings, "France, Great Britain and the Repression of the Slave Trade, 1841–1845," *French*

and slavery questions were closely associated in the French mind, as were British and French abolitionists.

A close examination of French newspapers, pamphlets, and legislative debates demonstrates the extent to which the terms "slavery" and "slave trade" became confused or synonymous in France as emotions peaked at the height of the controversy. Defenders of French slavery readily seized the opportunity to interconnect the two and employ this device to indict both British abolitionists and their French allies. One of the long-standing charges of French colonial spokesmen even in the 1830s had been that British abolitionists were not disinterested philanthropists, but clever schemers determined to destroy French colonial holdings and commerce by undermining slavery.[17] After the outbreak of the right of search controversy this litany increased with a vengeance. In the Chamber of Deputies, Jean Etienne Ducos of Bordeaux and Adolphe Augustin Marie Billault (deputy of Rennes), the latter a fierce defender of slavery, joined in decrying British motives in general.[18] Among the press, *Le Commerce*, still under colonial influence, published an article on both the right of search and abolitionism in which it insisted that, behind "the entirely generous facade of suppressing slavery," the "secret motives of British philanthropy" were to undermine French staple-producing colonies. Similarly, *Le Courrier de la Gironde* (Bordeaux) charged that Britain's long-term objective was "to destroy the colonies of the West" through the right of search and the abolition of slavery.[19]

At the same time that they were attempting to diminish the stature of British humanitarianism, French pro-slavery forces strove to discredit French abolitionists by portraying them as either the unwilling dupes or naive followers of their British mentors. At the height of the search crisis the *Courrier de la Gironde* referred to the Société française pour l'abolition de l'esclavage as "a club of Anglo–French negrophiles." *La Presse*, the large distribution paper of Emile de Girardin that was constantly in the pay of French *colons* under the July Monarchy, claimed

---

Historical Studies 10(1977): 101–125; Jennings, *French Reaction*, 146–67; and Daget, *La répression de la traite*, 480–536. Tudesq (*Les grands notables*, II, 837, 842) is the only historian to attribute enough credit to the right of search episode in derailing the French abolitionist cause in the 1840s.

[17] Jennings, *French Reaction*, 85–7, 153–5.

[18] *Le Moniteur universel*, Jan. 31, Feb. 1, 2, 1842;

[19] *Le Commerce*, Dec. 10, 1842; *Le Courrier de la Gironde*, March 10, 1842.

that more English than French attended the assembly in Paris to "raise questions menacing the existence of our colonies."[20] Delegate Charles Dupin asked in one of his pamphlets how French abolitionists could be so unpatriotic as to "consent to being the collaborators of England, the clients of its pretensions, the advocates of its errors."[21] Colonial defenders of slavery were employing the right of search episode to vilify French abolitionism through its British connections in a concerted effort to weaken the anti-slavery movement. French emancipationists were being made to pay dearly for their close association with the British.

Given the circumstances surrounding the right of search affair, French anti-slavery itself felt obliged to loosen its ties with the British. Isambert explained the phenomenon well when he reflected at the height of the crisis that "the greatest injury one can do a French patriot is to suspect him of being an ally of England."[22] Because of the search question, even important elements of the French abolitionist press became wary of or turned away from British humanitarianism. *Le Constitutionnel*, staunchly anti-slavery and favorable to the British initiative until now, became suspicious that "philanthropy is only a pretext" for Britain's crusade against slavery and the slave trade; like the *colons*, it came to believe that London's real objectives were commercial hegemony. The fervently abolitionist *Le Siècle* also became alienated from a nation which, "under the mask of humaneness," infringed upon the rights of others. By late 1842 it was convinced "that the right to emancipate [slaves] or retain them in servitude is one of

[20] Ibid., Feb. 25, 1842; *La Presse*, Jan. 20, 1843. The term "negrophile" was used here by colonial spokespersons as signifying "pro-Negro" or "pro-black," not as a racist epithet. Research undertaken for this book has shown that "black" and "Negro" were used interchangeably under the July Monarchy as simple substantives without racist connotations. Indeed, abolitionists as well as plantocrats employed the two terms indiscriminately. Another study has shown that little value judgment can be placed either on the employment of the phrases "black," "Negro," or "slave" in the discourse over the abolition of the French slave trade in the early nineteenth century (Serge Daget, "Les mots esclave, nègre, Noir, et les jugements de valeur sur la traite négrière dans la littérature abolitionniste française de 1770 à 1845," *Revue française d'histoire d'outre-mer* 60 (1973), 511–48). As Tudesq (*Les grands notables*, II, 848) has pointed out, it is anachronistic to try to read a late nineteenth- or twentieth-century racist message into pre-1848 French colonial phraseology.

[21] Charles Dupin, *Second mémoire: Situation comparée des colonies françaises et colonies anglaises* (Paris: Firmin-Didot, 1844), 15–16.

[22] Rhodes House Anti-Slavery Papers, G103, Isambert to Scoble, Aug. 1, 1842.

internal sovereignty with which foreign countries cannot meddle." The equally anti-slavery *Le National* adopted a similar stand when it insisted that in light of the right of search it became imperative for France to act alone in abolishing slavery; to "accomplish" this "under English injunction would be to stigmatize it forever in French eyes."[23] Because of the right of search episode, the French abolitionist movement, which had so relied in the past on British encouragement and the British precedent, felt obliged to distance itself from the British model. Although French and British abolitionists continued to remain in contact, the frequency and detail of their confidential communications diminished between 1842 and early 1844. Their exchanges also decreased. When the British staged another anti-slavery conference in London in 1843, only one delegate of the Société française, Amédée Thayer, attended.[24] By 1845 the organ of the French abolition society, *L'Abolitoniste français*, was forced to avow that British "influence is felt less than ever in France."[25] As a result of the right of search question, French abolitionism had distanced itself temporarily at least from the British example upon which it had always heavily relied for sustenance and inspiration. French anti-slavery itself emerged sullied and weakened in the process.

In turning public opinion against what was seen by many as English-inspired anti-slavery, the right of search episode dealt a major setback to the abolitionist cause in France. Already during the banquet of March 9, 1842, attended by the British delegation, Barrot saw the repercussions these developments would have for French anti-slavery. He warned his listeners that "to place sentiments of humanity in confrontation with national pride, to constitute a conflict between two noble passions, would not create a force favorable to the abolition of slavery, but conjure up a great danger to it."[26] In like manner, Tracy, speaking within the confines of the Broglie commission, bemoaned the fact that public opinion had turned against England so much that it would cause "veritable difficulties for the solution of the problem of slavery" in France.[27]

---

[23] *Le Constitutionnel*, Jan. 6, 23, 1842; *Le Siècle*, Jan. 4, Sept. 25, 1842; *Le National*, March 28, 1843.
[24] See Jennings, *French Response*, 179–180.
[25] Jan.–Feb. 1845.
[26] No. 19, 49; *Le Siècle*, March 12, 1842.
[27] Broglie Commision, Minutes, part 3, pp. 54–5, Feb. 14, 1842.

In his confidential report to the British in the summer of 1842 Isambert confirmed the fears of his colleagues. He avowed that "public opinion is everywhere in such a state that we dare not speak of the abolition of slavery.... We shall do nothing for four months, circumstances are not propitious; public feeling must be permitted to calm itself." His conclusion was that "philanthropy hangs its head in France," and that only "Mr. Bissette courageously continues his *Revue* and replies to our enemies."[28] Unbeknown to Isambert, Bissette's *Revue des colonies* had just published its last issue, and its financially strapped author was forced to return to the pamphlet media. The right of search crisis had left French anti-slavery in a state of debility and disarray. Having lost any possibility of gaining momentum, French abolitionism was obliged to retreat and bide its time, much to the relief of the government and *colons* alike.

It was in the midst of this inauspicious atmosphere caused by the right of search that the Broglie commission met between late January and the end of May 1842 – a full two years after its creation – to carry out the bulk of its work and prepare its report. Predictably, the responses of the colonial councils for which the commission had waited for over a year were totally negative. The first option proposed, that of progressive emancipation through the liberation of newborn children and *rachat*, was rejected as disruptive and having no advantages over full emancipation. The second proposal, that of simultaneous emancipation with blacks purchased by the state, was criticized as having all the disadvantages of an interim system. The third possibility, that of simultaneous emancipation followed by apprenticeship, was turned down as being condemned by the British experience. The Martinique colonial legislature asserted that it would not even take the three systems into consideration unless a full indemnity of slaves and property was paid in advance. Those of Guadeloupe and Guiana proclaimed that the moment had not yet come for emancipation and that only time could resolve the slavery question. More surprisingly, some of the newly appointed special councils, consisting of high colonial administrators, revealed themselves to be as opposed to any meaningful change as the colonial councils they were supposed to circumvent; the former, did, however, emit more constructive

---

[28] Rhodes House Anti–Slavery Papers, G103, Isambert to Scoble, Aug. 1, 1842.

suggestions.[29] The colonies remained steadfastly opposed to considering slave liberation in any form whatsoever.

Broglie succinctly summarized the colonial reaction when he opened the first meeting in 1842 of the commission on January 31. He remarked that colonial council responses were "unanimously negative on the principle of emancipation" and "very incomplete" in their treatment of the three systems presented them: "therefore an examination of their deliberations sheds little light" on the issues as a whole.[30] As Broglie commented in his report, the colonial councils wished "to protest against all ideas of emancipation near or distant" and refused to commit themselves to cooperating in any way in the process.[31] The Broglie commission's deliberations had been delayed while awaiting colonial replies that were foreseeably negative. Tracy was quick to note that the commission had been constituted for two years already but had achieved nothing.[32]

As soon as it met in 1842 the Broglie commission decided to proceed by scrutinizing the different options on emancipation that it had proposed already in 1840. This detailed examination of possible approaches to emancipation entailed going over the massive amount of documentation provided by the colonial department and interviewing several witnesses. Early on in the proceedings a fourth possibility besides the original three was raised, that of rapid liberation without apprenticeship of any kind. The debate on this latter proposal underscored the divisions that existed within the commission, and in particular the lack of unison in abolitionist ranks. A detailed examination of the position of abolitionist members of the Broglie commission provides a rare opportunity to gauge the attitude of French abolitionist leaders who as a whole rarely disclosed their exact feelings on the slavery issue.

Commission members fell within three loose categories: radical abolitionists, moderates and colonial defenders. Among the abolitionists, Tracy, for one, supported the possibility of outright slave liberation as

---

[29] ANCAOM, Gén. 184 (1437), Résumé of the replies of the colonial councils, Sept. 27, 1841; Gén. 184 (1441), Résumé of the advice of the colonial councils and special councils, Feb. 7, 1841.

[30] Broglie Commission, Minutes, part 3, pp. 1–2, Jan. 31, 1842.

[31] Ibid., Report, 235.

[32] Ibid., Minutes, part 3, p. 4, Jan. 31, 1842.

being similar to the choice made by Antigua in 1834 to move directly to slave liberation without an intermediary stage. Rossi, one of the principle proponents of this idea, tried to neutralize opposition by pointing out that such a move need not be implemented immediately, but in two or three years. Passy, known as an advocate of immediate emancipation, supported this concept during the debate on it, but then abstained in the vote, saying that he favored another system. Sade retreated totally from advocating rapid abolition, claiming that a delay of six or seven years was needed for its implementation. Perhaps the resolve of some abolitionists had been weakened by the concerted opposition to this measure by Audiffret, Jubelin, Wustemberg, Saint-Hilaire, and especially Mackau, all of whom insisted that slaves were not yet prepared; they also maintained that it was financially impossible to grant an indemnity in the near future. Even Tocqueville and Broglie ended up siding with the opposition. Tocqueville pointed out that he could not support general emancipation without laws to encourage the maintenance of work. Broglie opined that French slaves were not yet prepared for freedom; besides, he argued, their situation did not require immediate emancipation, for they were well cared for by their masters. In this sense, Broglie seemed impervious to the argumentation to the contrary put forth a year earlier by members of the French abolition society over which he presided.

Broglie's stance confirmed what had been evident already in the 1830s. He was an extremely moderate abolitionist, willing to support slave liberation only if it were implemented slowly, cautiously, and with extensive preparations. This position by the president of the abolition society reflected that of the majority of its members until the late 1840s. More revealing yet are the positions of Passy and Tocqueville, for they show an evolutionary process that was also typical of many members of the Société française pour l'abolition de l'esclavage, who steadily altered their attitudes and envisaged emancipation differently from year to year. Passy, perhaps the most radical, immediatist-oriented member of the society in the 1830s, had developed certain reservations by the 1840s. Tocqueville, ever since he put forth his option of the government acting as a tutor of the slaves, seemed progressively more concerned about adequately preparing slaves; he too, in other words, was evolving along more cautious and gradualist lines. While some French abolitionists were becoming more radical as time went on, others seemed to be regressing. Moderates of the 1830s like Agénor de Gasparin and Schoelcher turned to immediatism by the early 1840s, but their radicalization was offset by the backtracking of other progressives, such as Passy and Tocqueville. Shifting of positions within the ranks of the French abolition society was a factor weakening it, limiting its influence, and often rendering it difficult to fathom.

In the end, when the rapid emancipation option came to a vote, Sade, Tocqueville, and Passy abstained, with only Rossi, Tracy, and – surprisingly – Reynard voting for the measure. All three of the latter, however, qualified their vote by insisting that indemnity be unfailingly provided the masters. Everyone else, including Broglie, voted against the measure. In the process, the entire commission sanctioned the idea of granting an indemnity to the slave owners, something that some abolitionists had been reluctant to concede, at least when speaking within the confines of the French abolition society.[33] During the debate, the majority of the commission also revealed itself favorable to either a gradual, protracted emancipation approach or at least one containing some intermediary stage. From the outset it became apparent too that this body contained no determined core of radical abolitionists who would push for a decisive solution to the slavery question. Quite to the contrary, the president of the Société française pour l'abolition de l'esclavage revealed himself as extremely conservative on the emancipation issue. In this sense the debates within the commission afford a rare opportunity to perceive the deep divisions, even hesitations and contradictions, within anti-slavery ranks. Most of the abolitionist members of the Broglie commission reflected the cautious, elitist outlook of the mainstream of French anti-slavery, contented to work within government channels as responsible administrators should, and not inclined to decisive measures. And the abolitionists on the commission as a whole, be they the moderate majority or the more radical minority, were outnumbered by a nucleus of colonial backers who usually voted as a bloc, showing few of the divisions apparent in abolitionist ranks.

The commission rapidly disposed also of another option, the one inspired by the Tocqueville commission report. The chances of this

[33] Ibid., 40–94, Feb. 14, 21, 1842.

project were dashed when Sade, a member of the original Rémusat–Tocqueville commission of 1839, announced that he could no longer back it. Sade explained that the investigations carried out by the Broglie commission had demonstrated that it was currently impossible for the planters, in their present economic predicament, to pay freedmen enough salary for the state to be able to recuperate eventually the indemnity from the blacks. Tocqueville himself agreed that this was the case, even if he continued to support the plan he had put forth in 1839. Saint-Hilaire, like Sade, also changed his stance on this option, revealing that if he had favored the idea in 1839 it was because it had then seemed to be a system that could save the government the cost of paying an indemnity. Only Passy, Tracy, and Tocqueville provided a spirited defense of this procedure, though Rossi and the unpredictable Reynard joined in the end to support it. Still, it was defeated by a vote of seven to five, as the moderate abolitionists Broglie and Sade voted with its opponents.[34] Once again the abolitionist vote had divided, while among colonial proponents only Reynard had wavered. On the one hand, Passy demonstrated that he had shied away from immediatism in favor of the Tocqueville plan. On the other, Sade had abandoned the Tocqueville proposal in favor of a gradualist model. With this vote evaporated the last chance of the Broglie commission recommending a relatively rapid approach to slave liberation.

The next option debated was that of the British system, that is, general slave liberation at a certain date, followed by an intermediary regime of apprenticeship. The British apprenticeship experience, however, had few defenders in either Britain or France in the 1840s. Even the abolitionists on the commission agreed with the argument of their British counterparts that apprenticeship had been little more than a liberalized version of prolonged slavery. Only Broglie, Tracy, and Tocqueville had good words for the British system, while Mackau charged that apprenticeship would result in a "veritable calamity" if applied to French holdings. As a result, by a strange sort of reasoning the commission rationalized that if apprenticeship amounted to slavery in disguise, it would be better to prolong servitude itself for a longer time period than the four to six years that had been projected

---

[34] Ibid., 123–144, 150–182, March 7, 14, 1842.

for British possessions.[35] A subcommittee was struck to study the matter, and it recommended that slavery be retained ten years after the promulgation of any emancipation law. Although Sade argued in vain that the maximum should be eight years, ten years was finally accepted as the time necessary for reimbursing the master in labor the equivalent of half the value of a slave. Such a maneuver would conveniently reduce by half the amount of any indemnity paid out by the government. This estimation was based upon the assertion of the special council of Guadeloupe that a slave redeemed his value in labor over a twenty-year period. By examining average slave prices in Martinique, Guadeloupe, and Guiana, the committee then chose for the basis of its calculations the average price for the good years of 1825–1834, the very high rate of 1,200 francs per slave. Because there were about 250,000 slaves in French possessions, this meant that, by permitting masters to retain slaves for ten years longer, a huge total indemnity of 300 million francs could be reduced to 150 million. Perhaps, in fact, these calculations were a subterfuge to justify the retention of slavery for an additional ten years or to assure the masters an exceptional settlement. The total sum could have been less if the years 1835–1839 had been included in the calculations, but the price of slaves had fallen in Martinique by 37 percent between 1834 and 1839, and the commission did not wish to see the *colons* suffer from lower slave values brought on by British emancipation and the threat of impending French slave liberation.[36] In the process the commission showed how solicitous it was of planter interests, while totally neglecting the basic rights of slaves. This was not surprising, however, for cautious, gradualist abolitionists had a propensity – like the government and planters – to be preoccupied with the necessity for sustained labor and the needs of masters as the basis of any settlement to the slavery problem.

The proposal based on a distorted version of the British model received its final form after two further amendments. A resolution by

[35] Ibid., 11–22, Feb. 7, 1842.

[36] Although few reliable statistics on slave prices are available in the French colonial archives, Fallope has calculated that in Guadeloupe too the average price of slaves declined from 1264.91F in 1825–1829 to 1,168.50F in 1830–1834, and finally to 955,72F for 1835–1839 (*Esclaves et ciyoyens*, 260–261). Fuma claims (*L'Esclavagisme*, 45) that slave prices increased steadily during the July Monarchy in Bourbon, due to the labor-starved condition of the island. Still, he provides no statistics to corroborate this.

Rossi set the date for freeing the slaves as ten years after January 1, 1843, or January 1, 1853. However, after further discussion, it was decided to add on for good measure an additional five years of *engagement*, or indentureship, following 1853, something which the commission did not equate with apprenticeship. This was justified by the specious argument that between slavery and freedom a transitional period was required after all.[37] The contorted reasoning surrounding this entire discussion demonstrated to what extent the commission was determined to find reasons to postpone emancipation into the distant future. Because all members agreed on the necessity of an indemnity – a reimbursement that all also agreed could not possibly be paid by the government in the early 1840s – the commission was offering a compromise that would be generous to both the planters and the national treasury. The only ones who would not benefit from this, quite clearly, were the slaves. The vast majority of the commission believed, though, that the slaves needed extra time for preparation anyhow. The argument prevalent among radical abolitionists that it was contradictory to try to moralize slaves under slavery, was rejected by the majority of commission members, including some abolitionists. Only Passy, Rossi, Tocqueville, and Sade defended this idea. Broglie firmly believed that "moralization" could be achieved only under slavery. Once again, the majority on the commission shared in the beliefs of colonial defenders. The so-called "British option" had been denatured and bastardized to the point where it would be unrecognizable to any confirmed abolitionist, whether British or French. Unfortunately, however, there were still few immediatist-oriented British-style abolitionists in France in the early 1840s, and none on the Broglie commission. Furthermore, the progress of British-style immediatism was being obstructed by the Anglo–French search crisis that was raking France at the very time that the Broglie commission was arriving at its conclusions.

In such a prevailing atmosphere, the tendency in France in general, and within the Broglie commission in particular, was to concentrate on the negative rather than positive elements of the British precedent. Since British emancipation in 1834, and especially after the

---

[37] Broglie Commission, Minutes, 202–210, 248–81, 292–306, March 19, 24, April 4, 25, 1842.

termination of apprenticeship in 1838, much of the debate in France about the British example had revolved around its economic short-comings. By the early 1840s the dominant opinion in France held that the British accomplishment demonstrated how slave liberation could be effected peacefully and in a manner beneficial to blacks, but not without grave economic consequences. In defense of the British record, determined French abolitionists pointed out that most ex-slaves had continued to work, shifting their production from staples to victuals, and they strove to show that freedmen were much better off than they had been under slavery. In fact, though, these arguments tended to carry little weight with the French government, the *colons*, French business circles, the public at large, and even many abolitionists. The decline in sugar production that had been so manifest in British colonies after 1838 was the predominant element of concern for most Frenchmen. In the 1840s even French abolitionists had been obliged to concede that sugar production had plunged between 25 and 35 percent in British possessions after the end of apprenticeship.[38]

Within the Broglie commission the overriding issue concerning the British precedent involved the extent to which emancipation had failed from an economic point of view. A speech by Lord Stanley, the British Colonial Secretary, in the House of Commons on March 22, 1842, which admitted the economic shortcomings of the British experience, was bantered about by most of the colonial defenders on the commission. Joseph Henri Galos, who was added to the body in 1842 when he replaced Saint-Hilaire as Director of the Colonies, decisively employed Stanley's testimony to show that British results might be "favorable in the moral and social spheres," but that they proved "disastrous in the domains of work and production." This idea was so prevalent among commission members that moderate abolitionists like Broglie became convinced that their revamping of the British emancipation model constituted an improvement on it.[39] That French slaves would have to wait until 1858 for complete liberty under this

---

[38] See Jennings, *French Response*, 69–80, 105–115. One historian has calculated that between 1839 and 1846 British colonial sugar production fell a total of 36 percent (Philip D. Curtin, "The British Sugar Duties and West Indian Prosperity," *Journal of Economic History* 14 (1954): 157–73). See also Green, *British Slave Emancipation*, 229, 245–6.

[39] Broglie Commission, Minutes, part 3, p. 384, May 23, 1842.

scheme was overshadowed in their minds by the fact that the colonies and French commerce would suffer less. The commission's project for general emancipation had been watered down to the point where in the final vote it became the preferred plan of the majority. Broglie, Tocqueville, Tracy, Sade, Rossi, Passy, Reynard, Bignon, and Galos rallied to it. Only the diehard colonial advocates, Audiffret, Mackau, Wustemberg, Jubelin, and Saint-Hilaire – who had remained on the commission despite his retirement from the French colonial office – favored the idea of partial and progressive emancipation.[40] In the end, though, the commission decided to retain both of these options.

The partial and progressive emancipation plan was based upon the old Passy proposal of freeing newborn children, along with legalizing *pécule* and *rachat*. Added to it was a clause stipulating that this system would be in effect for twenty years, after which all remaining slaves would be freed. As Broglie reflected, both proposals were now similar, with one calling for liberty for the slaves after fifteen years (ten plus five of *engagement*), the other after twenty.[41] By this point, in late May 1842, the commission had finished all its business except completing Broglie's report and studying some documents from Bourbon that had not as yet arrived. Broglie informed his colleagues that he could not provide them with his conclusions before September, so they decided to suspend their meetings until early 1843, when the chambers reopened. When the commission reconvened on February 17, 1843, it took seven rapid sessions to hear the report and adopt it.

The commission's final meeting concluded on March 16, 1843. Its work was then presented to the Minister of the Navy and Colonies, printed up, and made public. The report put forth both of the commission's final options, the one for general or simultaneous and the other for partial and progressive emancipation, while indicating nevertheless that the majority preferred the former. The intention was to "give the government more latitude of choice following the political considerations in its control, and to impose on it a greater responsibility in presenting it two paths instead of one to arrive at a solution."[42] The Broglie commission had accomplished its task after three years of sitting and had presented two possible emancipation plans to the

---

[40] Ibid., 388–90.
[41] Ibid., 388.
[42] Ibid., 148–9, March 12, 1842; p. 390, May 23, 1842; Report, 176–7, 334, 342.

government. Broglie informed Isambert that the commission had done its duty, and that it was now time for the government to do the same.[43] Both of its plans, however, fell drastically short of the expectations held by many abolitionists when the commission was first formed.

Some abolitionists, such as Isambert, harbored few illusions about the recommendations of the Broglie commission. Isambert informed the British that the Broglie report, when finished, might have the positive effect of attracting French opinion to the slavery question. However, he was not optimistic about the "conclusions of the Commission," for "the system of slow and progressive abolition makes new progress in the public mind every day."[44] The *British and Foreign Anti-Slavery Reporter* and its Paris correspondent – invariably Isambert – were bitterly disappointed once they read the minutes of the Broglie commission. On the crucial point of "the immediate and general abolition of slavery," they remarked that "it is painful to perceive how few of the members of the Commission were governed in their decisions by sound principles of morals." Only Tracy and Rossi, the British organ explained, could be praised for championing this measure; the support given it by Reynard of the port city of Marseille had been a pleasant surprise. Broglie, president of the commission and of the abolition society, "declared himself to be opposed to it; whilst Sade and Tocqueville, two other members of the Society for the Abolition of Slavery, who were on the Commission, expressed themselves as doubtful or adverse." In particular, the British periodical stressed its disappointment with the attitude of a "distinguished . . . early and eloquent advocate in France of the abolition of the slave trade," an obvious reference to Broglie.[45] There was little doubt in the minds of avid anti-slavery spokesmen that the Broglie commission's debates had not advanced in France the cause of rapid emancipation.

The official report by Broglie inspired no more enthusiasm in radical abolitionist circles than did the commission proceedings. *Le Siècle*, for example, displayed disappointment with the unoriginality

---

[43] Bibliothèque Nationale, Paris, n. a. f. 23770, Papiers F. A. Isambert, part 2, pp. 26–7, Isambert to an unidentified colonial person of color, Jan. 27, 1843.

[44] Rhodes House Anti-Slavery Papers, G103, Isambert to Scoble, May 9, 1842; *British and Foreign Anti-Slavery Reporter*, June 1, 1842.

[45] Ibid., Feb. 21, 1844.

and time-worn nature of the commission's two proposals.[46] The most abolitionists could say was that the report was infused with Enlightenment- and religious-inspired humanitarianism, and was written with "talent" and "eloquence."[47] After all, the report had emphasized the belief that blacks were not prepared for liberty and that emancipation should not occur until after at least a decade and a half of special preparation. Its approach was an extremely conservative, gradualistic one, very near to that of the government, and closer to that of the *colons* than to the stance of immediatist abolitionists of the 1840s like Bissette, Isambert, or Schoelcher. Needless to say, though, pro-slavery advocates, wedded to the policy of defending the absolute status quo, found the Broglie report as unattractive as the abolitionists had. Their reactions ranged from the mild disapproval of the port city newspaper *Le Breton* (Nantes), to dire predictions by the Chamber of Commerce of Le Havre that the Broglie emancipation plans would lead to "the decadence of civilization in the Antilles and the ruin of our navy and colonies."[48]

Even before the report was made public, abolitionists wondered how the government might respond to it. In the spring of 1842, when parliamentary debates were centered upon the right of search issue to the point where the slavery question was hardly mentioned, Roger du Loiret, a mainstay of the French abolition society, questioned the navy-colonial minister as to whether his administration planned to follow through on the work of the commission. Admiral Duperré replied enigmatically that the body had not yet come to its conclusions, but that the government's intentions had not changed.[49] A year later, when the report was complete, French abolitionists again expressed concern as to whether the Soult–Guizot administration would act upon its recommendations. Early in 1843 Isambert apprehensively uttered his fears that the administration was espousing the colonial cause "and repudiating all the liberal doctrines" it had advocated prior to the right of search crisis. "In a word," he wrote to London, "there is no person in France who can foresee even afar off

[46] April 14, 1843.
[47] Rhodes House Anti-Slavery Papers, G103, Isambert to Scoble, April 13, 1843.
[48] *Le Breton*, April 19, 27, 1845; Le Havre, Chambre de Commerce du Havre, Régistre des delibérations, vol. 14, p. 17, session of Nov. 17, 1843.
[49] *Le Moniteur universel*, May 29, 1842.

the epoch in which the government will occupy itself seriously with emancipation."[50]

Once again, abolitionists employed their time-tested tactic of interpellations in the chambers in an attempt both to prod the government and receive clarifications as to its intentions. In 1843, as in the previous year, Roger du Loiret spoke up in the lower house, profiting from the discussion on the navy-colonial budget to query the Cabinet as to "what follow-through" it intended to give the Broglie report. This time Guizot replied on behalf of his administration, speaking in a highly dilatory manner. He pointed out that the government had to take into consideration the fact that a new sugar bill favorable to the colonies had not been passed by the chambers, and that a major earthquake had disrupted production in Guadeloupe.[51] Moreover, he maintained, the Broglie report had just been issued and its two systems were under consideration by the authorities. Contrary to what the commission had expected, Guizot also suggested that by offering two different options the commission had complicated the decision-making process. Most important, though, he stressed that the need to pay an indemnity of 250 million francs was "a grave fact" that it was impossible for the government to realize. Tracy captured the gist of Guizot's intervention when he exclaimed that the de facto head of the Cabinet had placed too much emphasis on purely "financial dispositions." Barrot blurted out that what the *colons* and government wanted was "an indefinite adjournment, but they dare not say it."[52] Guizot had reneged on his promise of March 1841 to act upon the Broglie commission recommendations as soon as they were issued.

There was a despondent tone in Isambert's assessment of the debate over the Broglie report in the lower house. He confided to the British that in France "the spirit of liberty backtracks every day." Guizot

---

[50] Rhodes House Anti-Slavery Papers, G103, Isambert to Scoble, Jan. 19, 1843.

[51] The chambers had just approved a new sugar law aimed at increasing the tax on beet sugar as a step toward the evenual equalization of tariffs on beet and cane sugar, much to the disapprobation of the administration, which had wanted to take more drastic measures to assist the colonies by outlawing the production of beet sugar (which had increased to 31 million kilos in 1841–1843) and indemnifying beet producers. The colonies had lobbied strongly for the suppression of beet sugar, because cane sugar production reached 89 million kilos in 1842, the market was flooded, prices fell, and the colonial establishment cried impoverishment once again (Boizard and Tardieu, *Histoire de la législation des sucres*, 70–85).

[52] *Le Moniteur universel*, June 29, 1843.

might want emancipation, Isambert remarked, but above all he wished to serve his master, the King, and not stray from the conservative policy of maintaining the status quo. The chambers were "very poorly disposed [toward emancipation] because our finances are tied up until 1853 with large public works" projects. Because of this, Isambert claimed, Guizot had exaggerated the amount of the indemnity – indeed, the commission had envisaged a reduced cost of only 150 million – to frighten the conservative majority from acting on the slavery problem.[53] Colonial spokesmen, to the contrary, rejoiced over the emphasis Guizot had placed on the fiscal impediments to emancipation and the little support abolitionists seemed to have in the chambers. Jollivet, delegate of Martinique, reported to his colonial council that the situation had changed dramatically since 1841 and that "the abolitionists are losing terrain every day" within the French legislature.[54]

There are a multiplicity of reasons why French slaves were not freed earlier than 1848. There was the effective opposition of the colonial party, the do-nothing policy of the July Monarchy wedded to the status quo in most matters, and the extremely moderate nature of mainstream French anti-slavery, unwilling or unable to appeal to pubic opinion. Such opinion, perhaps the key element in the entire equation, was never successfully tapped by French abolitionism. It remained alienated from the abolitionists because of government restrictions or discouragement, the Anglophobia concomitant with the Egyptian crisis of 1840, and especially because of the right of search controversy which plagued French anti-slavery from 1842 to 1845. Another leading element, though, was the unwillingness of the French chambers to provide the funding to cover an indemnity for slave owners, something underlined once more by Guizot's statement in the Chamber of Deputies. Here again, public opinion, unswayed by abolitionism, played a role, for in Great Britain too in the early 1830s the government would not have voted the immense sum of 20 million pounds to free its colonial slaves if public pressure – successfully orchestrated by British abolitionists – had not weighed heavily on British officialdom. Without such pressure in France the chambers followed their credo of responsible fiscal policies and steadily refused

---

[53] Rhodes House Anti-Slavery Papers, G103, Isambert to Scoble, June 29, 1843.
[54] Schoelcher Papers, N. a. f. 3631, pp. 26–7, Jollivet to President of Colonial Council, June 28, 1843.

to consider disbursing the sums necessary for slave liberation. More-over, in the early 1840s the government debt had grown due to increased expenditures. It was at this time that the legislature began financing the surge in French railway construction, laying the infra-structure for the railway network by providing capital outlays and loans for the new railroad companies. This resulted in a upswing in French railway investment until the speculative bubble burst in the late 1840s. Once agricultural difficulties also set in – the same process that brought famine to Ireland – as of the mid-1840s and led to indus-trial downsizing, the French government fell deeper in debt than ever and retained still fewer options. Besides, the war scare of 1840 led to a massive public works program for the fortification of Paris that sur-rounded the capital with an impressive series of forts. The debt ensu-ing from all of these obligations could not be amortized, according to calculations of the time, until 1853. The July Monarchy had arranged its fiscal options in such a manner as to leave little room for financing humanitarian endeavors like slave liberation. Quite clearly, liberating French slaves remained low on the Orleanist regime's list of priorities. And abolitionist pressures proved totally inadequate to oblige the government to place the slavery question higher on its agenda.

Abolitionists were well aware of these fiscal impediments to eman-cipation. The gradualist abolitionist Charles Joseph Dussillion thought it impossible for the government to disburse a large sum in 1843 when "all its resources are committed for ten years by the immense works required by the fortifications of Paris and the railroads."[55] The Insti-tut d'Afrique, whose members were generally well connected with the upper echelons of the administration, reported that the Council of Ministers examined in "five or six sessions" the recommendations of the Broglie commission, and especially the one calling for emancipa-tion in ten years, followed by a period of *engagement*. According to the organ of the Institut, the Cabinet had decided that "the proposi-tions of Mr. the duc de Broglie must be adjourned until France had finished its great works of the fortification of Paris and the railroads that should absorb all its resources for several years."[56] In one of a

[55] Charles Joseph Dussillion, *Considérations sur l'esclavage aux Antilles françaises et de son abolition graduelle, suivie d'un aperçu analytique et critique du système d'apprentis-sage et de ses résultats dans les colonies anglaises* (Paris: Dussillion, 1843), 105.
[56] *Annales de l'Institut d'Afrique*, March, April 1843.

series of articles on slavery that Tocqueville published in *Le Siècle* in the autumn of 1843, he too argued that a leading impediment to emancipation was the unwillingness by the government to increase the debt for the humanitarian act of freeing the slaves. He also feared that now that the Broglie commission had made its recommendations, the government might not put them into effect.[57] Similarly, Bissette informed his British interlocutors that "the French government does not have the intention to accomplish the grand work of slave abolition." The black abolitionist was convinced that, despite the Guizot administration's "false semblance of humanity for blacks," it "only wishes to befool us and gain time."[58] The government had received the Broglie report but done nothing with it. Its recommendations remained a dead letter, and many abolitionists feared that the entire report would simply be shunted aside.

Other developments in 1842 and 1843 also dampened abolitionist spirits. Saint-Hilaire, who had been Director of the Colonies since 1825, retired. He was replaced on March 27, 1842, by Galos, a native of Bordeaux, and, like Wustemberg, a deputy from the Gironde department, which traditionally had strong ties with the colonies. According to *Le Constitutionnel*, the appointment was made to appease the maritime cities, displeased with the slight progress that had been made in improving the legislation and tax structure on colonial sugar, of which Bordeaux and other Atlantic ports were important refiners.[59] The French correspondent of the *British and Foreign Anti-Slavery Reporter* – probably Isambert – saw the move as the displacement of Saint-Hilaire, whom he believed to have been prepared to yield on the emancipation question, for someone "decidedly adverse to it." *The Reporter* held that Saint-Hilaire had been purged from a French colonial office that was "filled with men who are avowed adversaries of emancipation."[60] Judging from his stance in the Broglie commission, where he consistently took a hard line on the slavery issue, Saint-Hilaire had regressed considerably from his

---

[57] *Le Siècle*, Dec. 15, 1843. For English translations of the articles Tocqueville submitted to the *Siècle* in late 1843, see Drescher, *Tocqueville and Beaumont*, 137–173.

[58] Rhodes House Anti-Slavery Papers, C13/116, Bissette to British and Foreign Anti-Slavery Society, July 27, 1843.

[59] *Le Constitutionnel*, March 30, 1842. For a discussion of the role played by French ports and their hinterland in refining colonial sugar, see Fiérain, *Les raffineries*.

[60] *British and Foreign Anti-Slavery Reporter*, April 20, 1842.

flexible position of 1839, and the Paris correspondent of the British journal was being far too generous in his evaluation of him. Still, the fact remains that Galos also had been decidedly procolonial in his interventions on the Broglie commission, revealing himself as highly critical of the economic outcome of British emancipation.[61] Quite revealingly, upon assuming office, Galos had written to Charles Dupin to assure him of his "desire to be useful to the colonies and to contribute to advance their important and legitimate interests."[62] It could be said that Saint-Hilaire had at least wavered on the slavery question. Galos was of unknown quality, with a background and early actions that seemed to augur poorly for the future.

Worse yet for the abolitionist cause was the appointment of Admiral Mackau as Minister of the Navy and Colonies in 1843. Already his predecessor, Admiral Roussin, who made a brief reappearance as minister from February to July 1843, had been judged retrograde on the slavery scene by the abolitionists.[63] Married to a Creole, Mackau had served during the 1830s first as commander-in-chief of the French naval station in the West Indies, and then for two years as governor of Martinique. As such, like most high colonial administrators, he had been exposed to the influence of the *colons* and had come to identify with them. Already as governor, Mackau had tended to view servitude through colonial eyes. However, it was on the Broglie commission that Mackau distinguished himself as the member most committed to protecting colonial interests. Mackau went far beyond other colonial defenders in proving himself inimical to any emancipation concept except the most cautious, long-term approach to the problem. Mackau revealed his position early in the hearings when he insisted that "the interests of the proprietors, far from having a secondary weight in the question" of slave liberation, "should be placed in the first rank of considerations." He felt that there could be no emancipation without guarantees for the continuation of work or without a generous indemnity, something that was the slave owners' right, but which was "impossible to realize" at this time. Thus, Mackau rejected

---

[61] Broglie Commission, Minutes, part 3, pp. 384–5, 430–2, May 23, 1842, Feb. 22, 1843.

[62] ANCAOM, Série Colonies EE (personnel dossiers), 960 (1), Galos, Henry, letter dated April 8, 1842.

[63] Rhodes House Anti-Slavery Papers, G103, Isambert to Scoble, April 13, 1843; *British and Foreign Anti-Slavery Reporter*, April 19, 1843.

outright the British example of any system stipulating general or rapid emancipation. He claimed to favor "sincerely the amelioration of the plight of the blacks, as a means of permitting them to arrive later at liberty," but he also insisted that France had "very serious duties to fulfill toward Frenchmen established beyond the seas."[64] In light of this, Mackau advocated simply continuing colonial department policies that called for religious and moral preparation of slaves. After all, he pointed out, one had to take into consideration "the limited intelligence of the black." Besides, "the blacks of our colonies," he believed, "are not in a moral condition that would render immediate and general emancipation a service for them." In order to moralize them and give them "the habit and taste for work," Mackau intoned the colonial line that it was "necessary to accept the benefits of time."[65]

Mackau was repeating the standard argument that the plantocracy had employed since the mid-1830s for refusing emancipation by postponing it far into the distant future. As the Paris correspondent of the British abolitionists – again probably Isambert – noted, on the Broglie commission Mackau had displayed "an almost implacable enmity to abolition."[66] And this was the person now named navy-colonial minister and thus placed in charge of the slavery question. Mackau's appointment marked a definite victory for the colonial cause. Given the fact that Mackau was not particularly close to Guizot,[67] it can be assumed that the appointment had been made under the influence of King Louis Philippe – who was also solicitous of colonial interests – because of the way Mackau had stood out on the Broglie commission as the most staunch defender of the colonial establishment. Furthermore, in August of 1844 Mackau was joined by Jubelin – whose background was also that of a colonial advocate – as under-secretary of state for the navy and colonies, a position Jubelin would hold until the Revolution of 1848. With Mackau, aided by Jubelin and Galos, in control of the French colonial office, it appeared that there would be token ameliorations for slaves, but no real movement on the emancipation front as long as they held the ministerial reins. Unfortunately

[64] Broglie Commission, Minutes, 8–9, 19–20, Jan. 31, Feb. 7, 1842.
[65] Ibid., 162, 165–66, March 14, 1842.
[66] *British and Foreign Anti-Slavery Reporter*, Feb. 21, 1844.
[67] Gabriel de Broglie, *Guizot* (Paris: Perrin, 1990), 338–9.

for the abolitionists and slaves, Mackau would retain his post until the spring of 1847.

If French anti-slavery fortunes had regressed in 1840–1841, they plunged even further in 1842–1843. Despite the setbacks afforded by the Egyptian crisis and the maneuvers of the Thiers administration, the French abolition society seemed determined and resourceful as late as the beginning of 1842. However, the main weakness of the French abolitionists since the 1830s had been their lack of popular support. Attempts by the society to remedy this by changing tactics and opening up to the public were dashed when the government again quashed moves along these lines in early 1842. At the same time, the right of search crisis intervened to fan renewed Anglophobia that the French public now associated directly with French abolitionists. French anti-slavery was sullied, forced to break with its British antecedents and support systems, and obliged to beat an ignominious retreat. All hopes of winning over public opinion in the immediate future were dissipated. The drawn-out proceedings of the Broglie commission – which met concurrently with the right of search imbroglio – showed how divided and impotent French abolitionism was in light of these new developments. They also demonstrated the lack of unity within abolitionist ranks, the absence of a common anti-slavery policy, and the tendency of individual abolitionists to waver constantly in their own convictions. The conclusions of the Broglie commission report and the installation of staunch colonial defenders in the French colonial office presaged a dim future for French opponents of slavery. Guizot, Mackau, Galos, and the King showed little inclination to act on either option put forth by the Broglie report, but much determination to continue in the policy of prevarication that marked the duration of the July Monarchy. Planters, government, even most abolitionists agreed on the necessity of a generous indemnity, while the government placed the slavery issue low on its list of fiscal priorities. The momentum and the spirit of French anti-slavery had been broken in the first years of the 1840s. French abolitionism reached its nadir in 1842–1843.

8

———

REDEFINING
ABOLITIONISM

French anti-slavery had touched bottom in 1842–1843, but by early 1844 there were several encouraging signs for abolitionists. These developments went beyond the annual revival of anti-slavery activity coinciding with the opening of the legislative session at the beginning of the year. In the first instance, the Société française pour l'abolition de l'esclavage took an important step in founding a bimonthly review that it would continue to publish for the remainder of the July Monarchy. The first issue of *L'Abolitioniste français* (sic) was dated January–February 1844. With the resumption of its annual sessions in early 1844, the "general committee" of the society deemed it wise "to resume its publications to propagate its principles and popularize them." The previous year the organization had interrupted its output of pamphlets that had totaled nineteen in number since 1835. The society now judged that, while these pamphlets had served to introduce the slavery question to the French public, "they did not provide enough continuity" in putting forth the group's message. The new bimonthly, society members believed, would permit them to counter the claims of their adversaries, report on developments in French and foreign colonies, and, especially, "remind the government incessantly of the need to carry out its promises." *L'Abolitioniste français* would enable the society to pressure the authorities in a more public and regular manner. The Société française had not altered its timeworn strategy of working through government channels, but was attempting to reinforce it. Forbidden to hold public meetings, the society was redoubling its effort to win over opinion through the press. The publication of this new journal indicates too that the society believed the right of search crisis to have receded to the point where it could once again freely publicize its message.

The statement of objectives accompanying the appearance of this new periodical also provides insight into the French abolition society's principles as it approached the mid-1840s. *L'Abolitioniste* postulated that slaves were "free by nature," requiring only the tutelage of the state to prepare them for liberty. In this sense, the society was still espousing the humanitarian–statist approach advocated by the Tocqueville report of 1839. The periodical went on to suggest, on the one hand, that emancipation should not be delayed by the difficulties of providing an indemnity, thus reflecting the opinion of its more radical members. On the other hand, though, it conceded that slave liberation could be achieved on "terms more or less long," and that it should not occur without the prerequisite preparatory measures.[1] These latter statements indicate that, while divisions continued to exist within the French abolitionist society between radicals and moderates, it was the cautious message of the moderates that still prevailed.

The publication of this new anti-slavery review was well received by liberal French newspapers with abolitionist inclinations, like *Le Semeur*. The *British and Foreign Anti-Slavery Reporter* also expressed its pleasure with the appearance of a French organ devoted exclusively to the abolitionist cause.[2] Indeed, the British were not foreign to the creation of the French bimonthly, for another element in the French abolitionist revival in 1844 involved its renewed ties with its cross-Channel colleagues. British emancipationists provided critical encouragement for the founding of this new organ through the purchase on a regular basis of 110 copies, 100 to be distributed in France and ten sent to England. British abolitionist organizations might also have provided further assistance to the fledgling publication. According to Isambert, only in the autumn of 1845 was the *Abolitioniste* able to "stand alone with the assistance offered by the [British] Society's subscription," implying initial financial aid beyond the subscriptions.[3] Whatever the amount the British contributed, though, their support had been crucial for the appearance of the new periodical.

The subsidization of the *Abolitioniste* was just one of the actions that marked increased British involvement with French anti-slavery in

---

[1] *L'Abolitioniste français*, Jan.–Feb. 1844, pp. 5–6, 10–11.

[2] *Le Semeur*, May 8, 1844; *British and Foreign Anti-Slavery Reporter*, May 1, 29, 1844.

[3] This was confided by Isambert to Scoble when the two met in the autumn of 1845 (Rhodes House Anti-Slavery Papers, Minute Books, Oct. 4, [17], 1845.

1844–1845. Alexander and Scoble, the treasurer and secretary of the British and Foreign Anti-Slavery Society, respectively, visited Paris in March 1844 to arrange for a French edition of one of their recent pamphlets advocating immediate emancipation. Consequently, the British group paid the Parisian publishing firm Firmin Didot 584.45 pounds for the printing of *Liberté immédiate et absolue de l'esclavage: Observations sur le rapport de M. le duc de Broglie.*[4] At the same time the two British delegates met with a series of French intellectuals, members of the bar, and Catholic clergymen in an effort to elicit publications from them favoring immediatism. They eventually joined up with two other British abolitionists, Josiah Forster and Joseph Gurney, to hold a meeting in Paris on March 29 with over fifty French abolitionists in an attempt to convert them to the immediatist cause. Subsequently, Gurney employed the services of three important Protestant bankers from Toulouse, the Courtois brothers, to make contact with a young theologian at the Protestant faculty of Montauban, Guillaume de Félice. At their meeting with him they requested that he write immediatist pamphlets and become the British group's "agent for the abolition of slavery in France." Félice agreed on the need in France for an active campaigner to "speak, write, agitate opinion, press the men in power, hold assemblies and provoke petitions." But Félice was obliged to decline the British offer to act on a full-time basis because of his heavy teaching duties.[5] Still, the British had judged the time appropriate to resume open contacts with French abolitionists now that the right of search controversy was waning. Moreover, the British were widening their contacts in France beyond the conservative French abolition society in an attempt to garner more widespread support for a radical and rapid approach to slave liberation.

The revival of French abolitionist activity in 1844, however, was not unduly dependent on British encouragement. Important new forces and figures were emerging within French emancipationism itself. By 1844 Agénor de Gasparin, son of an important count who had served in the Molé Cabinet, was distinguishing himself as a leading advocate

[4] Ibid., Oct. 4, 1844.
[5] *British and Foreign Anti-Slavery Reporter*, May 29, 1844; *Le Lien* (Paris), April 6, 1844; Rhodes House Anti-Slavery Papers, C157/66, Félice to F., L., and A. Courtois, July 4, 1844. The three Courtois brothers were also members of the Société française pour l'abolition de l'esclavage. Their bank is still an important Toulouse institution today.

of French anti-slavery. Like other former gradualist abolitionists, this Protestant deputy, himself a firm supporter of Guizot and thus holding close ties to the administration, had been converted to immediatism by his conviction that the government's slow gradualism would not free the slaves. In 1843 when Isambert received 1000 francs from persons of color in the colonies, he forwarded it to Mr. "G" (certainly a reference to Gasparin), whom he described as the best defender of the anti-slavery cause at the time, with the suggestion that the sum be shared with Bissette, who "is supported by no one here" and who had just been sued by the *colons*.[6] Agénor de Gasparin was also responsible, undoubtedly, for putting the slavery abolition question on the agenda of the Scientific Congress of France, held under the presidency of his father in the Protestant stronghold of Nîmes in 1844. Schoelcher read a long address before the congress on September 8, encouraging immediatism, and at the end of the scientific meeting the delegates expressed their formal wish for immediate slave liberation.[7] The Gasparin example indicates that the ranks of immediatist French abolitionists were growing in the mid-1840s and that this increase was probably due more to disillusionment with government policies and the gradualist French abolition society than to British inducements.

In 1843 Schoelcher had also published another important anti-slavery book, entrenching himself in the front ranks of French immediatist abolitionism.[8] The staunchly republican freemason Schoelcher also wove ties with the new Parisian leftist daily, *La Réforme*, which first appeared in 1843. He became its slavery expert and subsequently turned out a whole series of articles that publicized the radical anti-slavery cause. In one of its first issues *La Réforme* presented Schoelcher as an alternative to the "prudent and inoffensive" French abolition society, which, it said, offered the "ridiculous spectacle of a complete and incurable inertia," and which had done, was doing, and would do "nothing" to resolve the slavery question.[9] Its criticism of the Société française pour l'abolition de l'esclavage might have been justified to

---

[6] Bibliothèque Nationale, Isambert Papers, N. a. f. 23770, pp. 26–7, note by Isambert dated Jan. 27, 1843.

[7] Victor Schoelcher, *Historie de l'esclavage pendant les deux dernières années* (2 vols.; Paris: Pagnerre, 1847), II, 504, 522.

[8] *Colonies étrangères et Haïti: Résulatats de l'émancipation anglaise. Coup d'oeil sur l'état de la question d'affranchissement* (Paris: Pagnerre, 1843).

[9] *La Réforme*, Sept. 5, 1843.

a large extent, but its attack on it was not designed to foster unity among French abolitionists. Indeed, Schoelcher had often cooperated with the society, even speaking at its banquet for British delegates in Paris on March 10, 1842,[10] but he, like Bissette, became estranged with the group because of its Orleanist-establishment membership and its cautious approach to emancipation. The statement by the *Réforme*, like the positions adopted by Gasparin and Schoelcher, also suggested growing alienation from the gradualist cause and the beginning of a process of marginalization of the French abolition society embodying this approach.

By 1843–1844 divisions were apparent not only between the Schoelcher–*Réforme* faction and the French abolition society, but within the ranks of French immediatists. The growing fame of Schoelcher, his easy access to important channels of publicity, and his rapid promotion to a position of leadership in abolitionist circles infuriated Bissette, who, by the early 1840s, felt shunted aside, increasingly strapped for funds, and frustrated. Although Bissette had praised the earlier works of the relatively unknown Schoelcher, his harsh criticism of the republican abolitionist as of 1842 led to a bitter feud between the two men that lasted for the following ten years.[11] Bissette ranted against this "negrophile of recent date," this "newcomer into the arena," who had been highly cautious about the slavery question in the early 1830s when Bissette, who was as devoted an "abolitionist as Mr. Schoelcher," was already advocating emancipation.[12] The two carried on a rancorous exchange in brochures and the press. French anti-slavery might be reviving by 1844, but it was becoming increasingly fragmented too.

A more encouraging development for French abolitionism than its internal bickering centered around the working-class petition campaign that was suddenly launched in January 1844. Early in that month, Parisian typographers with the working-class newspaper *L'Union*, formerly *La Ruche populaire*, took the initiative of issuing a petition for immediate emancipation that they hoped would be signed

---

[10] *La Revue des colonies*, 8th year, no. 9, March 1842, pp. 337–49.

[11] See Jennings, "Bissette," 60–61, and Schmidt, *Schoelcher*, 71–5.

[12] C. C. A. Bissette, *Réfutation du livre de M. Victor Schoelcher intitulé "Des colonies françaises"* (Paris: Breton, 1843); *Deux-mots sur une note de Mr. V. Schoelcher* (Paris: Ebrard, 1843); *Réfutation du livre de M. V. Schoelcher sur Haïti* (Paris: Ebrard, 1844).

by several thousand workers.[13] All indications are that this was a spontaneous move by a small group of French printers, who might have become aware of the emancipation issue by printing abolitionist material, but who were acting independently of established anti-slavery channels. After the petition appeared in *L'Union*, dated January 22, it was actively supported by *L'Atelier*, another proletarian newspaper with a heavy representation of printers among its directors, and reprinted in some seventeen other French newspapers in the capital and the provinces, including the important Parisian governmental organ, *Le Journal des débats*.[14] Some eleven petitions were circulated by the workers in the first four months of 1844, and were then deposited individually in the Chamber of Deputies by different abolitionist deputies such as Isambert, Lamartine, Agénor de Gasparin, Carnot, and the leftist opposition leader Ledru-Rollin. By the time the last one was submitted in the lower house on May 4, some 8,832 signatures had been garnered.[15] It seems that the main method of soliciting signatures in Paris involved simply laying out the petitions at the *Union* offices.[16] However, not all the adherents were Parisian workers, suggesting that the printers had sought out certain adherents. The fourth petition, emanating from Paris and containing 476 names, had been signed mostly by people of letters, including the novelist Eugène Sue and the playwright Augustin Eugène Scribe. Other noted signatories included Jules Michelet, Schoelcher, Quinet, and the comte de Lasteyrie, a member of the French abolition society and nephew of Tracy.[17] Two

---

[13] Rhodes House Anti-Slavery Papers, G103, Isambert to Scoble, Jan. 24, 1844.

[14] *L'Union*, Jan. 1844, p. 1; March 1844, p. 4; *L'Atelier*, Feb. 1844, p. 80; *L'Abolitioniste français*, Jan.–Feb. 1844, pp. 56–7. For information on *L'Union* and *L'Atelier*, see Claude Bellanger et al., *Histoire générale de la presse française* (5 vols.; Paris: Presses Universitaires de France, 1969–1976), II, 131, and Armand Cuvillier, *Un Journal d'ouvriers: L'Atelier, 1840–1850* (1914; rpt., Paris: Editions ouvrières, 1954).

[15] These numbers are based upon statistics given in ANCAOM, Gén. 197 (1489). They seem preferable to the count of 9,026 provided in *L'Abolitioniste français* (May–June 1844, p. 122), for this review's account contains some textual errors rendering the reliability of the calculations suspicious. Augustin Cochin (p. 51) obviously based his total of 8,830 upon archival material, but made a small counting error. Be this as it may, there is only a difference of less than 200 between the archival and *Abolitioniste* figures. Gaston Martin is far off when he speaks of three petitions and more than 3,000 signatures (*Histoire de l'esclavage dans les colonies françaises* (Paris: Presses Universitaires de France, 1948), 288).

[16] *British and Foreign Anti-Slavery Reporter*, Feb. 7, 1844.

[17] *Le Moniteur universel*, April 28, 1844; ANCAOM, Gén. 197 (1489).

petitions were adhered to in the provinces, probably resulting from the document appearing in a number of provincial newspapers. The one from Metz and the Moselle had 603 signers, the one from Lyon, 1,705.[18] Most interestingly, one petition from Paris contained the names of what one colonial spokesperson referred to mockingly as "around one hundred maidens."[19] As such, it affords some rare evidence of female participation in the French anti-slavery campaign of the 1840s, albeit strikingly small in comparison to the massive female support obtained by the British abolitionist offensive of the 1830s.

One of the aims of the petitions was to challenge the oft-employed colonial contention that slaves fared better than many French workers. Such an assertion had been eloquently attacked by many abolitionists, such as when Agénor de Gasparin stated in the chambers that he would like to see the day when any worker would request to become a slave.[20] But it was best refuted by the workers themselves. Such a rejection of a cherished colonial theme, along with the request for immediate emancipation, infuriated the *colons*. As a result, colonial spokesmen like the delegate Jollivet attempted to belittle the workers' effort. Others challenged the legitimacy of petitions from a class without voting rights. The *Mémorial bordelais* remarked that workers were in no position to know much about slavery or to pass judgment on it. The *Courrier de la Gironde* (Bordeaux) was openly sarcastic in asserting that workers were "little suited at deciding social questions.... Masons are made for building houses and not systems."[21] The plantocracy could not countenance the undermining of one of their foremost theories in defense of slavery. *Colons* were probably also concerned by the fact that the workers' petitions of 1844 indicated the possibility of immediatism gaining increased support among the populace.

Contrariwise, pro-abolitionist organs applauded "this glorious initiative," this "beautiful and noble sentiment" on the part of the working class.[22] British abolitionists believed the petitioning significant as

[18] Ibid.; *L'Abolitioniste français*, May–June 1844, pp. 121–4.
[19] Schoelcher Papers, N. a. f. 3631, p. 49, Jollivet to President Colonial Council of Martinique, March 13, 1844.
[20] *Le Moniteur universel*, June 1, 1845.
[21] *Le Mémorial bordelais*, May 7, 1844; *Le Courrier de la Gironde*, March 22, 1845.
[22] *La Réforme*, April 28, 1844; *Le Siècle*, May 5, 1844.

"a popular movement" which "brings into action that very element which we have long deemed most useful, and wanting, to the advancement of emancipation in France."[23] The British probably hoped that the actions of the workers of *L'Union* would launch a series of petition campaigns that would, as in Great Britain, raise millions of signatures and play a role in obliging the government to move rapidly toward emancipation. But in France once again British hopes were dashed. There was no significant follow-through on the petitions of 1844 until different circumstances prompted a new campaign in 1846–1847 that raised only a few thousand more signatures than those collected by *L'Union*.[24] What the workers' petitions of 1844 did accomplish, though, was to help place the slavery issue once again on the docket of the French legislature, the arena in which most French emancipationist energies were still concentrated. It was one of the factors that also helped convince the government that the pause afforded it by the right of search controversy was over, and that it must take further measures on the slavery scene.

Well before the Parisian workers took the initiative of issuing their petitions, though, rumors indicated that Guizot and Mackau were drafting a plan for preparing slaves for liberation which would be presented in the chambers during the 1844 session.[25] At the end of the 1843 session abolitionists had lobbied hard for some action in the slavery-emancipation domain. Already at this time a division appears to have developed within the Cabinet over how to handle the slavery question. Indications were that Guizot favored more movement, while Mackau opposed concessions of any kind; however, Guizot seemed to have gained the upper hand.[26] Now that the Broglie commission had issued its report calling for emancipation in one of two ways, and now that the search crisis had crested, the government felt compelled to take some measures on the slavery front. Besides, by 1843 it was patently clear that preparatory measures implemented as of 1840 had had little effect.

[23] *British and Foreign Anti-Slavery Reporter*, Feb. 7, 1844.
[24] For a discussion of the paltry results of French petitioning in comparison with the massive anti-slavery campaigns in Britain, see Drescher, "Public Opinion and the Destruction of British Slavery," 25–9.
[25] *Annales de l'Institut d'Afrique*, no. 10, Oct. 1843.
[26] Schoelcher Papers, N. a. f. 3631, pp. 22–4, Jollivet to President of Colonial Council of Martinique, June 10, 1843; *L'Abolitioniste français*, Jan.–Feb. 1844, p. 9.

Already in the early 1840s, scattered reports circulated that legislation and funding applied to the colonies in 1840 and 1841 to prepare slaves religiously and educationally for liberty were without consequence. For example, Casimir Dugoujon, a priest who had spent two years as a missionary in Guadeloupe, wrote in September 1841 that religious preparatory measures for the slaves were still "nil," and would continue to be so, for everything necessary to "civilize" blacks under slavery was missing.[27] In effect, money that had been designated to build new chapels was being used instead by colonial councils to repair existing churches frequented by whites. Similarly, new schools or classes that were being opened systematically excluded slaves.[28] The slow progress on the moralization of slaves was amply confirmed by the Broglie commission hearings and its report, which demonstrated that very few slaves, especially those working on plantations, were being given access to religious or primary education. There was also a severe problem with the availability and training of priests, not to mention their priorities. Only Catholic clergy or missionaries were allowed to practice in the islands; they were insufficient in number and "mediocre" in quality to carry out effective missionary service among slaves; their many duties in towns kept most of them off plantations, where they were not particularly welcome anyhow by masters.[29] In a dispatch sent to the governor of Martinique in the summer of 1843, the navy-colonial minister himself admitted that he had received "the most distressing news" on the progress of instruction among slaves. In late 1843 Mackau again acknowledged to colonial authorities that the religious education of slaves was progressing much slower than anticipated.[30] Mackau himself had come to realize that additional preparatory moves for slaves were required. The

[27] *La Revue des colonies*, 8th year, no. 3, Sept. 1841, pp. 93–6. For more on Dugoujon, see Père Camille Fabre, "Un Préfet apostolique de la Guadeloupe en 1848: Casimir Dugoujon, des prêtres de Sainte-Croix du Mans," *La Province du Maine* 85 (1983): 47–77; and Paule Brasseur, "Libermann et l'abolition de l'esclavage," *Revue française d'histoire d'outre-mer* 73 (1986), 340–41.

[28] *L'Abolitioniste français*, Jan.–Feb. 1844, pp. 41–3.

[29] Broglie Commission, Report, pp. 92–105, 121–2. For more information on the failure of the ameliorative measures of 1840 in Guadeloupe, Martinique, and Bourbon, respectively, see Fallope, *Esclaves et citoyens*, 302–308; Delisle, *Renouveau missionnaire*, 172–7, 189–98; and Prudhomme, *Histoire religieuse*, 76–79.

[30] ANCAOM, Corr. Gén. 199, 1843, Minister to Governor of Martinique, Aug. 29, 1843; Minister to Governor of Bourbon, Dec. 1, 1843.

ineffectiveness of gradualist measures that was slowly but surely driving more and more gradualist abolitionists into the ranks of the immediatists was becoming increasingly apparent even in the corridors of the French navy-colonial ministry.

When the abolitionists made their annual interpellations in the chambers in early 1844, the government was in the final stages of drafting a new preparatory package. This time the Société française pour l'abolition de l'esclavage decided that Sade would question the administration on the first possible occasion. He received his chance to do so when Agénor de Gasparin – probably not a member of the society – intervened during a discussion of the right of search on January 23, 1844. Gasparin contended that the best means of repressing the slave trade was through the abolition of slavery – a favorite theme of British abolitionists too – "something which," he added, "is unfortunately still a distant measure." Mackau replied by expressing his surprise that the slavery issue would be brought up during a debate on the right of search, as if he assumed the latter would prevent discussion of the former. Having seen Gasparin steal the initiative, Sade then blurted out his question as to when the minister intended to submit concrete proposals to the chambers. Mackau retorted simply that in a few weeks the government would be prepared to explain its program in front of the assembly.[31] After consulting Mackau about this, Isambert correctly predicted that no real emancipation bill was in the works and that the minister would merely offer legislation improving the condition of slaves and giving them minimal rights.[32]

A similar impression pervaded procolonial circles. When colonial delegate Dupin spoke with Mackau, the latter assured him of his "best intentions toward the colonies," indicating to Dupin that the minister was "personally fighting within the Cabinet to prevent putting forth any inopportune measure." In February, though, Jollivet reported that while the Council of Ministers had definitely rejected any project to change the political constitution of the colonies – that is, the law of 1833 – Mackau would introduce a proposal containing *pécule* and *rachat*, something Jollivet promised to combat by every possible

---

[31] *Le Moniteur universel*, Jan. 24, 1844; *L'Abolitioniste français*, Jan.–Feb. 1844, pp. 55–6; Rhodes House Anti-Slavery Papers, G103, Isambert to Scoble, Jan. 24, 1844.
[32] Ibid.

means.[33] Once again, the abolition society forced the issue by having Isambert deposit the first emancipation petition from the Parisian workers in the Chamber of Deputies on February 19. Isambert also wrote to Mackau to inquire whether the minister would be prepared to present his new projects when the petition came up for discussion in the lower house, and Mackau replied affirmatively.[34] While pro-slavery elements dug in their feet against any alterations in the existing state of affairs, abolitionists employed their oft-used political skills to oblige the government to put forth its program without further delay and to make emancipation one of its eventual objectives.

The setting of the agenda for the debate on slavery and emancipation led to frantic interparliamentary maneuvering by colonial delegates and abolitionists alike. Jollivet lobbied in the parliamentary bureaus and was pleased to have Amaranthe Alphonse Dugommier Denis, a personal friend, appointed reporter of the Chamber of Deputies commission that was to examine the workers' petition. Denis pledged to Jollivet that he would push for the rejection of the petition, and thus of emancipation, while calling for a return to the order of the day. At the same time Denis made it known that he had spurned attempts by Isambert to influence him by telling the abolitionist point-blank that "he was a determined partisan of slavery." Jollivet also strove to involve the press in the issue, and to influence Mackau once again. Mackau did confirm to the delegate that he would support Denis's efforts to reject the petition, and thus rapid emancipation, but he remained adamant about putting forth his own proposal of *pécule* and *rachat* for slaves. Jollivet concluded quite rightly that colonial objectives could be met only partially. The navy-colonial minister, Jollivet believed, was inclined to reject the call for immediate emancipation contained within the workers' petition, but intent on advancing along the lines of cautious, gradual, partial emancipation by proposing a new preparatory plan.[35] As it turned out, Jollivet should not have been overly concerned. The Mackau proposal proved so

---

[33] Schoelcher Papers, N. a. f. 3631, pp. 46–7, Dupin to President Colonial Council of Martinique, Jan. 29, 1844; pp. 47–9, Jollivet to President Colonial Council Martinique, Feb. 27, 1844.

[34] *L'Abolitioniste français*, Jan.–Feb. 1844, pp. 56–7.

[35] Schoelcher Papers, N. a. f. 3631, pp. 49–52, Jollivet to President of Colonial Council of Martinique, March 13, April 12, April 28, 1844.

gradual in its implementation that it did little to advance emancipation. Still, colonial interests remained steadfastly opposed to change of any kind.

When the commission on the workers' petition made its report on May 4, 1844, in the lower house, Denis, predictably, termed immediate emancipation "an unfortunate measure" and requested its rejection through a return to the order of the day. After Gasparin spoke up to criticize Denis's remarks as a step backward, Mackau intervened as he had told Isambert he would. The navy-colonial minister announced that it was inopportune to adopt either of the Broglie commission proposals, but that the government intended to improve the condition of slaves and prepare them for liberty. Thus, the Cabinet had decided to "develop, in strengthening and completing them, the beneficent dispositions of the ordonnances of January 5, 1840, and September 16, 1841" covering the condition of slaves and their religious, primary, and moral education. This led to an immediate rejoinder by Ledru-Rollin, charging that "the promise made today by the minister is nothing but a dilatory and valueless measure without consequence" because the *colons* had obstructed previous measures of this kind and would continue to do so. Jollivet's attempts to defend the colonial position were inconsequential, and Guizot was forced to intervene to calm spirits in the chamber. Guizot testified that his administration desired emancipation, but that more preparation was necessary. This tended to reassure Tracy and some other abolitionists, to the point that the marquis Henri de La Rochejaquelin exclaimed that, although he had deposited one of the workers' petitions, he did not favor immediate slave liberation either. Still, the call for returning to the order of the day was rejected almost unanimously. Instead, the assembly voted to forward the petitions to the minister and Council of Ministers for consideration.[36] The government, for its part, had admitted that the ameliorative legislation implemented in 1840 had been inadequate and ineffective. The Chamber of Deputies in turn was calling the government to attention by informing it that some action was required on the slave liberation front.

Only ten days later Mackau followed through on his commitment by introducing into the Chamber of Peers a draft law. It clarified the

---

[36] *Le Moniteur universel*, May 5, 1844.

legislation of 1833 by specifying certain domains in which the government could act by ordonnances or legislative means concerning the colonies. It also promised to regulate the nourishment and upkeep of slaves, their hours of work and discipline, and it contained provisions encouraging marriages, religious instruction, and elementary education. Most important, it proposed legalizing, even encouraging, *pécule* and *rachat*.[37] The entire package presumed removing certain prerogatives from the masters' hands and giving them to government authorities. As such, it would certainly be opposed by the colonial establishment. Its timid measures, offering little more than the hope of self-redemption for slaves, had been seriously considered already in the mid-1830s, and could not expect to receive enthusiastic support from most abolitionists either. Moreover, the fact that it was introduced late in the legislative session raised serious questions about the government's real interest in its rapid passage through both houses.

Once again, colonial advocates and abolitionists swung into action to try to influence the legislative process. Bitterly opposed to peculium and self-redemption, the delegates protested against the proposed law and contacted as many peers as possible. The colonial representatives were pleased when the upper house chose five members from the "colonial party" to staff the commission studying the bill in comparison to only two abolitionists, Broglie and Rossi. Charles Dupin himself became one of the five procolonial commissioners, and Joseph Mérilhou – proslavery despite his Freemason background – was elected reporter of the body instead of the abolitionist candidate, Broglie. The colonial strategy centered around amending and retarding the legislation to the point where it could not be voted upon in 1844. The commission arranged to have each delegate appear and make a long presentation before it; Mérilhou promised to draw out the proceedings as much as possible. All of this maneuvering reportedly angered Mackau, who claimed to have hoped to pass the legislation through the two houses in two weeks each.[38] Ironically enough, the French abolition society had also worked for the adjournment of the bill until the following year, so that its members could better

---

[37] Ibid., May 15, 1844.
[38] Schoelcher Papers, N. a. f. 3631, pp. 57–8, Dupin to President Colonial Council of Martinique, May 28, 1844; pp. 62–4, Jollivet to President Colonial Council of Martinique, June 29, 1844.

prepare their attack on it.[39] By mid-July, Mérilhou confided to Jollivet that the law would not even be discussed during the 1844 session.[40] The government finally decided to withdraw the bill and not provoke a debate in the Peers on the Mérilhou report. To vote on the bill but not have it passed in both houses this late in the parliamentary year would have required the presentation of a new law the following session, while leaving it in the report stage meant that it could be revived in 1845.[41] Given its past record of deferring the slavery question, one can presume that the French government was not overly indisposed by the postponement once again of this issue.

One abolitionist organ, Le Semeur, asserted as much with its comment that Mackau, in putting forth his bill in the manner in which he had, probably intended to delay emancipation.[42] Other abolitionist advocates also criticized the proposed legislation for its temporization and shortcomings.[43] Schoelcher bemoaned the fact that "abolition is not advancing," for government leaders "do not want it, and the parliament displays a disappointing luke-warmness" toward it. "The question seems to be of so little importance that they are adjourning it to next year's session."[44] In the Abolitioniste français, Isambert viewed the Mackau law as essentially an adjournment of the two proposals put forth by the Broglie commission; in other words, the government had chosen once again amelioration rather than even gradual emancipation as suggested by Broglie's group. Besides, Isambert contended, by proposing to make slavery more tolerable, the law was designed to "relegate emancipation into the indefinite future." In a letter to London, Isambert confided the society's disappointment with a piece of legislation that "so revolts reason and principles." He explained its introduction as the result of a Cabinet struggle between Guizot and Mackau in which the latter had gained the upper hand.[45] Bissette was equally blunt in his categorization of the Mackau proposal

---

[39] Rhodes House Anti-Slavery Papers, G103, Isambert to Scoble, July 29, 1844.

[40] Schoelcher Papers, N. a. f. 3631, pp. 70–71, Jollivet to President Colonial Council of Martinique, July 13, 1844.

[41] ANCAOM, Corr. Gén. 201, 1844, Minister to Governors, July 16, 1844.

[42] May 22, June 26, 1844.

[43] Le Siècle, May 15, June 17, 1844; Le National, May 15, 1844.

[44] Schmidt, La correspondance, 159, Schoelcher to Legouvé, July 21, 1844.

[45] L'Abolitioniste français, May–June 1844, pp. 182–3; Rhodes House Anti-Slavery Papers, G103, Isambert to Scoble, July 29, 1844.

as a major step backward that must be combatted. To the black abolitionist it amounted to "a veritable deception to mislead the partisans of emancipation and obtain their cooperation in measures whose insignificance is their lesser vice."[46] Bissette described the project to the British as "a deception, a work of bad faith, to amuse us and gain time." According to him, the French Cabinet, "poorly disposed toward the abolition question," was pleased to cede to the anti-English, anti-slavery public opinion prevalent in France and "do nothing" about slave liberation.[47] Among organs favorable to the abolitionist cause, only the extremely moderate *Annales de l'Institut d'Afrique* stood out in praising the Mackau bill.[48]

The Institut d'Afrique has been depicted incorrectly as the culmination of the French abolitionist movement and its deflection toward imperialism.[49] It was, in fact, a minor abolitionist group which seemed to have little effect upon the government, the press, or most other abolitionists. Organized as an African promotion society at a time when French trade with Africa in such products as palm oil was increasing, it was interested in all aspects of the continent: its people, geography, history, commerce, and resources. In this sense the Institut was a precursor of late nineteenth-century imperialism, for its main objective was to promote trade with Africa and encourage European involvement there. It even formed in 1845 a Compagnie d'Afrique to attempt to exploit the vast riches of the continent, though there is no evidence that this scheme ever got off the ground. Thus, the formation of the Institut d'Afrique coincided with a period when French trade with Africa was developing, and it reflected a desire to expand this commerce.

Founded in 1839 according to its publication, the *Annales*, the Institut had a considerable membership list with hundreds of adherents, honorary or otherwise, including numerous French notables, educators, ecclesiastics, lawyers, and diplomats. One scholar has indicated that the Institut was of Christian inspiration, and contained a good number of prominent Catholics and Protestants.[50] Surprisingly,

[46] C. A. Bissette, *Du Projet Mackau, tendant à violer la loi du 24 avril sur le régime législatif des colonies* (Paris: Dupont, 1844), 3, 13, 15.

[47] Rhodes House Anti-Slavery Papers, C13/118, Bissette to Scoble, June 3, 1844.

[48] No. 6, June 1844, p. 45.

[49] Daget, "A Model of the French Abolitionist Movement," 75–9.

[50] Paule Brasseur, "A la recherche d'un absolu missionnaire: Mgr. Truffet, vicaire apostolique des Deux-Guinées (1812–1847)," *Cahiers d'études africaines* 15 (1975), 262.

though, there were few identifiable businessmen or bankers within the organization, indicating that its objectives were more theoretical than practical. Judging from the lists of new adherents published in the *Annales*, over half of its members were foreigners, with diplomats, men of letters, and ecclesiastics once again predominating, along with an occasional doctor or engineer. It even claimed the adherence of the presidents of Mexico and Chile. It drew in a number of English abolitionists, some of them affiliated with the ill-fated Niger expedition.[51] Thomas Buxton, William Forster, George Thompson, and Daniel and Joseph Gurney were members; the latter, an important cog in the British and Foreign Anti-Slavery Society, was even one of the Institut's vice-presidents. Its presidents, the duc de Montmorency and the prince de Rohan-Rochefort, emanated from French Legitimist circles. Its long-standing secretary general was Hippolyte Daniel de Saint-Antoine, a medical doctor and proprietor in the French West Indies who had been an active member of the Société française pour l'abolition de l'esclavage in the 1830s. In reality, it appears that executive officers really ran the organization, and that passive membership remained the norm for most adherents to the Institut.

The mission statement of the Institut d'Afrique was put forth in the first issue of its periodical the *Annales* (published on January 1, 1841) and elaborated on in subsequent numbers. The Institut aimed to work for the end of the slave trade and slavery, to "civilize" Africa through European influence, to promote trade both north and south of the Sahara, and to press for European settlement on the entire continent. As just such settlement was under way in Algeria at the time, the Institut concentrated its attention on North as well as Black Africa. Its interests were primarily political, economic, and cultural. It opposed slavery in Africa and elsewhere, but the slavery question was only peripheral to its principle preoccupations. At times the organization appeared well informed about government intentions, probably thanks to its high-placed officers. However, the *Annales* proffered an extremely vague and general discourse about the French colonial slavery question, uttering such current sophisms as the superiority of

---

[51] On the Niger expedition carried out by British abolitionists as a civilizing crusade to Africa in these very years, 1841–1842, see Howard Temperley, *White Dreams, Black Africa: The Antislavery Expedition to the Niger, 1841–1842* (New Haven: Yale University Press, 1991).

free over slave labor and the need to alleviate the misery of slaves, often with little concrete knowledge or evidence. From 1841 to 1848 the *Annales* typically reproduced second-hand information on the slavery and emancipation issues, praised other countries for their actions against slavery, and encouraged the French government to follow suit. But its language was always extremely moderate and gradualist, stressing the need for adequate deliberation and preparation.[52] In sum, the Institut d'Afrique was the most moderate, least influential, and most marginal of the French anti-slavery groupings under the July Monarchy. It certainly was not representative of the entire abolitionist movement .

The Institut d'Afrique aside, other abolitionists opposed the Mackau proposals and prepared to counter them in 1845. Commenting on abolitionist strategy, Isambert remarked that it would be necessary to prepare new worker petitions for 1845, though in reality none ever developed. One of the problems in France, Isambert suggested, was that French opinion was still Anglophobic because of the right of search affair, and therefore cool toward anti-slavery. Isambert also alluded to opposition to emancipation by the head of state when he inquired of his British colleagues whether Lord Brougham, who praised the French king in many ways, "could not try to convert him" to abolitionism.[53] The *Abolitioniste français* and the Catholic *Univers*, for their part, tried to refocus French opinion on the iniquities of colonial slavery itself and underline the shortcomings of the previous ameliorative moves. According to the latter organ, the treatment of slaves had even regressed since 1840. *Le Constitutionnel* too published a long critique of the treatment of French slaves despite the ameliorative legislation of 1840.[54] The condemnation of the Mackau laws by Rouvellat de Cussac, a colonial magistrate who had recently returned to France after some fifteen years service in Guadeloupe and Martinique, amounted to a harsh indictment of colonial society which, he charged, had constantly afflicted horrible abuses upon slaves. It was so poignant that, in retrospective, *L'Abolitioniste français* termed it "one

---

[52] For the above, see the entire run of the monthly, the *Annales de l'Institut d'Afrique*, 1841–1848.

[53] Rhodes House Anti-Slavery Papers, G103, Isambert to Scoble, June 5, Oct. 3, 1844.

[54] *L'Abolitioniste français*, Sept.–Oct. 1844, pp. 315, 336; *L'Univers*, Sept. 27, 1844; *Le Constitutionnel*, Oct. 5, 1844.

of the most useful publications for the cause of emancipation."[55] In making such points, French abolitionist advocates intended to remind the government and public opinion that truly meaningful measures needed to be taken against slavery. In many ways, though, by the autumn of 1844, with the sessions of both the legislature and abolition society suspended for six months, French anti-slavery had again lost much of the momentum it seemed to be developing at the beginning of the year. French abolitionists were reacting to the Mackau proposals rather than taking further initiatives of their own. As Isambert confessed to the British, "the cause of abolition in France is as if suspended during the interval of the parliamentary session." He promised, though, that the French abolition society would "wage an all-out attack" on the Mackau bill during the legislative year of 1845.[56] The highly organized and effective British anti-slavery movement could not but be struck with the lack of continuity – despite the appearance of *L'Abolitioniste* – and commitment in the ranks of the Société française pour l'abolition de l'esclavage ten years after its formation.

In 1845 all eyes were fixed on the legislative debates over the Mackau bill. Mérilhou finished his report in March, and the discussion of it and the law commenced in the Peers on April 3. In the meantime Mérilhou's pro-slavery commission had amended the law to the advantage of the *colons* by tying on clauses stipulating that any slave who achieved freedom through self-redemption must continue to work for his master for five years, and that slaves not be given a free Saturday – a privilege many of them exercised already under slavery. The debate then engaged over the bill and these alterations that had weakened it even further from an emancipationist point of view. In the Peers, unlike in the Deputies, a whole cohort of procolonial spokesmen unabashedly stood up to attack the Mackau bill, even in its now emasculated form, and to advocate the continuation of the status quo. Delegate Dupin, a member of the Peers, launched the attack with the typical colonial reproach, during these times of continued if attenuated Anglophobia, that emancipation was a ploy advocated by Englishmen. He then went on to oppose ameliorative projects, and *pécule* and *rachat* in particular, by arguing that slaves were well off already.

[55] Rouvellat de Cussac, *A Messieurs les membres*, 7–13; *L'Abolitioniste français*, 1849, 1–3 livraisons, p. 12.
[56] Rhodes House Anti-Slavery Papers, G103, Isambert to Scoble, Oct. 3, 1844.

He did this, as *L'Abolitioniste français* remarked, through the use of statistics, a device "in which no one believes any more."[57] He was supported by General Amédée Louis Despans Cubières, former minister of war in the Thiers Cabinet – and the object of a major corruption scandal later in the 1840s that would blacken the image of the July Monarchy – who in turn encouraged France not to cede to British efforts to destroy its colonies. Cubières admitted openly to opposing emancipation, while contending at the same time that servitude must be perpetuated to preserve colonial production. The prince de Moskowa, Joseph Napoleon Ney, son of the famous marshal, also denounced slave liberation as a British machination, while Audiffret pleaded for immobility pure and simple. They were supported in other interventions by Mérilhou, comte Ferdinand de Tascher, and comte Marthe Camille Bachasson de Montalivet – a close confidant of King Louis Philippe and an important power-broker under the July Monarchy – all of whom wished to leave reforms totally in the hands of the *colons*.[58] Procolonial advocates still dared to utter pleas for stalemate and regression on the slavery front, reflecting the continued strength of the slavery system ten years after the organization of the French abolitionist movement.

The debate over the Mackau bill also demonstrates the extent to which the top echelons of *notable*-dominated French society represented in the nonelective upper house – appointed by the king – were still prepared, even in the mid-1840s, openly to defend colonial interests and property. The very fact that the Mackau ministry chose to introduce its bill on slavery in the Peers rather than the Deputies makes one question its objectives. By turning first of all to the Peers it had in effect permitted a commission dominated by proslavery elements to refine the legislation rather than one from the anti-slavery-oriented Chamber of Deputies. This procedure might have reflected the navy-colonial department's belief that any measures leading toward emancipation needed colonial support to be implemented smoothly, and that the law, therefore, should be reworked by the Peers in a fashion as favorable to colonial interests as possible. If this were the case, though, it would confirm the fact that the July Monarchy's

---

[57] *Le Moniteur universel*, April 4, 1845; *L'Abolitioniste français*, March–April–May 1845, p. 57.

[58] *Le Moniteur universel*, April 5, 6, 9, 10, 13, 1845.

first concerns still lay with the colonies rather than the slaves. Besides, the government should have understood by this point that the only policy the *colons* were willing to accept was one of strict adherence to the status quo.

Anti-slavery forces in the Peers faced the triple task of confronting the Mérilhou amendments, defending abolitionism, and doing what they believed best for the slaves. Arthur Auguste Beugnot, perhaps a member of the French abolition society, attempted to blunt the Mérilhou clause that self-redeemed slaves must remain for half a decade with their previous owner by introducing an amendment permitting freed slaves to choose any master they wished for five years. His motion, however, was bitterly attacked by Dupin and Raymond Jean François Marie Lacave Laplagne-Barris, a faithful friend of the Orleans family and one of the executors of the will of King Louis Philippe. The personal intervention of Mackau and Guizot was required to assure the motion's passage. The procolonial establishment also put up a fierce fight against another Beugnot amendment guaranteeing slaves a Saturday rest day. Although the motion was defended by Mackau and Passy and eventually passed, Mérilhou combatted it with the argument that it interfered with planter rights to the point where it would result in a situation "where it is the slave who will be superior to the master."[59] As a whole, Beugnot took the lead in the Peers as defender of abolitionism, even though he personally found the Mackau bill inadequate.

Other abolitionists also distinguished themselves in the Peers debates. The duc d'Harcourt, member of the Société française pour l'abolition de l'esclavage, was one of the first to defend British intentions and justify emancipation as a humanitarian act. Passy and the comte Joseph Portalis also spoke up in hearty support of the bill, even though they too realized its limitations.[60] When Passy had been appointed a Peer in 1843, Jollivet had rejoiced, for "it is in the Chamber of Deputies that all measures that can affect the colonies are born; Mr. Passy will no longer be there, and we will be freed from our most powerful and dangerous enemy."[61] In this case, however, Passy's promotion came back to haunt the pro-slavery faction.

---

[59] Ibid., April 9, 1845.
[60] Ibid., April 5, 8, 9, 1845.
[61] Schoelcher Papers, n. a. f., 3631, p. 37, Jollivet to President Colonial Council of Martinique, Dec. 28, 1843.

Still, it was the liberal Catholic Charles Forbes comte de Montalembert, another member of the French abolition society, who stood out most of all among the anti-slavery contingent in the Peers. Montalembert spoke at length and with talent in defense of slave liberation. As a member of a family that had held lands in Saint-Domingue, and as someone who still possessed estates in the British colonies, he protested that it was not enough to accept the abolition of slavery in principle; it was necessary to take concrete measures to prepare for emancipation within a short time span. He praised the British example as one that France should follow, and suggested that British success was attributable to the work that Protestant ministers had carried out in preparing the slaves for freedom. Unfortunately, he remarked after examining the situation carefully, "in our colonies moralization and religious instruction are in a state of fiction." This situation could be blamed, he held, upon the clergy itself, the state, and the *colons*. With the exception of the Christian brothers, the Catholic clergy was only "lukewarm" about instructing slaves, because colonial churchmen were not independent of planter influence. The government, he charged, was responsible for not establishing bishoprics within French colonies which could have given ecclesiastics the discipline and leadership required to counter planter leverage. Finally, he contended, slave owners discouraged religious instruction of slaves, which they viewed as a prelude to emancipation. Montalembert concluded that French slaves needed preparation, and that this bill would begin the process. Pointing out that no colonial body had ever made a bona fide emancipation proposal and that *colons* simply wanted to preserve the current state of affairs, Montalembert insisted that the impasse could be broken with legislation of this kind.[62] It took impassioned, well-argued pleas like this to get the Mackau bill through the Peers.

The upper chamber finally approved the bill by a vote of 103 to 56. Despite its earlier condemnation of it, the French abolition society swung around to supporting it in the end. The organization justified its decision by reasoning that this bill was better than nothing; besides, the legislation promised to improve the plight of slaves. Even here, though, the society's journal reflected some doubts and

---

[62] *Le Moniteur universel*, April 8, 1845.

second thoughts. The *Abolitioniste* predicted, quite correctly, that the Mackau bill, like preparatory legislation in the British colonies before 1833, would do little except alienate the planters and give slaves false hopes of liberty. It would probably lead to few actual cases of self-redemption, for no maximum price for *rachat* was set.[63] While writing to the British, Isambert provided additional insight into the society's stand. French abolitionists had made few attempts to amend the legislation because they feared compromising its passage, he explained. He personally felt that if Guizot had chosen to push for one of the Broglie commission options it could have been forced through the Peers with no more difficulty than the amelioration project, but that Guizot was mired in the retrograde atmosphere which ossified movement of any kind in the mid-1840s July Monarchy. Isambert was also convinced that, once the Mackau bill was enacted, slavery "will last many more years." After mentioning that it was up to the abolition society to take measures to ensure that this would not be the case, Isambert could only suggest that the society use the occasion of new petitions before the Chamber of Deputies to remind the government of its commitments. Isambert then concluded his letter with the accurate observation that the difficult passage of the Mackau bill through the Peers indicated how a majority of that body was willing to grant certain civil rights to slaves but not freedom.[64] He might have added, though, that the entire episode showed that the Société française pour l'abolition de l'esclavage was still incapable of promoting any moves against slavery except through the press and traditional government channels. Once again, no new petitions appeared in 1845. Then too, the volte-face of the French abolition society in supporting a bill that it had at first denounced indicated that the gradualists had once again displayed their dominance within the organization.

If a large number of upper house members were prepared to defend slavery, the abolitionists enjoyed a much better distribution of forces in the lower chamber. The debate in the Deputies was engaged in late May. A commission, dominated by abolitionists and with French abolition society member Jules de Lasteyrie as reporter, deposited on

---

[63] *L'Abolitioniste français*, March–April–May 1845., p 280.
[64] Rhodes House Anti-Slavery Papers, G103, Isambert to Scoble, April 16, 1845.

May 22 a report couched in language entirely different from that of Mérilhou in the Peers. Repeating the charge made by Montalembert that "religious instruction is nil" in the colonies, the commission expressed the opinion that profound improvement for slaves was impossible under servitude. Still, while the commission might have preferred direct moves toward emancipation, it supported the present project because it promised some amelioration for the slaves. Besides, as Lasteyrie warned, if the current law were to prove ineffective, it would be necessary to reject the concept of a preparatory state and move directly to emancipation. Finally, the commission proposed one amendment to which Mackau agreed. The government would commit itself to freeing within five years what were called "domain slaves" (*esclaves du domaine de l'état*), or those 1,469 slaves owned by the government itself in the colonies.[65] Abolitionists hoped that liberating crown slaves would set an example in the colonies, and perhaps serve to destabilize slavery as a whole.

Within the Chamber of Deputies pro-slavery defenders were far less numerous and effective than in the Peers. Still, before the debate began Guizot, who supported the legislation, seemed concerned about the continuing lobbying of the colonial party, and the "lukewarm attitude of decent people."[66] Jollivet led the attack against the bill with many of the same arguments that his colleagues had employed in the Peers. He was joined by Wustemberg (the Protestant from Bordeaux who had been on the Broglie commission), Charles Levavasseur, and the marquis Henri Charles Louis Boniface de Castellane, the nephew of Molé. Castellane put forth the standard argument in the colonial arsenal: *Rachat* amounted to emancipation without indemnification by the state. Pierre Antoine Berryer, Legitimist leader in the lower house, also charged that England stood behind the legislation, and that the colonies retained the right to regulate their own institutions. Admiral Théodore Constant Leray, a former administrator in the colonies, was one of the most forceful speakers defending slavery. He too pleaded for colonial control over servitude, and denounced in particular the Beugnot amendment that would bring the government to disrupt slavery by freeing its own domain slaves. As a whole, though,

---

[65] *Le Moniteur universel*, May 23, 25, 1845; May 15, 1846.
[66] Guizot Papers, 42AP214, Guizot to Broglie, April 1, 1845.

these isolated speakers received little support from the ranks of the deputies.[67]

Pro-abolitionist spokesmen dominated the proceedings in the lower house. Tocqueville delivered one of the most effective speeches, underlining his opposition to slavery while still supporting the bill. Tocqueville conceded that few slaves would actually be freed under the self-redemption provisions, but, true to his belief put forth in 1839 that the state must play an intermediary role in the emancipation process, he stood behind the Mackau bill because it promised to give the government some control over both slave and master. He insisted that this was absolutely essential because the *colons* had steadfastly combatted any changes in the structure of slavery. Tocqueville also gave an impassioned defense of the beneficent nature of British emancipation, a move which he insisted France should imitate. Still, Tocqueville felt obliged to admit that few deputies were present for the debate on the Mackau legislation, showing what little enthusiasm the slavery question still inspired in the French chambers.[68]

It was, however, Agénor de Gasparin who emerged as the dominant speaker on the issue and the one who set the tone for the debates. Already in 1844 Bissette had joined Isambert in singling out to the British this "rising sun" in French anti-slavery. According to Bissette, Gasparin was "the one who feels the most vividly all that is hideous and degrading in slavery," someone prepared to castigate it "with the most conviction and heated spirits."[69] In the chambers Gasparin lived up to his billing by indicting the Mackau bill as ineffective, while demanding numerous amendments to render it palatable. He agreed with Tocqueville that the colonies would never act on their own against slavery, "the greatest question that is under our purview, a question of civilization and liberty." He also suggested that most French abolitionists, accused by colonial advocates of being impatient and overly demanding, actually "wait and hardly act."[70] While mainstream French anti-slavery was prepared to accept the Mackau proposal with minor revisions as the only option achievable at the time,

---

[67] *Le Moniteur universel*, May 30, 31, June 1, 3, 4, 1845; Tudesq, *Les grands notables*, II, 840.
[68] *Le Moniteur universel*, May 31, 1845.
[69] Rhodes House Anti-Slavery Papers, C13/118, Bissette to Scoble, June 23, 1844.
[70] *Le Moniteur universel*, May 31, June 3, 1845.

Gasparin upset this strategy with his impassioned attack on servitude itself and his demand for a more efficient piece of legislation. His remark about the inaction of most abolitionists also betrayed his distance from the French abolition society on the slavery question.

Gasparin's demands for amendments sent government officials and members of the French abolition society scurrying to recoup their position and save the legislation. Mackau immediately exclaimed that he had discussed the law in depth with the deputies' commission, that his administration approved of it in its current form, and that it should not be further amended. Then, to placate the plantocracy, he emphasized that this was only a preparatory bill, not an emancipation proclamation. He insisted too that the latter, if proposed, would always guarantee planters "a large indemnity." Abolitionists also stepped up to support the bill. Isambert avowed that he would have preferred an outright emancipation law, something that Guizot had earlier seemed ready to support. However, because the Cabinet judged the chambers unprepared to pay an indemnity, Isambert believed the current legislation the best achievable at this time. Ledru-Rollin, like Isambert, espoused emancipation and favored amending the bill under debate. Nevertheless, he too recognized that any changes voted by the Deputies would not have time to be approved by the Peers; therefore, he conceded that the proposal must stand untouched in order to pass during the 1845 session. In the debates, Isambert and Ledru-Rollin demonstrated their immediatist inclinations, countered by a willingness to follow the French abolition society line and accept the legislation as a lesser of two evils. Tocqueville too displayed more immediatist tendencies than he had as a member of the Broglie commission.

Odilon Barrot also intervened in the debates to request that all amendments be dropped so that the bill could pass this year; to fail to do so, he pointed out, would be to play in the hands of those who wished to procrastinate. Among members of the Société française pour l'abolition de l'esclavage only Roger du Loiret supported Gasparin's pleas for strengthening Mackau's legislation. Gasparin's proposed amendments for forbidding the whipping of women and setting a maximum price for *rachat* were eventually withdrawn or defeated. Mackau helped deflect support for these amendments by suggesting that all such objectives could be achieved by royal ordonnances originating in his office.[71] The law finally passed by a large majority, 193 to 52, according to one source.[72] It was accompanied by another bill providing funds for implementing the legislation, for encouraging European emigration to the colonies, and for assisting slaves to achieve *rachat*. This complementary bill then went before the Peers, where it experienced a much more difficult passage in early July by a vote of only 63 to 38. The two pieces of legislation finally received royal sanction on July 18 and 19, respectively. They were henceforth referred to as the Mackau laws.

The Mackau legislation authorized the navy-colonial minister to regulate through ordonnances the feeding, upkeep, and disciplining of slaves. It also provided for the establishment of special government magistrates to oversee the humane treatment of slaves. Moreover, it permitted the minister to introduce new ordonnances to establish measures for the primary and religious education of slaves, as well as for means to encourage marriages. It did cater to colonial concerns, though, in stipulating that no regulations on ameliorations could be issued without consultation with the colonial councils, granting the latter what amounted to a suspensive veto. In all of this the Mackau laws reiterated many of the points for moralization and preparation already implemented in 1840, showing to what extent this earlier legislation had remained a dead letter. They went beyond earlier measures, however, in legalizing *pécule* and *rachat*, and in initiating procedures to assist slaves in paying their *rachat*; they also provided for the mediation of self-redemption prices in cases of disagreement between slaves and masters. Still, the Mackau laws had few real attractions for slaves, because they required them to remain tied to a master for five years after *rachat*.[73] The legislation was bound to displease abolitionists as doing too little, and to anger planters for infringing upon their rights over slaves. It certainly did not open the road to slave emancipation, as some historians have believed.[74]

Abolitionist uneasiness with the Mackau laws had been apparent during the entire course of the debates in the Peers and Deputies. Isambert presented what amounted to the abolition society's excuses

---

[71] Ibid., May 31, June 1, 3, 4, 1845.
[72] *L'Univers*, June 5, 1845.
[73] ANCAOM, Gén. 40 (316), law of July 18, 1845.
[74] Gaston Martin, *Histoire de l'esclavage*, 290.

for supporting the bill in his correspondence with London. Free men of color – but certainly not Bissette – he said, had advised the society to content itself for the time being with the Mackau proposals. Moreover, while it was cruel to make slaves purchase their own freedom, abolitionists would try to aid them with this as much as possible – in fact the Société française never made any concerted efforts along these lines. Besides, he explained, the government had committed itself to introducing a new law within two years if the colonies attempted to block implementation of this legislation – something which never occurred either. Isambert also repeated the justification that if the abolitionists had insisted on amendments the government and Peers would have opposed them, compromising the bill for the 1845 session.[75] Still, in the end, Isambert seemed embarrassed and discouraged by the entire affair. It had, after all, demonstrated once again the extent to which mainstream French anti-slavery was still willing to settle for extreme gradualism.

British abolitionists, for their part, were livid over the Mackau laws. In examining this legislation the *British and Foreign Anti-Slavery Reporter* lost the reserve that had always accompanied its commentary on French developments. In referring to the Mackau proposals as "this worthless measure," it expressed its "regret that the abolitionists of France can do nothing more effectual for the advancement of the great interests which are at stake."[76] When the debate finally ended in the Deputies the *Reporter* uttered its amazement that "the most illustrious men ... in France have been concentrated for not less than fourteen days" on a bill for "purchased freedom." It was "a painful, a miserable disappointment. The world had been given to expect a measure of emancipation; and behold a measure of amelioration!" Like "all similar measures of which we have had experience," it would prove "tantalizing and abortive." Fortunately, though, Tocqueville and Gasparin had displayed "an admirable spirit," and together with Isambert, had defended British abolitionist integrity. The only good the British journal could say about the entire bill was that it promised to free slaves belonging to the French government.[77]

The *Reporter* reacted even more impetuously when the French

[75] Rhodes House Anti-Slavery Papers, G103, Isambert to Scoble, June 5, 1846.
[76] April 16, 1845.
[77] Ibid., June 25, Oct. 29, 1845.

government tarried in implementing the ordonnances without which the legislation remained stillborn. In the late autumn *Le National*, Schoelcher in *La Réforme*, and *L'Abolitioniste français* all pointed out what they viewed as temporization by French authorities. The Mackau law had received royal assent only on July 18, even though it had been passed on June 4. It had been sent to the colonies so late that it arrived there only in November. The first ordonnance, implementing *rachat*, had been issued on October 23, but legalized by insertions in the *Bulletin des lois* only on November 12. Besides, as Schoelcher pointed out, the ordonnance was phrased in such a manner as to impede rather than encourage the slave to seek self-redemption. There was no time limit set on the processing of a request for *rachat*; the procedure was costly for the slave; and the colonial commissioners overlooking the process were themselves *colons*. The *Abolitioniste* itself charged that once again laws had been passed only to have the navy-colonial minister permit the colonies to avoid implementing them.[78] This sent the *British and Foreign Anti-Slavery Reporter* into a frenzy and led it to utter its least diplomatic remarks yet about the French administration. After receiving *Le National*'s account of the situation, the *Reporter* exclaimed: "We do not hesitate to say that a more contemptible juggle was never played off upon a people or upon a legislature, even by the most eminent professors of the art of thimble rig." Moreover, it charged: "The tendency of the ordinances is rather to obstruct the redemption of the slaves than to promote it, rather to consolidate the system of slavery than to break it up. They might have been drawn up by Mr. Jollivet himself." The journal's diatribe culminated with an attack upon Mackau, who, it proclaimed, "is not an honest man, but a man of trick and chicanery. His word is not to be taken, otherwise than as a studied effort to deceive." Besides, now "the whole of the French government is implicated in his hypocrisy and deceitfulness." According to the *Reporter*, "it is but too plain that the 'rulers' of France do not mean to abolish colonial slavery. Are Frenchmen willing to have it perpetuated?" Finally, the newspaper expressed the wish that "the friends of humanity and freedom" would call Mackau "to a rigorous account."[79] British abolitionists had been

[78] *Le National*, Nov. 1, 1845; *La Réforme*, Dec. 7, 1845; *L'Abolitioniste français*, Oct.–Nov.–Dec. 1845, pp. 663–9.
[79] *British and Foreign Anti-Slavery Reporter*, Nov. 12, 1845.

correct in their assessment of the French government's attitude toward emancipation. Furthermore, their remarks indicated a growing chasm between radical British and conservative French abolitionist circles whose ineffective actions were exasperating London.

Despite the encouragement of their British colleagues, members of the Société française pour l'abolition de l'esclavage were in no position to act decisively in late 1845 and early 1846. At the end of its October–November–December issue, *L'Abolitioniste français* announced Isambert's resignation as secretary of the society as of January 6, 1846. It noted that for some time already he had wanted to step down, finding this task, combined with his duties as lawyer and deputy, too heavy. Still, "until the present he had yielded to the intense pressure of his colleagues," who had striven to retain the services of such a devoted and selfless campaigner against slavery and the true mainstay of their society. Isambert did give assurances, though, that he would in every way remain active in supporting the abolition society and its cause. He was now succeeded as secretary by Dutrône, honorary councilor at the Royal Court of Amiens, one of the founders of the society and a low-key but active member in it since its inception.[80]

There is undoubtedly some truth to the fact that Isambert, born in 1792, was tired and overworked, for without fanfare he had ceased in mid-1844 his role of official manager–proprietor (*propriétaire-gérant*) of *L'Abolitioniste*, a position he had held since its founding. He had handed this position over temporarily to his son, Alfred Isambert, himself a lawyer, who then also stepped aside. Still, Isambert recounted a slightly different story to his English confreres. To them he reaffirmed that he did not wish to distance himself from the Société française, and that he had made his decision because his duties required "a mass of monetary and administrative detail, incompatible with my position of magistrate and deputy." But he also revealed the profound disillusionment of both himself and his colleagues with the political situation in France and the discouraging circumstances facing anti-slavery at the time.

By the mid-1840s the July Monarchy had become wedded to the status quo in all matters, steadfastly refusing growing demands for parliamentary, electoral, and social reform from an increasingly active

---

[80] *L'Abolitioniste français*, Oct.–Nov.–Dec. 1845, pp. 682–3.

opposition. In writing to the British, Isambert showed little optimism about the prospects of French abolitionism faced with what he described as the administration's markedly retrograde policies. "Mr. Guizot," he claimed, "has put his talent to serving the small, petty, egotistical interests of his master," meaning King Louis Philippe. He also charged that "they have stifled all public spirit in France by material interests," adding that "I have bitterly fulfilled my duties of good citizen by protesting." Isambert was also disheartened that "my friend of twenty years" – an evident reference to Odilon Barrot – seemed to be ceding the leadership of the opposition to Thiers, who was unfavorable to abolitionism. More significant, he remarked, Passy no longer attended meetings of the Société française pour l'abolition de l'esclavage. "It is Mr. de Tracy who now presides over us," for Broglie too had stepped aside.[81] A hemorrhage was occurring among the leadership of the French abolition society, especially in its more liberal faction. Despite Isambert's attempts to minimize these developments, it seems likely that an increasing number of devotees to the abolitionist cause, in particular immediatists like Passy and himself, were no longer prepared to carry the administrative load within a society which could not bring about noteworthy movement on the slavery scene. Part of their disillusionment might have arisen from a feeling that Guizot, in whom many abolitionists had placed their trust, had betrayed their cause and would not advance it significantly. Part of it was probably due also to the realization that gradualism would not work, and that the moderately oriented French abolition society could not succeed in freeing the slaves. Even Broglie might have stepped aside as president of the French abolition society because of the government's refusal to accept either of the two gradualist proposals for slave liberation that his commission had recommended.

If the passing of the Mackau law had rendered many abolitionists despondent, one might expect that the very insignificance of this legislation would have pleased colonial advocates. When first hearing of the new law, one Martinique planter, Dessalles, did utter a sigh of relief that emancipation had been postponed at least until 1853.[82] But this was not the typical reaction of colonial spokespersons. Throughout

[81] Rhodes House Anti-Slavery Papers, G103, Isambert to Scoble, March 6, 1846.
[82] Forster and Forster, *Sugar and Slavery*, 178.

the July Monarchy, French colonial defenders had espoused a policy of absolute immobility even to a greater extent than the government. In 1843 one official observer reported that colonial councils were convinced that their fierce resistance over the previous five years had prevented metropolitan authorities from adopting abolitionist projects that they had appeared ready to implement in the late 1830s.[83] Since the mid-1830s the *colons* had coyly exploited their stance of accepting the principle of abolition while postponing its implementation indefinitely by every means possible. A basic premise of this policy was to oppose even the minor changes which the legislation of 1845 proposed to implement.

Throughout the late 1830s colonial proponents had employed the press as their prime vector for advocating immobility. Despite the legislation of 1839–1841 preventing *colons* from using funds provided by Paris for this purpose, they had continued to devote hundreds of thousand of francs raised in the colonies for buying off the metropolitan press. In the previous decade Charles Dupin had coordinated much of this effort; in the 1840s it was his colleague representing Martinique, Jollivet, who led the colonial press lobby. The sums the delegates disbursed were phenomenal for the times. For example, from the autumn of 1841 to the spring of 1842, some 105,695 francs were distributed to the minor Paris paper *Le Globe* alone. From late 1841, the delegates began spending much more than this in bribing the very important *La Presse* of Emile de Girardin, which enjoyed one of the largest press runs of the July Monarchy (22,170 copies daily in 1836) and was a highly influential independent conservative daily. Besides this, the delegates gave generous stipends to much of the Legitimist press, all newspapers in Le Havre, and several other Parisian journals of all political proclivities, including the Fourierist daily *La Démocratie pacifique*.[84] In his lavishness Jollivet even succumbed to a daft scheme by Alphonse Ride, who had resided for some time in the American South and who requested a subsidy to contact newspapers

---

[83] ANCAOM, Gén. 171 (1379), Admiral Moges, Commander of French naval forces in the West Indies, to Minister, Nov. 21, 1843.

[84] For more detail on all of the above, see Jennings, "Venality of the July Monarchy Press." Because of the Fourierist orientation of *La Démocratie pacifique*, some historians have incorrectly categorized it as anti-slavery. See, for example, Philippe Vigier, "La recomposition du mouvement abolitionniste français sous la monarchie de Juillet," in *Les abolitions de l'esclavage*, 287–8.

in Southern cities of the United States to "prepare an alliance between the states of the South of the Union, the Spanish states, Brazil, Guadeloupe and Martinique." Ride requested an initial payment of 200 francs per month in January 1843, then 250 francs monthly, a sum matched by the delegate of Guadeloupe, Chazelles. By the end of November, though, Jollivet reported that Ride had done nothing but run up additional expenses; Jollivet now described his erstwhile agent as a former tax collector from Troyes who had been dismissed for irregularities and who was not worthy of confidence.[85] Ride did, however, produce a large but superficial study providing a primitive defense of slavery, something for which the delegates probably also paid, for they regularly subsidized pamphlets and books as well as the press.[86]

If Jollivet had yielded so readily to Ride's entreaties, it was no doubt because he himself entertained the possibility of forging an "alliance with Louisiana and Cuba" to counter the international anti-slavery convention held in London in the summer of 1843. In other instances he claimed to have been in contact with the ministers of several slave-holding states (Brazil, Spain, the United States, Denmark, the Netherlands, and Texas) to discourage them from abolishing slavery. He even suggested that "an alliance with Cuba etc. could furnish us with the resources that we lack."[87] There is no evidence, though, that the Martinique colonial council ever gave any serious follow-up to his extravagant suggestions. Perhaps all of this was part of the constant attempt by Jollivet to pry additional funding from his employers to build up the huge slush fund that he employed to defend the colonial cause in Paris by all possible means, including giving large stipends for articles from Bissette's nemesis, Granier de Cassagnac, whom the British termed "the great enemy of the blacks."[88] The colonial councils of

---

[85] Schoelcher Papers, N. a. f. 3631, pp. 8–9, Jan. 29, 1843; pp. 9–10, Feb. 13, 1843; pp. 35–6, Nov. 29, 1843, Jollivet to President Colonial Council of Martinique.

[86] Alphonse Ride, *Esclavage et liberté, existence de l'homme et des sociétés en harmonie avec les lois universelles* (2 vols.; Paris: Dalloye, 1843).

[87] Schoelcher Papers, N. a. f. 3631, pp. 20–2, May 28, 1843; pp. 35–6, Nov. 29, 1843; p. 39, July 13, 1844, Jollivet to President Colonial Council of Martinique.

[88] *British and Foreign Anti-Slavery Reporter*, July 28, 1841. Even certain planters, such as Dessalles, expressed disdain for Granier de Cassagnac, who, he claimed, sold his pen to the highest bidder and was "a mere confidence man" (Forster and Forster, *Sugar and Slavery*, 156).

Martinique and Guadeloupe came up in late 1842 and early 1843 with their own idea of developing "an alliance between viticulture proprietors and the colonies for the defense of their mutual respective interests" in the French chambers at a time when both sugar and wine legislation was on the docket. Once again, however, there is no evidence that anything came of this, even though the colonial legislatures proposed to devote all possible resources to it, except those already committed to the press.[89] The colonies were spending widely and considering every method possible to defend their interests in the 1840s as in the 1830s. As Bissette aptly remarked, "the *colons* are rich; their resistance to emancipation is thus a formidable one."[90]

The colonial lobby did indeed put up a formidable resistance to the Mackau laws. The delegates representing Martinique blamed the Mackau proposals on Guizot and referred to them as the "sad law of Mr. Mackau ... against the colonies."[91] The minister's attempts to reassure the colonies that his ameliorative legislation in fact "leaves intact the question of emancipation" were of little avail.[92] Mackau's efforts to discourage colonial opposition by insisting that it was "useless" to try to "shake the government's resolve" did not work either.[93] The Council of Delegates in Paris fought the Mackau measures tooth and nail through political intrigue and the press for every stage of their passage through the legislature. Not only had Jollivet influenced the reporter of the Peers commission, but he had provided procolonial peers with information to defend their position, had spoken with the most influential ones, and had invited some twenty of them over for dinner to encourage them to attack the legislation. The delegates even sent a circular to the presidents of the port city chambers of commerce to ask them to pressure the deputies representing their regions to vote against the Mackau law.[94] Dupin reported that for fourteen months he

---

[89] Schoelcher Papers, N. a. f. 3632, pp. 8–10, Jan. 17, 1843; pp. 10–11, Jan. 28, 1843, President of Colonial Council of Martinique to President Colonial Council of Guadeloupe; N. a. f. 3631 , pp. 12–13, March 13, 1843, Jollivet to President Colonial Council of Martinique.

[90] *La Revue des Colonies*, 8th year, No. 7, Jan. 1842, pp. 257–61.

[91] Schoelcher Papers, N. a. f. 3631, pp. 58–60, May 29, 1844, Jollivet to President Colonial Council of Martinique; pp. 64–6, June 29, 1844, Dupin to President Colonial Council of Martinique.

[92] ANCAOM, Corr. Gén. 205, 1845, Feb. 6, 1845, Minister to Governors.

[93] Ibid., Corr. Gén. 201, 1844, Sept. 13, 1844, Minister to Governors.

[94] Schoelcher Papers, N. a. f. 3631, pp. 177–8, Jollivet to President Colonial Council of

had devoted himself entirely to battling the "unfortunate" bill. His colleague Jollivet attributed their failure in defeating the legislation to "the union of abolitionists and of the ministry" that had pushed it through.[95] Dupin, though, took solace in the fact that he had spoken at length with the King about the matter and that the monarch had "no enthusiasm for the law" but saw it as a political necessity. Dupin also reported that the King's son, the duc de Nemours, had left the Peers during a vote on part of the bill because "he does not approve of what is being done against us."[96] The royal reaction to the Mackau laws, if accurately reported by Dupin, might indicate that if the legislation had been put on the docket in the first place it was because Guizot had insisted upon some gesture to satiate public opinion, the opposition, or the British with whom France was trying to improve relations.

Be this as it may, the colonies themselves reacted with predictable defiance to the Mackau legislation. News merely of the introduction of the bill led the Colonial Council of Guadeloupe to refuse to vote the colonial budget in protest, something which Jollivet warned the Martinique legislature not to imitate, because such actions could lead Mackau to call new colonial elections or even suppress the colonial councils entirely.[97] If Martinique later in the 1840s swung around to accept the Mackau law as a de facto dilatory measure, initially the passage of the bill strained relations between the colonies and the navy-colonial office. Mackau, so close to the colonies in most ways and truly protective of their interests, showed displeasure with the strong colonial reaction by temporarily withholding invitations to colons or their representatives to attend navy-colonial department receptions. He also tightened up further the restrictions against the use of government funds by the delegates in an attempt to control them somewhat.[98] In the end, nevertheless, this temporary strain between Paris and the colons probably worked to the advantage of

Martinique, March 13, 28, 1845; pp. 182–3, Circular to presidents of chambers of commerce, April 30, 1845.
[95] Ibid., pp. 82–3, Dupin to President Colonial Council of Martinique, April 13, 1845; p. 86, Jollivet to President Colonial Council of Martinique, May 30, 1845.
[96] Ibid., pp. 81–2, 84, Dupin to President Colonial Council of Martinique, April 12, 1845.
[97] Ibid., pp. 71–3, Jollivet to President Colonial Council of Martinique, July 29, 1844.
[98] Ibid., pp. 91–2, Jollivet to President Colonial Council of Martinique, Dec. 13, 1845; pp. 92–4, Mackau to President Colonial Council of Martinique, Aug. 24, 1845.

the latter. The reactions of the plantocracy certainly registered with Mackau, who definitely was favorable to its cause and wished its cooperation in all matters. Diehard colonial defense of the status quo was certainly an element helping to convince the government to act slowly in implementing the relatively innocuous provisions of the Mackau legislation. It also helped deter the administration from considering more radical moves toward emancipation, and even from taking rapid action to liberate domain slaves.

In reflecting upon the situation of French anti-slavery in general, the abolitionist *Le Semeur* made an insightful statement in 1844. The newspaper remarked that "since 1830, one cannot but be struck by the progress and the retrograde steps" that emancipationism "had taken one after another," by "the flux and reflux that have succeeded each other without interruption."[99] This assessment more than any other captures the essence of French abolitionist forces under the July Monarchy. Few movements were marked by more false starts, unfulfilled expectations, interruptions, dashed hopes, setbacks, and fresh starts. Some of this inconsistency could be attributed to the very cautious nature of the leading French anti-slavery organization. Negatively affected by international crises of the early 1840s, French abolitionism seemed poised for another take-off in early 1844 when a new abolitionist organ appeared, anti-slavery petitions emerged, and immediatism seemed to progress. At the same time fresh hopes were stirred by word that the government was preparing to issue legislation leading toward emancipation. In reality, though, such optimism was short-lived. The government, true to its record, replied to political pressure by passing ineffective preparatory legislation with no immediate impact. The introduction of the Mackau laws might have been stimulated by the desire to make some concessions to abolitionists and to strengthen existing but ineffective ameliorative measures, but in reality these moves did little to speed up the slave liberation process. Instead, they managed to displease both the *colons* and the abolitionists, but they especially disarmed and discouraged the latter. Already during debate on the Mackau bills, abolitionists opposed them as inadequate, only to swing around to support them as slight improvements to the status quo. That the legislation passed with the assistance

[99] May 8, 1844.

of the French abolition society showed how the latter formation was willing to compromise its principles. The society had been unable to profit from the modest worker petitions of 1844, and still had no credible solution of its own for the slavery problem. Its support for the Mackau laws alienated the British, who became increasingly persuaded that this moderate organization could not resolve the French slavery question. It also perturbed more radical members within its ranks, such as Isambert and Passy, who receded into the background, temporarily at least. Furthermore, immediatist anti-slavery was still underdeveloped in France, with its radical components within the ranks of the abolition society isolated, others such as Gasparin opposed to the society's objectives, and still others such as Bissette and Schoelcher at loggerheads. French anti-slavery was revealing itself as disillusioned and divided; it also remained as ineffective as ever after the passage of the Mackau laws. Despite the hopes born in 1844, by late 1845 there was little evidence of French abolitionist success. After nearly a dozen years of existence, the French abolition society had accomplished little more than its British comrades had achieved in the mid-1820s. In early 1846 it would have been hard to convince any French abolitionist that French slavery would be abolished in just two years time.

9

TOWARD
IMMEDIATISM

The Société française pour l'abolition de l'esclavage seemed debilitated after the passage of the Mackau laws. The necessary stimulus came once again from across the Channel. An improved atmosphere for cooperation was provided by the resolution of the right of search imbroglio that had haunted Franco–British anti-slavery activities since 1842. Anxious to end the impasse, in early 1845 Paris and London appointed two trusted abolitionists, Broglie and Stephen Lushington, to work out a settlement in negotiations held in the British capital. Their discussions, undertaken at the very moment when the French chambers were voting the Mackau laws, proved embarrassing at times for French authorities, for they afforded the colonial lobby the chance to claim once again British inspiration for French emancipationism. Indeed, during the London talks, well-intentioned British abolitionists played into French colonial hands when they issued a statement enjoining their government to exploit efforts to settle the right of search as a means to pressure France to emancipate.[1] Broglie, fortunately, defused the issue by informing Lushington that "the greatest harm of the right of search ... was that as long as it continued, the words abolition of slavery could no longer be pronounced in France."[2] Subsequently, the right of search dispute was settled on its own terms, with no overt reference to the slavery question. The convention of May 29, 1845, abolished Anglo–French search procedures on the high seas while committing each country to police its own merchant ships off the slave coasts.[3] In so doing, it laid

[1] Rhodes House Anti-Slavery Papers, Minute Books, February 7, 21, May 2, 1845.
[2] Guizot Papers, 42AP214, Broglie to Guizot, March 19, 1845.
[3] For more detail, see Jennings, *French Response*, 159–76.

to rest an issue which, as Broglie had recognized, had done irreparable damage to the anti-slavery cause in France. With the termination of the right of search dispute a yoke was lifted from the shoulders of French abolitionism. This development also permitted once again much more concerted Franco–British cooperation on the anti-slavery scene.

British abolitionists renewed their contacts with their French colleagues in 1845–1846. After the settlement of the right of search problem, a French abolitionist, Caillet, addressed a meeting of the British and Foreign Anti-Slavery Society in London about the current state of the movement in France. In the process, he stressed the desirability of further British abolitionist visits to France.[4] The British needed little encouragement along these lines. In July 1845 William Forster, and his wife, traveled to France and met with leading French abolitionists. Upon returning to London he reported the disappointing news that the French still lacked a provincial organizational network of the kind that had led to the success of the cause in Britain. Forster pointed out that "it appeared that the Anti-Slavery operations" in France "are mostly confined to Paris and that great ignorance exists in the provinces relating to the question." He also believed, though, that "Anti-Slavery exertions in the provinces would be well repaid." Consequently, the secretary of the British body, Scoble, announced his intention to visit Southern France in the autumn, journeying to the Protestant center of Montauban to hold another meeting with Félice. At a subsequent session of the British organization it was suggested that he carry on discussions with Isambert along the way.[5] The British had clearly perceived the weaknesses of the Société française and its limited possibilities of achieving much more that the Mackau laws. In light of this, the British seemed more determined than ever to make overtures to different sectors of French society apt to foster an English-style, Protestant-inspired, nationwide French abolitionist movement. London had not yet given up entirely on the French abolition society, but it had decided to try itself to forge the provincial links that French anti-slavery so sorely lacked.

During an October meeting of the British abolitionist group, Scoble

---

[4] Rhodes House Anti-Slavery Papers, Minute Books, June 6, 1845.
[5] Ibid., Aug. 1, Sept. 5, 1845.

recounted his trip across the Channel. It had begun with a three-day sojourn in Paris, where the British abolitionist had gathered information on the Mackau laws. Then, on his way South he had spent forty-eight hours with Isambert at his country home in the Loiret, where the French abolitionist had explained his society's stand on the new legislation. Following this, Scoble had remained nine days in Montauban with Félice, the emergent Protestant abolitionist who had been contacted by Gurney in 1844 and who now pledged to devote more time to the cause. They had discussed in detail emancipationism, "setting the ground upon which it shall henceforth be based by himself and his friends, viz., that slavery is a crime before God and ought therefore to be abolished." Félice had also committed himself to preparing "a pamphlet forthwith. After which an attempt will be made," he had explained, "to organize Committees on that principle." Discouraged with the achievement so far of the Catholic-dominated French abolition society, Scoble and his British associates obviously hoped to found a Protestant-dominated anti-slavery network to complement it. Exasperated with both the Mackau laws and the French abolition society, the British abolitionists were attempting to take things into their own hands. Given the mixed economic record of British emancipation, they were also encouraging the French to continue stressing the moral basis for slave liberation.

From Montauban, Scoble had journeyed to nearby Toulouse for four days. There he had been received by the Protestant bankers the Courtois brothers, "who rejoice that the question will now be placed on the right ground." His next stop had been the town of Saverdun, where he had spoken to several pastors and Mr. Laurens, "an influential member of the *Conseil général* of Lot and Garonne [department], who will also lend his best assistance to the cause." On his way back to London his journeys took him through Bordeaux and Nantes, where he had met with pastors.[6] These ports were bastions of pro-colonial sentiment, but Scoble obviously thought he could sway their small, longstanding Protestant element. Apparently the British felt that Protestants in these two port cities with strong ties to the colonies could be more open to the emancipation idea than Wustemberg, the important wine merchant of Prussian extraction and leader of the

---

[6] Ibid., Oct. [17], 1845.

Bordeaux chamber of commerce who so vociferously defended slavery, despite his Protestant faith. They failed to realize that Protestants as a whole in Bordeaux had connections to colonial trade and were as pro-slavery as the rest of the population.[7]

Upon returning to London, Scoble seemed highly pleased. He explained that "at the several places" he had stayed, he had met "at private soirées many influential persons ... all of which will co-operate on the ground of immediate and entire emancipation. The plan proposed is first to issue Mr. de Félice's pamphlet, then to organize, and afterward, to move the Protestant Consistorie [sic] and the *conseils-généraux* throughout France to petition the Chambers, and then by a succession of well-written and judicious pamphlets to awaken every portion of society to take an interest in the question, to accomplish which the friends of the Anti-Slavery cause in France will require the cordial sympathy and generous support of the Abolitionists in Great Britain."[8] The presumption of the British was manifest in believing it possible to set up an effective Protestant-based network in a country in which only 2 percent of the population was of that faith. Still, the determination of London to find an alternative path to the gradualist French abolition society was apparent. Much of the British effort would not succeed, for abolitionists across the Channel could not impose their model upon a nation so foreign in anti-slavery culture to their own. Nevertheless, the British were propagating certain concepts that would take root in the future.

Despite the British initiative, traditional French abolitionism seemed to be marking time once again after the passage of the Mackau laws. Isambert's hopes that new petitions would refocus attention on emancipation remained unfulfilled for the time being. After the noble effort by the workers of *L'Union* in early 1844, the only petition the abolitionists could muster in 1845 was one of Protestant inspiration from ten inhabitants of Neuville (Loiret) – a department represented by the determined abolitionist Roger du Loiret and where Isambert had his country home – that Agénor de Gasparin deposited in the Chamber of Deputies on February 12.[9] Following the hiatus occasioned by the intersession period, in early 1846 the British abolitionist

---

[7] Jennings, "Slavery and the Bordeaux Press," 281.

[8] Rhodes House Anti-Slavery Papers, Minute Books, Oct. [17], 1845.

[9] *L'Abolitioniste français*, Jan.–Feb. 1845, p. 43; Tudesq, *Les grands notables*, II, 835.

formation stepped in again to encourage its cross-Channel allies. In a public letter to the Société française pour l'abolition de l'esclavage, the British organization suggested that it was time to move toward more rapid emancipation now that the right of search dispute had been terminated and "the general question of emancipation can be discussed with calm." The British body also expressed its belief that the voting of the Mackau laws should convince even the most skeptical abolitionist that the only possible remedy for slavery was its complete eradication. The French abolition society replied rapidly to its British counterpart with an open letter of its own, signed by its new secretary, Dutrône, and president, Tracy. It vowed that the French group was well aware of the inadequacies of the 1845 legislation and of the fact that the *colons* would elude its provisions. However, it insisted that its approach would be its time-tested one of gathering evidence to demonstrate in the chambers the weaknesses of the laws.[10] Perhaps as a sop to the British, the French abolition society began featuring as of 1846 on the front of issues of its journal, *L'Abolitioniste*, a new rendition of the old seal borrowed from the English that French abolitionist societies had employed since the Amis des Noirs. This time, though, the chained and kneeling slave was facing leftward, and under it was a statement that the society owed this design to Wilks, who had been associated already with the Société de la morale chrétienne. All of this was symbolical, both of the society's past and continued indebtedness to the British. The fact remains, however, that the Société française, still employing its parliamentary tactics of the mid-1830s, remained true to its gradualist self despite British pressures.

In late 1845 and early 1846 the French anti-slavery community persisted in its strategy of demonstrating how ineffective the Mackau legislation had been so far in altering conditions in the colonies. *La Réforme* of November 1, 1845, denounced "continued mistreatment of slaves"; the article made such an impact that Mackau wrote to his governors to request their investigation of the matter.[11] When an apologist for the *colons*, the Abbé Joseph Rigord, a curate in Martinique, published a booklet insisting that more time was needed to prepare slaves, Schoelcher in reviewing his work remarked that priests had

[10] *L'Abolitioniste français*, 1846, 2nd issue, pp. 78–83, 84–6.
[11] Ibid., 93; *La Réforme*, Nov. 1, 1845.

already had 300 years to moralize slaves with little effect. He also exclaimed: "More time to prepare the negroes for liberty. But that amounts to an indefinite adjournment; no one is dupe to that formula" any more.[12] Abolitionists were striving to underline the immutability of the colonial situation despite the Mackau laws.

In 1846 as in late 1845 the abolitionists also persisted in denouncing the French government's slowness in implementing the Mackau legislation. Delays in issuing ordonnances to activate the different clauses of the Mackau law were partly imputable to the provision stipulating that all initiatives must be discussed with the colonies or their representatives. This stipulation afforded the latter the opportunity to delay the implementation of any measures. The delegates lobbied against every ordonnance put forth by the navy-colonial office, criticizing them, demanding their revision or withdrawal, or stalling in commenting on them. As Jollivet avowed, the delegates tried "to buy time" as much as possible, offering their advice only when Mackau threatened to issue his decrees forthwith if their procrastination continued.[13] Still, these very delays were convincing evidence that the Mackau laws did not provide the means for bringing rapid improvement for slaves or preparing them for liberation in the near future. Indeed, modern scholarship tends to confirm that none of the July Monarchy's ameliorative moves measurably improved the material condition of colonial slaves.[14] Already at that time, the abolitionists never missed an opportunity to point out this basic weakness in the Mackau legislation. During the discussion of the colonial budget in the Deputies in the spring of 1846, Isambert, still active despite his resignation as secretary of the abolition society, demanded that the minister give an account of what elements of the 1845 laws had been implemented so far. He accompanied this request with the accusation that since the promulgation of the ordonnance on forced *rachat* the previous autumn not one slave had had recourse to this measure. His

---

[12] *L'Abolitioniste français*, 1846, 2nd issue, pp. 107–21. The study by Rigord was entitled: *Observations sur quelques opinions relatives à l'esclavage, émises à la Chambre des Pairs à l'occasion de la discussion de la loi sur le régime des esclaves aux colonies* (Fort Royal: Ruelle, 1845). For more detail on Abbé Rigord, see Delisle, *Renouveau missionnaire*, 199–201.

[13] Schoelcher Papers, N. a. f. 3631, pp. 244–6, Jollivet to President Colonial Council of Martinique, April 27, June 13, 1846.

[14] Fallope, *Esclaves et ciyoyens*, 308.

colleague Jules de Lasteyrie then joined in to criticize once again the slow record of the government in issuing its *ordonnances*.[15] Only after these deliberations in the lower house did the navy-colonial office move quickly to issue on May 18, 1846, *ordonnances* on religious and elementary education, and on June 4 and 5, regulations covering the disciplining, nourishment, and upkeep of slaves.

The most noteworthy provisions were those forbidding the whipping of women and children, measures denounced by the plantocracy as "disorganizing" for plantation work teams. Still, it was clear that these regulations too could not possibly begin to be implemented in the colonies until the end of 1846 at the earliest, for they were not inserted in the *Bulletin des lois* until June 23. By mid-1846 new information indicated that only twenty-nine slaves had resorted to *rachat*, largely because *colon*-dominated commissions were setting the price so high as to be dissuasive.[16] As late as March 1847 the procolonial organ *Le Courrier du Havre* admitted that "amelioration measures are barely beginning, moral and religious instruction are just being introduced in the colonies."[17] Abolitionists could not fail to see that improvements in a basic area such as religious education, a domain upon which the government was supposedly concentrating its efforts and into which it had been pumping funds since 1839–1840, were still sorely lagging. Modern studies, while suggesting some progress in Christianization after 1845, confirm the ineffectiveness of the Mackau laws in questions of slave education.[18] It was becoming

---

[15] *Le Moniteur universel*, May 16, 1846. Isambert's claims were exaggerated, but his pessimism not entirely misplaced; out of 205 slave requests for *rachat* with or without assistance between July 1845 and Dec. 1846 in Guadeloupe alone, five came to settlements with their masters, 15 paid the entire sum themselves, 35 received the assistance of state funding, and 151 had their requests adjourned because they could not themselves pay for their self-redemption (Fallope, *Esclaves et ciyoyens*, 293). A government document did assert, though, that in all the colonies by October 1847, some 2,017 slaves had been freed by *rachat* under the provisions of the law of 1845 (ANSOM, Guadeloupe 258 (1554), Minister to Governor of Guadeloupe, Feb. 14, 1848), though these numbers might be inflated. In 1848 the commission formed to grant an indemnity to slave owners estimated at around 3,000 the total number of slaves manumitted for the period 1845–1848 (Schmidt, *Schoelcher*, 85–6).

[16] *L'Abolitioniste français*, 1846, 4th issue, pp. 262–3; 5th issue, pp. 287–301; Schoelcher Papers, N. a. f. 3631, p. 249, Jollivet to President Colonial Council of Martinique, Sept. 12, 1846.

[17] Article in ANCAOM, Gén. 197 (1489).

[18] Delisle, *Renouveau missionnaire*, 201–6; Nelly Schmidt, "Suppression de l'esclavage,

steadily apparent to many abolitionists that the Mackau laws could not improve the plight of slaves or affect their liberation in the foreseeable future.

Gradualist emancipation theories were increasingly discredited and undermined by the failure of the Mackau laws. This was one of the principle points articulated by Félice in a booklet, *Emancipation immédiate et complète des esclaves: Appel aux abolitionistes,* that he turned out in the late spring of 1846. In this work Félice argued that slavery was a crime, and that the idea of preparing slaves gradually for emancipation was "a great and deplorable illusion." Moreover, he pointed out that gradualist approaches had obtained little, the Mackau laws bringing only "sterile reforms." Thus, he insisted, Frenchmen should work relentlessly for immediate slave liberation by forming associations, agitating, writing, and petitioning.[19] This was obviously the book advocating immediatism that Félice had promised in the autumn of 1845 to produce for Scoble.

In fact, the British abolitionists appear to have had a direct hand in the publication and distribution of Félice's *Emancipation immédiate.* In a long, detailed letter, Félice recounted to the British that the Courtois brothers of Toulouse had arranged for 1,500 copies to be printed by a Protestant religious publishing group, while Félice had paid for more than 2,000 additional copies with funds provided by Gurney. What monies remained after the publication costs had been used by Félice to mail out 900 copies in the capital and an equal number in the provinces to members of the chambers, men of letters, Catholic and Protestant religious leaders, and the principal newspapers. He pointed out that while some Protestants criticized the book for not being sectarian enough, he was insistent that his work be directed to all people believing in "justice and humanity," for "we will attain our objective only by going beyond Protestant circles." According to Félice, "the Cabinet will do nothing decisive for the slaves if it is not pushed by the legislative chambers, and the chambers in turn will do nothing if they are not pushed by national opinion." The "best informed people were

système scolaire et réorganisation sociale aux Antilles: Les Frères de l'instruction chrétienne, témoins et acteurs, instituteurs des nouveaux libres," *Revue d'histoire moderne et contemporaine* 31 (1984): 212–3.

[19] Guillaume de Félice, *Emancipation immédiate et complète des esclaves: Appel aux abolitionistes* (Paris: Delay, 1846), 11–24, 34, 43, 107, 112–3.

convinced" that the Mackau laws were "a new dupery *to gain time*" (emphasis in the original), and that the "Cabinet would rather come to an arrangement with the *colons* than emancipate the slaves." Moreover, he was certain that "the King Louis Philippe himself [was] personally unfavorable to emancipation." It was therefore necessary to "stir things up, agitate, conquer national opinion" by issuing more and more pamphlets directed at different layers of French society. He suggested that the British could help French abolitionists achieve the goal of producing at least three or four immediatist pamphlets per year by subsidizing their writing, publication, and distribution, and by turning to people such as Schoelcher and Bissette, assisting them as they had aided him.[20] As far as publications were concerned, Félice was clearly trying to conform the French anti-slavery effort to the successful British model. Moreover, as the British "agent for the abolition of slavery in France," he was attempting to entice the British into more involvement on the French scene. His efforts in this latter sense testify to the fact that there was still no established French anti-slavery network for immediate slave liberation. French immediatism remained dependent upon a handful of activists, some of them heavily reliant upon British encouragement and support. Besides, with the exception of the workers' petitions of 1844, it was still unable to move beyond the traditional printed medium in advancing its cause.

The very publication of Félice's booklet, however, seems to have had the effect of stirring up some immediatist sentiment in France. *Emancipation immédiate* was well received by abolitionist organs such as *Le Semeur*, *La Réforme*, *L'Espérance*, and *L'Abolitioniste français*. The latter described it as perhaps the best work written so far in favor of emancipation.[21] According to Félice, even such provincial organs as *Le Journal de Calais*, *Le Journal de Lyon*, and two newspapers from Toulouse – city of the Courtois brothers – had issued reviews favorable to immediate emancipation. Félice had heard that Isambert, Tracy, and Lutheroth – another low-key mainstay of the French abolition society – had reacted positively to his work; Lamartine, Tocqueville, Rémusat, and Gasparin had actually written kind

---

[20] Rhodes House Anti-Slavery Papers, C157/68, Félice to [Scoble], July 21, 1846.
[21] *Le Semeur*, June 10, 1846; *La Réforme*, June 16, 1846; *L'Espérance*, Aug. 11, 1846; *L'Abolitioniste français*, 1847, 1st issue, pp. 51–6.

words to him about it. Félice also reported to London that Bissette had sent him a touching letter concerning the booklet. At the same time the black abolitionist had asked Félice to draw up a petition for immediate slave liberation which Bissette offered to have signed by 5,000 to 6,000 of his acquaintances in Paris.[22]

Félice's remarks concerning Bissette's suggestion of turning to petitioning to advance the immediatist cause is significant, for, after finishing his booklet, Félice proceeded to draw up just such a document in August 1846. Petitioning, like pamphleteering, had been advocated by the British as a prime means of popularizing the abolitionist cause. It had even proved to be the most effective weapon in the British anti-slavery arsenal in the late 1820s and early 1830s. Still, it appears that in France in 1846 the encouragement for petitioning came from Bissette and was then picked up by Félice without direct British involvement at first. In his booklet, Félice had already praised the petitioning process, especially the example put forth by the French workers in 1844; the idea that Bissette would promote and distribute a large petition in Paris was probably the decisive factor in Félice deciding to draft his petition for immediate slave liberation dated August 17, 1846. In a letter to Schoelcher, Félice avowed that it was Bissette who had asked him to draw up a draft of a petition along the same principles as his book; accordingly, Félice had accomplished his mission and sent the draft to Bissette. Félice explained his role to Schoelcher by pointing out that Bissette was a man of action, while Félice himself was an "office person," isolated in the provinces. Then, once the process began, other petitions were produced, usually with identical wording to that of August 17, and distributed elsewhere. Indeed, many of them showed the same date on them; some were turned out by the same printing house in Toulouse, by friends of Félice, indicating that the Courtois brothers too probably had a hand in the process. That some considerable thought went into the final drafting process is evidenced by the fact that the petitions of 1846–1847 tended to be better organized and presented than those of 1844, with neatly drawn squares or columns for signatures. The petitions, like Félice's booklet, all depicted slavery as a crime that must be eliminated rapidly. At the same time they insisted that all attempts

[22] Rhodes House Anti-Slavery Papers, C157/68, Félice to [Scoble], July 21, 1846.

at amelioration, as provided by the Mackau law and its subsequent ordonnances, were illusory.[23]

The first petition, containing some 300 signatures, was deposited by the dissident conservative, comte Charles de Mérode, brother-in-law of Montalembert, in the Chamber of Deputies on September 3, 1846, for discussion during the 1847 legislative session. It had been rapidly circulated by Bissette himself. Among the signatories of this initial petition were notable figures such as the republican scientist François Arago (the future navy-colonial minister), the writer-historian Michelet, and the prominent Protestant leader Adolphe de Monod, along with the abolitionists Dutrône, Saint-Antoine, Isambert, Lutheroth, and Gatine. This initial effort was followed up by some twenty-four other petitions from Paris and twenty-five from other towns or cities, most with identical wording. They were dated from August 17, 1846, to April 15, 1847. Among those from the capital was a "Petition from the women of Paris," which cited the plight of slave women. In analyzing this small women's petition, Schoelcher remarked that the number of signatures had been limited because French women feared compromising themselves with a "too eccentric act" and did not wish to have the "pretention of putting themselves forward." Contrasting this with British women who had signed such documents by the thousand, Schoelcher hoped that French women would strive to rival their cross-Channel sisters.[24] Already in 1842 Schoelcher had reproached French Catholic women like Madame Legouvé, wife of his good friend, for a distinct lack of ardor for the abolitionist cause in sharp contrast to British and American women.[25] In speaking of the 1847 campaign, though, Schoelcher did claim that abolitionism had been the first cause in France to draw some female signatures on petitions read before the legislative chambers.[26]

The 1837 petitions totaled some 10,737 signatures, 8,080 from Paris and 2,657 from the provinces. One addressed to the inhabitants of Lyon, a city that had already contributed to the 1844 campaign,

---

[23] ANCAOM, Gén. 197 (1489); L'Abolitioniste français, 1846, 5th issue, pp. 274–87; Victor Schoelcher, Sa correspondance inédite, part 2: Lettres martiniquaise (1829–1881) (Paris: Revue mondiale, 1935), pp. 32–4, Félice to Schoelcher, Nov. 29, 1846.

[24] Schoelcher, Histoire de l'esclavage, II, 453–4.

[25] Schmidt, La correspondance, 126, undated letter from 1842 to Legouvé.

[26] Schoelcher, Histoire de l'esclavage, II, 453–4.

was followed by 1,638 names, but has not been included in the total. Although in the archives this document was found among other 1847 petitions, evidence suggests that this large submission that only began circulating in February 1847 was not completed in time for the April 1847 debate and was held over for the 1848 campaign that never came to fruition because of the intervening February Revolution. If the Lyon petition were to be added to the others the total would be 12,395.[27] Most of the petitions submitted from the provinces had relatively few signatures, ranging from two dozen to 300. Many small provincial petitions emanated from areas with relatively high Protestant representation: Toulouse (198 signatures), Laverdun (Ariège, 20 signatures), Uzès (Gard, 24), Castres-Mazamet (Tarn, 233), communes around Castres (42), Brassac (Tarn, 127), Puy-Laurens (Tarn, 142), Calmot-Gabel (Ariège, 75), Réalmont (Tarn, 166), Mazères (Ariège, 56), Albi (Tarn, 54), Strasbourg (23), Montauban (148), Saint-Antonin (Tarn et Garonne, 116), Samatan (Gers, 67), and Nimes (181). Given the fact that fair-sized towns (Albi, Montauban) and cities (Toulouse, Strasbourg, Nimes) often garnered no more signers that villages, it would seem that a local pastor or activist was probably in charge of circulating the documents. Other petitions originated from disparate regions of France whose motives for submission are more difficult to decipher: Vizelle (Isère, 83), Mens (Isère, 25), Marennes (Charentes-Maritimes, 55), St. Martin-La Flotte-Ile de Ré (Charentes-Maritimes, 75), Metz (49), Nancy (242), Saint-Quentin (Aisne, 156), and Fontainebleau (172). Because nearby towns in the same provinces sometimes submitted petitions, it is possible that the word spread or that one individual in each area distributed one or two petitions. In Nancy, it was a friend of Bissette who gathered signatures, including that of the bishop. There were even two petitions originating in the planter-dominated colonies, indicating support there among the free of mixed race, some of whom possessed slaves. The one from Guadeloupe presented 267 names and specified that it was from *hommes de couleur*

---

[27] ANCAOM, Gén. 197 (1489). Circumstantial evidence also suggests that that the sum of 10,737 is correct, for several contemporary references by abolitionists who were in a position to know mention the round figure of 11,000. Seymour Drescher, a reliable quantitative historian, also cites 10,700 (Drescher, "Public Opinion and the Destruction," 29). There is no evidence, however, to support the assertion of one recent student of the topic that there were 16,000 signatures for 1847 (Motylewski, *La Société*, 102).

libres. That from St. Pierre, Martinique, addressed to Schoelcher, contained sixty-four signers, many of them listing the number of slaves they owned. Schoelcher and his organ *La Réforme* had also played a role in collecting Parisian signatures. The newspaper pleaded for support for the cause in its issue of December 20, 1846, reproduced Félice's petition, and even offered copies of it for distribution.[28] All of this implies a better organized and more widespread petition campaign than in 1844. An embryonic anti-slavery network, with solid Protestant participation, had formed in the provinces at least for this specific effort. Still, it was Bissette who played the leading role in raising many of the signatures on the petitions, and probably also in their distribution.

In a letter to London, Félice emphasized that it was "due to Mr. Bissette especially, I would like to repeat here, that we owe the greatest number of signatures. He demonstrated in this matter a never failing zeal and devotion." Félice then added that while Schoelcher, with whom he had been in correspondence over the matter, had shown "much good will in supporting the petitions," it was regrettable that he and Bissette were at loggerheads, despite Félice's attempts to work out a rapprochement between them.[29] A fierce opponent of Bissette, delegate Jollivet, also reported that "Bissette had carried door to door a petition requesting immediate emancipation, and had had it signed by a rather large number of workers of Paris."[30] It was Bissette himself, though, who offered the most complete account of his concerted petitioning efforts. Writing to Scoble in London in January 1847, Bissette explained that in cooperation with Félice – who seems to have remained in Montauban most if not all of the time – he had circulated petitions in Paris since August and had alone collected over 6,000 signatures. Every day he had carried petitions door to door. Because the campaign continued into the spring, it can be assumed that he collected several hundred, if not thousands, more by the time

[28] ANCAOM, Gén. 197 (1489); Rhodes House Anti-Slavery Papers, C13/119, Bissette to Scoble, Jan. 19, 1847; *L'Abolitioniste français*, 1846, 5th issue, pp. 274–87; *La Revue abolitioniste* (Paris), no. 1, pp. 110–12. This latter journal also reproduced the "Petition from the Women of Paris," pp. 33–9.
[29] Rhodes House Anti-Slavery Papers, C157/69, Félice from Montauban to London, May 8, 1847.
[30] Schoelcher Papers, N. a. f. 3631, p. 253, Jollivet to President Colonial Council of Martinique, Dec. 29, 1846.

the petitions were submitted to the chambers. He had also targeted certain specific sectors of the population. By March 1847, for instance, he had obtained the signatures of some 800 Catholic priests and had won over the Archbishop of Paris to the cause; the latter had confirmed to Bissette that emancipation was "the constant wish of the Church."[31] It was the combination of Félice's petition and Bissette's diligence in collecting adherents that accounted for the success of the 1846–1847 petition campaign, as limited as this success might have been when compared with the millions of signatures the British had mustered some fifteen years earlier.[32] While Schoelcher is fully deserving of his fame as the liberator of French slaves in 1848, the team of Bissette and Félice was more important for the advancement of the immediatist ideal under the July Monarchy than the celebrated liberator of French blacks.

Bissette had reason to be proud of his decisive role in the petition campaign of 1846–1847, but the small network centered around him and a handful of Protestant activists was not very extensive. Bissette, for example, complained bitterly about the total lack of assistance he had received from the Société française pour l'abolition de l'esclavage. He had asked the secretary of the society to aid him in any way possible, but the group's "assistance ... had been completely nil"; it had not even agreed to reprint copies of the petition as Bissette had requested. Bissette insisted to the British that he alone had covered, with much difficulty, the costs of his petitioning effort. He did, however, thank Scoble for the 10 pounds the British society had sent him for these purposes. Still, he complained that his resources had been so limited that he had been unable to campaign outside of Paris, and he regretted the British decision not to provide additional assistance to permit him to travel to French port cities.[33] In his letter to London of May 8, 1847, Félice too bemoaned the fact that he had not heard from his British correspondent for a long time, and that the British abolitionists had not replied positively to his request for financing on a

---

[31] Rhodes House Anti-Slavery Papers, C13/119, 122, Bissette to Scoble, Jan. 19, March 19, 1847.

[32] For an excellent account of the essential role played by massive petitioning in the eventual British anti-slavery victory over slavery, see Seymour Drescher, "Public Opinion and the Destruction of British Colonial Slavery," 22–48.

[33] Rhodes House Anti-Slavery Papers, C13/119, Bissette to Scoble, Jan. 19, 1847.

wide scale French anti-slavery activities. Indeed, in January 1847 the British and Foreign Anti-Slavery Society had judged Félice's recommendation "impracticable."[34] Quite clearly, the British were willing to supply much encouragement and small sums of start-up money for French immediatist activities, just as they had helped with the launching of *L'Abolitioniste français*. But they undoubtedly came to realize the limitations to their involvement in France and the necessity for the French to stand on their own as much as possible. British abolitionists would not extensively fund a French abolitionist movement unable to support itself. The paucity of funding available to immediatist-oriented abolitionists in France also indicates to what extent an effective abolitionist network, adequate financial resources, and thus popular support in general were still lacking in France less than one year prior to the Revolution of 1848. The continuing differences between Bissette and Schoelcher, between the Bissette–Félice faction and the French abolition society, also show that French anti-slavery remained as divided as ever.

In early 1847, as in previous years, the slavery question remained centered in the legislative sphere. With the discussion of the immediatist petitions in the chambers set for late March 1847, both the abolitionists and colonial delegates undertook concerted lobbying efforts. Bissette arranged with several abolitionist deputies to introduce the many petitions one at a time at a few days' interval after the opening of the legislative session in order to obtain the maximum exposure possible for the cause. Bissette also saw the deputy who had been appointed reporter on the petitions in the lower house. This was Paul de Gasparin, a recently elected representative and brother of Agénor, who had split with Guizot over the latter's refusal to reform, had failed to be reelected in 1846, and thereafter had largely withdrawn from politics. The two spent hours debating strategy. Bissette spoke at length too with Montalembert, who promised to try to have his friend, the abolitionist Beugnot, named reporter of the petitions in the upper house. Then, when Beugnot was appointed, Bissette discussed matters with him in detail, only to discover that the Peers commission as a whole was unfavorable to the petitions and would try to "choke

---

[34] Ibid., C157/69, Félice from Montauban to London, May 8, 1847; Minute Books, Jan. 15, 1847.

all discussion" with the argument that the 1845 Mackau laws were adequate to prepare emancipation. Mackau was uncooperative with both Bissette and Paul de Gasparin, but Guizot told Gasparin that he would weigh upon the navy-colonial minister to "render his colleague more tractable."

Bissette also seized the occasion to approach the British abolitionists about a subsidy to enable him to begin a new abolitionist monthly to fight for immediate emancipation. In the process he informed London that he would have the collaboration of Félice in his new endeavor. Bissette asked specifically for 300 francs per month for three months, with the remark that the British could cease supporting his review after this trial period if it did not meet their expectations. As cautious as ever in terms of stipends, the British and Foreign Anti-Slavery Society committed funding for the first three monthly issues, but only after it had extracted a pledge from Bissette that "all personal polemics" would be banned from the new publication.[35] The British had obviously become wary of the black abolitionist because of the controversies swirling around him due to his caustic, combative, volatile nature. True to his commitment, Bissette issued the first number of his short-lived *Revue abolitioniste* in early March 1847, just as the chamber debates were about to begin. In its very first issue Bissette emphatically proclaimed that the review's primary objective would be "the complete and immediate abolition of slavery."[36]

As for the *colons*, in 1846 the president of their Council of Delegates had been confident that the colonies had "time before them." Dupin believed that the deputies, peers, and the King would not want to vote hundreds of millions of francs for an indemnity at a time when "the treasury has no money."[37] But the deposition of the abolitionist petitions caused consternation in colonial ranks, all the more so because these submissions mentioned only a small token indemnity for slave owners. In early 1847 the delegates noted with dread that the Catholic clergy was subscribing to the petitions and had therefore broken out of its heretofore neutral position on the emancipation issue.

---

[35] Ibid., C13/119–120, 122, Bissette to Scoble, Jan. 19, Feb. 2, March 19, 1847; Minute Books, Feb. 12, 1847.

[36] *La Revue abolitioniste*, 1847, 1st issue, p. 3.

[37] Schoelcher Papers, N. a. f. 3631, pp. 210–13, Dupin to President Colonial Council of Martinique, June 29, 1846.

The delegates remained optimistic, though, that the Peers would reject the petitions; the decision within the lower chamber, they believed, would depend upon the attitude of the Cabinet. The Council of Delegates acted by asking to speak before the petition commissions in both houses. In so doing, its members were disappointed when Paul de Gasparin confirmed to Jollivet that he intended to support the petitions. The delegates reacted also through their press, and by calling a meeting of Martinican planters residing in Paris, along with representatives from the two chambers who were favorable to the colonies.[38] The upshot of this action was a counter-petition from a little-known Martinican planter, submitted to the navy-colonial minister in late March. In typical *colon* fashion, it argued that emancipation was unnecessary, unwise, and unaffordable at the time.[39] Bissette treated with scorn this attempt by the plantocracy to negate the abolitionist petition campaign with such a pitiful effort.[40] Still, the delegates received some reassurances when they learned that the Council of Ministers would discuss the issue. The result was that the Cabinet decided unanimously to call for the rejection of the petitions, reassert its faith in the legislation of 1845, and request a return to the order of the day.[41] Once again the administration and *colons* concurred in their stance in opposition to abolitionist aspirations. Moreover, the government's intention of continued adherence to the ameliorative option that had marked July Monarchy policy for the previous fifteen years as an alternative to rapid emancipation now rendered the Mackau laws more appealing to part of the colonial lobby that had often been so critical of them since their passage in 1845.

The government's strategy was facilitated by the recommendation of the petitions commission of the Chamber of Peers. Despite Beugnot's efforts, it declared itself, as predicted, against taking into consideration the abolitionist petitions containing some 3,000 signatures that had been submitted to the upper house. Expressing its belief that the Mackau laws would eventually lead to slave liberation, it advocated

---

[38] Ibid., pp. 106, 115, Jollivet to President Colonial Council of Martinique, Jan. 26, 29, March 13, 1847.

[39] ANCAOM, Gén. 197 (1439), Benjam to Minister, March 26, 1847.

[40] Rhodes House Anti-Slavery Papers, C13/122, Bissette to Scoble, March 19, 1847.

[41] Schoelcher Papers, N. a. f. 3631, pp. 226–7, Dupin to President Colonial Council of Martinique, March 30, 1847.

returning to the order of the day. Mackau and his supporters employed the same arguments as the commission during the Peers debate on the petitions on March 30, 1847. According to the minister, the legislation of 1845 was just beginning to have its effect, and the gradualist solution it proposed should not be superseded by the dangerous one of immediate emancipation that could lead to "the total overthrow of established order." The petitions were especially pernicious, the minister suggested, because they "put into doubt" the property rights "of our compatriots" by questioning the need for a generous indemnity. In reply to this attack, only Montalembert stood out among abolitionists in defending the petitions and the radical option they offered. The Peers proceeded to reject nearly unanimously the petitions, demonstrating that the appointive upper house was still far from favoring emancipation.[42] Bissette complained bitterly that Broglie, who had promised to intervene, had not done so, and that Harcourt and Passy, who had encouraged Montalembert earlier, had not spoken up to support him. Despite his promises of good behavior to the British, this led Bissette to launch into a tirade against the French abolitionist establishment. He ridiculed "these gentlemen who amuse themselves in playing with the abolition of slavery, like young children who play ... with little soldiers. They do not think about coming together to set a plan to follow."[43] At one point Gustave de Beaumont had blurted out to an English abolitionist that the Société française pour l'abolition de l'esclavage had not admitted Bissette to its ranks because "he is a colored man." But the real reason was undoubtedly the gap between the elitist members of the society and the acerbic, mud-raking, radical Bissette, who had also become somewhat of a pariah because of his unpaid debts at a time when such practices were castigated by respectable members of the upper classes.[44] As the anti-slavery cause faced adversity in the spring of 1847, the division between moderate and radical abolitionists seemed to be accentuated. Bissette's criticism of the French abolition society for its inaction in the Peers and its attitude toward the petition campaign also reveals how moderate mainstream French anti-slavery still remained.

[42] *Le Moniteur universel*, March 31, 1847.
[43] Rhodes House Anti-Slavery Papers, C13/123, Bissette to Scoble, April 3, 1847.
[44] Quote by Beaumont cited in Drescher, *Dilemmas of Democracy*, 163. On the social stigmatization attached to Bissette as a borrower and debtor, see Jennings, "Bissette," 55–6.

While government and colonial representatives might take solace in their victory in the Peers in late March 1847, they faced a different alignment of forces in the elective lower house a month later. Even before the debate opened there, Jollivet anticipated that the Cabinet might lack resolve during the discussions; he feared that the petitions commission would be divided, and that the navy-colonial minister would be hesitant in the face of pressure from Guizot.[45] Things went even worse than Jollivet expected. When Paul de Gasparin made his report in the Deputies on April 24, it set the tone for the ensuing debate. Gasparin's report concluded that preparatory measures had not worked, that self-redemption and amelioration could not end slavery, and that the petitions should be referred to the minister of the navy and the Cabinet so that the government could fix a date for emancipation. Jules de Lasteyrie and Ledru-Rollin then made moving speeches showing how the *colons* had displayed bad faith toward implementing the 1845 laws, and how slaves were still being horribly mistreated. They especially underlined the prejudice and injustice of colonial magistrates toward slaves. Mackau and Jollivet tried to defend the 1845 laws and argue for the return to the order of the day, but both appeared overwhelmed. Mackau even flinched before the accusations about colonial magistrates and offered to investigate the matter. When the request was finally made to take the petitions into consideration and refer them to the Cabinet and minister, Guizot intervened to support this motion. The lower house then proceeded to vote decisively for taking the petitions into consideration.[46] The overwhelming support that the abolitionist petitions had generated in the Chamber of Deputies had led Guizot to turn against his navy-colonial minister. The colonial lobby had suffered a worst defeat in the lower house than the abolitionists had in the upper one. Bissette could rejoice at finally winning a battle.[47]

The *colons*, to the contrary, were shocked by their setback. Jollivet exclaimed that the outcome in the Deputies surpassed his worst fears. Abolitionism, he reported to Martinique, had advanced by ten years. Still, Jollivet often purposefully exaggerated developments in order to

---

[45] Schoelcher Papers, N. a. f. 3631, pp. 116–7, Jollivet to President Colonial Council of Martinique, April 13, 1847.

[46] *Le Moniteur universel*, April 25, 27, 1847.

[47] *La Revue abolitioniste*, 1847, 1st issue, pp. 113–21.

draw more monies from his frightened colonial council.[48] Mackau himself, though, reacted precipitously to the developments in the lower chamber. He had been personally humiliated, even contradicted publicly by Guizot, leader of the Cabinet. His policies of immobility had been questioned by the elective house. As a result, he resigned as navy-colonial minister a few days after the debate in the chambers. According to the delegates of Guadeloupe, Mackau said he resigned because "it was impossible for him, in light of the present majority, to do good for the colonies, and because he could not consent to be a part of and to cooperate in the destruction of our overseas possessions."[49] The duc de Montebello, Napoleon Lannes, Peer, minister under Molé, and former member of the Morale chrétienne, was recalled from his diplomatic position in Naples to replace him. In the meantime, though, Guizot assumed the position of interim Minister of the Navy and Colonies along with his other duties. As Jollivet remarked, Mackau had harmed the colonial position through his 1845 legislation, but he was better than Guizot, who had maintained connections with the abolitionists in the past.[50] The reaction of the delegate of Martinique, however, was mild in comparison with that of his counterparts representing Guadeloupe.

In 1846 Guadeloupe had elected two progressive delegates to represent it in Paris, Eimar de Jabrun and Eugène de Reizet (also spelled Reiset), both large landowners in the island, and thus men who could most profit from a generous indemnity. Their positions on slavery contrasted with that dominant in Martinique. By 1847 Jollivet and Dupin, along with the Martinique colonial council, had swung around to accepting the Mackau legislation.[51] They came to judge it objectionable in principle, but harmless in reality. Martinican *colons*, in sum, had rightly concluded that the 1845 laws would not advance significantly the emancipation of slaves and really amounted to an annoying but effective delaying tactic. Jabrun and Reizet, to the contrary,

---

[48] Schoelcher Papers, N. a. f. 3631, pp. 117–20, Jollivet to Colonial Council of Martinique, April 29, 1847.
[49] ANCAOM, Gén. 173 (1388), Reizet and Jabrun to President Colonial Council of Guadeloupe, May 30, 1847.
[50] Schoelcher Papers, N. a. f. 3631, pp. 120–2, Jollivet to President Colonial Council of Martinique, May 14, 1847.
[51] Ibid., pp. 108–9, Nov. 12, 1847; ANSOM, Corr. Gén., Martinique 122, Colonial Council 1847, statement during colonial council meeting of July 17, 1847.

adhered to that colonial concept dating back to the 1830s which held that emancipation with an inflated indemnity and guarantees of work was preferable to projects like the Mackau laws that gradually undermined servitude and diminished planter indemnities.

The addition of Jabrun and Reizet to the Council of Delegates in Paris brought the first evidence of serious disagreement in colonial ranks over what strategy best suited the situation. Already in late 1846 Jollivet ruminated about the fact that there were "two opinions in the colonies, one more disposed to concessions, the other to resistance."[52] Now, these differences between Guadeloupe and Martinique developed into an open schism. Immediately after the April 1847 debate in the Deputies, Jabrun and Reizet panicked. Fearing rapid slave liberation on terms totally unacceptable to the planters, the two now recommended that the Guadeloupe colonial council announce its willingness to accept emancipation on certain conditions favorable to the colonies. They urged their colonial legislature to inform the King that Guadeloupe wished direct representation in the French chambers, emancipation with indemnity, and guarantees of sustained black labor through the adoption of "association."[53] Association was a concept put forth earlier by the socialist Charles Fourier which proposed the integration of capital and workers as a means of organizing labor.[54] The leading Fourierist newspaper in France, *La Démocratie pacifique*, immediately hailed the move as heralding a veritable social revolution in the colonies that would also set an example for Europe to follow.[55] This newspaper, however, was receiving heavy stipends from the Guadeloupe delegates at this time, so its enthusiasm is highly suspect.[56]

[52] Schoelcher Papers, N. a. f. 3631, pp. 103–4, Jollivet to President Colonial Council of Martinique, Dec. 13, 1846.

[53] ANCAOM, Gén. 173 (1388), Reizet and Jabrun to President Colonial Council of Guadeloupe, May 30, June 29, 1847. For more detail on this entire question of association and Guadeloupe, see Lawrence C. Jennings, "French Slave Liberation and Socialism: Projects for 'Association' in Guadeloupe, 1845–1848," *Slavery and Abolition* 17 (1996): 93–111.

[54] On the term association, its ambiguity, roots, and variations in 1840s France, see Maurice Tournier, "Quant un mot en cache d'autres; le vocabulaire de 'l'association' en 1848," *Prévenir* no. 13 (1986): 113–26. For a thorough examination of Fourier and his role in pre-Marxian socialism, see Jonathan Beecher, *Charles Fourier: The Visionary and his World* (Berkeley: University of California Press, 1986).

[55] *La Démocratie pacifique*, vol. 9, no. 21, July 24, 1847; no. 34, Aug. 8, 1847.

[56] See Jennings, "Slavery and the Venality," 976.

Guadeloupe's proposal for emancipation-association in 1847 was not the first of its kind in the French colonies. Already during the French Revolution, Guadeloupe had experimented with association as a coerced labor alternative to slavery. More recently and significantly, the colony of Guiana had considered several plans for colonization, emancipation, and association in the early and mid-1840s. Guiana, the largest, most underdeveloped, and least populated of all French plantation colonies, realized it could not hope to prosper until new sources of capital and labor were attracted to it. It was in line with these needs that in early 1840s Jules Lechevalier, a Fourierist adventurer and native of Martinique, formulated several similar plans calling for the development of colonization and the attraction of metropolitan capital through the formation of a company to take over all the agricultural land of Guiana, abolish slavery in the process, and replace it with association. Lechevalier's basic design was to attract capital through a guarantee to investors from the government assuring an annual return of 4 percent, just as the July Monarchy was doing for some of the burgeoning railway companies in metropolitan France at the time. Then, with this funding the company intended to compensate planters generously for their lands and slaves, achieving the ultimate dream of slave owners of paying off their debts, enriching themselves on the emancipation process, and obtaining managerial positions in a new company. Besides, the ex-slaves, liberated in the process, would still remain attached to the soil and forced to work under conditions harsher than those prevailing under servitude at the time. The liberated slaves were to be considered associates in the company because they would be given a pittance of a wage – much less than what free labor was paid in the colonies – and promises of a small percentage of eventual profits if the company were to achieve net gains superior to 4 percent. The latter was a near impossibility, for this rate of return was rarely attained on the most efficiently run Guianese plantations even in the best of years.[57]

---

[57] For a detailed account of this entire issue, see Lawrence C. Jennings, "Economic Development, Associative Socialism, and Slave Emancipation in French Guiana, 1839–1848," article submitted for publication. A different and briefer interpretation of Lechevalier's activities is available in Jack Hayward, "From Utopian Socialism, via Abolitionism to the Colonisation of French Guiana: Jules Lechevalier's West Indian Fiasco, 1833–1844," in Daget, ed., *De la Traite à l'Esclavage*, II, 603–626.

The governors of Guiana immediately saw through this project as a scam, and forcefully denounced it as such to Paris. Governor André Aimé Pariset reported that association would arbitrarily fix at a low rate the wages of supposedly freed blacks, abolish their right to a Saturday rest, eliminate their garden plots, and generally offer conditions worse than slavery. As Pariset remarked, "under the cover of their socialistic and humanitarian ideas ... never would so grave an exploitation of man, a more absolute servitude have been organized" under "a supposed title of emancipation."[58] Besides, the proposal was fiercely opposed by the many small landowners in Guiana who feared the loss of their lands and slaves to the company. The large landholders could hope to make a profit, return to France, or manage the enterprise; the small ones would be left with nothing once they paid off their debts and lost their slaves. A spokesman for the smaller owners, T. F. Ronmy, decried the association idea as an "ill-conceived plan," a "half-baked enterprise," a "utopia" more fit for the previous century than the 1840s.[59] With reports like this reaching Paris, there was no chance of the government accepting the colonization-emancipation scheme. In 1846, Mackau finally informed Lechevalier and his associates that no exception could be made for Guiana, and that the colony must abide by the government's program of amelioration and preparation outlined in the 1845 legislation.[60]

The Guadeloupe association proposal of 1847 strongly resembled that put forth earlier by Guiana. Following the advice of its delegates in Paris, on July 10, 1847, President Ambert of the Colonial Council of Guadeloupe issued a preliminary address to the King indicating that his island was prepared to advance with France "down the path of emancipation" if this were accompanied by association to guarantee the maintenance of work.[61] During the detailed debate that ensued on this proposal in the Guadeloupe colonial council it became evident that the *colons*, like those of Guiana, were preoccupied particularly with guaranteeing themselves indemnification and sustained labor if

---

[58] ANCAOM, Guyane 50 (25), Governor to Minister, Feb. 18, March 31, 1846; Gén. 173 (1388), Governor to Minister, Feb. 21, 1846.

[59] Ibid., Guyane 50 (25), Ronmy to Governor, Aug. 24, 1845; T. F. Ronmy, "Observations sur le projet de la colonisation de la Guyane," June 30, 1845.

[60] Ibid., Minister to Governor, April 17, 1846.

[61] Ibid., Gén. 173 (1388), Colonial Council of Guadeloupe to King, July 10, 1847.

the government were to proceed with slave liberation. The Guadeloupe plan called for emancipation with a generous indemnity of 1,200 francs per slave and the establishment of a regime of association under which freedmen would continue to be attached to their former owners. Besides, the association, managed by the masters, would work blacks from sunrise to sunset, and give them a small portion of any profits that might develop. Not only would this plan guarantee the plantation owners an indemnity and reliable labor source, but it would enable the association to avoid paying salaries to blacks at a time when there was an insufficient supply of currency floating in the colonies to cover wages. Thus, as colonial councilor Payen proclaimed, association, "justly lauded by the socialists," would provide freedmen with "food, lodging, and care."[62] All of this, of course, singularly resembled the current state of slavery and amounted to a mockery of the Fourierist concept of an open association of free workers. Governor Layrle of Guadeloupe exposed the plan to authorities in Paris as "nothing but the continuation of slavery with indemnity for the masters."[63] Many abolitionists also castigated the Guadeloupe proposal. According to Le Semeur, it amounted to nothing but "disguised servitude." The Lyonnais abolitionist Hector Fleury also condemned this "favorable financial operation" that Guadeloupe was attempting to realize through a "new slavery veiled only behind a hypocritical lie."[64]

Although both colonial authorities and abolitionist circles castigated the Guadeloupe association proposal, the most determined opponents of the plan were the representatives of Martinique. Jollivet declared bluntly that "Guadeloupe has joined the enemy." And he and his colleague Dupin fought the proposal mercilessly through lobbying and the press. The Colonial Council of Martinique denounced association as "impracticable," and imputed Guadeloupe's errors to its "despair." It concluded that the Mackau legislation, "as bad as it might be, is still better than what is proposed" by Guadeloupe.[65] Presented with the initiative by Guadeloupe, French Guiana briefly

---

[62] Ibid., Corr. Gén., Guad. 237, Colonial Council 1847, July 3, 1847.
[63] Ibid., Gén. 173 (1388), Governor to Minister, Nov. 25, 1847.
[64] Le Semeur, Nov. 3, 1847; Hector Fleury, De la société coloniale et des garanties de régime servile dans les possessions françaises (Lyon: Boursy, 1847), 34–5.
[65] Schoelcher Papers, N. a. f. 3631, pp. 108–9, Jollivet to President Colonial Council of Martinique, Nov. 12, 1847; ANCAOM, Corr. Gén., Martinique 122, Colonial Council 1848, Dec. 21, 1847.

reiterated in the autumn of 1847 its willingness to accept emancipation accompanied by indemnity and an unspecified system of organized labor.[66] As a result, in late 1847 the Council of Delegates in Paris found itself deeply split over the slavery issue. By early 1848, though, the Colonial Council of Bourbon, which had wavered on the question, rallied to the stance of Martinique and regretted "the disastrous path into which the [Guadeloupe *colons*] had precipitated themselves."[67] Moreover, in the meantime the Guadeloupe colonial legislature itself retracted its support for association-emancipation and turned against the conciliatory delegates representing them in Paris. In late 1847, Governor Layrle reported that the association proposals put forth by Reizet and Jabrun were "no longer acceptable" in his colony, and that the "stationary, if not resistant, ideas" of Dupin of Martinique had won out in Guadeloupe too.[68] Be this as it may, the government in Paris had had no intention of accepting a highly suspect and unorthodox approach to emancipation that it had already rejected in 1846 for Guiana. The Chamber of Deputies debate of 1847 and the consequent proposals of Guadeloupe had, nevertheless, destroyed the remnants of colonial unity on the slavery issue. More elements than ever in the colonies were prepared to accept some form of emancipation, although they still made their offers of cooperation contingent upon absurd schemes that the government could not possibly accept. In this atmosphere of conditional acquiescence by some elements of the colonial establishment, a determined government could probably have pushed through a slave liberation bill of some kind if it had wished to do so. At least Jollivet believed this to be the case.[69] It was the government itself, though, which still rejected action along these lines. As throughout the July Monarchy, the authorities refused to open the door to reforms of any kind, had their priorities elsewhere, and did not wish to allocate the necessary funds for an indemnity.

Outside the Guadeloupe delegation, cooler heads prevailed in Paris by the late spring of 1847. Dupin remained convinced that, despite the vote in the Chamber of Deputies on April 26, the government would

[66] Ibid., Corr. Gén., Guyane 71, Colonial Council 1847, Oct. 8, 12, 23, 1847.
[67] Ibid., Corr. Gén., Réunion 64, Colonial Council 1848, Jan. 20, 1848.
[68] Ibid., Guadeloupe, 193 (1176), Governor to Minister, Dec. 24, 1847.
[69] Schoelcher Papers, N. a.f. 3631, pp. 117–20, Jollivet to President Colonial Council of Martinique, April 29, 1847.

make no concrete moves toward emancipation: "You can be persuaded that in the current state of our finances, the Chamber of
Deputies will not vote 300 million [francs] for an indemnity, nor 200,
nor even *100*" (emphasis in the original).[70] In the few days that he
served as interim navy-colonial, Guizot failed to budge on the slave
liberation front. He did, however, seize the occasion to propose two
preparatory measures to which Mackau had apparently been opposed.
On May 17 he reintroduced into the Chamber of Peers the bill permitting forced expropriation of property in the Antilles, a procedure
that Duperré had proposed to the two houses in 1842, that had been
passed by the Peers, but then withdrawn by the government. Five days
later he presented in the Chamber of Deputies a bill determining the
composition of colonial courts hearing cases involving slaves, an
apparent attempt to improve the quality of colonial justice.[71] Neither
measure, however, advanced noticeably the emancipation process. The
expropriation motion at best was a long-term move to prepare the
colonies for a new order by clearing them of unproductive indebted
elements and creating an atmosphere propitious to new investment.
Both measures were most likely intended as sops offered the abolitionists in an attempt to satiate their more moderate elements, a tactic
the government had been employing since the mid-1830s.

French authorities took other token moves on the slavery front in
the late 1840s, but outside the four traditional slave colonies. France
made commitments concerning Muslim slavery in both the French
territories of Mayotte and Algeria. The tiny Indian Ocean island of
Mayotte, acquired by France in 1841, had a total population of only
3,000, almost all of it Muslim, and half of it slave. Following the
African Muslim tradition, slaves here were treated in a paternalistic
fashion and were as likely to be domestic servants as agricultural
workers. French hopes to develop Mayotte as a port and plantation
establishment were dependent upon additional immigration from
Africa, but Paris realized that the importation of free blacks would be
construed by British cruisers crisscrossing the East African coast as
surreptitious slave trading as long as slavery existed on the island
itself. Accordingly, Mackau suggested to the King already in 1846 that

---

[70] Ibid., pp. 215–16, Dupin to President Colonial Council of Martinique, May 14, 1847.
[71] *Le Moniteur universel*, May 18, 19, 23, 1847; *Annales de l'Institut d'Afrique*, Sept.–Oct.
1847, nos. 9–10, pp. 68–70.

the development of a free market economy on Mayotte necessitated freeing the slaves and indemnifying their Muslim masters. The French chambers voted funding in the spring of 1847 to provide 200 francs per slave as compensation, but the liberation process began only in July 1847, after Mackau had fallen from power. The Mayotte experience was tangential to French colonial developments as a whole.[72] This minor instance of liberating Muslim-owned slaves on an island off the East African coast raised little interest in France in either abolitionist or *colon* circles, and was not viewed as a precedent for the abolition process by any of the parties involved. In the French mentality of the time, there was an immense difference between large-scale black tropical slavery and scattered cases of Muslim domestic slavery on the periphery of the French colonial empire.

Much the same can be said about the proposed project to abolish domestic Muslim slavery in those parts of Algeria conquered by July Monarchy France. The sectors of Algeria consolidated under French control as of 1844 harbored some 5,000 adult black slaves owned by Algerian Muslims and employed almost exclusively as domestic servants. French authorities in the War Ministry which controlled the colony – it was not under the purview of the Minister of the Navy and Colonies even for matters of slavery – did all they could to stop the movement of slaves by sea off Algeria, not wishing to contravene the anti-slave trade agreements of 1831–1833 and antagonize the British. However, they hesitated to attack the institution of slavery itself for fear of angering their Muslim subjects and perhaps even instigating new uprisings.[73] Despite the fact that no Frenchmen in Algeria owned slaves, French abolitionists brought the matter to the fore in the spring of 1846 when they introduced a small petition in the Peers that was reported upon on May 22. Citing recent moves against slavery made by Tunis, Egypt, and the Ottoman Empire, they asked for a definite end to the Algerian slave trade, that all slave markets be closed, and that slavery be abolished in the North African territory as soon as possible.[74]

---

[72] Jean Martin, "L'affranchissement des esclaves à Mayotte, décembre 1846–juillet 1848," *Cahiers d'études africaines* 16 (1976): 207–33.

[73] ANCAOM, Algérie F80 728, note for the minister, Feb. 1846; Governor General of Algeria to Minister of War, May 10, 1849.

[74] Ibid., copy of petition dated April 2, 1846, signed Hain, Dufau, Gatine, Schoelcher, Charles d'Aspailly, Thayer, Dutrône, and Lutheroth; *Le Moniteur universel*, May 22–23, 1846.

Perhaps by mere coincidence – but probably to deflect any possible abolitionist intervention in the lower house on the issue – on April 24, 1847, as Gasparin made his report on the immediatist petitions, the Minister of War informed the Governor General of Algeria that he must begin preparations for the freeing of Muslim slaves under his jurisdiction.[75] Conceding the need for terminating slavery in Algeria, along with taking minor preparatory measures in the plantation colonies, could help convince abolitionists of the government's good intentions.

In reality, though, Muslim slaves in Algeria had to wait longer than black slaves in the plantation colonies to obtain their freedom. Orders were given to close slave markets in Algeria, and officials were instructed to use every means possible to stop the flow of slaves from black Africa into the south of Algeria. But the situation was complicated by the fact that France did not control all of Algeria, and that French military authorities constantly feared that the disruption of this Muslim tradition could incite uprisings in the areas under their jurisdiction. A plan was eventually drawn up providing for the ending of servitude as of January 1, 1851, in all areas of Algeria occupied by the French army, and the carrying out of efforts in the meantime to persuade Algerian Muslim leaders of the necessity of such measures.[76] Guizot himself became implicated in the process in early 1848 when, as foreign minister, he was pressed by the British to end slavery and the slave trade in France's African possessions. But he simply deflected the British request by restating France's desire to abolish slavery eventually in all its possessions.[77] Military considerations seemed to prevail in Algeria. A commission of authorities within Algeria recommended in 1849 that a payment of 300 francs be made to most Arab slave owners; the governor general agreed with this, but suggested that, once this was accomplished, officials "close their eyes" on the entire issue in the future.[78] Despite the involvement of Guizot in the question in early 1848, the holding of black slaves by Muslims was still tolerated in Algeria as late as 1849.

---

[75] ANCAOM, Algérie F80 728, Minister to Governor General, April 24, 1847.

[76] Ibid., note "On the abolition of slavery in Algeria," Ministry of War, May 1847; "Projected ordonnance for the abolition of slavery in Algeria," June 2, 1847.

[77] Ibid., Guizot to Minister of War, Jan. 21, 1848.

[78] Ibid., Governor General to Minister of War, May 10, 1849.

Moreover, Guizot failed to speed up procedures for freeing govern-ment-domain slaves in the colonies during his brief term as interim navy-colonial minister. As with all matters concerning emancipation, Mackau had moved as slowly as possible along these lines, despite his commitment in 1845 to liberate all 1,469 government-owned slaves within five years. Mackau had decided to free first of all only those domain slaves not involved in agricultural labor, so as not to disrupt work patterns on plantations; he had also made the arbitrary decision to require of any liberated domain slave five years of *engagement* as stipulated by the 1845 law for self-redeemed blacks. Finally, he had also asked the governors to free in the first instance only those domain slaves of good moral standing. As a result, only 126 were freed in 1846 and another 218 in 1847, most of them in both years being from the colony of Guiana. In the Chamber of Deputies, Guizot had blunted colonial opposition to freeing any slaves at all by declaring that the state had the indubitable right to liberate those it owned in the colo-nies.[79] But while in power briefly as colonial-navy minister he took no measures to advance the process. Despite the vote of April 26, 1847, the government was clearly not launching itself onto the path of emancipation. Most domain slaves obtained liberty with their fellow blacks only following the Revolution of 1848.

Still, plantocratic elements deemed even the minor measures of amel-ioration or preparation put forth by Guizot to be menaces to the colo-nial status quo. As a consequence, they orchestrated several actions to oppose the administration's motions. The delegates approached the new navy-colonial minister, Montebello, and were pleased to find him better disposed toward the colonies than Guizot.[80] They also launched one of their typical lobbying efforts against the two Guizot bills in the press, the commissions of the two houses, and the legislative chambers themselves. They held a meeting of *colons* living in Paris to determine means of countering charges made by abolitionists about the cruelty of slave owners. Some fifty-three Paris-based Martinicans then signed

[79] Ibid., Corr. Gén. 205, 1845, Minister of Navy and Colonies to Governors, Aug. 21, 1845; Corr. Gén. 209, 1846; Minister to Governors, July 27, 1846; Corr. Gén 213, 1847, Minis-ter to Governor of Guiana, Nov. 11, 1847; *Le Moniteur universel*, May 15, June 14, 1846.
[80] Schoelcher Papers, N. a. f. 3631, pp. 215–16, Dupin to President Colonial Council of Martinique, May 14, 1847; pp. 139–40, Jollivet to President Colonial Council of Mar-tinique, July 13, 1847; ANCAOM, Gén. 173 (1388), Reizet and Jabrun to President Colonial Council of Guadeloupe, June 29, 1847.

an address to the government on May 10 against the bills Guizot had proposed.[81] By the summer, Martinique's delegates were able to report that both bills had passed in the chambers in which they had been introduced, but that it had been too late in the session for them to be approved by the other house. Thus, their final passage had been put off until 1848.[82] Jollivet and Dupin also attempted to rally the colonial Council of Delegates around a four-point plan that they established to counter the demands of Guadeloupe for emancipation-association. According to the Martinique delegates, if menaced with slave liberation the colonies should steadfastly request preparation of slaves, revision of the sugar laws, organization of free labor, and absolute guarantees of an indemnity. They claimed to be supported in this strategy by delegate Dejean de la Batie of Bourbon.[83] Finally, the Martinique delegates campaigned against a petition that their colleagues from Guadeloupe had had signed in May by some twenty to twenty-four Guadeloupe planters residing in Paris in favor of their project.[84]

The Guadeloupe petition constituted an attempt by Reizet and Jabrun to influence the chambers in favor of emancipation-association. Because they feigned their goal to be emancipation, they also strove to rally support for their idea among people they considered to be "conservative abolitionists." Broglie and Tocqueville were two abolitionists whom the plantocracy believed fell within this category because of the concern of the former with adequate preparation for slaves and of the latter with an interim period of government-controlled apprenticeship. Accordingly, the delegates contacted Broglie in 1847, told him their aim was slave liberation and direct representation in the chambers, and obtained his commitment to submit their petition in the Peers before he had even seen a written copy of it. They then approached Tocqueville about introducing their petition into the Chamber of Deputies, but Tocqueville was more circumspect; he demanded to see

---

[81] Schoelcher Papers, N. a. f. 3631, pp. 213–15, Dupin to President Colonial Council of Martinique, April 29, 1847; pp. 116–17, Jollivet to President Colonial Council of Martinique, April 29, 1847; pp. 120–2, Jollivet to President Colonial Council of Martinique, May 14, 1847.

[82] Ibid., pp. 216–17, Jollivet to President Colonial Council of Martinique, May 30, 1847; p. 228, Dupin to President Colonial Council of Martinique, June 14, 1847; pp. 123–4, Jollivet to President Colonial Council of Martinique, Aug. 29, 1847; p. 128, Jollivet to President Colonial Council of Martinique, Nov. 29, 1847.

[83] Ibid., pp. 122–3, Jollivet to President Colonial Council of Martinique, June 13, 1847.

[84] Ibid., p. 228, Dupin to President Colonial Council of Martinique, June 14, 1847.

the document, found it too vague concerning slave liberation, and declined sponsoring it. Later they reported that Tocqueville, in the course of his discussion with him, confessed his alienation from the abolitionist cause. According to the delegates, Tocqueville avowed that: "I have given up a long time ago on the slavery question, and no longer occupy myself with it, for on the one hand I could not agree with the *colons* whose principles are unacceptable, and on the other hand I did not wish to ally myself with men who wish to advance and resolve it at any price, and whose ideas could bring ruin and disaster."[85] If the delegates of Guadeloupe were reporting correctly, this could indicate that Tocqueville, like so many of his anti-slavery colleagues, had become alienated from the French abolition society by 1848. This would suggest, though, that, unlike his more radical associates, Tocqueville felt ambivalent about the radicalization of French abolitionist forces, which were increasingly under the influence of the left-wing opposition to the July Monarchy, in the form of people such as Schoelcher, Bissette, and Ledru-Rollin. If this were the case, the radical Tocqueville of the late 1830s, known then as an advocate of rapid emancipation, had become much more moderate by the late 1840s, constituting another case of evolution – and not always toward immediatism – on the part of important French abolitionists under the July Monarchy

Be this as it may, Tocqueville was not gullible enough to sponsor the Guadeloupe petition. It was finally deposited in the upper house by Broglie, as promised, and in the lower chamber by Bignon. The latter might have been a member of the radical left in the Chamber of Deputies, but he remained a true defender of port city interests concerning slavery. The delegates of Martinique fought the petition, which was opposed by most abolitionists too.[86] The Guadeloupe initiative died after Guizot made a declaration in the chambers on July 13, 1847, against direct representation for the colonies.[87] Throughout the July Monarchy, the idea of establishing colonial deputies persisted

[85] ANCAOM, Gén. 173 (1388), Reizet and Jabrun to President Colonial Council of Martinique, May 30, 1847.

[86] Schoelcher Papers, N. a. f. 3631, pp. 142–4, Jollivet to President Colonial Council of Martinique, May 29, 1847; pp. 229–33, Dupin to President Colonial Council of Martinique, Aug. 30, 1847.

[87] *Le Moniteur universel*, July 14, 1847.

in being unacceptable to both the government and the abolitionists as long as the existence of slavery in the colonies skewered the popular franchise. Moreover, the government was in no mood to broach the question of parliamentary reform in the summer of 1847. By this time a reformist banquet campaign was under way in France against electoral and parliamentary restrictions, a movement that the government adamantly opposed and that eventually led to the Revolution of 1848.

While colonial apologists were struggling to advance their cause in mid-1847, the abolitionists were building upon the momentum they had achieved in April. In the spring of 1847 Schoelcher published his *Histoire de l'esclavage pendant les deux dernières années*, consisting of immediatist-oriented articles that he had written since 1845 for *La Réforme* and other newspapers. According to *L'Abolitioniste français*, there was no more zealous and capable advocate of emancipation in France at this time than Schoelcher.[88] And Schoelcher's was not the only new anti-slavery work appearing in 1847. Schoelcher himself exclaimed in the summer of 1847 that hardly a week passed without some new brochure or treatise coming out on the abolition question.[89] Many of these works were of an immediatist nature, showing growing disillusionment with government-sponsored preparatory measures Among them was another book by the Lyonnais Victor Fleury. In it he refuted the arguments made against slave liberation and proclaimed that, because ameliorative steps would not work, immediate slave liberation was the only solution to the slavery question.[90] Fleury's publication, the second book he had turned out that year on emancipation, constituted evidence of some increase in provincial support for the anti-slavery cause.

Lyon appears to have been the center of provincial abolitionist sentiment in the 1840s, for it had already rallied to the workers' petition in 1844 and mustered more signatures for the petition campaign of 1846–1848 than any other provincial city. Indeed, upon hearing that petitions were being circulated again for immediate abolition, an eleven-person committee had been established in Lyon on February 7, 1847, to bolster the effort. Its president, Gudin, was a merchant, but

---

[88] *L'Abolitioniste français*, 1st issue, 1847, pp. 57–60.
[89] Ibid., 5th issue, 1847, pp. 438–47.
[90] Victor Fleury, *De l'esclavage colonial et son abolition immédiate dans les colonies françaises* (Lyon: Boursy, 1847).

among its members were also an innkeeper and a cloth folder (Lardet, the vice-president), indicating middle-class and even artisan participation. This committee continued its anti-slavery activities well into the autumn. The establishment newspaper, *Le Censeur de Lyon*, organ of business interests within the city, first published Fleury's books, and also came out against slavery.[91] French abolitionism seemed to be widening its base by mid-1847. At the same time it appeared as though the Société française pour l'abolition de l'esclavage was being eclipsed by a series of smaller, more radical groupings, with the Bissette-Félice formation and the Schoelcher faction leading the way.

Despite the growing number of immediatist-oriented abolitionists, the French abolition society had not as yet deviated from its official stance of gradualism, even after the successful submission of the petitions calling for rapid slave liberation in April 1847. The Société française, true to its moderate past, remained a bastion of caution and circumspection, despite an increasing tendency for some of its members to espouse immediatism. The British, though, continued to pressure the French organization to alter its orientation. In January 1847 the British and Foreign Anti-Slavery Society dispatched a long address to Paris in an attempt to convince the French body that it should abandon gradualism because ameliorative measures could never prove effective.[92] Then Josiah Forster visited Paris in June on behalf of British anti-slavery. He contacted, "among others," Paul de Gasparin and Gustave de Beaumont and "engaged them to prepare a pamphlet containing the substance of the late debate in the French chambers relative to emancipation for circulation among the *Conseils généraux*" in advance of their autumn meeting. Forster also met with Lutheroth and Dutrône of the Société française "and found that the French [abolition society] met but rarely" even at this late date. However, concerning Bissette, "Dutrône spoke approvingly of his labours." As a result, the British organization accorded Bissette 30 pounds for distributing in the provinces petitions that were again in circulation in preparation for the 1848 legislative session.[93]

The news that the French society continued its policy of meeting

[91] Schoelcher, *Histoire de l'esclavage*, II, 145; *Annales de l'Institut d'Afrique*, Sept.–Oct. 1847; ANCAOM, Gén. 197 (1489); *L'Abolitioniste français*, 1st issue, 1847, pp. 41–3.

[92] Ibid., 5th issue, 1847, pp. 380–3.

[93] Rhodes House Anti-Slavery Papers, Minute Books, June 26, Aug. 27, 1847.

rarely must have disappointed but not surprised the British, who had complained about the group's ineffective anti-slavery strategies ever since the 1830s. To compensate for the lack of initiative by this organization, the British were more engaged than ever in supporting by limited means the different radical elements of French emancipationism. Still, even the Société française pour l'abolition de l'esclavage was beginning to display encouraging signs in some of its discourse. It had not assisted Bissette in his circulation of petitions, but its organ had nevertheless praised these efforts as "the most impressive manifestation that has taken place yet in our country in favor of" blacks. *L'Abolitioniste* was also becoming aware that "the very application of the impotent, temporizing and absolutely ineffective system of the Mackau laws has shown that it is necessary to finish with slavery." Or, as Dutrône remarked when the petitions were presented in the Peers, the government "has proved by the slowness and softness of its measures, that it will never carry out emancipation except under the whip of public opinion."[94] Some of the leaders of the Société française pour l'abolition de l'esclavage at least were associating themselves with the petitioning campaign and becoming increasingly disenchanted with the government's temporization.

Following Forster's report to London, the British abolitionist grouping publicly displayed its dissatisfaction with French mainstream anti-slavery in a September 1, 1847, article in its journal. After again denouncing the Mackau laws as ineffective "schemes of amelioration," the *British and Foreign Anti-Slavery Reporter* gave a brief historical account of the French abolition society in which it underlined its shortcomings and failures. It observed that, while the French organization contained:

the most eminent statesmen and philanthropists.... they did not, however, organize on the principle of immediate and entire abolition – in fact they had no plan, at least they never presented one to the Chambers – but they provoked frequent discussions there, and were instrumental in circulating a large amount of information on the subject of slavery, and of extorting from the government and the Chambers a decision that slavery ought and must be abolished. Thirteen years have now passed since the institution of the society, and slavery is not abolished.[95]

[94] *L'Abolitioniste français*, 5th issue, 1846, pp. 273–4; 1st issue, 1847, pp. i–iv.
[95] *British and Foreign Anti-Slavery Reporter*, Sept. 1, 1847.

The British were correct in depicting the Société française pour l'abolition de l'esclavage as a group of individualistic intellectuals who opposed servitude through the written media and parliamentary methods, but who could not over the years even arrive at a sustained common stand for combatting slavery effectively. The tone of the British evaluation read almost like an obituary, as if the French abolition society were a thing of the past, no longer counting in British eyes as an important force on the French anti-slavery scene.

At this very time, however, apparently unbeknown to London, a transformation occurred within the Paris organization. On September 16, 1847, the French abolition society finally replied to the address sent by the British in January. It took the form of a pronouncement signed by First Vice-President Passy – who had become active again within the society – and Secretary Dutrône. The society admitted too much hesitation in the past, but announced that it had now come to believe that "the fate of slaves cannot effectively be ameliorated," and that "the only remedy to slavery" involved its abolition. Its aim from now on, it declared, would be "complete and immediate emancipation of slaves."[96] Immediatism had finally emerged victorious within the ranks of the Société française pour l'abolition de l'esclavage. As could be expected, this pledge to pursue "the great doctrine of immediate and entire emancipation" gave "great satisfaction" to the British once it became known in London.[97]

Evidence suggests that this change in French abolition society policy actually occurred in the course of July–August 1847. If the British had been unaware of these developments before the publication of their negative assessment on September 1, it is probably because the exchange of confidences by letter between the two organizations had apparently ceased with the resignation of Isambert as secretary of the French group. The fact remains that already at the end of August the Société française pour l'abolition de l'esclavage had drawn up its own petition for complete and immediate slave liberation. The society also began circulating some hundred copies of this petition, dated August 30, in the provinces. Not only did the petition contend that the laws of 1845 had been futile, but it argued that it was no longer possible to postpone slave liberation simply because a few hundred million francs

[96] L'Abolitioniste français, 5th issue, 1847, pp. 384–6.
[97] Rhodes House Anti-Slavery Papers, Minute Books, Oct. 1, 1847.

would have to be paid out to planters. Indeed, it seems that the Société française had turned to Schoelcher to draw up its petition, attesting to renewed and closer association between the two abolitionist forces. The society also accompanied its petition with an address to abolitionists throughout France, requesting them to form committees in all the principle cities of the country, such as the one already operating in Lyon, to publicize the concept of "complete and immediate abolition of slavery" through publishing brochures and signing petitions. This statement affirmed that French honor could not permit the nation to remain behind Britain, Tunis, Sweden, Valachia, and Egypt, all of which had all taken measures of some kind against slavery over the previous dozen years. Finally, it beseeched daughter societies that might form in the provinces to communicate with Paris, for it acknowledged that until now French anti-slavery had lacked "unity of action." After inserting these two notices in its November-December 1847 issue, L'Abolitioniste announced that some 30,000 signatures had already been collected throughout France to be presented the following year in the chambers.[98] These two pronouncements were jointly signed by Dutrône and Passy, confirming the continued activity of the latter within the society now that it had abandoned its gradualist policies. The Société française pour l'abolition de l'esclavage was becoming at once more active, ecumenical, and radical.

This alteration in the stance of the abolition society was in line with the immediatist tendencies that an increasing number of its members had been displaying since the passage of the Mackau laws. English prodding, the success of the April petitions in the lower house, and the radical inclination of some of its leadership had probably all played a role in effecting this transformation. Perhaps too, the Société française began to feel bypassed by events, and reluctant to be left behind as immediatism gained more adherents with advancing time. Most likely, the society had finally come to realize after the April debates that gradualism could never free the slaves, and that outright and immediate emancipation was the only possible solution to the slavery problem.

[98] L'Abolitioniste français, 6th issue, 1847, pp. 462–78, 457–61; Société française pour l'abolition de l'esclavage, pétition aux chambres pour demander l'abolition de l'esclavage dans les colonies françaises (Paris: Duvillers, 1847). A handwritten note on the petition indicates that it was drafted by Schoelcher; and the catalogue of the French Bibliothèque Nationale attributes it to Schoelcher.

Right after the April 1847 debates in the lower house, Protestants also began contemplating the possibility of organizing themselves more effectively to circulate immediatist petitions.[99] On June 19 a Bureau de Correspondance was established by Protestants at 8, rue Rumford in Paris. This correspondance bureau immediately called for all French Protestants and their pastors in particular to gather as many signatures as possible; it also reflected religious rivalry over the emancipation issue when it encouraged Protestants to outperform Catholics who were also gathering signatures. This appeal of the bureau appeared in most of the Protestant journals of Paris.[100] One Protestant organ boasted in late 1847 that the objective was to raise 100,000 signatures to submit to the chambers in 1848.[101] Other sources corroborate the fact that Protestants were playing an important role in petitioning. According to Félice, himself a Protestant leader, there were four different petition campaigns under way by late 1847, one of which was Protestant uniquely. He recounted that the petitions emitted by the French abolition society and by Bissette were the most widely distributed, while the one put out by the Bureau de Correspondance was mostly adhered to by his religious fellowmen and pastors. The fourth, he explained, had been composed with the specific purpose of gathering the signatures of Catholic clergy.[102] No longer were petitions being left for signatures in workers' organizations or circulated largely by one person, Bissette – although the latter, according to Félice, continued to be active in this campaign too. By late 1847 it appears that the French had finally developed a sustained and multifaceted petition movement that promised to gather many more signatures for presentation in 1848 than in 1847 or 1844. The first elements of an anti-slavery network were finally beginning to coalesce in France.

---

[99] *Le Semeur*, April 28, 1847

[100] Ibid., July 7, 1847; *Archives du Christianisme*, June 26, 1847; *L'Espérance*, July 15, 1847; *Le Lien*, July 17, 1847; *La Sentinelle, journal des familles protestantes*, Sept. 1, 1847.

[101] *Archives du Christianism*, Nov. 27, 1847. This paper, under Adolphe Monod, seemed to be the best informed of the Protestant publications concerning the petitioning process, indicating that the Bureau de Correspondance might have been closely connected with Monod's faction, which was inspired by the same Methodism that had played such a significant role in firing up British emancipationism. For more on Monod, see James L. Osen, *Prophet and Peacemaker: The Life of Adolphe Monod* (Lanham, Md.: University Press of America, 1984).

[102] Rhodes House Anti-Slavery Papers, C157/70, Félice to London, Dec. 8, 1847.

During his sojourn in France in the summer of 1845, Scoble had encouraged his French associates to have recourse once again to the *conseils généraux*, the departmental legislatures, in an attempt to stir up public opinion outside Paris. As French abolitionists had diverted their attention away from these bodies during the early 1840s, the number of departmental councils expressing wishes for slave liberation had declined markedly from the eleven requests for emancipation issued in 1839. Anti-slavery statements decreased to five in 1840, then climbed back up to seven the following year, before plummeting to four in 1842 and then only three for the next three years. If the decline to five in 1840 was due to the negative impact of the Egyptian crisis, the low score for 1842–1845 certainly reflected the anti-abolitionist sentiment permeating France during the right of search dispute. Those few general councils that did continue to express anti-slavery feelings when French abolitionism was at its nadir were invariably from the same departments: the Ariège, where its deputy, French abolition society member Dugabé, continually influenced his local council; the Allier, the district of Tracy; at times the Loiret, stronghold of Roger; and the Nord. Their votes were consistently discounted during these years by officials in the French navy-colonial office as weak remnants of abolitionist lobbying. Colonial office functionaries often wrote the names of individual abolitionists in the margins of these statements, such as "Mr. Roger" for the Loiret, as if to characterize them as emanating from the efforts of one person. As for the Nord department, which had voted steadily against slavery since 1836, on different occasions navy-colonial department officials made disparaging marginal remarks about the fact that this was the leading beet sugar-producing area of France. For instance, in 1841 they intimated that "this smells of sugar beet"; in 1842 the comment was a simple "sugar beet." Similarly, when the Pas-de-Calais department, which voted against slavery irregularly (1837–1839, 1847), did so in 1841, this too was denoted in marginal notes as "again the odor of sugar beet!"[103] Colonial spokesmen always claimed that a strong sugar beet lobby was behind the anti-slavery movement in France, and the vote of the Nord department in particular provides some scant evidence substantiating

---

[103] ANCAOM, Gén. 156 (1301). Concerning Dugabé's actions, see *La Revue abolitioniste*, 1847, p. 200.

such a charge. However, to impugn the vote of the Nord department only to its economic interests is probably exaggerated, for an influential member of the French abolition society, Delespaul, an important magistrate in Lille and deputy from 1834 to 1848, had been responsible for this vote as early as 1837, and his department's wishes as expressed in its *conseil général* might have been due to the pressure from this individual abolitionist as much as those of the Ariège and Allier were due to their *notable* anti-slavery figures. Moreover, the wishes of the Nord department in 1847 were particularly solicitous of the rights of *colons* and the well-being of the colonies themselves, hardly indicative of a statement reflecting an economic struggle between beet and cane sugar interests.[104] That the navy-colonial office should react the way it did to the scant evidence of sugar beet areas lobbying against the sugar cane-producing colonies and their institution of slavery is indicative particularly in the way it demonstrates the extent to which French officialdom was receptive to self-serving colonial discourse.

Increased abolitionist attempts to mobilize the general councils in the late 1840s are not only attributable to British inducements. Once again it was Bissette who had taken the initiative in this direction already in 1846. At this time he wrote to the *conseil général* of the Seine department, requesting it to back "rapid and complete abolition of slavery" for religious, humanitarian, and economic reasons. During the November 1846 meeting of the council of the Seine, councilor Duperrier, a former *colon*, joined with other colleagues in taking up Bissette's argument and affirming that abolition would stimulate black consumption and thus increase French exports to the colonies, just as it had in the British case. In the process of expressing its wishes for emancipation to the government, the Seine council also acknowledged that its decision had been inspired by Bissette.[105] In 1846 five *conseils généraux* altogether came out against slavery, for the Drôme department also joined with the Seine and the three regular petitioners.[106] Although it had been a coup to win over the important Seine department representing Paris, five general councils remained still an

[104] Tudesq, *Les grands notables*, II, 836.
[105] *La Réforme*, Feb. 11, 1847; *L'Abolitioniste français*, 1846, 6th issue, pp. 350–8; *La Revue abolitioniste*, 1847, 1st issue, pp. 19–39.
[106] ANCAOM, Gén. 156 (1301).

insignificant number. The reinvigorated abolitionist community was determined to do better in 1847.

As the autumn of 1847 approached, Bissette dispatched a letter to all of the departmental councils, appealing for their support in the anti-slavery struggle. This time he was seconded by the Société française pour l'abolition de l'esclavage. Concurrently with the emission of its petition, the abolition society addressed an appeal on August 29 to the members of the *conseil généraux* throughout France.[107] This two-pronged approach met with success. By the end of 1847, a record twenty-four out of eighty-six general councils had expressed in some form their wish for slave liberation. Most of these statements came from departments that had not been active in the past, or that had fallen silent after 1839. Many of them indicated that their anti-slavery sentiment had been inspired by the appeals of either Bissette or the French abolition society.[108] One abolitionist organ optimistically opined that if all the departmental councils could be persuaded to declare their opposition to slavery, "parliament will cede to the voice of the country."[109] This sort of unanimity on the part of the *conseils* was still distant, and there were no guarantees how the government would react even if a majority of the departmental bodies could be won over to the cause. Nevertheless, the fact remains that the summer and autumn of 1847 witnessed some of the most impressive successes yet of French anti-slavery. Abolitionism was better organized than at any time in the past; it was inspired by its accomplishments both in the lower house and in the field; and its major components seemed more united than ever in their immediatist message. Everything depended, then, on keeping up the momentum gained, and on how the government would react to the strengthened abolitionist offensive.

Abolitionists had reason to be optimistic in late 1847. Still, there were indications that the anti-slavery battle was far from over entering 1848. Some disquieting signs remained about the true efficiency and unity of the movement and about the real level of popular support it enjoyed. In 1847 as in earlier years, Bissette continued to devote much energy to pleading for funds from the British. It is noteworthy in this sense that it was still the British who were financing the mailing of

---

[107] *Le Semeur*, Sept. 1, 1847.
[108] ANCAOM, Gén. 156 (1301).
[109] *Annales de l'Institut d'Afrique*, Sept.–Oct. 1847.

Bissette's petitions into the provinces in the summer and autumn of 1847.[110] And Bissette's *Revue abolitioniste*, launched in 1847 and heavily subsidized by London for its first three issues, immediately folded after the third. Likewise, in late 1847 it was Josiah Forster personally who arranged to pay the cost of publishing and distributing in France a large, new edition of Félice's anti-slavery brochure.[111] Radical French anti-slavery still seemed to be highly dependent upon the efforts of a few determined individuals, and still centered for the most part upon the written media rather than a wide-based popular appeal. It was also greatly underfunded, a sign of meager support among the French public.

Although the unity of French abolitionism had progressed significantly when the French abolition society rallied to the immediatist cause, its efforts were still somewhat dispersed, uncoordinated, and divided. In the summer of 1847, Agénor de Gasparin, formerly a convinced advocate of immediate slave liberation but less present on the anti-slavery scene after his failure to be re-elected, requested funds from fellow Protestants to help in the *rachat* of slaves in accordance with the stipulations of the 1845 legislation.[112] The question could be asked whether Agénor de Gasparin had regressed and fallen in line with conservative policy under pressure from his erstwhile friend and former close associate Guizot, whether he had been alienated by the increased republican role in radical anti-slavery, or whether he had simply been forced into a reduced role by his withdrawal from active politics. By late 1847 too Félice had abandoned all hope of reconciling Bissette and Schoelcher.[113] The two would remain bitter enemies even after the end of slavery, when they would fiercely contest national assembly seats in Martinique and Guadeloupe.[114] Even in late 1847, despite improvements, France did not yet possess an elaborate anti-slavery network, capable of rallying hundreds of thousands of supporters or millions of signatures, as the British had in the early 1830s. French abolitionism as late as 1847 was still artisanal in approach,

---

[110] Rhodes House Anti-Slavery Papers, Minute Books, June 4, Aug. 27, Dec. 10, 1847.
[111] Ibid., C157/70, Félice to London, Dec. 8, 1847.
[112] *La Sentinelle, Journal des familles protestantes*, Aug. 15, 1847.
[113] Schoelcher, *Lettres mantiniquaises*, 34–6, Félice to Schoelcher, Dec. 8, 1847.
[114] Pâme, "Cyrille Bissette," 302–56; Schmidt, *Victor Schoelcher*, 123–33; Fallope, *Esclaves et citoyens*, 382–6; Forster and Forster, *Sugar and Slavery*, 245, 247–9; 259–60.

and extremely limited in scope. In confiding to the British in May 1847, one astute French abolitionist observer, Félice, remarked that even after the April victory in the chambers, "at the most we are at the point where you were in 1824," that is, with a government wedded to amelioration, and ten years short of slave liberation.[115]

The analyses that Félice made in both May and December 1847 concerning the situation facing French anti-slavery are detached, incisive, and basically accurate. In May, not only did he insist that abolitionists would be fortunate if, with all their best efforts, they succeeded in ending slavery in ten years' time, but he disclosed what he believed to be the chief factor retarding the emancipation process in France. He confided to the British: "The King is opposed to emancipation, not for any love of slavery, if I am well informed, but because he has adopted the maxim of *not touching questions which time can resolve* [emphasis in the original] when he is not absolutely forced to do so. The emancipation of slaves would threaten to alienate several allies of his government, weaken the majority, and pose obstacles to his great objective" of assuring a peaceful succession to the crown. "Louis Philippe will therefore resist" slave liberation, Félice was convinced:

as long as he is not *forced* to accord liberty by a strong, energetic, *general* manifestation of pubic opinion.

There is the truth.

Mr. Guizot is *personally* favorable to emancipation. But, as minister, he will abstain from actively speaking or acting. He knows very well that, despite his great talent and his services, he would be dismissed by Louis Philippe if he really wished to free the slaves.

In its recent sessions the majority of the Chamber of Deputies voted when carried away by sentiment rather than by principles. It had heard revolting facts [about the treatment of slaves]; it was indignant, and therefore sent the petitions to the minister. Nothing more. There is only *a very small* minority [in the lower house] that has adopted the principle of immediate emancipation.

Even supposing that the majority in this chamber were to pronounce itself for emancipation (which is completely improbable), Louis Philippe and his government will use the Chamber of Peers to resist....

If the government is pushed a little, it will put forth a reform project, then another, having no other aim than *to gain time.*

---

[115] Rhodes House Anti-Slavery Papers, C157/69, Félice to London, May 8, 1847.

Félice went on to add that, only when the government became convinced that slave liberation would be more of an advantage than a liability to its stability and to a smooth dynastic succession, would it move in that direction, and not one moment earlier. "Until now we have been considered insignificant agitators, and the government has let us alone. Our 11,000 signatures are something, no doubt, but too little, infinitely too little to move the crown. Even when we will have 100,000 signatures, there will be few changes. We would need *a million* signatures, and especially the names of *electors*, to obtain our end." Therefore, he stressed, abolitionists must work diligently through the spoken and written word to try to sway the public. He ended by saying that those on whom one could count the most were the Protestants, but that their numbers were much smaller in France than in England, and that it was necessary to act outside Protestant circles.[116] In his incisive, probing manner, Félice had gone to the heart of the matter in explaining the failures of anti-slavery in France as of the late spring of 1847.

At the end of 1847 Félice offered a new evaluation of the situation in his country. After mentioning the conversion of the Société française pour l'abolition de l'esclavage to immediatism, he conceded that the emancipation question had progressed within the year. He then added:

However, I fear that we are still far from our goal.... Some members of the government, and in particular Mr. Guizot, are well disposed toward emancipation. The new Minister of the Navy and Colonies, Mr. de Montebello, is neutral: he is better than Mr. Mackau. But other ministers of state are little favorable to this cause; and I fear, between the two of us, that the King, Louis Philippe, will apply himself by every means to *temporize*. He likes the *status quo* in all things; he dreads, he avoids as much as possible the least changes; and everything suggests that he will try to *adjourn* until the end of his life the grand question of emancipation by paltry *mitigations*. To surmount the tergiversations of the King a *strong pressure of national opinion* would be necessary. Will we obtain this manifestation in France? There is the entire question. [emphasis in the original]

Félice went on to explain that in reply to requests from Bissette and the French abolition society, some of the *conseils généraux* had replied

[116] Ibid.

positively, but not the majority of them. In his opinion most of the Catholic clergy also "gave no signs of sympathy for the cause of the slaves." The same was true of most newspapers, that is to say, those not in the pay of the planters. As for the political scene:

The majority of the liberal or radical party, finally, does not care about this subject either. We have been able to see this in the reformist banquets [of 1847] where the orators spoke of everything – everything except the emancipation of the blacks! Republicanism, socialism, even Fourierism had found advocates in their banquets, but not the sacred principle of emancipation: this is a sign of the state of public spirits.

There is the real balance-sheet of the situation concerning the emancipation question. As for the mass of the people, it is ignorant of or foreign to the debate. They hardly know that slaves exist in our colonies!

In repeating the argument that the deputies would not agree to spend even 150 million francs for an indemnity in the current sad state of the government's finances, he concluded that "the struggle" for abolition "will still be long and hard."[117] The radical abolitionist newspaper *Le Semeur* agreed that the slavery question was "far from being resolved." It too noted such an "indifference in national opinion" toward emancipation that during the reform banquet campaign everything had been mentioned except slavery.[118] More significant, though, Félice had reiterated his contention that Louis Philippe's regime would never agree to emancipation, despite the redoubled efforts of the abolitionists. His analysis of the situation was basically correct. It was the institution of the July Monarchy itself, and Louis Philippe in particular, who were the main obstacles to emancipation in the French colonies.[119] Only the determined behind-the-scene opposition of the monarch to any significant movement toward emancipation – because of his commitment to the status quo in all things – can

[117] Ibid., C157/70, Félice to London, Dec. 8, 1847.
[118] Feb. 16, 1848.
[119] Historians have too often assumed that because Louis Philippe was a self-proclaimed liberal, opposed to slavery in principle, he was actually favorable to freeing the slaves. See, for example, Cochin, *L'Abolition*, 35; Antoine Gisler, *L'Esclavage aux Antilles françaises (XVIIIe–XIXe siècle): Contribution au problème de l'esclavage* (1965; rpt., Paris: Karthala, 1981), 128; Tomich, *Slavery in the Circuit*, 58.

explain the fact that every Cabinet that broached the slavery question under the July Monarchy limited itself in the end to ameliorative-preparatory measures. Félice could not realize that at the moment he was writing, however, the July Monarchy was approaching its end, and that as soon as it fell slavery would receive its final death blow at the hands of a republican regime that empowered Schoelcher to deal with the emancipation question.

As the year 1848 opened, Frenchmen were unaware that within two months the February Revolution would establish the Second Republic. The abolitionists once again prepared to confront the government over the slavery issue in the chambers, armed this time with more petitions than ever. On February 14 – a week before the outbreak of the Revolution and ten days prior to the fall of the monarchy – Dupin reported that the abolitionist Beugnot was prepared to interpellate the navy-colonial minister in the Peers "in a few days" on what his office intended to do concerning emancipation.[120] Quite clearly, the Société française still retained its penchant for operating through official parliamentary channels. The question, of course, is how the government would have reacted to this renewed questioning by the abolitionists, for the Revolution of 1848 occurred before Beugnot had a chance to broach the issue. All indications are, however, that the government would have made no substantial concessions on the slavery question.[121] Hard pressed by an increasingly vocal opposition that had opened a banquet campaign in mid-1847 to call for parliamentary and electoral reform while avoiding laws against public meetings, the government was in no mood to yield to what Félice himself described as a troublesome but ephemeral group of abolitionists. Emancipation, after all, constituted a reform, and the government was increasingly digging in its heals against any and all concessions. This was apparent in a speech that Guizot made before the Chamber of Deputies on February 12, 1848, when he rejected innovations or reforms of any kind.[122] It even appeared that the gains made by

---

[120] Schoelcher Papers, N. a. f. 3631, pp. 232–5, Dupin to President Colonial Council of Martinique, Feb. 9, 14, 1848.

[121] This interpretation differs markedly from the more optimistic one put forth by Seymour Drescher, "British Way, French Way: Opinion Building and Revolution in the Second French Slave Emancipation," *American Historical Review* 96 (1991): 725–34.

[122] *Le Moniteur universel*, Feb. 13, 1848.

anti-slavery during 1847 might be submerged by an overriding political crisis that could relegate abolition to a secondary plane and reduce its chances of advancement as the government doggedly defended the existing state of affairs.

If the Revolution of 1848 had not occurred, and if political pressures had calmed down to the point where the emancipation question could have been broached again, it seems that the July Monarchy would have reacted to abolitionist actions in 1848 as it had in the past. Indications are that the government would have faced down a new petition campaign with additional token measures, as Félice had predicted. It was common knowledge that abolitionist petitioning was continuing, that more signatures would be presented to the legislature in 1848, and that the government stood poised to present a contingency plan in face of such an eventuality. After the April 1847 setback in the lower house, Director of the Colonies Galos told one of the delegates that the government would reply to any additional petitions that the abolitionists might present by offering to free newborn slave children. In other words, the administration would have put forth the most gradualist and least costly of the two plans recommended by the Broglie commission report, something which would have aimed at abolishing slavery twenty years hence. Much to the chagrin of the delegates, Guizot spoke openly of this option, which the government was convinced it could persuade the chambers to pass, to different deputies who questioned him on the next move by his administration if it were faced with determined abolitionist pressures.[123]

The prospect of a piecemeal, partial, long-term solution to the slavery question that might reduce indemnification infuriated the *colons* in 1847, of course, just as it had in the late 1830s and mid-1840s. It was especially disquieting to them because it was accompanied by rumors that the government might even attach to its proposed plan for freeing newborn children one encouraging the *rachat* of slave women. The plantocracy shuddered at eventualities apt to disorganize work and reduce the sacrosanct indemnity. These fears were so great that they even helped inspire the delegates of Guadeloupe to put forth their

---

[123] ANCAOM, Gén. 173 (1388), Jabrun and Reizet to President Colonial Council of Guadeloupe, May 30, June 29, 1847; Jabrun to President Colonial Council of Martinique, Sept. 14, 1847; Schoelcher Papers, N. a. f. 3631, pp. 135–6, Jabrun to President Colonial Council of Guadeloupe, June 15, 1847.

recommendation for emancipation-association.[124] Nevertheless, the fact remains that these were options that the government had considered and proposed to the colonies already in the previous decade. They were exceedingly gradual moves that would have had little immediate effect. Besides, given the government's record of proposing measures only to retract or dilute them in face of determined colonial opposition, there is no certainty that even these modest proposals would have been implemented in 1848. Guizot's reintroduction of the forced expropriation bill, the general indebtedness of the treasury, and the proposals of freeing newborn children all indicate that the administration envisaged retaining slavery for at least another decade or more and phasing it out very slowly. This sort of policy is also in line with the government's general tendency to grant reforms grudgingly and gradually. Until the very end, the July Monarchy proved itself determined to avoid taking meaningful steps toward rapid slave liberation. Félice had been correct in his analysis of the situation. Only the termination of King Louis Philippe's rule would bring an end to French colonial slavery. The end came faster than anyone expected.

The Revolution of 1848 broke out on February 22, when crowds took to the streets of Paris after the authorities banned a monster reform banquet scheduled to meet in the capital that day. Fierce fighting broke out between demonstrators and the forces of order, during which the delegate Jollivet was accidentally killed on his way to the legislative chambers.[125] Despite attempts to assuage the insurgents with the dismissal of Guizot and the formation of a liberal Cabinet under Barrot, within three days the monarchy fell. Louis Philippe fled to England, like Charles X before him, and a Provisional Government, stacked with opposition deputies, and cliques surrounding the republican newspapers *Le National* and *La Réforme*, proclaimed the Second Republic.[126] This eleven-man government that would rule France

---

[124] Ibid.

[125] It is perhaps due to this that Schoelcher, once he was appointed under-secretary of state for the colonies, obtained access to so many of the compromising secret letters exchanged between the delegates and their colonies, documents that constitute the backbone of his collection of slavery papers now in the French Bibliothèque Nationale.

[126] For the February Revolution and the Provisional Government, see, among others, Maurice Agulhon, *1848 ou l'apprentissage de la République, 1848–1852* (Paris: Seuil, 1973); and Roger Price, *The French Second Republic: A Social History* (Ithaca: Cornell University Press, 1972). The old multivolume studies by Daniel Stern (pseud. comtesse d'Agoult),

until May – after elections by universal male suffrage gave France a National Constituent Assembly – contained several noted abolitionists. Ledru-Rollin, the radical abolitionist and one of the leaders of the left opposition under the July Monarchy, assumed the title of Minister of the Interior. Lamartine became the highly influential foreign minister.[127] Other abolitionists included Ferdinand Flocon, editor of *La Réforme*, and Crémieux, the justice minister who, like Lamartine, had been a member of the Société française pour l'abolition de l'esclavage. The new regime was not only republican, but stocked with abolitionists.

Colonial delegate Dupin was aware already on February 28 that the establishment of a republic meant that "emancipation is inevitable," for the new republican navy-colonial minister, François Arago, had informed the colonial governors that the republic meant liberty. Although François Arago was the brother of Etienne Arago of the *Réforme*, and a close associate of the republican Schoelcher, Dupin also claimed to be his acquaintance. Therefore, Dupin proceeded immediately to see the new minister to try to influence him to carry out the transformation to freedom with the preservation of work, order, and the interests of the *colons* in mind. Dupin left their meeting of February 28 convinced that he was in "perfect accord" with Arago and Mestro, who had been promoted to Director of the Colonies, because "they will act according to conservative principles" concerning colonial rights.[128] It is not surprising that Dupin should wish to sabotage any emancipation move or that the navy-colonial department, in which Mestro had played an important role since 1830, should be inclined toward caution and circumspection in this matter as it had always been under the July Monarchy. Martinique *colons* in Paris had also formed a committee on February 26 and had proceeded to meet with Mestro and Arago. The committee, like the delegates,

Histoire de la Revolution de 1848 (3 vols; 1851; rpt. Paris: Calman Lévy, 1896–1897), and Louis Antoine Garnier-Pagès, *Histoire de la Révolution de 1848* (10 vols.; Paris: Pagnerre, 1861–72), still offer the best detailed factual accounts.

[127] On the role of Lamartine in 1848, see William Fortescue, *Alphonse de Lamartine: A Political Biography* (New York: St. Martin's, 1983), and Lawrence C. Jennings, *France and Europe in 1848: A Study of French Foreign Affairs in Time of Crisis* (Oxford: Clarendon, 1973).

[128] Schoelcher Papers, N. a. f. 3631, pp. 233, 236, Dupin to President Colonial Council of Martinique, Feb. 28, 1848.

impressed upon the new minister the need for a cautious approach, an adequate indemnity, measures to guarantee work, and a new law favoring cane sugar. One of its leaders, Lepelletier de Saint-Rémy, left the meeting too with the conviction that Arago would not act immediately, but put off a final decision until the formation of a regularly constituted national assembly. Indeed, the message that François Arago had sent the governors on February 26 had stipulated that the final decision on the emancipation question would be made by the popularly elected National Assembly after it was constituted, thus postponing slave liberation for a few months at least. Despite the Provisional Government's determination to free the slaves, the colonial faction could still entertain hopes that it would have an opportunity to influence the government's decision, gain more time, and work for guarantees of both an indemnity and coerced labor.[129]

All hopes that Dupin and the *colons* might have entertained about influencing Arago and the emancipation process were abruptly dashed, though, in early March when Schoelcher returned from a trip to Senegal. This French possession, like Mayotte and Algeria, was peripheral to the general question of French colonial slavery. Senegal in the 1840s amounted to little more than a handful of trading stations. Among them there were at most 6,000 "captives," as they were called, or enslaved blacks brought into French-controlled territory. Almost all were owned by black or mixed-race inhabitants rather than whites, and, as in Mayotte and Algeria, few worked the land, most being employed as servants, workers in towns, or sailors.[130] As the emancipation issue advanced in France, though, the situation in Senegal was raised by the Broglie commission in 1842, and studied by a commission set up in the colony itself. The latter, quite understandably, recommended against freeing the slaves. However, in 1845 the

[129] Ibid., p. 175, Procès-verbal d'un comité permanent près du Gouvernement Provisoire, Feb. 26, 1848; Jacques Adélaïde-Merlande, "L'Abolition de l'esclavage: Les événements en métropole," in *Historial Antillais*, IV, 12–13.
[130] François Renault, "L'Abolition de l'esclavage au Sénégal: L'Attitude de l'Administration française (1848–1905)," *Revue française d'histoire d'outre-mer* 58 (1971): 5–6; Roger Pasquier, "A propos de l'émancipation des esclaves au Sénégal en 1848," *Revue française d'histoire d'outre-mer* 54 (1967): 191–2. Schoelcher wrote to his friend Legouvé from Gorée on Sept. 22, 1847, that because "in Senegal, as in most Muslim countries," slavery "is domestic rather than agricultural," the captives were "exposed to less cruel requirements" (Schmidt, *La correspondance*, 165).

Mackau ministry committed itself to resolving the problem eventually by royal ordonnances, just as it promised for the *esclaves de domaine* in the traditional colonies. In this case too, though, Mackau moved slowly once abolitionist pressure was deflected. Only in 1847 did the navy-colonial office formulate a plan to free Senegalese slaves in 1849 in exchange for an indemnity, but this proposal too was never presented to the chambers. By the late 1840s abolitionists decided to renew the pressure, and Schoelcher undertook his fact-finding mission to expand abolitionist knowledge on a slave territory "about which nothing was known in France."[131] Immediately upon returning to France from the African coast Schoelcher learned that the Revolution of 1848 had occurred and that a republic had been established.

Schoelcher rushed to see Arago on March 3, and obtained from him the mandate to deal with the slavery question. The radical abolitionist and long-standing republican convinced the navy-colonial minister that postponing even briefly the final decision on emancipation could cause impatient slaves to rise up in revolt. Schoelcher had feared that placing the issue in the hands of the National Assembly, preoccupied as it would be with organizing the new republic, could have postponed slave liberation once again. As a result of Schoelcher's intervention, Arago forthwith issued decrees on March 4 naming the abolitionist as under-secretary of state for the navy and colonies and placing him in charge of a commission to end slavery. According to one source, he had been supported in his decision within the Provisional Government by Ledru-Rollin. Basically, Schoelcher had forced the issue by persuading Arago to reverse his previous inclination to delay the matter until the calling of the National Assembly. Instead, the decree of March 4, signed by all members of the Provisional Government, proclaimed that Schoelcher's commission would "prepare, as rapidly as possible, the act of immediate emancipation." This decree called for the immediate termination of servitude, but made no mention of an indemnity.[132] The radical abolitionist solution to the slavery problem was being imposed on France by Schoelcher and his

[131] Pasquier, "A propos de l'émancipation," 193–4; Adélaïde-Merlande, "L'Abolition," 13.
[132] Ibid, IV, 13–14; Jacques Adélaïde-Merlande, "La commission d'abolition de l'esclavage," *Bulletin de la société d'histoire de la Guadeloupe*, nos. 53–4 (1982): 4; Schmidt, *Victor Schoelcher*, 103–4; Stern, *Histoire de la Revolution*, II, 70.

republican allies. The British were "delighted" with the "marvelous events" bringing emancipation to France.[133] However, according to Dutrône, some members of the Société française pour l'abolition de l'esclavage, true to their moderate convictions, felt that the Republic had gone too far too fast with its abolition decree.[134]

The Commission for the Abolition of Slavery, presided by Schoelcher and formed officially on March 5, contained three other abolitionists from the Orleanist regime within its midst: Paul de Gasparin, the brother of Agénor and a former supporter of Guizot; Jules de Lasteyrie, the brother-in-law of Rémusat and a member of the moderate opposition under the July Monarchy; and Adolphe Gatine, the lawyer and long-time member of the Société française pour l'abolition de l'esclavage, who had been a noted defender of blacks in the colonies. A token worker was appointed to the commission, Charles Gaumont, who had originated from the Antilles and who had been involved in the workers' anti-slavery petition campaign of 1844. He was joined by a moderate man of color and naval officer, François Auguste Perrinon, a friend of Schoelcher and his future political ally in the Antilles; however, Perrinon had also been a member of the Martinican *colon* delegation of February 26, and thus had close ties with the colonists. On the commission the administration was represented by Mestro. And its two secretaries were Henri Wallon and L. Percin. There was no colonial spokesman within the commission, and no Bissette. Schoelcher undoubtedly considered Perrinon as a black alternative to his opponent Bissette. The latter proposed his services, but Schoelcher persuaded Arago not even to reply to a person, whom, Schoelcher claimed, was a "debtor . . . disdained by the whites, and no less by the abolitionists."[135] Nevertheless, Bissette and a delegation of five *hommes de couleur libres* met with the Provisional Government on April 7. They expressed their joy and gratitude for the abolition of slavery, and pledged their full-fledged cooperation in the emancipation process. Bissette and his friends also formed a short-lived Club des Amis des Noirs – like under the first Revolution – to vent their ideas.[136]

---

[133] *British and Foreign Anti-Slavery Reporter*, April 1, 1848.
[134] *L'Abolitioniste français*, 1849, 1–3rd issues, p. 78.
[135] Adélaïde-Merlande, "L'Abolition," 14–5; Schmidt, *Victor Schoelcher*, 105–9.
[136] *Annales de l'Institut d'Afrique*, March–April 1848, nos. 3–4, pp. 21–2; Drescher, "British Way, French Way," 731; "Adélaïde-Merlande, "L'Abolition," 16.

It appears, though, that Schoelcher, as de facto assistant navy-colonial minister, had a free hand in choosing and refusing whomever he wished to sit on the commission. He also completely dominated commission proceedings.

The commission met from March 6 to July 21, 1848, but the essential part of its business was concluded by April 13. In the course of its meetings it received testimony from numerous functionaries, from several free men of color, and from abolitionists such as Isambert; even Bissette made a presentation before it. The body was besieged at the same time by a series of procolonial delegations attempting to influence its final decrees. All the delegates of Guadeloupe, Bourbon, and Martinique, including Jollivet's temporary replacement, Froidefond-Desfages, testified before the Schoelcher commission. So did representatives of the port cities of Le Havre, Nantes, and Marseille, along with different *colons* residing in Paris. Even the port cities of Dieppe and St. Malo wrote to the commission, evidencing a well-orchestrated campaign by colonial advocates. Schoelcher revealed later that all of them professed their willingness to accept emancipation, but on two conditions: an "indemnity and the organization of work." The Guadeloupe delegation even tried to reintroduce its proposal for organizing work through an associative scheme, though this option was rejected outright by Schoelcher, who insisted that the abolition decree be uniform for all colonies. On the very day that the Provisional Government issued its abolition decree of April 27 the delegates of Guadeloupe presented a protest to the government about the precipitousness of the commission's proceedings.[137] As late as July 1848, when the Republic had taken a more conservative course after the repression of the workers' revolt of June, the port cities supposedly approached the then French head of state, General Eugène Cavaignac, to appeal for a reversal of the March and April decrees and a reversion to a gradual emancipation approach.[138] Rare were the colonials who rallied to the emancipation decree, such as the twenty-five young *colons* of Réunion (formerly Bourbon) – including a certain Sully-Brunet who likely was the son of the delegate of the island – and applauded with their youthful enthusiasm the emancipation

[137] Ibid.; *L'Abolitioniste français*, 1848, 2–4th issues, pp. 20–30.
[138] *Le Journal des débats*, July 15, 1848; *L'Abolitioniste français*, 1849, 1–3rd issues, pp. 26–42.

proclamation as "a grand act of justice and fraternity."[139] Apart from these young rebels, the French colonial establishment continued to fight its rear-guard action against the emancipation decree and its consequences for the colonies.

Schoelcher and his commission, however, would have nothing to do with such retrograde tactics.[140] The body dutifully listened to the diverse testimony, studied official documents provided by the navy-colonial ministry, and posed a whole series of questions as to how the slave liberation process should proceed. In the process the commission examined a great many issues, such as the right of planters to an indemnity, the need to preserve work on the plantations, and the desirability of encouraging immigration to the colonies. Most of all, however, it remained adamant that emancipation must be immediate and complete.[141]

After much research, reflection, and debate, the commission drafted the general abolition decree of April 27, 1848, that was signed by all the members of the Provisional Government.[142] The decree proclaimed that French slaves would be freed within two months of its promulgation in the colonies, that it was forbidden for French citizens anywhere to possess slaves, that the colonies would be given direct representation in the National Assembly rather than delegates, and that the National Assembly would decide on the indemnity for slave owners.[143] The new republican government, at the urging of Schoelcher and his commission, had proven uncompromising in its principles. Abolition would be general and unconditional. It would be applied as soon as the order could be transmitted to the colonies and preliminary measures taken for its implementation. At the same time, though, preoccupied like all nineteenth-century regimes with promoting the work ethic, the Republic issued a number of decrees in 1848

[139] *Le Courrier français*, March 21, 1848; *L'Abolitioniste français*, 1848, 2–4th issues, pp. 110–11.
[140] Ibid., p. 30.
[141] Ibid., pp. 17–21; Adélaïde-Merlande, "La commision d'abolition," 17–21.
[142] Adélaïde-Merlande, "L'Abolition," 15–7; Adélaïde-Merlande, "La commission d'abolition," 5–13.
[143] *Le Moniteur universel*, May 3, 1848; *L'Abolitioniste français*, 1848, 2–4th issues, 44–6. For the implications of this decree for French slave-owning citizens living outside French possessions, see Lawrence C. Jennings, "L'Abolition de l'esclavage par la IIe République et ses effets en Louisiane, 1848–1858," *Revue française d'histoire d'outre-mer*, 56 (1969): 375–97.

encouraging free labor through government incentives, and regulations controlling vagabondage.[144]

Schoelcher resigned as under-secretary of state on May 17, 1848, but he and other abolitionists, such as Isambert and Tocqueville, were named members of a new commission, appointed on June 17, 1848, that studied the indemnity question. The indemnity commission eventually recommended in 1849 an indemnity of 90 million francs for the 248,310 slaves estimated to exist in French colonies in 1848: 87,087 in Guadeloupe; 74,447 in Martinique; 60,951 in Réunion; 12,525 in Guiana; 9,800 in Senegal; and 3,500 in Ste. Marie and Nossibé (Madagascar).[145] However, when the Second Republic finally promulgated its indemnity law of May 2, 1849, it provided only for the meager sum of 6 million francs in cash and 6 million in credit, with one-eighth of the latter going toward the establishment of colonial banks. Because the final sum was proportioned differently to the various colonies according to slave values, this meant that the cash payment per slave amounted to only 20.49 francs in Martinique, 23.01 in Guadeloupe, 29.41 in Guiana, and 33.59 in Réunion.[146] The Broglie commission had recommended 1,200 per slave some five years earlier, but the Republic was much less solicitous of planter interests than the July Monarchy had been.

In the meantime slaves in Martinique had contributed to their own liberation by revolting and thereby speeding up the emancipation process. Word reached Martinique by British ships that the monarchy had been overthrown and that the Republic had proclaimed its intentions on March 4 to abolish slavery. This brought increased unrest among slaves. Finally, on May 20–23 slaves and persons of color in several parishes of Martinique demonstrated, especially those in the region around the main commercial town of Saint-Pierre. Skirmishes occurred with the forces of order, with several blacks and whites being killed and wounded. The arrest of one slave led to a veritable

[144] Adélaïde-Merlande, "L'Abolition," 18–21.
[145] M. A. I. Fischer-Blanchet, "Les travaux de la commission de l'indemnité coloniale en 1848," *Espaces caraïbes* I (1983), 37–56.
[146] *L'Abolitioniste français*, 1849, 4–5th issues, pp. 109–12; Alain Buffon, *Monnaie et crédit en économie coloniale: Contribution à l'histoire économique de la Guadeloupe, 1635–1919* (Basse-Terre: Société d'histoire de la Guadeloupe, 1979), 144; Buffon, "L'Indemnisation des planteurs après l'abolition de l'esclavage," *Bulletin de al Société d' histoire de la Guadeloupe*, nos. 67–8 (1986): 63.

insurrection on May 23. Slaves invaded Saint-Pierre and set fire to a house occupied by armed *colons*, leading to thirty-five deaths and as many wounded. Fearing a general slave revolt, the municipal council requested the interim governor, General Rostoland, to declare emancipation immediately. He complied that very day, after consulting with his private council. Upon hearing of the events in Martinique, Governor Layrle first declared a state of emergency on Guadeloupe, and then, after consultations with his council, proclaimed slave liberation on his island on May 27. Thus, freedom came to the slaves of the two islands eleven days before the official act of April 27 reached the colonies and some two months earlier than the legislation stipulated.[147] Freed from the constant threat of repression, French colonial slaves were able to participate in the emancipation process once it had been initiated in Paris. Only in Guiana and Réunion were slaves freed according to schedule, on August 10 and December 20, 1848, respectively.

L'Abolitioniste français, still edited by Dutrône, duly reported these developments. However, the abolitionist journal was a mere shadow of its former self. It had suspended publication for the first two-thirds of 1848, and simply concentrated upon reproducing government reports, assembly debates, and news from the colonies or abroad concerning slavery when it appeared once again in late 1848. From then until its final issue in 1850 it hardly ever editorialized or discussed events in France. Its last issue of late 1850 contained only skeletal reports, and no commentary whatsoever on why it was suspending publication. The review simply disappeared.[148] This reflected the fate of the Société française pour l'abolition de l'esclavage itself, which also suspended its activity once French emancipation was completed. Indeed, according to Dutrône, the society had looked forward with anticipation to the moment when its objectives were achieved and it could disband.[149] The French abolition society had prepared the way for an eventual emancipation, but was much too tied to the legislative chambers of the July Monarchy to continue beyond its demise. During its final months its members had contributed by testifying

---

[147] Fallope, *Esclaves et ciyoyens*, 344–5; Armand Nicolas, *La Révolution antiesclavagiste de mai 1848 à la Martinique* (Fort-de-France: Imprimerie Populaire Carénage, 1967), 20–7.

[148] For the above, see the entire press run of *L'Abolitioniste français*, 1848–1850.

[149] Drescher, "Two Variants of Anti-Slavery," 54.

before or serving on different commissions ending the slave regime, but the spotlight had switched to Schoelcher after the Revolution of 1848. The Société française had kept the issue of emancipation in the news and on the legislative docket for nearly fifteen years, but could not topple slavery under an unyielding monarchy. Though the society had undergone a major change in the summer of 1847 when it finally espoused immediatism, even this had not shaken the Orleanist regime's resolve to continue in its policy of postponing slave liberation. Emancipation came to French colonial possessions only with revolution in France, which toppled the Orleanist government, brought the republicans and the immediatist Schoelcher to power, and enabled him to glorify himself as the liberator of French slaves.

CONCLUSION

The Société française pour l'abolition de l'esclavage had been unable to bring about slave liberation in the French colonies. Under the July Monarchy anti-slavery had not proved strong enough to overcome the opposition of the plantocracy and the procrastination of the government. To the very end it remained too removed from public opinion to win over the support necessary to counter the resistance of an effective colonial lobby combined with the determined immobility of French authorities. Like its predecessors during the Revolutionary and Restoration periods, the Société française was dominated by members of the elite who feared the masses and felt at ease propagating its message only through the printed media and parliamentary channels. Besides being restricted by its own reticence toward the populace, its efforts were stymied by the government every time it attempted to expand its activities even to include a larger section of the middle classes. The Société française fell under the July Monarchy's laws on associations and was not permitted to organize public meetings. It could not imitate the British, draw funding and support from the public, or use these resources to pressure the government. The very nature of the French abolition society as an appendage to the ruling classes limited its actions. It could not overcome the firm determination of King Louis Philippe and his various administrations to rebuff anti-slavery demands. Believing in the continued importance of the colonies, unwilling to disburse the sums necessary for an indemnity, and wedded to preserving the colonial along with the metropolitan status quo, the King and his Cabinets would not consider any moves on the slavery front beyond token ameliorative or preparatory measures. The regime's tendency to reconcile competing interests rather than to alienate any one, along with its own conservative attitude toward servitude, enforced its immobility. Inaction rather than movement remained the priority of the July Monarchy. Without public support the abolitionists could not sway it. Only when Louis Philippe was removed from power could emancipation be imposed by radical abolitionist forces.

Other factors also impeded the progress of French anti-slavery under the Orleanist regime. Dominated by legalistic, *notable* legislators, French abolitionism relied upon individual initiative and brio. The French abolition society often harbored as many different approaches to the slavery problem as it had members. It rarely adopted a precise policy, or held it for very long. Instead, it advocated, like its predecessors, a general policy of gradualism which could rally, with various degrees of enthusiasm, almost all of its members. At a time when there were no set political parties in France, but a series of loose formations centered around particular individuals, French anti-slavery suffered from a similar structure. By the 1840s there was a steady growth in immediatism within the ranks of anti-slavery, but positions of various abolitionists continued to differ. Much of the membership of the abolition society was very cautious during the 1830s, with only Passy, Tracy, Isambert, Dutrône, and Lutheroth steadily stressing the need to move rapidly toward slave liberation. By the 1840s there was a definite trend for the gradualists of the 1830s – like Agénor de Gasparin, Montalembert, Jules de Lasteyrie, not to mention Schoelcher – to become immediatists. However, other progressives of the 1830s, such as Tocqueville and Tracy, regressed or became more detached from the cause for one reason or another in the 1840s. Still others, such as Lamartine, wavered constantly, or issued eloquent but empty, if not contradictory, pleas for emancipation in general. Furthermore, the exact stances of many members of the abolition society were not publicized, and impossible to decipher. In this sense, there was no disciplined French anti-slavery force in the modern sense. Not only was the Société française weakly knit and indecisively organized, but it also broke its momentum continually by abiding by the parliamentary calendar and suspending its meetings for nearly half a year. Its generally disorganized efforts, when faced with determined opposition, go far to explain the hesitant, seesaw nature of French anti-slavery under the July Monarchy. Unlike their British counterparts, most French abolitionists did not place the eradication of slavery at the top of their lists of priorities. As a result of the irresolute nature of the French abolition society, radical immediatist abolitionists, like Bissette, Schoelcher, and Félice, chose to operate largely outside its parameters. French anti-slavery was weakened not only by its disorganization and wavering, but by its divisions.

Distant from the French public, and divided within itself, anti-slavery under the July Monarchy, like under preceding regimes, became highly dependent upon the British for support. London inspired the formation of the French abolitionist movement and provided it with advice, encouragement, even funding. The British also made constant voyages to France to try to stimulate immediatist thought or form a Protestant network with this inspiration. But Protestantism was too underrepresented in France to provide the sort of evangelical network that had experienced such success in Britain. Indeed, immediatists like Bissette and Félice, often operating individually or with few allies, tended to be even more dependent upon the British than their more moderate colleagues within the ranks of mainstream French anti-slavery. French abolitionists under the July Monarchy remained highly indebted to their British brethren. But British succor constituted a double-edged sword. On the one hand, French friends of the slaves were dependent upon it because of their general lack of popularity within France. On the other hand, this very dependence, widely known and constantly denounced by the plantocracy, tended to distance further French anti-slavery from a firmly Anglophobic public. At two times when French anti-slavery seemed poised for advances, in 1840 and 1842, a crescendo of Anglophobia concomitant with the Egyptian and right of search crises forced abolitionists into retreat and enabled the government to table the emancipation issue. Identified in the public mind with the British, French anti-slavery was seriously hobbled at least until the right of search affair was finally resolved in the mid-1840s. In the end, it is questionable whether French abolitionism profited more than it suffered from its British connections.

Although French anti-slavery under the July Monarchy struggled under inherent weaknesses and ultimately failed in its objective of freeing the slaves, it nevertheless attained certain achievements that should not be underestimated. As during the Napoleonic and Restoration epochs, French emancipationists under the Orleanist regime served as the conscience of the French nation faced with the horrors of colonial slavery. Once the slave trade was repressed, abolitionists concentrated their humanitarian efforts against colonial slavery and insisted upon its transformation and ultimate eradication. Realizing full well that only the government could improve the plight of slaves and decree their eventual liberation, the Société française pour l'abolition de l'esclavage devoted itself to influencing the various Cabinets and pressing them to act. Although often outmaneuvered by the powerful colonial lobby whose objectives were closely aligned with those of the authorities, the abolitionists persisted year after year in reviving the emancipation question. They were most effective during the 1830s when high-placed officials of the Société française held influential Cabinet posts, but managed to keep the emancipation question alive even when excluded from the corridors of power. Given the orientation and objectives of the Orleanist regime, it is evident that it would have made few real ameliorations on the slavery front without abolitionist pressure in parliament. Interpellations and motions by abolition society members within the lower house brought the formation of parliamentary commissions and the production of commission reports that embarrassed the government and pushed it slowly forward. The taking into consideration of anti-slavery motions by majorities in the Deputies showed not that the lower chamber was abolitionist, but that it too wanted some movement on the slavery scene. It was in reply to these pressures that the government took its first real ameliorative and preparatory moves in 1839–1840. The authorities were able to disembarrass themselves of the issue only due to the outbreak of the Egyptian and right of search crises. Nevertheless, emancipationists had achieved a consensus within France already in the late 1830s that slavery must be terminated sometime in the future. In this sense, the French abolition society brought the slavery problem out into the open, slowly acquainted Frenchmen with it, and ultimately gained their acceptance of the need for its gradual eradication. All in all, the French abolition society played the important role of preparing the terrain for eventual slave liberation.

The cautious, intermittent, gradualist modus operandi of the abolition society also had another significant consequence. It, along with government stalling, kindled the fires of immediatism in France. From its meager beginnings in the mid-1830s as a concept advocated by the British and a handful of radical French abolitionists, immediatism began to gain an increasing number of adherents after gradualism proved its shortcomings by the early 1840s. Marginalized at first, it progressively grew beyond the individualistic efforts of a Bissette or a Schoelcher, a workers' petition campaign, or a small batch of publications. By the mid-1840s, it was given additional impetus by the inconsequential ameliorative legislation that constituted the ultimate concession of an anti-reform government. By the late 1840s, immediatism had its axis in a Bissette–Félice–British formation, and one centered around Schoelcher and *La Réforme*. Late in the July Monarchy, radical French anti-slavery adopted the British-inspired tactic of petitioning, and even won over the adherence of the French abolition society six months before the Revolution of February 1848. Despite all this, though, in the face of a July Monarchy determined to maintain the status quo, it could only muster a handful of publications and a few thousand signatures on petitions even in the late 1840s. Immediatists too were far from establishing the complex anti-slavery network that had rallied millions in Great Britain and forced abolition upon the London government. Their limited accomplishments were based largely upon individual efforts, especially those of the heroic, if irascible, black abolitionist Bissette, probably the most important figure in French anti-slavery under the July Monarchy. Without the Revolution of 1848 that overthrew the Orleanist regime, slavery undoubtedly would have endured many more years in the French colonies. Nevertheless, the radical abolitionists had managed to establish and build a rudimentary immediatist culture in France. Once the February Revolution swept away the unyielding July Monarchy, the republican Schoelcher was able to implement these immediatist concepts when he came to power as under-secretary of state for the colonies under the Second Republic. Schoelcher encapsulated and implemented the achievements of radical French abolitionism. He took advantage of a revolutionary situation to institutionalize them. Buffeted under Napoleon, resuscitated under the Restoration, French anti-slavery nurtured, developed, and matured under the July Monarchy to the point where it could achieve its objectives under the new republican regime that emerged in 1848.

BIBLIOGRAPHY

ARCHIVAL SOURCES

This study is based upon an exhaustive analysis of the dossiers in the French colonial archives concerning slavery and its abolition and upon abolitionist and slavery papers in both French and British depositories, listed below.

France, Archives Nationales, Centre des Archives d'Outre-Mer, Aix-en-Provence
    Généralités
    Correspondance Générale
    Série géographique: Guadeloupe, Guyane, Martinique, Réunion
    Dossiers du personnel

France, Archives Nationales, Paris
    Series F7
    Guizot Papers
    Mackau Papers

Bibliothèque Nationale, Paris
    Isambert Papers
    Schoelcher Papers
    Thiers Papers

Bordeaux, Chambre de Commerce de Bordeaux

Le Havre, Chambre de Commerce du Havre

Archives départementales de la Loire-Atlantique, Chambre de Commerce de Nantes

Bodleian Library, Oxford, Rhodes House Anti-Slavery Papers

NEWSPAPERS AND JOURNALS

L'Abolitioniste [sic] *français* (Paris), 1844–1850
Annales de l'Institut d'Afrique (Paris), 1841–1848
Annales maritimes et coloniales (Paris), 1830–1847
Archives du Christianisme (Paris), 1832–1834, 1837–1846, 1848
Archives philanthropiques (Paris), 1830–1831
L'Atelier (Paris), 1844
Le Breton (Nantes), 1832–1848
British and Foreign Anti-Slavery Reporter (London), 1840–1848
Le Commerce (Paris), 1831–1845
Le Constitutionnel (Paris), 1830–1848
Le Courrier de la Gironde (Bordeaux), 1838–1845
Le Courrier francais (Paris), 1830–1842
La Démocratie pacifique (Paris), 1844–1848
L'Espérance (Paris), 1841–1848
La Guienne (Bordeaux), 1833–1848
L'Indicateur (Bordeaux), 1830–1845
Journal de la Société de la morale chrétienne (Paris), 1822–1829, 1832–
     1847, 1850
Le Journal des débats (Paris), 1832–1845, 1847
Le Journal du Havre (Le Havre), 1831–1848
Le Lien (Paris), 1841–1848
Le Moniteur du commerce (Paris), 1833–1836
Le Moniteur universel (Paris), 1830–1848
Le National (Paris), 1830–1848
L'Outre-mer (Paris), 1839–1840
La Presse (Paris), 1836–1848
La Réforme (Paris), 1843–1848
La Revue abolitioniste (Paris), 1847
La Revue coloniale (Paris), 1843–1848
La Revue des colonies (Paris), 1834–1842
La Sémaphore de Marseille (Marseille), 1831–1845
Le Semeur (Paris), 1831–1848
La Sentinelle, Journal des familles protestantes (Valence), 1844–1847
Le Siècle (Paris), 1836–1848
Le Temps (Paris), 1830–1842
L'Union (Paris), 1844
L'Univers (Paris), 1836–1842

PRIMARY PRINTED WORKS

Bissette, Cyrille. *C. C. A. Bissette, homme de couleur de la Martinique, à un colon, sur l'émancipation civile et politique appliquée aux colonies françaises*. Paris: Imprimerie Gaultier-Laguionie, 1830.

Bissette, Cyrille. *Deux-mots sur une note de Mr. V. Schoelcher*. Paris: Ebrard, 1843.

Bissette, Cyrille. *Du Projet Mackau, tendant à violer la loi du 24 avril sur le régime législatif des colonies*. Paris: Dupont, 1844.

Bissette, Cyrille. *Examen rapide des deux projets de loi relatifs aux colonies, adressé à la Chambre des députés*. Paris: Impr. d'Everat, 1833.

Bissette, Cyrille. *Mémoire au Ministre de la Marine et des Colonies, et à la Commission de législation coloniale sur les améliorations legislatives et organiques à apporter au régime des colonies françaises*. Paris: Impr. A. Mie, 1831.

Bissette, Cyrille. *Note sur le projet de loi relatif au régime legislatif des colonies*. Paris: Impr. Dupont & Laguionie, 1833.

Bissette, Cyrille. *Observations sur les projets de lois coloniales, présentés à la Chambre des députés*. Paris: Impr. A. Mie, 1832.

Bissette, Cyrille. *Pétition des hommes de couleur de la Martinique, déportés aux colonies étrangères par Général Donzelot en décembre 1823 et janvier 1824*. Paris: E. Duverger, 1828.

Bissette, Cyrille. *Polémique sur les évènements de la Grande Anse*. Paris: Impr. J. S. Cordier, 1834.

Bissette, Cyrille. *Réfutation du livre de M. V. Schoelcher sur Haïti*. Paris: Ebrard, 1844.

Bissette, Cyrille. *Réfutation du livre de M. Victor Schoelcher intitulé "Des colonies françaises."* Paris: Breton, 1843.

Bissette, Cyrille, and Louis Fabien. *Demande en grâce pour Adèle, jeune esclave de la Martinique condamnée à la peine de fouet pour avoir chanté la Parisienne*. Paris: Impr. August Mie, 1831.

Bissette, Cyrille, Louis Fabien, and Mondésir Richard. *Pétition à la Chambre des députés, relative à l'amélioration du sort des esclaves aux colonies*. Paris: Impr. P. Dupont & Laguionie, 1832.

Buxton, J. [Thomas Fowell]. *Discours prononcé dans la Chambre des Communes d'Angleterre à l'appui de la motion pour l'adoucissement et l'extinction graduelle de l'esclavage dans les colonies anglaises*. Paris: Crapelet, 1824.

Cochin, Augustin. *L'Abolition de l'esclavage*. 1861; rpt., Fort-de-France: Désormeaux, 1979.

Dugoujon, Abbé Casimir. *Lettres sur l'esclavage dans les colonies françaises*. Paris: Pagnerre, 1845.

Dupin, Charles. *Mémoire adressé par le conseil des délégués des colonies à MM. les membres du conseil des ministres.* Paris: Didot frères, 1842.

Dupin, Charles. *Second mémoire: Situation comparée des colonies françaises et colonies anglaises.* Paris: Firmin-Didot, 1844.

Dussillion, Charles Joseph. *Considérations sur l'esclavage aux Antilles françaises et de son abolition graduelle, suivie d'un aperçu analytique et critique du système d'apprentissage et de ses résultats dans les colonies anglaises.* Paris: Dussillion, 1843.

Fabien, Louis. *Appel aux amis de l'humanité contre un épouvantable arrêt.* Paris: Impr. Dezauche, 1834.

Félice, Guillaume de. *Emancipation immédiate et complète des esclaves: Appel aux abolitionistes.* Paris: Delay, 1846.

Fleury, Hector. *De la société coloniale et des garanties de régime servile dans les possessions françaises.* Lyon: Boursy, 1847.

Fleury, Victor. *De l'esclavage colonial et son abolition immédiate dans les colonies françaises.* Lyon: Boursy, 1847.

France, Administration des douanes. *Tableau décennal du commerce de la France avec ses colonies et les puissances étrangères, 1837–1846.* Paris: Impr. Nationale, 1848.

Garnier-Pagès, Louis Antoine. *Histoire de la Révolution de 1848.* 10 vols. Paris: Pagnerre, 1861–72.

Gasparin, Agénor de. *Esclavage et traite.* Paris: Joubert, 1838.

Granier de Cassagnac, Adolphe. *De l'abolition des esclaves par l'éducation religieuse.* Paris: Impr. H. Fournier, 1837.

Granier de Cassagnac, Adolphe. *De l'émancipation des esclaves: Lettres à M. de Lamartine par M. Granier de Cassagnac.* Paris: Delloye, 1840.

Guéroult, Adolphe. *De la question coloniale en 1842: Les colonies françaises et le sucre de betterave.* Paris: Gosselin, 1842.

L'Instant, S. *Essai sur les moyens d'extirper les préjugés des blancs contre la couleur des Africains et des sangs-mêlés.* Paris: Pagnerre, 1841.

Jollivet, Thomas Marie Adolphe. *Analyse des délibérations et avis des conseils coloniaux et des conseils speciaux sur l'abolition de l'esclavage dans les colonies françaises.* Paris: Impr. de Cosse et Gaultier-Laguionie, 1842.

Jollivet, Thomas Marie Adolphe. *La commission présidé par M. le duc de Broglie, et les gouverneurs de nos colonies, théorie et pratique.* Paris: Impr. de Boulé, 1843.

Macaulay, Zachary. *Faits et renseignements prouvant les avantages du travail libre sur le travail forcé.* Paris: Hachette, 1835.

Ministère de la Marine et des Colonies. *Avis des conseils coloniaux de la Martinique, de la Guadeloupe, et de la Guyane française, sur diverses propositions concernant l'esclavage.* Paris: Impr. Royale, 1839.

Ministère de la Marine et des Colonies. *Colonies françaises: Exécution de l'ordonnance royale du 5 janvier 1840 relative à l'instruction religieuse, à l'instruction primaire et au patronage des esclaves. Exposé sommaire.* Paris: Impr. Royale, 1842.

Ministère de la Marine et des Colonies. *Commission instituée par décision royale du 26 mail 1840 pour l'examen des questions relatives à l'esclavage et à la constitution politiques des colonies.* 2 vols. Paris: Impr. Royale 1840–1843.

Ministère de la Marine et des Colonies. *Exposé générale des résultats du patronage des esclaves dans les colonies françaises, imprimé par l'ordre du ministre secrétaire d'état de la Marine et des Colonies.* Paris: Impr. Royale, 1844.

Ministère de la Marine et des Colonies. *Notices statistiques sur les colonies françaises.* Paris: Impr. Royale, 1837–1838.

Ministère de la Marine et des Colonies. *Questions relatives à l'abolition de l'esclavage: Instructions adressées à MM. les gouverneurs des colonies. Circulaires du 18 juillet 1840. Avis des conseils coloniaux. Délibérations et avis des conseils spéciaux.* Paris: Impr. Royale, 1843.

Montrol, François Mongin de. *Des colonies anglaises, depuis l'émancipation des esclaves, et de l'influence de cette émancipation sur les colonies françaises.* Paris: Impr. E. Duverger, 1835.

Rémusat, Charles de. *Mémoires de ma vie.* 5 vols. Paris: Plon, 1958–1967.

Ride, Alphonse. *Esclavage et liberté, existence de l'homme et des sociétés en harmonie avec les lois universelles.* 2 vols. Paris: Dalloye, 1843.

Rigord, Abbé Joseph. *Observations sur quelques opinions relatives à l'esclavage, émises à la Chambre des Pairs à l'occasion de la discussion de la loi sur le régime des esclaves aux colonies.* Fort-Royal: Ruelle, 1845.

Rouvellat de Cussac, Jean Baptiste. *A Messieurs les membres de la Chambre des députés: Quelques observations sur le projet de loi relatif à l'esclavage dans les colonies.* Paris: Pagnerre, 1845.

Schoelcher, Victor. *Colonies étrangères et Haïti: Résulatats de l'émancipation anglaise. Coup d'oeil sur l'état de la question d'affranchissement.* Paris: Pagnerre, 1843.

Schoelcher, Victor. *Des colonies françaises: Abolition immédiate de l'esclavage.* Paris: Pagnerre, 1842.

Schoelcher, Victor. *De l'esclavage des noirs et de la législation coloniale.* Paris: Paulin, 1833.

Schoelcher, Victor. *Histoire de l'esclavage pendant les deux dernières années.* 2 vols. Paris: Pagnerre, 1847.

Schoelcher, Victor. *L'Abolition de l'esclavage: Examen critique du préjugé contre la couleur des Africains et des sangs-mêlés.* Paris: Pagnerre, 1840.

Schoelcher, Victor. *Sa correspondance inédite.* Part 2: *Lettres martiniquaise (1829–1881)* Paris: Revue mondiale, 1935.

Société française pour l'abolition de l'esclavage. *4ème Publication.* Paris: Bourdon, 1836.

Société française pour l'abolition de l'esclavage. *Analyse de la discussion de la Chambre des Députés et de la Chambre des Pairs relative à l'émancipation des esclaves, par M. F. de Montrol (Troisième Publication).* Paris: Impr. Paul Dupont, 1835.

Société française pour l'abolition de l'esclavage. *No. 5. Année 1837.* Paris: Duverger, 1837.

Société française pour l'abolition de l'esclavage. *No. 6. Année 1838.* Paris: Duverger, 1838.

Société française pour l'abolition de l'esclavage. *No. 7. Analyse de la discussion de la Chambre des députées, relative à la proposition de M. Passy sur l'émancipation des enfans [sic] et le rachat des esclaves dans les colonies françaises, par M. F de M[ontrol].* Paris: Hingray, 1838.

Société française pour l'abolition de l'esclavage. *No. 8. Année 1838.* Paris: Hingray, 1838.

Société française pour l'abolition de l'esclavage. *No. 9. Rapport fait au nom de la commission chargée de l'examen de la proposition de M. Passy sur le sort des esclaves dans les colonies françaises, par M. de Rémusat, député de la Haute-Garonne.* Paris: A. Henry, 1838.

Société française pour l'abolition de l'esclavage. *No. 10. La Société française pour l'abolition de l'esclavage à MM. les membres des Conseils Généraux des départements.* Paris: Hingray, 1938.

Société française pour l'abolition de l'esclavage. *No. 11.* Paris: Hingray, 1838.

Société française pour l'abolition de l'esclavage. *No. 12.* Paris: Hingray, 1839.

Société française pour l'abolition de l'esclavage. *No. 13.* Paris: Hingray, 1839.

Société française pour l'abolition de l'esclavage. *No. 14.* Paris: A. Henry, 1839.

Société française pour l'abolition de l'esclavage. *No. 15.* Paris: E. Duverger, 1840.

Société française pour l'abolition de l'esclavage. *No. 16. Banquet offert à la députation de la Société centrale britannique pour l'abolition universelle de l'esclavage, 10 février 1840.* Paris: Hingray, 1840.

Société française pour l'abolition de l'esclavage. *No. 17.* Paris: Hingray, 1840.

Société française pour l'abolition de l'esclavage. *No. 18.* Paris: Hingray, 1840.

Société française pour l'abolition de l'esclavage. *No. 19.* Paris: Hingray, 1842.

Société française pour l'abolition de l'esclavage. *Pétition aux chambres pour demander l'abolition de l'esclavage dans les colonies françaises.* Paris: Duvillers, 1847.

Société française pour l'abolition de l'esclavage. *Prospectus de la Société française pour l'abolition de l'esclavage (Programme de la Société).* Paris: Impr. E. Duverger, 1835

Stern, Daniel [pseud. comtesse d'Agoult]. *Histoire de la Revolution de 1848.* 3 vols. 1851; rpt., Paris: Calman Lévy, 1896–1897.

SECONDARY SOURCES

Adélaïde-Merlande, Jacques. "L'Abolition de l'esclavage: Les événements en métropole." In *Historial Antillais,* IV, 11–24. 5 vols. Fort-de-France, Dajani, 1980–1.

Adélaïde-Merlande, Jacques. "La commission d'abolition de l'esclavage." *Bulletin de la société d'histoire de la Guadeloupe,* nos. 53–4 (1982): 3–34.

Adélaïde-Merlande, Jacques. *Documents d'histoire antillaise et guyanese, 1814–1914.* Noyon: Finet, 1979.

Adélaïde-Merlande, Jacques. "La loi Mackau et son application vue par Victor Schoelcher." *Cahiers de la Fondation Schoelcher,* no. 1 (1982): 7–20.

Agulhon, Maurice. *1848 ou l'apprentissage de la République, 1848–1852.* Paris: Seuil, 1973.

Alexandre-Debray, Janine. *Victor Schoelcher, ou la mystique d'un athée.* Paris: Perrin, 1983.

Anderson, M. S. *The Eastern Question, 1774–1923.* London: Macmillan, 1966.

Anstey, Roger. "The Pattern of British Abolitionism in the Eighteenth and Nineteenth Centuries." In *Anti-Slavery, Religion and Reform: Essays in Memory of Roger Anstey,* ed. Christine Bolt and Seymour Drescher, 19–42. Folkstone, Kent: Dawson, 1980.

Beecher, Jonathan. *Charles Fourier: The Visionary and His World.* Berkeley: University of California Press, 1986.

Bellanger, Claude, et al. *Histoire générale de la presse française.* 5 vols. Paris: Presses Universitaires de France, 1969–1976.

Bénot, Yves. *La démence coloniale sous Napoleon*. Paris: La Découverte, 1992.

Bénot, Yves. *La Révolution française et la fin des colonies*. Paris: La Découverte, 1988.

Blackburn, Robin. *The Overthrow of Colonial Slavery, 1776–1848*. London: Verso, 1988.

Boizard, E., and H. Tardieu. *Histoire de la législation des sucres (1664–1891)*. Paris: Impr. Dubreuil, 1891.

Brasseur, Paule. "A la recherche d'un absolu missionnaire: Mgr. Truffet, vicaire apostolique des Deux-Guinées (1812–1847)." *Cahiers d'études africaines* 15 (1975): 259–85.

Brasseur, Paule. "De l'abolition de l'esclavage à la colonisation de l'Afrique." *Mémoire spiritaine*, no. 7 (1998): 93–107.

Brasseur, Paule. "La littérature abolitionniste en France au XIXe siècle: L'Image de l'Afrique." In *Culture and Ideology in Modern France: Essays in Honour of George Rudé (1910–1993)*, ed. F. J. Fornasiero, 18–39. Adelaide: University of Adelaide, 1994.

Brasseur, Paule. "Les campagnes abolitionnistes en France (1815–1848): L'Afrique sans l'Afrique." In *De la traite à l'esclavage: Actes du colloque international sur la traite des Noirs, Nantes, 1985*, ed. Serge Daget, II, 331–41. 2 vols. Nantes: Centre de Recherche sur l'Histoire du Monde Atlantique, 1988.

Brasseur, Paule. "Libermann et l'abolition de l'esclavage." *Revue française d'histoire d'outre-mer* 73 (1986), 335–46.

Brasseur, Paule. "Le mot 'Negre' dans les dictionnaires encyclopédiques français au XIXe siècle." In *Libermann, 1802–1852, une pensée et une mystique missionnaires*, eds. Paul Coulon, Paule Brasseur, et al., 581–94. Paris: Editions du Cerf, 1983.

Braudel, Fernand, and Ernest Labrousse. *Histoire économique et sociale de la France*. 4 vols. Paris: Presses Universitaires de France, 1976–1982.

Braunstein, Dieter. *Französische Kolonialpolitik, 1830–1852: Expansion, Verevaltung, Wirtschaft, Mission*. Weisbaden: Steiner, 1983.

Broglie, Gabriel de. *Guizot*. Paris: Perrin, 1990.

Buffon, Alain. "L'Indemnisation des planteurs après l'abolition de l'esclavage," *Bulletin de la société d'historie de la Guadeloupe*, nos. 67–8 (1986): 53–72.

Buffon, Alain. *Monnaie et crédit en économie coloniale: Contribution à l'histoire économique de la Guadeloupe, 1635–1919*. Basse-Terre: Société d'histoire de la Guadeloupe, 1979.

Bury, J. P. T., and R. P. Tombs. *Thiers, 1797–1877: A Political Life*. London: Allen & Unwin, 1986.

Cahier de marronnage du Moule (1845–1848). Basse-Terre: Société d'Histoire de la Guadeloupe, 1996.

Cohen, William B. *The French Encounter with Africans: White Response to Blacks, 1530–1880*. Bloomington: Indiana University Press, 1980.

Collingham, H. A. C. *The July Monarchy: A Political History of France, 1830–1848*. London: Longman, 1988.

Craton, Michael. "Slave Culture, Resistance and the Achievement of Emancipation in the British West Indies, 1783–1836." In *Slavery and British Sociey, 1776–1846*, ed. James Walvin, 100–122. London: Macmillan, 1982.

Craton, Michael. *Testing the Chains: Resistance to Slavery in the British West Indies*. Ithaca: Cornell University Press, 1982.

Curtin, Philip D. "The British Sugar Duties and West Indian Prosperity." *Journal of Economic History* 14 (1954): 157–73.

Cuvillier, Armand. *Un journal d'ouvriers: L'Atelier, 1840–1850*. 1914; rpt., Paris: Editions ouvrières, 1954.

Daget, Serge. "L'Abolition de la traite des noirs en France de 1814 à 1831." *Cahiers d'études africaines* 11 (1971): 14–57.

Daget, Serge. "The Abolition of the Slave Trade by France: The Decisive Years 1826–1831." In *Abolition and Its Aftermath: The Historical Context, 1790–1916*, ed. David Richardson, 141–67. London: Frank Cass, 1985.

Daget, Serge. "A Model of the French Abolitionist Movement and its Variations." In *Anti-Slavery, Religion, and Reform*, eds. Christine Bolt and Seymour Drescher, 64–79.

Daget, Serge. "France, Repression of the Illegal Slave Trade, and England, 1817–1850." In *The Abolition of the Atlantic Slave Trade: Origins and Effects in Europe, Africa and the Americas*, ed. David Eltis and James Walvin, 193–217. Madison: University of Wisconsin Press, 1981.

Daget, Serge. "J. E. Morenas à Paris: L'Action abolitionniste, 1819–1821." *Bulletin de l'Institut fondamental d'Afrique Noire*, series B, 31 (1969): 875–85.

Daget, Serge. "Les mots esclave, nègre, Noir, et les jugements de valeur sur la traite négrière dans la littérature abolitionniste française de 1770 à 1845." *Revue française d'histoire d'outre-mer* 60 (1973): 511–48.

Daget, Serge. *Répertoire des expéditions négrières françaises à la traite illégale*. Nantes: Centre de Recherches sur l'Histoire du Monde Atlantique, 1988.

Daget, Serge. *La répression de la traite des Noirs au XIXe siècle:*

L'Action des croisières françaises sur les côtes occidentales de l'Afrique (1817–1850) Paris: Karthala, 1997.

Daget, Serge. *La traite des Noirs: Bastilles négrières et velléités abolitionnistes.* Evreux: Ouest-France Université, 1990.

Davis, David Brion. "The Emergence of Immediatism in British and American Antislavery Thought." *Mississippi Valley Historical Review* 49 (1962): 209–230.

Davis, David Brion. *The Problem of Slavery in the Age of Revolution, 1770–1823.* Ithaca: Cornell University Press, 1975.

Davis, David Brion. *Slavery and Human Progress.* New York: Oxford University Press, 1984.

Debbasch, Yvan. "Poésie et traite: L'Opinion française sur le commerce négrier au début du XIXe siècle." *Revue française d'histoire d'outre-mer* 48 (1961): 311–52.

Delisle, Philippe. "Eglise et esclavage dans les vieilles colonies françaises au XIXe siècle." *Revue d'histoire de l'église de France* 84 (1998): 55–70.

Delisle, Philippe. *Renouveau missionnaire et société esclavagiste: la Martinique, 1815–1848.* Paris: Publisud, 1997.

Démier, Francis. "Esclavage, économie coloniale et choix de développement français durant la première industrialisation, 1802–1840." In *Les abolitions de d'esclavage, de L. F. Sonthonax à V. Schoelcher, 1793, 1794, 1848. Actes du colloque international tenu à l'Université de Paris VIII les 3, 4 et 5 février 1994,* ed. Marcel Dorigny, pp. 273–81. Paris: Editions Unesco, 1995.

Deveau, Jean Michel. *La France aux temps des négriers.* Paris: France-Empire, 1994.

Dimakis, Jean. "La Société de la morale chrétienne et son action en faveur des Grecs lors de l'insurrection de 1831." *Balkan Studies* 7 (1966): 27–48.

Dorigny, Marcel. "Mirabeau et la Société des amis des Noirs: Quelles voies pour l'abolition de l'esclavage." In *Les abolitions de l'esclavage,* ed. Marcel Dorigny, 153–64.

Drescher, Seymour. "British Way, French Way: Opinion Building and Revolution in the Second French Slave Emancipation." *American Historical Review* 96 (1991): 709–34.

Drescher, Seymour. *Capitalism and Antislavery: British Popular Mobilization in Comparative Perspective.* New York: Oxford University Press, 1987.

Drescher, Seymour. *Dilemmas of Democracy: Tocqueville and Modernization.* Pittsburgh: University of Pittsburgh Press, 1968.

Drescher, Seymour. *Econocide: British Slavery in the Era of Abolition.* Pittsburgh: University of Pittsburgh Press, 1977.

Drescher, Seymour. "Public Opinion and the Destruction of British Slavery." In *Slavery and British Society*, ed. James Walvin, 22–48.

Drescher, Seymour, ed. *Tocqueville and Beaumont on Social Reform*. New York: Harper, 1968.

Drescher, Seymour. "Two Variants of Anti-Slavery: Religious Organization and Social Mobilization in Britain and France, 1780–1870." In *Anti-Slavery, Religion, and Reform*, eds. Christine Bolt and Seymour Drescher, 43–63.

Dubois, Laurent. *Les esclaves de la République: L'Histoire oubliée de la première émancipation, 1789–1794*. Paris: Calmann-Lévy, 1998.

Duchêne, Albert. *La politique coloniale de la France: Les ministres des colonies depuis Richelieu*. Paris: Payot, 1928.

Elisabeth, Léo. *L'Abolition de l'esclavage à la Martinique*. Fort-de-France: Archives départementales, 1980.

Duprat, Catherine. *"Pour l'amour de l'humanité": Le temps des philanthropes: La philanthropie parisienne des Lumières à monarchie de Juillet*. Paris: Editions du C.T.H.S., 1993.

Eltis, David. *Economic Growth and the Ending of the Transatlantic Slave Trade*. New York: Oxford University Press, 1987.

Engerman, Stanley L. "Some Considerations Relating to the Property Rights in Man." *Journal of Economic History* 33 (1973): 43–65.

Fabre, Père Camille. "Un préfet apostolique de la Guadeloupe en 1848: Casimir Dugoujon, des prêtres de Sainte-Croix du Mans." *La Province du Maine* 85 (1983): 47–77.

Fallope, Josette. *Esclaves et ciyoyens: Les Noirs de la Guadeloupe au XIXème siècle dans les processus de résistance et d'intégration, 1802–1910*. Basse-Terre: Société d'Histoire de la Guadeloupe, 1992.

Fallope, Josette. "Résistance d'esclaves et ajustement du système: Le cas de la Guadeloupe dans la première moitié du XIXe siècle." *Bulletin de la Société d'Histoire de la Guadeloupe*, nos. 67–8 (1986): 31–52.

Federini, Fabienne. *L'Abolition de l'eslavage en 1848: Une lecture de Victor Schoelcher*. Paris: L'Harmattan, 1998.

Fiérain, Jacques. *Les raffineries de sucre des ports français, XIXe–au début du XXe siècle*. New York: Arno, 1977.

Fischer-Blanchet, M. A. I. "Les travaux de la commission de l'indemnité coloniale en 1848." *Espaces caraïbes* 1 (1983): 37–56.

Forster, Elborg, and Robert Forster, eds. *Sugar and Slavery, Family and Race: The Letters and Diary of Pierre Dessalles, Planter in Martinique, 1808–1856*. Baltimore: Johns Hopkins University Press, 1996.

Fortescue, William. *Alphonse de Lamartine: A Political Biography*. New York: St. Martin's, 1983.

Fuma, Sudel. *L'Esclavagisme à la Réunion, 1794–1848*. Paris: L'Harmattan, 1992.

Geggus, David. "Haiti and the Abolitionists: Opinion, Propaganda and International Politics in Britain and France, 1804–1836." In *Abolition and Its Aftermath*, ed. David Richardson, 113–40.

Geggus, David. "Racial Equality, Slavery, and Colonial Secession during the Constituent Assembly." *American Historical Review* 94 (1989): 1290–308.

Genevray, Pierre. "Gabriel Delessert, préfet, puis préfet de police, résistance en politique, apaisement dans les questions religieuses, 1834–1848." *Bulletin de la Société de l'histoire du Protestantisme français* 103 (1957): 10–36.

Genovese, Eugene D. *Roll, Jordan, Roll: The World the Slaves Made.* New York: Pantheon, 1974.

Gershman, Sally. "Alexis de Tocqueville and Slavery." *French Historical Studies* 9 (1976): 467–83.

Gisler, Antoine. *L'Esclavage aux Antilles françaises (XVIIIe–XIXe siècle): Contribution au problème de l'esclavage.* 1965; rpt., Paris: Karthala, 1981.

Gobert, David L., and Jerome S. Handler, eds. and trans. "Barbados in the Apprenticeship Period: The Report of a French Colonial Official." *Journal of the Barbados Museum and Historical Society,* 36 (1980): 108–28.

Gobert, David L., and Jerome S. Handler, eds. and trans. "Barbados in the Post-Apprenticeship Period: The Observations of a French Naval Officer." *Journal of the Barbados Museum and Historical Society* 35 (1978): 243–66, 36 (1979): 4–15.

Green, William A. *British Slave Emancipation: The Sugar Colonies and the Great Experiment, 1830–1865.* Oxford: Clarendon, 1976.

Gross, Izhak. "Parliament and the Abolition of Negro Apprenticeship, 1835–1838." *English Historical Review* 96 (1981): 560–76.

Hart, Richard. *Slaves Who Abolished Slavery.* 2 vols. Mona, Jamaica: Institute of Social and Economic Research, University of the West Indies, 1980–1985.

Hayward, Jack. "From Utopian Socialism, via Abolitionism to the Colonisation of French Guiana: Jules Lechevalier's West Indian Fiasco, 1833–1844." In *De la Traite à l'Esclavage*, ed. Serge Daget, II, 603–626.

Hurwitz, Edith F. *Politics and the Public Conscience: Slave Emancipation and the Abolition Movement in Britain.* London: Allen & Unwin, 1973.

Jennings, Lawrence C. "L'Abolition de l'esclavage par la IIe République et ses effets en Louisiane, 1848–1858." *Revue française d'histoire d'outre-mer* 56 (1969): 375–97.

Jennings, Lawrence C. "Cyrille Bissette, Radical Black French Abolitionist." *French History* 9 (1995): 48–66.

Jennings, Lawrence C. "Economic Development, Associative Socialism, and Slave Emancipation in French Guiana, 1839–1848." Article submitted for publication.

Jennings, Lawrence C. *France and Europe in 1848: A Study of French Foreign Affairs in Time of Crisis.* Oxford: Clarendon, 1973.

Jennings, Lawrence C. "France, Great Britain and the Repression of the Slave Trade, 1841–1845." *French Historical Studies* 10 (1977): 101–125.

Jennings, Lawrence C. "French Anti-Slavery under the Restoration: The Société de la morale chrétienne." *Revue française d'histoire d'outre-mer* 81 (1994): 321–31.

Jennings, Lawrence C. "French Perceptions of British Slave Emancipation: A French Observer's Views on the Post-Emancipation British Caribbean." *French Colonial Studies* 3 (1979): 72–85.

Jennings, Lawrence C. "French Policy towards Trading with African and Brazilian Slave Merchants, 1840–1853." *Journal of African History* 4 (1976): 515–28.

Jennings, Lawrence C. "The French Press and Great Britian's Campaign against the Slave Trade." *Revue française d'histoire d'outre-mer* 67 (1980): 5–24.

Jennings, Lawrence C. *French Reaction to British Slave Emancipation.* Baton Rouge: Louisiana State University Press, 1988.

Jennings, Lawrence C. "French Slave Liberation and Socialism: Projects for 'Association' in Guadeloupe, 1845–1848." *Slavery and Abolition* 17 (1996): 93–111.

Jennings, Lawrence C. "French Views on Slavery and Abolitionism in the United States, 1830–1848." *Slavery and Abolition* 4 (1983): 19–40.

Jennings, Lawrence C. "The Interaction of French and British Antislavery, 1789–1848." *Proceedings of the Fifteenth Meeting of the French Colonial Historical Society, Martinique & Guadeloupe, May 1989,* pp. 81–91. Lanham, Md.: University Press of America, 1992.

Jennings, Lawrence C. "La Presse havraise et l'esclavage." *Revue historique* 272 (1984): 45–71.

Jennings, Lawrence C. "Réflexions d'un observateur sur l'émancipation des esclaves britanniques à l'île Maurice." *Revue d'histoire moderne et contemporaine* 29 (1982): 462–470.

Jennings, Lawrence C. "Slavery and the Venality of the July Monarchy Press." *French Historical Studies* 17 (1992): 957–78.

Jennings, Lawrence C. "Slave Trade Repression and the Abolition of

French Slavery." In *De la traite à l'esclavage*, ed. Serge Daget, II, 359–372.

Jurt, Joseph. "Lamartine et l'émancipation des noirs." In *Images de l'africain de l'antiquité au XXe siècle*, ed. Daniel Droixhe and Klaus H. Kiefer, 113–28. Bern: Peter Lang, 1987.

Kates, Gary. *The "Cercle Social," the Girondins, and the French Revolution*. Princeton: Princeton University Press, 1985

Kennedy, Emmet. *A Philosophe in the Age of Revolution: Destutt de Tracy and the Origins of "Ideology."* Philadelphia: American Philosophical Society, 1978.

Kennedy, Melvin D. "The Bissette Affair and the French Colonial Question." *Journal of Negro History* 45 (1960): 1–10.

Lecuir-Nemo, Geneviève. "Femmes et vocation missionnaire, permanence des congrégations feminines au Sénégal de 1819 à 1960: Adaption ou mutations? Impact et insertion." 2 vols. Doctorat, Université de Paris, 1994–95.

Léotin, Marie-Hélène. *La révolution anti-esclavagiste de mai 1848 en Martinique*. Fort-de-France: Apal, 1991.

Louis-Joseph, Christian. "La Monarchie de Juillet et la guerre des deux sucres." In *Historial Antillais*, III, 352–7.

Lucas, Edith E. *La littérature anti-esclavagiste au dix-neuvième siècle: Étude sur Madame Beecher Stowe et son influence en France*. Paris: Boccard, 1930.

Mancini, Matthew. "Political Economy and Cultural Theory in Tocqueville's Abolitionism." *Slavery and Abolition* 10 (1989): 151–171.

Martin, Gaston. *L'Abolition de l'esclavage, 27 avril 1848*. Paris: Presses Universitires de France, 1948.

Martin, Gaston. *Histoire de l'esclavage dans les colonies françaises*. Paris: Presses Universitaires de France, 1948.

Martin, Jean. "L'Affranchissement des esclaves à Mayotte, décembre 1846–juillet 1848." *Cahiers d'études africaines* 16 (1976): 207–33.

Martin-Frugier, Anne. "La formation des élites: Les 'conférences' sous la Restauration et la Monarchie de Juillet." *Revue d'histoire moderne et contemporaine* 36 (1989): 211–244.

Maxwell, John Francis. *Slavery and the Catholic Church: The History of Catholic Teaching Concerning the Moral Legitimacy of the Institution of Slavery*. Chicester: Barry Rose, 1975.

McCloy, Shelby. *The Negro in the French West Indies*. Lexington: University of Kentucky Press, 1966.

Merriman, John, ed. *1830 in France*. New York: New Viewpoints, 1975.

Moitt, Bernard. "Slave Resistance in Guadeloupe and Martinique, 1791–1848." *Journal of Caribbean History* 25 (1991): 136–59.

Motylewski, Patricia. *La Société française pour l'abolition de l'eslavage, 1834–1850*. Paris: L'Harmattan, 1998.

Necheles, Ruth F. *The Abbé Grégoire, 1787–1831: The Odyssey of an Egalitarian*. Westport, Conn.: Greenwood, 1971.

Nicolas, Armand. *La Révolution antiesclavagiste de mai 1848 à la Martinique*. Fort-de-France: Imprimerie Populaire Carénage, 1967.

Offen, Karen. *Paul de Cassagnac and the Authoritarian Tradition in the Nineteenth Century*. New York: Garland, 1991.

Osen, James L. *Prophet and Peacemaker: The Life of Adolphe Monod*. Lanham, Md.: University Press of America, 1984.

Pâme, Stella. "L'Affaire Bissette, 1823–1830." In *Historial Antillais*, III, 222–39.

Pâme, Stella. "Cyrille Bissette, 1795–1858." Doctorat de 3e cycle, Université de Paris, 1978.

Pasquier, Roger. "A propos de l'émancipation des esclaves au Sénégal en 1848." *Revue française d'histoire d'outre-mer* 54 (1967): 188–208.

Peabody, Sue. *"There Are No Slaves in France": The Political Culture of Race and Slavery in the Ancien Regime*. New York: Oxford University Press, 1996.

Pinkney, David. *The French Revolution of 1830*. Princeton: Princeton University Press, 1972.

Price, Roger. *The French Second Republic: A Social History*. Ithaca: Cornell University Press, 1972.

Prudhomme, Claude. *Histoire religieuse de la Réunion*. Paris: Karthala, 1984.

Quinney, Valerie. "Decisions on Slavery, the Slave Trade and Civil Rights for Negroes in the Early French Revolution." *Journal of Negro History* 55 (1970): 117–30.

Renault, François. "L'Abolition de l'esclavage au Sénégal: L'Attitude de l'administration française (1848–1905)." *Revue française d'histoire d'outre-mer* 58 (1971): 5–80.

Resnick, Daniel P. "Political Economy and French Anti-Slavery: The Case of J.-B. Say." *Proceedings of the Third Annual Meeting of the Western Society for French History, 1975*, 177–187. N.p.: Western Society for French History, 1976.

Resnick, Daniel P. "The Société des amis des Noirs and the Abolition of Slavery." *French Historical Studies* 7 (1972): 558–69.

Rigoulet-Roze, David. "A propos d'une commémoration: L'Abolition de l'esclavage en 1848." *L'Homme: Revue française d'anthropologie*, no. 145 (1998): 127–36.

Sainville, Léonard. "La condition des noirs dans les Antilles françaises de 1800 à 1850." 4 vols. Doctorat d'état, Université de Paris, 1970.

Schefer, Christian. *L'Algérie et l'évolution de la colonisation française: La politique coloniale de la Monarchie de Juillet.* Paris: Champion, 1928.

Schmidt, Nelly, ed. *La correspondance de Victor Schoelcher.* Paris: Maisonneuve et Larose, 1995.

Schmidt, Nelly. *L'Engrenage de la Liberté: Caraïbes–XIXe Siècle.* Aix-en-Provence: Publications de l'Université de Provence, 1995.

Schmidt, Nelly. "Suppression de l'esclavage, système scolaire et réorganisation sociale aux Antilles: Les Frères de l'Instruction chrétienne, témoins et acteurs, instituteurs des nouveaux libres." *Revue d'histoire moderne et contemporaine* 31 (1984): 203–45.

Schmidt, Nelly. *Victor Schoelcher et l'abolition de l'esclavage.* Paris: Fayard, 1994.

Schnakenbourg, Christian. *Histoire de l'industrie sucrière en Guadeloupe aux XIXe et XXe siècles.* Vol. 1: *La crise du système esclavagiste, 1835–1847.* Paris: L'Harmattan, 1980.

Stein, Robert. *Léger Félicité Sonthonax: The Lost Sentinel of the Republic.* Cranbury, N.J.: Fairleigh Dickinson University Press, 1985.

Stein, Robert. "The Revolution of 1789 and the Abolition of Slavery." *Canadian Journal of History* 17 (1982): 447–67.

Strong, Robert A. "Alexis de Tocqueville and the Abolition of Slavery." *Slavery and Abolition* 8 (1987): 204–15.

Tarrade, Jean. "Les colonies et les principes de 1789: Les assemblées révolutionnaires face au problème de l'esclavage." *Revue française d'Histoire d'Outre-Mer* 76 (1989): 9–34.

Tarrade, Jean. *Le commerce colonial de la France à la fin de l'Ancien Régime; l'évolution du régime de l'Exclusif de 1763 à 1789.* 2 vols. Paris: Presses Universitaires de France, 1972.

Temperley, Howard. *British Antislavery, 1830–1870.* Columbia: University of South Carolina Press, 1972.

Temperley, Howard. *White Dreams, Black Africa: The Antislavery Expedition to the Niger, 1841–1842.* New Haven: Yale University Press, 1991.

Thesée, Françoise. "Autour de la Société des amis des Noirs." *Présence africaine,* no. 125 (1983): 3–82.

Thésée, Françoise. *Le général Donzelot à Martinque: Vers la fin de L'Ancien Régime colonial, 1818–1826.* Paris: Karthala, 1997.

Thésée, Françoise. "La révolte des esclaves du Carbet à la Martinique (oct.–nov. 1822)." *Revue française d'histoire d'outre-mer* 80 (1993): 551–84.

Tomich, Dale W. "'Liberté ou mort': Republicanism and Slave Revolt in Martinique, February 1831." *History Workshop* 29 (1990): 85–91.

Tomich, Dale. *Slavery in the Circuit of Sugar: Martinique and the World Economy, 1830–1848.* Baltimore: Johns Hopkins University Press, 1990.

Tournier, Maurice. "Quant un mot en cache d'autres; le vocabulaire de 'l'association' en 1848." *Prévenir,* no. 13 (1986): 113–26.

Tudesq, André Jean. *Les grands notables en France (1840–1849): Étude historique d'une psychologie sociale.* 2 vols. Paris: Presses Universitaires de France, 1964.

Turley, David. *The Culture of English Antislavery, 1780–1860.* London: Routledge, 1991.

Tyrrell, Alex. "The 'Moral Radical Party' and the Anglo-Jamaican Campaign for the Abolition of the Negro Apprenticeship System." *English Historical Review* 99 (1984): 135–44.

Vigier, Philippe. "La recomposition du mouvement abolitionniste français sous la monarchie de Juillet." In *Les abolitions de l'esclavage,* ed. Marcel Dorigny, 285–91.

Walvin, James. "The Propaganda of Anti-Slavery." In *Slavery and British Society,* ed. James Walvin, 49–68.

Walvin, James. "The Public Campaign in England Against Slavery, 1787–1834." In *The Abolition of the Atlantic Slave Trade,* eds. David Eltis and James Walvin, 63–79.

Walvin, James. "The Rise of British Popular Sentiment for Abolition, 1787–1832." In *Anti-Slavery, Religion and Reform,* eds. Christine Bolt and Seymour Drescher, 149–62.

Weissbach, Lee-Shai. *Child Labor Reform in Nineteenth-Century France: Assuring the Future Harvest.* Baton Rouge: Louisiana State University Press, 1989.

INDEX

L'Abolitioniste français, 193–5, 283
Académie des Sciences et Belles Lettres de
    Lyon, 13
Académie des Sciences morales et poli-
    tiques, 128
Académie Française, 12–13
Agency Committee (Great Britain), 38
Alexander, William, 144, 195
Algeria, 150, 208, 254–6, 277
Ambert, General, 78, 251
Amis des Noirs. *See* Société des Amis des
    Noirs
Anglophobia, 166, 187, 287; as result of
    Egyptian crisis, 154; as result of right
    of search crisis, 171–6, 192, 209, 229
Antigua, 111, 177
apprenticeships, 40, 113, 120, 131, 144–5,
    179–81
Arago, François, 239, 276, 278
Arnous Dessaulsay, René, 78
Audiffret, Charles Louis Gaston, marquis
    d', 148, 177, 211

Barante, Amable Guillaume Prosper
    Brugière, baron de, 10
Barbados, 121
Barrot, Odilon: and Broglie commission
    debates, 186; Cabinet formed under,
    275; and emancipation petitions,
    143–4; and Mackau bill, 217; member
    of Tocqueville commission, 126; and
    right of search crisis, 174; Société
    française activities of, 51, 64, 166
Batie, Dejean de la, 258
Beaumont, Gustave de, 61, 261
Berryer, Pierre Antoine, 107, 108, 215
Beugnot, Arthur Auguste, 212, 273

Bignon, François, 148, 259
Billault, Adolphe Augustin Marie, 172
Billiard, Auguste, 61, 65
Bissette, Cyrille, 24, 136 fig., 289; attempts
    to mobilize *conseils généraux,* 267–8;
    Club des Amis des Noirs formed by,
    279; comments on the press, 81; Com-
    mission for the Abolition of Slavery
    testimony, 280; concern for slaves,
    36–7, 47; consulted by commission on
    colonial legislation, 31; critical of
    Rigny's bill, 35; and emancipation
    petitions, 238–9, 241–2, 265; emer-
    gence as immediatist, 70–73, 75;
    enmity with Cassagnac, 80, 224;
    enmity with Schoelcher, 50n4, 161,
    197, 243, 269, 279; fears of govern-
    ment inaction, 189; and Félice, 238,
    241; Freemason affiliation of, 60;
    funding from British abolitionist soci-
    ety, 244, 261, 268; and indemnity for
    slave owners, 66, 90, 143; and Isam-
    bert, 29, 71–2, 118–19; as mandatory
    of the men of color, 29–30; as martyr
    to colonial injustice, 29, 122n52;
    opposition to Mackau bill, 206–7,
    219; opposition to waiting periods,
    34; praise of Gasparin, 216; praise of
    Rémusat report, 118; publications of,
    49, 104, 153, 175; relations with colo-
    nial interests, 49–50, 77, 83, 84, 196;
    review of Foignet's speech, 63; slave
    liberation plan of, 92–3; and slave
    uprising (Martinique, 1822), 43; and
    Société française, 72, 93, 242, 246;
    and sugar question, 116; tirade against
    abolitionist establishment, 246

Blanqui, Jerome Adolphe, 71
Bonald, Louis Jacques Maurice de, 142
Bonaparte, Napoleon. *See* Napoleon I
Bourbon. *See* Île de Bourbon
Brissot, Jacques Pierre, 1, 3
Brissotin faction, 3
British and Foreign Anti-Slavery Society, 144, 208; Caillet's address to, 230; correspondence with the French, 130, 146, 153, 243; members' visits to France, 195; pressure on Société française to abandon gradualism, 261, 263
Broglie commission, 148–52, 154, 164, 192; and apprenticeships, 179; concluding deliberations of, 175–84; and indemnity for slave owners, 66, 179–80, 282; members' views on slavery question, 176–7; reaction to British emancipation, 181–2; Soult-Guizot government not supportive of, 162, 169–70; Thiers government not supportive of, 156–7
Broglie, Victor, duc de, 140 fig.; anti-slave trade speech of, 12; early abolitionist activities of, 5, 8; and emancipation petitions, 87, 143–4, 246, 258–9; influence on navy-colonial office, 83, 84; influence within Cabinet, 101; member of Mackau bill study commission, 205; as Prime Minister, 67, 70, 86; and right of search settlement, 229; and slavery debate, 68–70; and slavery question commission (Broglie commission), 148; slavery question views of, 13, 177, 184; and Société de la morale chrétienne, 10, 14, 16; and Société française, 51, 67, 97, 148n15, 167
Brougham, Henry Peter, Lord, 67, 209
Bureau de Correspondance, 265
Buxton, Thomas, 208

Caillet (French abolitionist), 230
Carnot, Hippolyte, 10, 198
Cassagnac, Bernard Adolphe Granier de: accused of planning disruptions of Société française's public meeting, 168; British opinion of, 224; as delegate for Guadeloupe, 156–7, 158; enmity with Bissette, 80, 224; proslavery writings of, 80–81, 85

Castellane, Henri Charles Louis Boniface, marquis de, 215
Castelli, abbé Pierre Paul, 129
Catholics: church's role in religious education of slaves, 110–12, 142, 201, 213; church's toleration of servitude, 128–9; participation in abolitionist movement, 8–9, 242
Chamber of Deputies: Broglie commission report, 185–6; colonial courts reforms, 254; colonial garrisons funding, 68; emancipation petitions, 143, 198, 203, 232, 239, 247–8; Guadeloupe emancipation-association petition, 259; interpellations, 99–100, 156; Mackau bill, 214–18; Passy motion, 106–8, 124; Passy-Tracy emancipation proposal, 85–6; sugar question proposals, 143, 147; Tracy motion, 126, 143
Chamber of Peers: colonial garrisons funding, 69; emancipation petitions, 68, 87–8, 143, 245–6, 255; Guadeloupe emancipation-association petition, 259; indebted colonial property proposals, 142–3, 145, 169, 254; interpellations, 273; Mackau bill, 204, 210, 213
Chateaubriand, François René de, 4
Christian Brothers, 110, 213
Clarkson, Thomas, 2, 159, 160
Clavière, Etienne, 1, 3
Colonial Councils. *See Conseils coloniaux*
colonies: disagreements over strategies, 249; government consultations with, 104–5; indebted property proposals, 142–3, 145, 169, 254; insistence on status quo slavery system, 125, 128, 168, 204, 212, 227; military deployments in, 43–4, 153–4; military garrisons funding, 68–9; port cities' support of, 78–9, 148; religious structure of, 110–12; and sugar question, 25–8, 115–18, 266; support for emancipation decree (1848), 280
colons: and Council of Delegates, 76; dependence on sugar monoculture, 27, 117; and emancipation petitions, 199, 244–5, 247; emancipation postponement strategy of, 79–80; and indemnity for slave owners, 65–7, 90–91,

94, 115, 180; Mackau's strained relations with, 226–7; opposition to rights for free persons of color, 32; reaction to British emancipation, 48, 181; reaction to Mackau laws, 222–5; reaction to Saint-Domingue uprising, 121; relations with Société française, 63–4; repression of Martinique uprising (1831), 37; testimony to Commission for the Abolition of Slavery, 280; use of the press, 80–81, 223–4. *See also* plantocracy/planters

Commission for the Abolition of Slavery, 279–81

commissions: Broglie commission, 148–55, 175–85; Commission for the Abolition of Slavery, 279; commission on colonial legislation, 31–2; Guizot-Rémusat commission, 109; indemnity commission, 282; Mackau bill study commission, 205; Martin-Passy commission, 34–5; special on slavery question, 146; as strategy for emancipation, 288; Tocqueville commission, 126. *See also specific names*

Compagnie d'Afrique, 207

Condorcet, Antoine, marquis de, 2, 3

Congrégation du Saint-Esprit, 110, 128, 130

Conil (delegate, Île de Bourbon), 91

Conseils coloniaux (Colonial Councils), 76, 158; government consultations with, 94–6, 114–15; legislative structure reforms, 34–5, 131–2; responses to Broglie commission, 175–6

Conseils généraux (General Councils), 96; legislative structure reforms, 34–5; Société française's appeals to, 85, 92, 103–4, 120, 266–8

Constant, Benjamin, 5, 8, 10, 12

contests: catechism for blacks, 130; essay, 13, 16, 18, 128; Grégoire prize, 103, 119, 161, 165; poetry, 13

Cooper, James, 52

Coquerel, Charles, 10, 14, 16

Corcelles, François de, 85

Council of Delegates, 76–8; and emancipation petitions, 244–5; government consultations with, 83; letter to *conseils généraux*, 96–7; resistance to Mackau laws, 225; split over slavery,

253; testimonies before Commission for the Abolition of Slavery, 280; use of the press, 78, 80–81, 225

Courtois brothers, 231, 236, 238

Crémieux, Adolphe, 52, 276

Croissant, Jean François Xavier, 108

crown slaves, 215, 257

Cubières, Amédée Louis Despans, 154, 211

Cussac, Jean Baptiste Rouvellat de, 44, 209

d'Argout, Antoine Maurice, comte, 10, 31

Daumier, Honoré, 138 fig.

Declaration of Rights (1789), 50

De Cools (delegate, Île de Bourbon), 112, 128

Degérando, Joseph Marie, baron, 9, 13, 14

d'Eichtal, Auguste, baron, 10

Delespaul, Adolphe Clément Joseph, 104, 267

Delessert, François, 10, 14

Demerara slave uprisings, 121

Denis, Amaranthe Alphonse Dugommier, 203–4

domain slaves, 215, 257

Duchâtel, Tanneguy, 167

Ducos, Jean Etienne, 172

Dugabé, Charles Casimir, 126

Dugoujon, Casimir, 129

Dumas, Alexandre, 49

Duperré, Victor Guy, baron, 45, 87; and Broglie commission report, 185; and colonial-metropolitan reorganization proposals, 132; and indebted colonial properties proposals, 254; and indemnity for slave owners, 90; member of Mackau bill study commission, 205; return to navy-colonial office, 124; and slave abuse debates, 156, 158; and slavery debates, 68–9, 82, 88, 125

Dupin, Charles, baron: attacks abolitionists for British connection, 173; attempts to influence Arago, 276; as colonial delegate, 77, 129; and colonial press lobby, 223; and Galos, 190; on government's unwillingness to move on emancipation, 253–4; gradualist approach of, 79; and Guadeloupe emancipation-association proposals, 252, 258; on Louis Philippe's colonial stance, 105; and Mackau bill, 210, 212, 225–6;

Dupin, Charles, baron (*cont.*)
  opinion of Mackau, 202; opinion of
  Passy, 86; and slavery debates, 88; and
  Tocqueville report, 127
Dupotet, Jean Henri Joseph, 45
Dussillion, Charles Joseph, 188
Dutrône, Henri: and emancipation peti-
  tions, 239; on government's emanci-
  pation postponement strategy, 262;
  opinion of Bissette, 261; and Société
  de la morale chrétienne, 14; and
  Société française, 221, 233, 263–4;
  views on slavery question, 286
Duvergier de Hauranne, Prosper, 10, 13

Egyptian crisis of 1840, 149, 153–4, 156,
  163, 166–7, 171, 192; Anglophobia
  resulting from, 187, 287
emancipation acts: automatic freedom on
  French soil (1836), 89; British (1833),
  38–40; Convention (1794), 3; free persons of color (1792), 2; free persons of
  color (1833), 35; general abolition
  decree (1848), 281
emancipation question. *See* slavery question
engagement, 181, 183, 257
Enlightenment, 1, 4, 21, 50, 185
essay contests, 13, 16, 18, 103, 119, 128
Etienne, Charles Guillaume, 14

Fabien, Louis, 34; concern for slaves, 36;
  consulted by commission on colonial
  legislation, 31; as mandatory of the
  men of color, 29; and *La Revue des
  colonies* (Paris), 49; Société française
  activities of, 61–2, 72
Félice, Guillaume de, 195, 230–1, 236–8,
  265, 269–72
Fleury, Victor, 260
Flocon, Ferdinand, 276
Foignet, Alexandre, 63–4
Forster, Josiah, 195, 261, 269
Forster, William Edward, 208, 230
fortification of Paris, 188
Fourier, Charles, 249
France, Joseph, 55
Freemasons, 59–60
free persons of color (*hommes de couleur
  libres*): abolitionists' goals under July
  Monarchy, 29–30; emancipation peti-
  tions from, 87, 240; equal rights for, 2,

31–5, 46; publications of, 49–50;
  religious needs of, 111; uprisings of,
  42, 44, 52, 122n52, 123
French abolition society. *See* Société
  française pour l'abolition de
  l'esclavage
Frossart, Benjamin Sigismond, 10

Galos, Joseph Henri, 182, 189–90, 192
Gasparin, Adrien Etienne Pierre, comte de,
  97
Gasparin, Agénor de, 97, 243; and emanci-
  pation petitions, 198, 199, 204, 232;
  and Félice's booklet, 237; gradualist
  approach of, 119; immediatist
  approach of, 178, 195–6, 286; and
  Mackau bill, 216–17; praised by Bissette, 216; requests funds to support
  rachat, 269; and right of search
  debates, 202
Gasparin, Paul de, 243, 245, 247, 261, 279
Gatine, Adolphe, 52, 60, 239, 279
Gaumont, Charles, 279
General Councils. *See Conseils généraux*
Girondins, 3
Goepp, pastor, 9
Goubert, Edouard, 129
gradualism/gradualists, 75, 145; British
  attempt to find alternative to, 232;
  Broglie commission support of, 150,
  183–4; colonial ecclesiastics support
  of, 129; discrediting of, 236; and
  emancipation petitions, 87; Foignet's
  speech at Société française, 63; Institute d'Afrique support of, 209; navy-
  colonial office plans for, 84; Passy
  motion support of, 134; Société des
  Amis des Noirs support of, 1; Société
  française support of, 14–17, 19, 155,
  261, 286
Grande Anse affair, 42, 44, 52, 123
Great Britain: abolitionists' reaction to
  Mackau laws, 219, 228, 262; colonial
  sugar production of, 182; emancipation bill, 38–40; public opinion support for emancipation in, 187; and
  right of search treaties, 32–3, 36,
  170–71, 174, 229
Grégoire, abbé Henri, 21; activities under
  Napoleon, 5; activities under the
  Restoration, 6–8; essay contest

(Grégoire prize), 103, 119, 128, 161, 165; and Société des Amis des Noirs, 2; and Société des Amis des Noirs et des Colonies, 3
Gregory XVI, 128–9
Guadeloupe: administrative reforms, 30–1; colonial council on emancipation, 94; colonial council's proposed alliance with viticulture proprietors, 225; colonial council's support of the press, 80–1, 225; dissolution of *conseil colonial*, 158; emancipation-association proposal of, 250–3, 274, 280; emancipation petitions from, 240; and Mackau laws, 226; military troops in, 43, 154n27; priests in, 111, 130; response to Broglie commission, 175; slaves of, 28, 122n53, 180, 282; slave uprising (1848), 123, 283; sugar production of, 25, 27, 116–17
Guérin, V., 64, 65
Guiana: administrative reforms, 30–1; colonial council on emancipation, 94; colonial council on indemnity for slave owners, 115; emancipation-association proposal of, 249–53; military troops in, 43, 154n27; priests in, 111, 130; response to Broglie commission, 175; slaves of, 28, 180, 282; sugar production of, 27
Guizot, François, 67, 275; attendance at World Anti-Slavery Convention, 152; and emancipation of Algerian slaves, 256; and emancipation of domain slaves, 257; and emancipation petitions, 247; as foreign minister, 156; and Guizot-Rémusat commission, 109; as interim navy-colonial minister, 248, 254; and interpellations, 98, 204; and Mackau, 191, 200, 206; and Mackau bill, 212, 215, 226; and Passy motion, 108; pledge to act on Broglie commission, 157, 158, 164, 186, 192; reply to Clarkson, 159–60; and Société de la morale chrétienne, 10; speech against governmental reforms, 273
Guizot-Rémusat commission, 109–10, 112–13, 124–5, 127, 130
Gurney, Daniel, 208
Gurney, Joseph, 195, 208

Harcourt, François Eugène Gabriel, duc d', 97, 212, 246
Hyde de Neuville, Jean Guillaume, baron, 12

Île de Bourbon (later Réunion): administrative reforms, 30–1; colonial council on emancipation, 94; colonial council on Guadeloupe's association proposals, 253; *colons*' support for emancipation decree (1848), 280; military troops in, 43, 154n27; priests in, 111, 130; slaves of, 28, 282; sugar production of, 25, 27
immediatism/immediatists, 54, 75; Bissette as first French, 73; British support of, 38, 145, 181, 237; colonial ecclesiastics support of, 129; Commission for the Abolition of Slavery support of, 281; growth of, 196, 217, 288; and Société française, 60, 145, 155, 263; Tocqueville report support of, 134
indemnity commission, 282
indemnity for slave owners, 65–7, 79, 90–1; abolitionists' support of, 107; and alienation of public opinion, 187; in British emancipation, 40, 65–6; Broglie commission discussions on, 179–80; Second Republic's final settlement of, 282; view of *conseils coloniaux* on, 94, 115; view of Société française on, 143
indentureship periods (*engagement*), 181, 183, 257
Institut d'Afrique, 188, 207–8
interpellations, 67, 82, 85, 98; on Broglie commission report, 186; on slave abuse, 156; on slavery and emancipation, 202, 273; as strategy for emancipation, 101–2, 106, 288
Isambert, Alfred, 221
Isambert, François, 135 fig.; appeals to *conseils généraux*, 85; assessment of Louis-Philippe's emancipation views, 146–8, 150, 169, 209; belief in duplicity of Thiers, 158; and Bissette, 29, 71–2, 118–19; and Broglie commission, 170, 184, 186–7; commission on colonial legislation membership, 31; communications with the British, 153–4, 158–9, 167, 169, 175, 185;

Isambert, François (*cont.*)
 correspondent for *British and Foreign
 Anti-Slavery Society Reporter,* 189,
 191; and emancipation petitions, 198,
 203, 209, 232, 239; faith in Guizot's
 principles, 159; and Félice's booklet,
 237; Freemason affiliation of, 59;
 and Gasparin, 196; on government's
 move toward emancipation, 149; on
 government's support for Tocqueville
 report, 130–1; gradual emancipation
 plan of, 65; and Guizot-Rémusat
 commission, 109; immediatist tendencies of, 146, 217; and indemnity for
 slave owners, 102, 282; and Mackau
 bill, 206, 210, 214, 217–19, 234;
 medal given to, 118–19; and religious
 needs of slaves, 112; and Rémusat,
 159; report on British colonial blacks,
 145; and right of search debates,
 202; and Saint-Hilaire, 89, 91; and
 slavery debates, 68, 88, 100; and
 Société française, 17, 51, 52, 64, 221;
 speech to World Anti-Slavery Convention, 152; testimony to Commission
 for the Abolition of Slavery, 280;
 views on limitation of colonial powers,
 160, 169–70; views on slavery question, 162, 286; visited by Forster,
 230–1

Jabrun, Eimar de, 112, 128, 157, 248–9,
 258
Jamaica, 111, 121, 123
Jollivet, Thomas Marie Adolphe, 187, 275;
 accused of planning disruptions of
 Société française's public meeting,
 168; advice on Mackau laws to Martinique legislature, 226; attacked in
 British abolitionist press, 220; and
 colonial press lobby, 223; and emancipation petitions, 199, 203, 247; and
 Guadeloupe emancipation-association
 proposals, 252, 258; and Mackau bill,
 215, 225–6; on Mackau's proposal,
 202; and Passy, 212; proposals for
 alliances with other nations, 224
Jubelin, Jean Guillaume: appointed under-
 secretary of state for navy and
 colonies, 191; and Broglie commission, 162–3, 164; on colonies'

response to emancipation, 104; on
 sugar question, 115; views on slavery
 question, 177
July Monarchy, 285–6; anti-slave trade
 legislation of, 32, 46; colonial administrative reforms of, 31–6, 46, 157–8;
 consultations with colonies, 104–5;
 consultations with *Conseils coloniaux,*
 94–6; consultations with Council of
 Delegates, 83; counters to abolitionist
 initiatives, 33–4; election campaigns
 devoid of anti-slavery themes, 168;
 emancipation action decision of, 133;
 emancipation postponement strategy
 of, 82, 100–101, 163, 170, 192, 206,
 284; emancipation preparatory initiatives of, 142–3; emancipation waffling
 of, 152, 158; fear of slave uprisings,
 120, 124; and government debt, 188;
 importance of colonies to, 26, 28; and
 indemnity for slave owners, 66–7,
 90–1; information gathering on British
 colonies, 44–5; leaders of, 22–3; legislative system of, 76; Louis-Philippe's
 exercise of power, 105–6; and Mackau
 laws, 218, 227, 234–5; public meetings, ban on, 97, 104, 166–8; reaction
 to British emancipation, 40–2, 46,
 113, 181; reaction to Broglie commission report, 185; right of search
 treaties, 32–3, 36, 170–1, 174, 229;
 slavery question stance, 69–70; and
 sugar question, 117–18

Laborde, Louis Joseph Alexandre, comte
 de: and Guizot-Rémusat commission,
 109; and Passy motion, 106–7; and
 slavery debates, 68; and Société de la
 morale chrétienne, 9; and Société
 française, 51, 152; and Tracy motion,
 143–4
Lacrosse, Bertrand Théobald Joseph,
 baron, 156
Lafayette, Marie Joseph Gilbert, marquis
 de, 2–3, 5, 6, 8, 24
Laffon-Ladabat, André Daniel, 14
Laisné de Villevêque, Gabriel Jacques, 65,
 152
Lamartine, Alphonse de: appeals to *conseils généraux,* 104; draft slave liberation plan, 97; and Félice's booklet,

237; as foreign minister, 276; and Passy motion, 107; and slave liberation plan, 92; and slavery debates, 68, 88; and Société française, 148n15; and sugar question, 116; views on slavery question, 144–45, 286; and working-class emancipation petitions, 198

Lanjuinais, Jean Denis, comte, 10

Laplagne-Barris, Raymond Jean François Marie Lacave, 212

La Rochefoucauld-Liancourt, François Alexandre Frédéric, duc de, 9

La Rochefoucauld-Liancourt, Gaëtan, duc de: appeals to *conseils généraux*, 103; gradualist approach of, 63; immediatist tendencies of, 19; opposition to government's cooperation with *colons*, 88; report on anti-slavery activities, 51, 61; and Société de la morale chrétienne, 16, 36

La Rochejaquelin, Henri, marquis de, 204

Las Cases, Emmanuel, comte de, 119

Lasteyrie, Ferdinand Charles Léon, comte de, 13, 14, 198

Lasteyrie, Jules, marquis de, 214, 235, 247, 279, 286

Layraud, André, 104

Lechevalier, Jules, 250–1

Lechevalier, Théodore, 81, 126

Ledru-Rollin, Alexandre Auguste, 198, 204, 217, 247, 276, 278

Legitimists, 22, 74, 107, 208, 215

Leray, Théodore Constant, 215

Levavasseur, Charles, 215

Lhorente (Catholic theologian), 14

liberals, 10, 11, 22, 51, 59

London Society for the Abolition of the Slave Trade, 1

Louis-Philippe (King of the French), 10, 22, 285–6; catechism for blacks prize contest of, 130; exercise of power, 23, 105–6; feelings on freed blacks, 130; flight to England, 275; Mackau's appointment influenced by, 191; reaction to Mackau laws, 226; reported colonial stance, 105; resistance to emancipation, 70, 134, 146, 147, 149–50, 270–1; response to Broglie commission report, 192

Louis XVIII, 6, 110

Lushington, Stephen, 229

Lutheroth, Henri, 65, 68, 237, 239, 261, 286

Macaulay, Zachary, 7–8, 52, 54, 85, 119

Mackau, Admiral: and apprenticeships, 179; attacked in British abolitionist press, 220; and Broglie commission, 148, 192; draft law introduced by, 204–5, 212, 217; and emancipation of domain slaves, 257; and emancipation of Mayotte slaves, 254–5; and emancipation of Senegalese slaves, 278; and emancipation petitions, 246, 247; and Guiana emancipation-association proposals, 251; and Guizot, 191, 200, 206; as Minister of the Navy and Colonies, 148, 190; policies toward *colons* after Mackau laws, 226–7; pro-colonial stance of, 202; and religious education of slaves, 201; and right of search debates, 202–4; views on slavery question, 177, 190–1

Mackau laws, 202–6, 209–20, 222, 225–9, 232–7

Madagascar, 282

Mahul, Alphonse, 17

Malouet, Pierre Victor, 4

mandatories of the men of color, 29–30, 36, 47, 87

maroons, 122

Marron, Paul Henri, 10, 13, 14

Martin du Nord, Nicolas Ferdinand Marie Louis Joseph, 34

Martinique: administrative reforms, 30–1; balance of trade with France, 26; colonial council on emancipation, 94; colonial council on Guadeloupe's association proposals, 252; colonial council on indemnity for slave owners, 115; colonial council's proposed alliance with viticulture proprietors, 225; colonial council's support of the press, 81, 225; *colons* meeting with Arago, 276–7; emancipation petitions from, 87, 241; free persons of color uprising, 42, 44, 52, 122n52, 123; Jollivet's advice on Mackau laws to legislature of, 226; military troops in, 43, 154n27; priests in, 111, 130; response to Broglie commission, 175; slaves of, 28, 180, 282; slave

Martinique (*cont.*)
uprisings, 33, 37, 43, 122n52, 123,
282–3; sugar production of, 25, 27,
116
Martin-Passy commission, 34–5
Mauguin, François, 77, 78; and *Le Journal
du commerce,* 81; and Passy motion,
107; and religious education of slaves,
111–12; on Saint-Domingue uprising,
121; and slavery debates, 79
Mayotte, 254–5, 277
Mérilhou, Joseph, 205, 210–11
Mérode, Charles, comte de, 239
Mestro, Henri Joseph, 42n52, 113, 120,
148, 276, 279
Michelet, Jules, 198, 239
military deployments to colonies, 43–4,
68–9, 153–4
Mirabeau, Honoré, comte de, 1
Mohamet Ali, 154
Molé, Louis Mathieu, comte de, 96,
99–100, 105, 107, 112
Monnet, Alexandre, 129
Monod, Adolphe de, 239
Montalembert, Charles, comte de, 10, 87,
213, 246, 286
Montalivet, Marthe Camille Bachasson,
comte de, 14, 211
Montebello, Napoleon Lannes, duc de, 14,
248
Montmorency, duc de, 208
Montrol, François Mongin de, 62, 65, 90,
102
Morale chrétienne. See Société de la morale
chrétienne
Morenas, Joseph Elzéar, 7
Muslim slavery, 254–6

Napoleon I, 3, 4, 6
navy-colonial office, 84, 95–6, 142;
colonial-metropolitan reorganization
proposals, 131–2; lack of concern
over slave uprisings, 124; reaction to
Guizot-Rémusat commission, 114;
religious education of slaves, 129–30,
201, 235; views on sugar question, 116
Nemours, duc de, 226
Ney, Joseph Napoleon, prince de la
Moskowa, 211
Niger expedition, 208
notables, 23, 73, 97, 120, 211

Orleanists/Orleanist regime, 22, 30–2, 51,
74, 101, 164, 188. *See also* July
Monarchy
Orléans, duc d', 10, 22
Orsini, abbé, 112

Pagnerre, Laurent Antoine, 55
Pariset, André Aimé, 251
Partarrieu-Lafosse, Jean Isidore, 14
Passy, Hippolyte: and Broglie commission,
148, 156; and emancipation petitions,
246; and government's move toward
emancipation, 134, 143, 163; and
Guizot-Rémusat commission, 109; as
immediatist, 86; and indemnity for
slave owners, 90, 102; influence
within Cabinet, 101; and Mackau bill,
212; and Martin-Passy commission,
34–5; as minister of commerce, 86, 96;
as minister of finance, 125, 146; Passy
motion, 106–8, 183; Passy-Tracy
emancipation proposal, 85–6; and religious needs of slaves, 112; and slavery
debates, 68; and Société française, 51,
53, 121, 263–4; and Tocqueville
report, 130–1; views on slavery question, 177–8, 286
patronnés, 32, 33, 35
pécule (peculium), 83, 91, 101, 107; colonial councils and, 87–8, 94–5, 99,
113; *colon* rejection of, 91; and
Mackau bill, 205; as part of Passy
motion, 183; tabling of, 105, 114
Percin, L., 279
Périer, Casimir, 10
Perrinon, François Auguste, 279
Persegol (from Guiana), 61–2
petition campaigns: on Algerian slave trade
and slavery, 255; Chamber of
Deputies, 247–8; Chamber of Peers
commission, 245–6; Félice/Bissette,
238–42; on Guadeloupe emancipation-association, 258; in Lyon, 260;
from Martinique, 87, 241; by Protestants, 232, 265; and Société française,
68, 143–4, 168, 262, 263–4; as
strategy for emancipation, 97, 289; by
working-classes, 197–200, 209, 228
Piscatory, Théobald, 10
plantocracy/planters: as critics of Bissette,
49; defense of slavery, 27, 76, 199;

emancipation postponement strategy of, 80, 101, 257–8; on indemnity for slave owners, 66, 79; Legitimists' support for, 107. *See also colons*
poetry contests, 13
Poncelet, abbé, 111
Portalis, Joseph, comte, 212
port cities, 78–9, 148, 189, 225; response to Broglie commission, 185; support of colonies, 78–9; testimony to Commission for the Abolition of Slavery, 280
the press: reaction to British emancipation, 39, 48–9; reaction to Broglie as prime minister, 70–1; and right of search controversy, 171–2; suppression and restriction of, 4, 8, 98; use by *colons*, 223–4; use by *conseils coloniaux*, 158; use by Council of Delegates, 78, 80–1; use by Société française, 193; use by working-class petitioners, 197–8
Price, Joseph, 13
Protestant participation in abolitionist movement, 9, 14, 18, 59, 231–2, 240, 265
provincial organization networks, 168, 230, 260, 264
public meetings, ban on, 97, 104, 166–68
public opinion: appeals to *conseils généraux* used to inform, 85, 92, 97, 103–4, 120; *conseils coloniax* and secret funds to influence, 132, 158, 223; essay and poetry contests used to inform, 12–13, 16, 18, 103, 128; inability of abolitionists to win, 187; petitions used to inform, 97, 168; Société française's renewed efforts to win, 166, 192, 193
public works programs, 188
Puerto Rico, 117

Quinet, Edgar, 198

rachat, 41, 61, 65, 83, 101, 107; colonial councils and, 87–8, 94–5, 99, 113; *colon* rejection of, 91; and Mackau bill, 205, 220; as part of Passy motion, 183; tabling of, 105, 114
Reizet, Eugène de, 248–9, 258
religious education of slaves, 110–12,

129–30, 142; criticisms of, 201, 213, 215; under Mackau laws, 235
Rémusat, Charles de, 10, 14, 18, 67; appeals to *conseils généraux*, 103; and Félice's booklet, 237; and Guizot-Rémusat commission, 109; Isambert's opinion of, 159; member of Tocqueville commission, 126; as Minister of the Interior, 145; and slave abuse debates, 157
Rémusat report. *See* Guizot-Rémusat commission
Rémusat-Tocqueville commission. *See* Tocqueville commission
republicanism/republicans, 5, 20, 74, 98
Restoration, 6, 22, 110–11, 116–17
Réunion, 141 fig., 280. *See also* Île de Bourbon
Revolution of 1848, 273, 275
Reynard, André Elysée, 148, 184
Richard, Mondésir, 29, 49
Ride, Alphonse, 223–4
right of search issues, 32–3, 36, 170–5, 192; and alienation of public opinion, 187, 193, 287; settlement of, 229
Rigny, Henry Gauthier, comte de, 24, 33–5, 39–41, 45
Rigord, abbé Joseph, 233
Robespierrists, 3
Roger [du Loiret], Jacques François, baron, 87; appeals to *conseils généraux*, 85, 103; and Broglie commission report, 185–6; and emancipation petitions, 232; Freemason affiliation of, 59; as immediatist, 60; indemnity plan of, 65; and Mackau bill, 217; member of Guizot-Rémusat commission, 109; member of Tocqueville commission, 126; and navy-colonial debates, 149
Rohan-Rochefort, prince de, 208
Rosamel, Claude Charles Marie de Campe de, 99, 107, 120
Rossi, Pellegrin Louis Edouard, 148, 177, 181, 184, 205
Roussin, Albin Reine, 145, 148–9, 151, 157, 190

Sade, Xavier, comte de: appeals to *conseils généraux*, 103; and apprenticeships, 180; and indemnity for slave owners, 179; member of Broglie commission,

Sade, Xavier, comte de (*cont.*)
148; member of Tocqueville commission, 126; and right of search debates, 202; views on slavery question, 177, 184
Saillant, Charles Philibert de Lasteyrie-du, 9
Saint-Antoine, Hippolyte Daniel de, 208, 239
Saint-Domingue: attempted reconquest by Napoleon, 4; slaves freeing themselves on, 122n52; slave uprisings, 3, 120–22; sugar production of, 25, 28
Sainte-Croix, Félix Renouard, marquis de, 14, 62, 63–4, 65
Saint-Hilaire, Edmé Jean Fileau de, 41, 182; and Broglie commission, 148, 152; and colonial policies, 70, 132; emancipation position paper, 99; and indemnity for slave owners, 66, 91, 179; and Isambert, 89, 91; movement toward emancipation, 84; replacement as Director of Colonies, 189; views on slavery question, 177, 190
Saint-Rémy, Lepelletier de, 277
Saint-Venant, Bory de, 4
Salverte, Eusèbe, 68
Saverdun, Laurant de, 104
Say, Jean Baptiste, 3, 5, 65
Schoelcher commission. *See* Commission for the Abolition of Slavery
Schoelcher, Victor, 47, 137 fig., 233–4, 289; and Commission for the Abolition of Slavery, 279–81; and emancipation of Senegalese slaves, 278; and emancipation petitions, 198, 241, 264; emergence as immediatist, 161, 178, 196, 260, 286; enmity with Bissette, 50n4, 161, 197, 243, 269, 279; Freemason affiliation of, 59, 196; Grégoire prize withheld from, 161, 165; and indemnity for slave owners, 66, 282; and Mackau bill, 206; on military deployments, 44; optimism about emancipation progress, 160; publications of, 161; and *rachat*, 220; and Société française, 55, 196–7; speech to Scientific Congress of France, 196; on women's abolition efforts, 239
Scientific Congress of France, 196
Scoble, John, 52, 130, 145, 162; trips to France, 144, 195, 230–2, 236, 266

Scribe, Augustin Eugène, 198
Sébastiani, General Horace, 10, 25
Second Republic, 275, 281–2
Seminaire du Saint-Esprit, 110, 128, 130
Senegal, 28n15, 277–8, 282
Simonde de Sismondi, Jean Charles Léonard, 6, 45–6
Sisters of Saint Joseph of Cluny, 110
slavery question: debates in legislative sessions, 68–9, 87–8, 98–100; and elimination of slave trade, 13, 21, 36; gradualist approaches toward, 1, 14–15, 16–17, 19, 53–4, 62, 102, 286; and Pope Gregory XVI, 128; and Second Vatican Council, 129; and Société des Amis des Noirs et Colonies, 3; Société française's individualistic approach to, 65, 74, 102, 286; special commission on, 146
slaves: abuse of, 156; and colonial courts reforms, 254; emancipation of Muslim, 254–6; growing focus on, 37; manumission of female, 19, 39; newborn slave children freedom proposal, 88, 94, 105, 114, 183; population statistics, 28, 282; reactions to British emancipation, 120, 123; religious education of, 110–12, 129–30, 142, 201, 213, 215; running away by, 122; self-liberation activities of, 122; uprisings of, 3, 33, 37, 43, 120–3, 282–3; value of, 91, 180
slave trade: abolitionists' focus on outlawing, 5–6; bans on, 6, 32; petition to eliminate Algerian, 255; right of search treaties, 32–3, 36; Société de la morale chrétienne's committee on, 12–15, 17–18; and Société des Amis des Noirs et Colonies, 3; Société des Amis des Noirs' offensive against, 1–2; surreptitious continuation of, 7
Société de la morale chrétienne, 8–12, 18–19; British encouragement and funding of, 21; emancipation petition of, 87; essay contests of, 16, 18; growing focus on slavery, 36; links to Société française, 59, 61; lobbying efforts of, 16–17; manumission of female slaves plan of, 19, 39; marginalization of, 19–20; publication

program of, 16, 19; slave trade/slavery committee, 12–14, 17–18
Société des Amis des Noirs, 1–3, 20–1, 233
Société des Amis des Noirs et des Colonies, 3
Société française pour l'abolition de l'esclavage, 19, 73, 84, 119–20, 285; activities tied to legislative schedules, 51–2, 92, 286; appeals to *conseils généraux*, 85, 92, 96, 103–4, 120, 268; British influence on, 52–3, 144, 233, 287; British pressure to abandon gradualism, 261, 263; and Broglie commission, 154–5; conservative approach to emancipation, 86, 102; disillusionment of leadership, 222, 228; and emancipation petitions, 68, 87, 143–4, 168, 228, 262, 263–4; end of, 283–4; essay contests of, 103, 119, 128, 161, 165; formation of provincial auxiliary bodies, 166, 230; government authorization of, 67, 168; gradualism supported by, 155, 261, 286; and immediatism, 155, 263; and indemnity for slave owners, 143, 155; individualistic approach to slavery question, 65, 74, 102, 263, 286; interpellation strategy of, 85, 102, 106, 156, 202, 273; links to Société de la morale chrétienne, 59, 61; and Mackau bill, 205–6, 213–14, 218–19, 228; marginalization of, 197, 261, 264; membership of, 54–60; and Passy motion, 108; Passy-Tracy emancipation proposal, 86; prospectus of, 53, 121; publication program of, 193–5; public meetings of, 97–8, 166–8, 193; relations with *colons*, 63–4; and Tocqueville report, 143; and Tracy motion, 143
Society for the Abolition of the Slave Trade, London, 1
Sonthonnax, Léger Félicité, 3
Soult, Nicolas-Jean de Dieu, duc de Dalmatie, 145, 156
Staël-Holstein, Auguste, baron de, 5, 8, 9, 12–14, 17
Staël-Holstein, Germaine, Madame de, 5–6, 7, 21
Stanley, Edward Geoffrey Smith, Lord, 182

Stapfer, Philippe Albert, 9
Ste. Marie and Nossibé (later Madagascar), 282
Sue, Eugène, 198
sugar question, 25–8, 115–18, 138 fig., 143, 147, 186
Sully-Brunet, Jacques, 91
Sully-Brunet of Réunion, 280

Tallyrand-Perigord, Charles Maurice de, prince of Benevento, 39
Tascher, Ferdinand, comte de, 211
Ternaux, Louis Guillaume, 14
Teste, Jean Baptiste, 142
Thayer, Amédée William, 60, 174
Thayer, Edouard, 17, 60
Thiers, Adolphe, 10; belief in duplicity of, 157–9; and Egyptian crisis, 156; interest in colonial status quo, 149–50; as Prime Minister, 86, 96, 145, 163–4, 192; and slavery debates, 147–8
Thompson, George, 208
Tocqueville, Alexis de: and apprenticeships, 179; and Félice's booklet, 237; on government debt and emancipation priorities, 189; and Guadeloupe emancipation-association petition, 258–9; immediatist tendencies of, 217, 259; and indemnity commission, 282; and indemnity for slave owners, 179; and Mackau bill, 216; member of Broglie commission, 148; member of Tocqueville commission, 126; and slavery debates, 147; views on slavery question, 177–8, 184, 286
Tocqueville commission, 126–8, 148, 163
Tocqueville report, 131, 132, 143, 146, 178–9, 194
Tracy, Victor Destutt de: appeals to *conseils généraux*, 85, 103; and apprenticeship, 179; and Broglie commission, 148, 176, 186; Chamber of Deputies speech, 33; commission on colonial legislation membership, 31; and Félice's booklet, 237; and indemnity for slave owners, 102; Passy motion becomes Tracy motion, 124–6; Passy-Tracy emancipation proposal, 85–6; and slavery debates, 68, 88, 99, 100; Société française's letter to British, 233; support for immediatism,

Tracy, Victor Destutt de (*cont.*)
    184; views on Anglophobia and anti-
    slavery success, 174; views on slavery
    question, 176–7, 286
Tredgold, J. H., 146
Turckheim, Jean Frédéric, baron de, 13

Ultraroyalists, 5, 26
Universal Abolition Society, 52

vagabondage, 155, 282
Verhuell, Carel Henrik, 10, 87
Vernes (*négociant*), 13, 14
Vielcastel, Horace de, 10

Villemain, François, 10

Wallon, Henri, 279
Whitehorne, James, 144
Wilberforce, William, 6
Wilder (*négociant*), 14
Wilks, Marck, 14, 233
women's abolition efforts, 199, 239
working-class emancipation petitions,
    197–200, 209, 228
World Anti-Slavery Convention, 145, 152
Wurstemberg, Jacques Henri, 148, 177,
    215, 231
Wurtz, Jean Geoffroi, 9